D0481436

THE COMPLETE ENCYCLOPEDIA OF

WARSHIPS

1798–2006

STEAM · TURBINE · DIESEL · NUCLEAR

THE COMPLETE ENCYCLOPEDIA OF

WARSHIPS

1798–2006

STEAM · TURBINE · DIESEL · NUCLEAR

JOHN BATCHELOR & CHRIS CHANT

Published by Rebo International b.v., Lisse, The Netherlands in association with Publishing Solutions (www) Ltd., England.

Text: Christopher Chant
Illustrations: John Batchelor
Production, layout and typesetting: The Minster Press, Dorset, England
Prepress services: Trilabit, Prague, The Czech Republic
Cover design: Trilabit, Prague, The Czech Republic
Proofreading: Sarah Dunham

ISBN: 978-90-366-1719-2

Contents

Introduction

The Battle of Waterloo in 1815 ended the Napoleonic Wars and ushered in a period of peace for Europe and much of the "Western world." A particular legacy of the war was the complete British mastery of the seas, for in the period since the start of the French Revolutionary Wars after 1789 the Royal Navy had grown to a great size and an even greater capability founded on the excellence of its ships and the vast experience of its officers and men. The Royal Navy was enormously trimmed in the aftermath of the Napoleonic Wars, but there was still no single European nation, or even a combination of two such countries, which could hope to rival, let alone better, the Royal Navy with its far-flung experience and ability to support itself in any part of the world.

An immediate consequence of peace and British naval supremacy was a huge growth in Great Britain's overseas trade, which had become ever more important during the Napoleonic Wars and now blossomed into a process by which raw materials were imported and finished goods exported to an ever widening market. With its feet placed firmly on this sound economic footing, Great Britain became the most powerful nation in the world.

With the Royal Navy's position assured, there was little impetus from within the British naval establishment for the adoption of novelties which might upset the balance. The Royal Navy was therefore more than happy to maintain its pre-eminent position using the strategies, tactics and even ships that had underpinned the defeat of Napoleon in 1815. This meant a fleet based on wooden ships armed with large numbers of broadside guns, even though this meant high manning levels. Many seamen were released from the service and turned to the mercantile service for continued employment, but the owners of merchant ships wished to reduce the cost of building and operating their ships, and therefore looked toward new technologies and ever-reducing manning levels.

By the 1840s, wood was reaching its limits, in capability as well as in quality also available in adequate quantity, as the prime material for ship construction as owners demanded ever larger vessels with still smaller crews. However, a new structural material for the manufacture of large vessels and, increasingly, their steam machinery had already made its appearance courtesy of the "industrial revolution." This was iron, which was increasingly available in its two primary forms as cast iron and wrought iron. With wrought iron available to them, ship designers could plan hulls that were considerably longer and beamier, yet still strong and rigid, in the confident knowledge that the "state of the art" in building such hulls was becoming ever more scientific. The limited number of yards which initially embarked on the construction of iron hulls at first retained their traditional practices for the construction of wooden hulls, merely seeking to reproduce parts and components of these hulls in wrought or cast iron. This began to change with the introduction of fresh ideas from that classic engineer, Isambard Kingdom Brunel. In 1843 Brunel's second steamship, the *Great Britain*, of 3,270 gross tons and the world's first ocean-going iron ship with propeller propulsion, highlighted significantly enhanced methods of ship construction. Brunel's innovations included girder-section stringers of iron extending the full length of the vessel to ensure longitudinal strength, an inner as well as an outer bottom combined in a cellular arrangement for greater strength, bulkheads to compartmentalize the ship into a number of watertight sections, and massive strength throughout the hull. There were many sceptics, but the patently clear advantages of

Brunel's concepts in the provision of great strength, large cargo-carrying volume and extensive watertight compartmentalization spurred a number of yards not so much to copy the whole concept but rather to attempt a type of hybrid construction. Thus iron came to be adopted for the frames, fore-and-aft stringers, floor plates, keelson and cross bracing, with wooden planking retained for the bottom, topsides and decks.

In much the same period there emerged a process that radically reduced the cost of turning iron into steel, and this again transformed the cost of ship construction in a material of greater strength/weight ratio and improved tensile strength. The qualities of steel thus made it feasible for a hull to be built with only about three-quarters of the material that would have been necessary with an iron hull. This significant weight saving offered the advantages of either lower coal consumption for a given speed, or slightly greater speed with the given engine power. On the other side of the material coin, however, was the fact that mild steel also corroded considerably more rapidly than wrought iron: this could be offset by coating all mild steel surfaces with a paint based on red lead, and by scraping and repainting as frequently as possible right through the relevant ship's life.

Just as important as the adoption of iron for the construction of larger and more sturdy hulls was the steady development of the steam machinery that was seen initially as a back-up to sail (itself steadily improved in terms of its spars, rigging and plans) when the wind was absent or in the wrong quarter, but then increasingly as the prime mover that would allow the relegation of sail to secondary importance and also permit crews to be reduced still further in number. In the period between 1820 and 1850, when the steam power began to come strongly to the fore, steam engines were notably wasteful as they were low-pressure units of great weight but only limited power. There were advances during the period, with typical boiler pressures increasing from 2 lb/sq in (0.14 kg/cm^2) to 20 lb/sq in (1.41 kg/cm^2), but it was after the mid-point of the 18th century that steam power become fully dominant as new compound engines, operating at 60 lb/sq in (4.22 kg/cm^2), offered not only greater power but also considerably improved economy. The compound engine was then itself superseded from the 1870s by the triple expansion engine, which used steam of 120 lb/sq in (8.44 kg/cm^2) in three mechanical processes before the spent steam was exhausted into a condenser before being returned to the boiler as water.

The type of steam engine that spelled the end of the age of sail was of the reciprocating type, in which a piston moves backward and forward inside a cylinder, its motion being transferred and translated into a rotary form by a connecting rod and crank on a driving shaft. Used to drive a propeller shaft, such engines were generally installed with their pistons moving in vertical cylinders, with horizontal cylinders more rare. The first major development from the single-cylinder reciprocating marine engine was the compound engine in which, after leaving the first cylinder, the steam passed through a second larger-diameter and lower-pressure cylinder before exhausting to a condenser for cooling and thus a return to feed water condition. This second use of the steam added to

the power generated by the engine from a given quantity of steam, and thus enhanced the efficiency of the engine. Although the concept of the compound steam engine had been patented in 1781, it was only in the 1860s and with the advent of boilers operating at higher pressures that this type of engine became practical for seagoing service.

In the following decade the reciprocating steam engine reached its conceptual apogee for seagoing purposes with the introduction of the triple expansion engine. This added a third cylinder to the two-cylinder compound engine. The new intermediate-pressure cylinder occupied the pressure gap between the high- and low-pressure cylinders, and thus allowed the steam to be used three rather than two times before being exhausted into the condenser. The arrangement drove three pistons connected to the same crankshaft and thus represented still more power transmitted to the crankshaft by a given quantity of steam, and was made feasible at the technical level by improvements in the design and construction of boilers to produce higher steam pressures. It is worth noting that shortly before the introduction of the steam turbine to power ships, a final stage in the development of the reciprocating engine was typified by the quadruple expansion engine. Such engines were comparatively rare, their most notable use being in four large German liners built between 1897 and 1902. A hybrid of reciprocating and turbine features also making use of the quadruple expansion capability provided by high-pressure boilers was based on a triple expansion reciprocating engine from which the steam was ducted to a low-pressure turbine which extracted the last of the steam's power.

The rotation of a crankshaft cannot, in itself, drive a vessel through the water. Thus the invention and steady perfection of the reciprocating steam engine was only of use in combination with a system to transfer the power to a propulsion arrangement. The earliest of these was the paddle wheel which, in primitive man- and animal-powered forms, had been known to the ancient Chinese and Egyptians from very early times. With the development of the steam engine in the latter half of the 18th century machine-powered paddlewheel propulsion was introduced in a number of forms, at first mounted between a pair of hulls or in the hull as in, respectively, Patrick Miller's boat of 1788 and William Symington's *Charlotte Dundas* of 1802. The first "standard" paddlewheel layout, however, was two such wheels athwartships on a common shaft driven by the steam engine. The earliest examples of the powered paddlewheel had six or more fixed blades (properly called floats), and in some cases these wheels could be taken apart carried on deck when the vessel was under sail. By about 1840 the paddle-wheel generally incorporated a device through whose agency radial rods, mounted on an eccentric, moved the floats in turn so that they remained all but upright between the moments of entering and exiting the water, in the process maximising propulsive power and minimising wash.

For the first half century of seagoing steam power, the paddlewheel was essentially unchallenged. The first regular transatlantic liners such as Brunel's *Great Western* were based on paddlewheel propulsion, as too were those of the companies which plied to and from Spain, the Mediterranean, India and China. From the beginning, though, owners, captains and engineers had been all too aware of the fact that the paddlewheel was far from ideal for ocean-going purposes. For example, paddlewheel propulsion was very vulnerable to the breaking of the drive shaft and damage to the engine if, in bad weather, the vessel rolled strongly and one wheel was in the water while the other was out of it. In naval service, moreover, large and almost wholly exposed paddlewheels on each side of the ship were immensely vulnerable to the enemy fire as well as collision.

The obvious solution to both problems was the adoption of a wholly submerged propulsion arrangement, and this became possible with the invention of the screw propeller, which was a straightforward development of the Archimedes screw, whose principle was already well established. Four engineers are usually credited with its invention independently of each other in the period between 1833 and 1836. These were the English Robert Wilson, French Frederic Sauvage, Swede John Ericsson and English Francis Pettit Smith. It was the last whose invention was finally awarded a patent. In 1835 Smith made a model boat driven by a spring-powered propeller, and in May of the following year Smith secured the first patent for propeller propulsion. With financial and technical aid, Smith then built a 10-ton vessel, driven by a wooden propeller powered by a small steam engine, and this successfully navigated the waters off the coast of Kent. The Admiralty was interested but demanded validation of the concept in a larger vessel, and a company was therefore established to build the 237-ton *Archimedes*, which in October 1839 achieved 10 kt and later cruised through British waters as well as travelling to Amsterdam and Oporto.

The decisive moment in the rivalry between the paddlewheel and the screw propeller came in 1845. The Admiralty had contracted for its first screw-propelled sloop, HMS *Rattler*, during 1841. This was an 880-ton frigate fitted with a 220-hp (164-kW) steam engine, and in March 1845 the

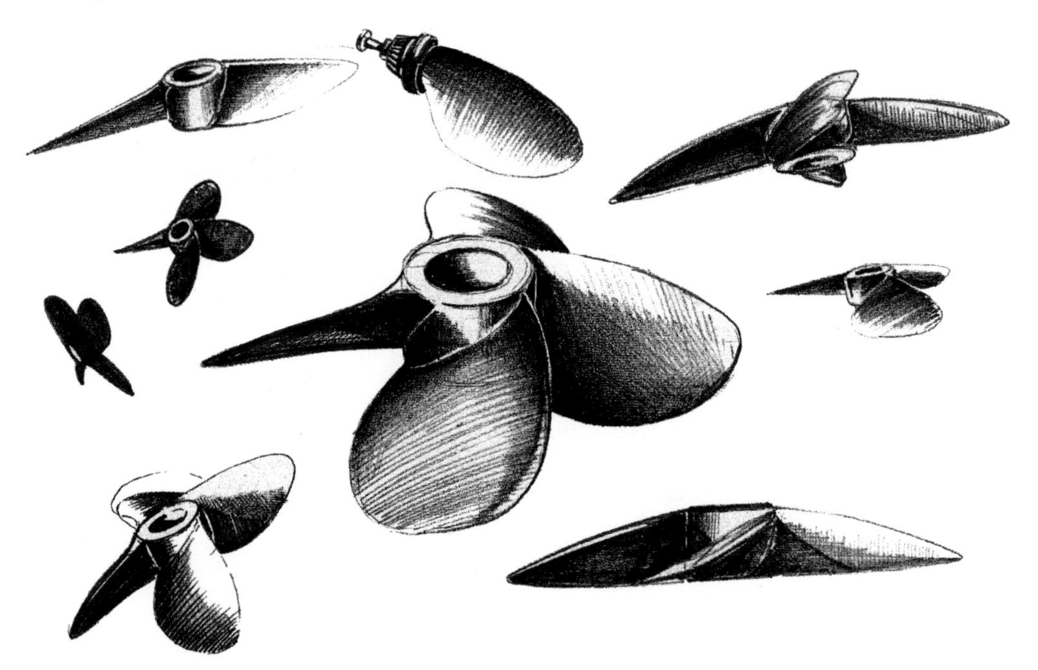

vessel was pitted again a paddlewheel-driven half-sister, HMS *Alecto*, in comparative trials. Over a course of 115 miles (185 km) the *Rattler* beat the *Alecto* by several miles, and when the two vessels were attached stern-to-stern the *Rattler* towed the *Alecto* stern first at 2.7 kt with both vessels' engines going full speed ahead. This proved that the propeller drove a ship faster through the water, and also exerted considerably more power.

The propeller was then developed into a remarkably efficient means of transforming a ship's engine power into forward thrust through the water. The first propellers had just two blades, long and narrow, and in many cases were designed to be lifted from the water when not being used. Launched in 1860 as the world's first ironclad battleship, HMS *Warrior* had a single two-blade propeller weighing 10 tons, but it required some 600 men to lift this clear of the water: turning at 56 revolutions per minute, this propeller nonetheless drove the *Warrior* at 14.3 kt.

The replacement of two-blade propellers by three- and four-blade units then followed quite soon. As engine power increased, especially as the original type of reciprocating engine was developed into the compound and triple-expansion engine, the number of propellers increased from the singleton unit, driven by a centerline shaft, to two units (one on each quarter) and for the largest ships to four units (two on each quarter). These multi-propeller arrangements not only made for greater propulsive efficiency through the provision of a less disturbed flow of water to the propellers, but were also of benefit in enhancing the steering of the vessel.

Before leaving the subject of steam machinery and propulsion, mention should be made of an alternative to reciprocating machinery, namely the rotating machinery represented by the turbine. Although the gas turbine, based on technology developed for the aviation industry, has been very popular for warships since 1960, the original type of turbine for maritime use was the steam turbine, in which a jet of steam is directed at a disc of blades set at an angle in a drum connected either direct or through gearing to the propeller shaft: the pressure of steam on the blades revolves the drum and the shaft attached to it. The steam turbine engine was invented by the Hon. Charles Parsons in the last decade of the 19th century, and demonstrated in his small Turbinia yacht, capable of an unprecedented 30 kt, at the Diamond Jubilee Review of the Royal Navy in 1897. Because of its admirable simplicity and high power/weight ratio, the steam turbine was soon adopted as the most efficient means of steam propulsion for any navy with scant pretension to modernity.

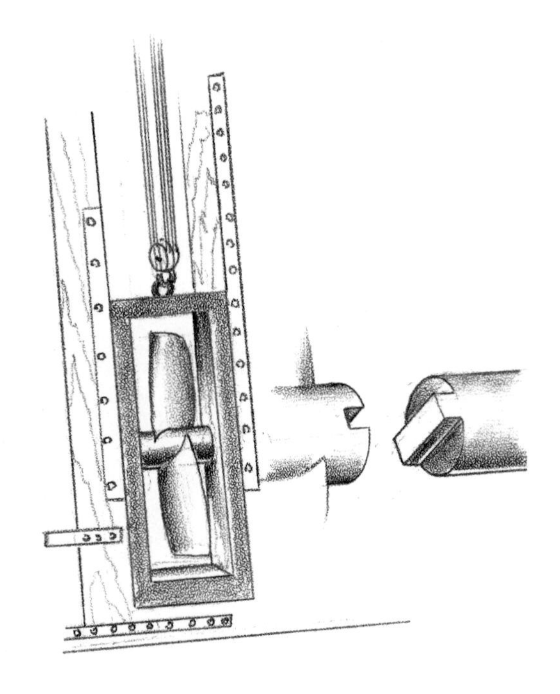

Up to the middle of the 19th century, the warship remained largely unaltered in conceptual terms from those which had fought in the French Revolutionary and Napoleonic Wars, the only major changes have been the limited adoption of metal in the structure, improved guns increasingly firing explosive shell as an alternative to solid shot, and steam propulsion to supplement the sails which still remained the primary form of propulsion. Then on November 30, 1853, during the preliminary stages of the Crimean War (1853/56), a Russian force of six line-of-battle ships appeared off the Turkish port of Sinope on the southern coast of the Black Sea and shelled a Turkish squadron of seven frigates, two corvettes, two transports and two steamers. Within just a few minutes all 13 Turkish vessels had been set on fire and completely destroyed. The naval world was stunned, and immediately planned the construction of warships built of iron or protected by iron plates and therefore "immune" to attack of this type.

This marked the birth of the ironclad, a designation which was used indiscriminately from this time up to 1906 for any warship built of metal or, more properly, built of wood under a protective sheathing of iron plate, the latter gradually developing into special protective armour built into the structure of the ship or added to the basic structure. The first such warship was a French vessel, *La Gloire*, a 5,600-ton frigate launched in 1859 with iron plates over an oak hull, while the first all-metal warship was HMS *Warrior*, a British 9,210-ton battleship launched in the following year and the real precursor of the modern warship, which came into being as a combination of iron (later steel) construction, steam-powered propeller propulsion and the shell-firing gun in place of wooden construction, sail propulsion and the shot-firing gun. The transformation did not take place overnight, but

wholly changed naval warfare and resulted in the creation of new types of warship.

The battleship was the equivalent of the sailing navy's line-of-battle ship, and the term is generally used for any capital ship (potentially battle-winning warship) of the period after the introduction of iron and later steel as the primary structural material. The introduction into naval warfare during the 1840s and 1850s of several important developments such as the explosive shell, the rifled and therefore more accurate gun, armour plate, and increasingly reliable and efficient steam machinery rendered obsolete the traditional two- and three-deck wooden line-of-battle ships, which had for some 300 years been the arbiter of naval warfare and during this period remained essentially unaltered in terms of its hull, rig, speed and offensive power. As noted above, the first seagoing ironclads were *La Gloire* and this French ship's British counterpart, the more ambitious *Warrior.* Both were classified as frigates and carried full sailing rig, but were capable of 13 kt on their steam engines, which delivered more than 3,000 hp (2240 kW) and could overtake, outmaneuver and comprehensively defeat any three-deck line-of-battle ship. In the absence of the spurs so often given to technical innovation and tactical thought by a major conflict, the ironclad battleship that emerged from these frigates was a monster which evolved through a number of phases, each a compromise derived from theoretical thinking in combination with technical developments in aspects such as metallurgy, gun construction and mounting, shell propellants, and the design of hulls and propulsive machinery.

By the middle of the 19th century's last decade, when Germany decided to create a navy to challenge Great Britain's naval supremacy, it seemed that virtually every conceivable mix of guns (large- and small-calibre), speed (high and moderate) and armour protection (thick and thin) had been considered and in most cases tried, and warship designers had at last fixed on a basic battleship scheme which combined a primary armament of four large-calibre guns, some 10 guns of perhaps two intermediate calibres), and a large number of quick-firing guns of small calibre to deal with the torpedo boat, which was the latest threat to the battleship. The "standard battleship" had a displacement in the order of 10,000 tons and a speed of some 16 kt. And while the last vestiges of a sailing capability had finally disappeared, the range capability of the new breed of breech-loading rifled gun appeared to have been entirely overlooked in the retention of a complete anachronism, the ram bow intended to provide a capability for the sinking of an enemy vessel by direct impact. The significance of the ram at this late stage was a complete miscalculation of the importance of the ram in the 2nd Battle of Lissa in July 1866, in which it proved effective against a tactically inept foe, and in accidental collisions such as that which led to the loss in 1893 of HMS *Victoria*, flagship of the Royal Navy's Mediterranean Fleet.

The development of the gun, armour and steam machinery proceeded so speedily during the technically

inventive period between 1870 and 1900 that the battleship became a readily distinguishable type with its limited number of main guns mounted in turrets, and most technically sophisticated navies embarked on the process of building such ships in homogeneous classes rather than just as singleton ships for experimental, development or even service use. This process was marked by a significant increase in displacement with each new class: so far as the Royal Navy's battleships were concerned, this escalation was between 9,210 tons in the *Warrior* of 1860 to 15,000 tons in the nine battleships of the "Majestic" class of 1896. Now approaching the conceptual horizon, though, was the "all-big-gun" battleship that completely revolutionised battleship design in its combination of high speed, adequate protection, and a main armament comprising large guns of just one calibre. The factors that paved the way to this new type of battleship were the threat posed to British naval supremacy by a relatively newly unified German nation, resulting changes in mercantile strength, altered balances of imperial power, tactical implications of naval warfare in the Russo-Japanese War (1904/05), and technical developments including the creation of effective torpedoes, submarines, and radio communications.

The British and Italians had experimented unsuccessfully with single-calibre battleship armament during the 1870s, and then reverted to the mixed-calibre main armaments that were standard but finally revealed as wholly inefficient in the naval fighting of 1904/05: ranging for the different calibres was altogether too complicated, and spotting the "splash" of the different-calibre shells in action proved impossible. Added to this, and to the surprise of the naval world in general, accurate fire with the heaviest guns out to a range of almost 20,000 yards (18300 m) proved possible. The implications were unchallengeable: the concentration of largest-calibre fire at maximum accurate range would sink or disable an enemy ship before its larger number of medium-calibre guns and his ship-launched torpedoes could be brought into action. Even before the decisive Battle of Tsushima, in which a Russian fleet was virtually destroyed during May 1905, the Japanese had laid down the *Aki* as the world's first "all-big-gun" battleship, and only financial limitations and delayed delivery of the guns prevented the completion of the *Aki* as the first example of the new breed of battleship. Both the Americans and the Russians had also seen the way naval developments were heading and were planning "all-big-gun" battleships by 1904.

However, it was the British who completed, in 1906 and some years before any other nation, the first "all-big-gun" battleship in the form of HMS *Dreadnought*, which gave its name to a genre which then continued in basic concept for another 40 years. There were many who contributed to the design of the *Dreadnought*, but if a single parent is demanded this should be Admiral Sir John Fisher, who had become First Sea Lord in 1904. Completed in less than a year, largely through the use of materials and components already in hand for other ships, the 17,900-ton *Dreadnought* carried the armament of 10 12-in (305 mm) guns in five twin turrets and had a maximum speed of 21 kt on her oil-fired steam turbines, and was altogether superior to any other battleship in the world. The ship's construction was not without controversy, for its completion rendered obsolete not only foreign but also current British battleships, and demanded an unprecedented industrial and financial effort in the immediate future to keep the Royal Navy ahead of the emergent German navy through the rapid completion of large numbers of the most modern ships. By the time Germany completed her first class of four dreadnoughts, Great Britain had seven in commission. The "naval race" in dreadnought construction continued at a steadily increasing tempo right past end of World War I (1914/18). Germany in fact ceased dreadnought construction in the later part of the war so that greater resources could be concentrated on the mass production of submarines, but rivalry with the USA and Japan lasted to the "battleship holiday" mandated by the Washington Naval Treaty of 1921/22. Great Britain completed 48 dreadnoughts up to 1918 and Germany 26, and in addition to the USA and Japan, France, Italy, Austria-Hungary and Russia built such ships, and modest numbers were also delivered to South American nations embroiled in their own "naval race."

The most impressive battleships of this generation were British, American and Japanese. Guns of 16-in (406-mm) calibre came into service,

and shell design, gun propellants and protection (both armour and internal design) were all significantly improved. Typical of the breed was HMS *Hood*, designed in World War I as a battle-cruiser and the largest capital ship in service between the two world wars, had a displacement of 41,200 tons, main armament of eight 15-in (381-mm) guns, and speed of 31 kt. Naval rearmament began in the mid-1930s and, despite the manifest and growing capability of air and submarine attack, the major naval powers embarked once again on the construction of battleships which were, in essence, improved versions of World War I thinking in their emphasis on high speed, sturdy protection and "all-big-gun" armament. The two major changes, much elaborated in World War II (1939/45), were the strengthened horizontal protection and the replacement of World War I's batteries of quick-firing guns (providing protection against the attacks of torpedo boats) by batteries of fast-firing anti-aircraft guns. Many battleship survivors of World War I, now modified and re-equipped, performed well in World War II, mainly in the escort and shore bombardment roles.

Early in World War II it might have been believed that the era of the battleship was over, for Italian and US losses at Taranto in November 1940 and Pearl Harbor in December 1941 to British and Japanese air attack respectively, suggested that the aircraft carrier was now paramount. Handled well, fitted with effective light and medium anti-aircraft armaments and operating with suitable escorts, the battleship was nonetheless revealed as a type which could still cope with punishment from the air and offer flexible and effective gun fire support in surface actions. However, as the

British discovered with their loss of the new battleship HMS *Prince of Wales* and the elderly battle-cruiser *Repulse* in December 1941, and the Japanese in their own turn with the loss of their new battleships *Musashi* and *Yamato* in October 1944 and April 1945, no battleship could itself fight off a hard-pressing onslaught by warplanes armed with torpedoes and armour-piercing bombs.

The *Yamato* and *Musashi*, completed in 1941 and 1942, were the greatest battleships ever completed. Each had a displacement of more than 67,000 tons, main armament of nine 18.1-in (463-mm) guns in three triple turrets and speed of 27 kt. Their only rivals, in terms of capability, were the four US battleships of the "Iowa" class completed just a short time later. These each had a displacement of 45,000 tons, main armament of nine 16-in (406-mm) in three triple turrets and speed of 33 kt. The last two of these ships, much modernized and fitted with 32 long-range land attack missiles, were the USS *Iowa* and USS *New Jersey*, which were the last battleships in commission anywhere in the world and finally decommissioned only in October 1990 and February 1991 respectively.

Essentially a contemporary of the dreadnought battleship, the battle-cruiser was a British concept, attributable to "Jackie" Fisher, for ships of battleship size to work as advanced scouts for the battle fleet, and therefore powerful enough to push home their reconnaissance right up to the enemy's main fleet, but also fast enough to outstrip it. The battle-cruiser had guns of the same calibre as their battleship relatives, but possessed some 4 kt more speed through the thinning of their protection. Fisher initially called the type a fast armoured cruiser, and it was only in 1912 that the designation battle-cruiser was accorded, perhaps inadvertently persuading some commanders to use them as if they were fast battleships. The one country which succeeded, at least partially, in producing such hybrids of battle-cruiser and battleship capabilities, was Japan. This reflected the country's lack of industrial and financial strength in the first 50 years of the 20th century, and resulted in the creation of general-purpose battleships combining good armament, high speed protection which could be regarded as scarcely adequate.

The first battle-cruisers were HMS *Invincible* and HMS *Indomitable*, which were 17,000-ton vessels armed with eight 12-in (305-mm) guns and capable of 25.5 kt. Once the type was more firmly established, evolution then led to greater size, heavier armament, considerably more power and much higher speed, culminating in the Hood, which was the last British battle-cruiser to be built. Other nations, including Germany and Japan, built battle-cruisers, although not in numbers equal to those of the British in a perhaps unconscious appreciation that the battle-cruiser possessed an inherent weakness in its lack of protection (especially the horizontal armour that could protect against long-range plunging fire and later against air attack) and its inability to stand up to the punishment of heavy fire from battleships carrying larger numbers of the same calibre of main gun. Their original task was conceptually valid by the standards of the 20th century's first decade, but was rendered wholly obsolete after the emergence of the airplane as the primary reconnaissance tool.

The carriage and operation of aircraft are, of course, the *raisons*

d'être of the aircraft carrier. The idea of operating aircraft from warships originated soon after the airplane became practical, and in 1911 the American aviator Eugene Ely both took off and alighted on platforms erected on cruisers. A few months later Commander C. R. Samson of the Royal Navy took off in a Short biplane from a similar platform on the forecastle of the pre-dreadnought battleship HMS *Africa*. Aircraft made many flights from British warships in World War I, and in 1917 a Sopwith Pup landed on the flight deck superimposed on the forecastle of the light battle-cruiser/aircraft carrier HMS *Furious*, but it was not until this ship was revised with a landing deck abaft her superstructure that landings were made on a regular basis. These were very difficult because of the turbulence streaming back from the superstructure. Thus it was not until 1918, when a ship with an unobstructed deck over her whole length was completed, that the problem of landing was solved in an effective manner. This pioneering ship was HMS *Argus*, which was able to do away with a conventional superstructure and funnel by incorporating a hydraulically lifted bridge and discharging her smoke and gases over the stern.

This pioneering aircraft carrier was followed in 1920 by HMS *Eagle*, which was produced as a conversion of an incomplete battleship. The *Eagle* had her superstructure and funnels offset to the starboard side of an otherwise unobstructed flight deck, as did HMS *Hermes*, which was completed in 1923 as the first ship laid down as an aircraft carrier.

The Americans and Japanese had also got into the act, both commissioning their first small carriers in 1922. These were the USS *Langley* and the *Hosho* respectively, and were flush-decked vessels with hinged funnels, on one side, which could be lowered to the horizontal position during flight deck operations. No further carriers were built until after the conclusion of the Washington Treaty, when the Americans and Japanese each opted to convert a pair of capital ships otherwise scheduled for scrapping. These were the battle-cruisers USS *Lexington* and USS *Saratoga*, and the battleship *Kaga* and battle-cruiser *Akagi*, which were each transformed as an island carrier of some 36,000 tons. The islands of the Japanese ships was comparatively small as they did not incorporate the funnels, which extended horizontally over the side. The British selected the light battle-cruisers HMS *Courageous* and HMS *Glorious*, originally sister ships of the *Furious*, for conversion into island carriers.

Later carriers built by the British, Americans and Japanese, together with the French *Béarn* converted from battleship standard, had the offset island that was standard from this time onward. From 1937, however, when the Royal Navy started work on HMS *Illustrious* as their first post-Washington Treaty carriers, the British took a conceptual step forward with the introduction of armoured flight decks and hangar sides. While this improved their survivability in the face of air attack, it also reduced the number of aircraft they could operate. War experience bore out the necessity for such increased protection, however, and both the Americans and the Japanese adopted it for fleet carriers laid down after the Battle of Midway, fought in June 1942 largely by carrierborne aircraft and resulting in the loss of one and four carriers respectively.

The aircraft carriers built up to the end of World War II fell into three main categories, namely large fleet carriers each carrying up to 100 aircraft, light fleet carriers each operating about 40 aircraft, and small escort carriers (originally converted from merchant ships and therefore comparatively slow) each carrying between 20 and 35 aircraft. The light fleet and escort carriers have now disappeared, the latter often after post-war service as helicopter-carrying amphibious assault ships, and the fleet carrier is now known as attack carriers in the US Navy, which is the only service still operating aircraft carriers in significant numbers. The largest of these are the "Nimitz" class ships with nuclear propulsion, a displacement of some 95,000 tons, an air group of up to 100 aircraft, and a crew of more than 5,000.

The monitor is a low-freeboard and shallow-draft ship mounting one or two large guns and intended for coastal bombardment. The name comes from the original USS *Monitor*, an ironclad designed by John Ericsson for the US Navy in 1862 during the American Civil War (1861/65). The British built monitors in large

numbers during World War I for coastal bombardment and riverine operations, and similar ships were built by other nations, seeing more limited service in World War II and surviving, in the case of some South American vessels, toward the end of the 20th century.

In the era of sail, the designation cruiser was commonly applied to a fourth-rate ship or large frigate detached from a fleet to cruise independently to find and then report the enemy, while frigates and smaller vessels used for the trade protection role were also known as cruisers. The one essential characteristic of any ship detached for duty as a cruiser was sailing speed superior to that of any enemy being sought. Following the large-scale adoption of steam machinery for propulsion and iron for construction and protection during the middle of the 19th century, the cruiser evolved into specific type of warship. This was built in three or four types extending between, at the upper end, the armoured cruiser which was a large ship with a displacement of up to 16,000 tons displacement, via the belted cruisers with only a waterline belt of armour and the second-class cruiser with only light armour, to the light cruiser with very little armour but notably high speed. For the British, who were faced with the requirements associated with imperial policing and protection by fleets and squadrons stationed permanent at overseas bases, the cruiser was a necessity which had to be constructed in large numbers and in various forms. On several of the farther flung overseas stations, such vessels were the core of local fleets or squadrons.

In fleet service, the cruiser was still the primary implement of scouting for the main fleet it supported, though they differed from their sailing predecessors in not being detached from the fleet but remaining in visual touch. During battle the cruiser's most important task was the adoption of a position from which it could observe and report any movement of the enemy fleet, but secondary tasks were gun and torpedo attacks as and when the opportunity offered, and fleet defence by defeating attack by the enemy's lighter vessels.

After the end of World War I there was a radical change in the nature of the cruiser, resulting in the scrapping of virtually all of the ships but those completed in the second half of the war. The reason for this change was the assumption of the reconnaissance and scouting roles by aircraft, and its result was the introduction of a single "cruiser" type differentiated by the calibre of its main armament as an 8-in (203-mm) cruiser of a 6-in (152-mm) cruiser. These ships were therefore of much the same basic concept, but those with large-calibre guns tended to be larger and to carry better protection. As fleet reconnaissance was no longer the primary role, the cruiser rapidly gained a number of tasks including trade protection, support of amphibious forces and, in a more specialized form, defence against air attack. Cruisers with 8-in (203-mm) guns gradually became known as heavy cruisers, those with 6-in (152-mm) guns as light cruisers and, in the case of a few ships built to heavy cruiser standards but with the size and armament of capital ships, large heavy cruisers. Sometimes, but wrongly, called battle-cruisers, these last were typified by the US Navy's "Alaska" class ships with 12-in (305-mm) guns. Occupying a somewhat intermediate position were vessels such as Germany's "Scharnhorst" class vessels, which were in fact small capital ships and often known as battle-cruisers.

As noted above, one of the secondary tasks allocated to the cruiser was defense against the torpedo boat. This was a type of warship developed in the period between 1880 and 1890 to exploit the capabilities of a new and potentially decisive weapon, the Whitehead "locomotive torpedo" with a warhead capable of punching through the armour of a battleship's waterline belt. The first real torpedo boat anywhere in the world was the 19-ton HMS *Lightning*, which had been launched in 1876 to carry spar torpedoes (charges at the tips of fixed poles), but was modified in 1879 with

above-water tubes for two Whitehead torpedoes. The success of this pioneering torpedo boat persuaded the Royal Navy to order 12 more such vessels, which were earmarked for coast defense.

Other navies followed suit and, as it combined low construction and operating costs with a high level of capability against considerably larger warships, the torpedo boat was built in large numbers in the first half of the 1880s for the navies of Austria-Hungary, France, Italy, the Netherlands and Russia, and in the period immediately after this for the navies of Chile, China, Greece, Portugal, Spain, Sweden and Turkey.

The capabilities of the torpedo boat, in the hands of many smaller navies, implied a significant threat to the Royal Navy's supremacy in the last stages of the 19th century, and the Admiralty therefore found itself in the position of trying to find the tactical counter to a type of vessel it had itself created. The first counter to the torpedo boat was the torpedo boat catcher, which was a vessel larger and faster than the basic torpedo boat, and carrying a 4-in (102-mm) quick-firing gun as well as torpedo tubes. The pioneer of this new type of small warship was HMS *Rattlesnake*, which was launched in 1886 but was found to have an insufficient margin of speed over the torpedo boat to guarantee interception. Further prototypes were also unsuccessful, and it was only in 1893 that the required solution was discovered in the torpedo boat destroyers HMS *Havock* and HMS *Hornet*. Characterized by a displacement of 250 tons, a speed of 27 kt, and an armament which combined three 18-in (457-mm) torpedo tubes with one 12-pdr and two 6-pdr quick-firing guns, these pioneering vessels had the speed and firepower to catch and overwhelm any torpedo boat, and themselves carried the torpedo boat's armament, of which the two deck-mounted tubes could be replaced by two more 6-pdr guns.

Thus the pure torpedo boat had been rendered obsolete only a few years after its introduction, but most navies nonetheless persevered with their torpedo boat procurement programs, and in British service the torpedo boat remained in service to World War I after the last had been built in 1908.

The torpedo boat destroyer was a far longer-lived type of warship, its name gradually being trimmed just to destroyer. The emergence of the destroyer as the answer to and also the successor of the torpedo boat was facilitated by two factors, namely the invention of steam turbine propulsion

to replace triple expansion steam engines and the adoption of oil in place of coal to fire the boilers. The combination of these two features wholly revolutionized destroyer design to provide greater speed and significant reduction in manning requirements. This opened the design floodgates at a time of the "naval race" between Germany and Great Britain in the years leading to World War I. The first turbine-engined destroyers were HMS *Viper* and HMS *Cobra*, completed respectively by Parsons and Armstrongs in 1900 and 1901 with a light displacement of 344 and 375 tons. By the outbreak of World War I the royal Navy had destroyers of up to 1,300 tons operating in flotillas led by super-destroyers (flotilla leaders) approaching 2,000 tons. The increase in displacement and size allowed the shipping of larger numbers of heavier weapon, and also provided a hull with improved seakeeping qualities and the volume for the bunkerage offering a significant endurance. As a result, therefore, the destroyer became an altogether more versatile warship than the small torpedo boat could ever have been, with the seakeeping and endurance to operate with squadrons of cruisers and battleships.

The classic roles of the destroyer in the fleet scenario were already the delivery of salvoes of torpedoes at an enemy's heavier warships and the defeat of the enemy's own torpedo boat attacks when, in World War I, the emergence of the submarine as a decisive weapon in World War I demanded the addition of another role. Up to this time the torpedo had been seen largely as a surface-launched weapon, but it was now shown to be just as deadly as a weapon launched under water by an unseen vessel. The destroyer was now additionally tasked with the screening of the battle fleet, every time it emerged from harbor, against submarine attack. World War I added further tasks, too, firstly and largely unsuccessfully in patrolling sea areas through which merchant ships, increasingly the submarines' most important targets, had to pass, and from 1917 in escorting convoys across the oceans. However, the destroyer was decisively hampered in the anti-submarine role by the lack of any genuinely effective means, except the simple hydrophone, of detecting and more importantly of fixing the position of a submerged submarine. Many destroyers were also outfitted as coastal minelayers in World War I, so adding a further string to the already considerable range of tasks these versatile ships could undertake.

Developments between the end of World War I and the end of World War II (1919/45) further magnified the capabilities and importance of the destroyer. The ever increasing importance of air power in naval operations required that some destroyers become as air direction ships to control the activities of carrierborne and shore-based aircraft. The development of ASDIC (later known as sonar) both to detect and to fix the bearing of a submerged submarine provided them with an enhanced anti-submarine capability when combined with specialized weapons more effective than the basic depth charge, which was dropped or fired "blind" over the stern and each quarter after the destroyer had passed over the submarine and lost sonar contact in the process. These new weapons fired ahead over the bows while the sonar still had contact with the target, and included the Hedgehog and the Squid. The former was located on the foredeck and fired a 24-round pattern of 30-lb (14-kg) impact-fused bombs, while the latter was located on the quarterdeck to fire a pattern of three full-size depth charges over the bridge to land in a pattern ahead of the ship.

After World War II, the destroyer gradually lost its importance in the anti-submarine role but only as it gained steadily more power in tackling air, surface and land targets as guided missiles became their primary armament, and as advanced radars and other systems became their primary sensors. Thus the destroyer had grown steadily in size, the average displacement increasing from perhaps 2,000 tons in 1945 to 5,000 tons and more in the first part of the 21st century. In this modern capability, therefore, the destroyer can be regarded as the latter-day counterpart of the light cruiser.

The term frigate effectively disappeared with the end of the era

of sail, but then reappeared in World War II to denote a type of specialized anti-submarine vessel created largely for the all-important convoy escort role with specialized weapons and sensors, and also characterized by moderate speed but long endurance. Typical of the breed were the "River" and "Loch" classes. The latter had a deep-load displacement of 2,260 tons, was armed with one 4-in (102-mm) DP gun, one quadruple 2-pdr pom-pom AA gun, one Squid projector and depth charges, and could reach 20 kt on its geared steam turbine propulsion arrangement. The US Navy counterpart of the frigates was the destroyer escort. Since the end of World War II, the frigate has increased steadily in size and capability, in the process assuming the destroyer's erstwhile "maid of all work" mantle. The modern frigate is therefore found in general-purpose form, but more importantly in anti-submarine and anti-aircraft forms.

In World War II the frigate was often partnered by the sloop and the corvette, both of these being names that had also died out with the end of the era of sail before being revived for anti-submarine vessels smaller than the frigate. In its World War II form, therefore, the sloop was a member of one of the classes of specialized but smaller convoy escort warships which were of so vital an importance to the allied war effort in the Battle of the Atlantic. Similarly, the corvette of World War II for small anti-submarine escorts used mainly the Battle of the Atlantic. First ordered in 1939 as a type that could be constructed quickly to help fill the gap in the British anti-submarine capability, the original design was based on that of the whale catcher and was driven by a triple expansion steam engine, the only design which

was readily available and could be made quickly, powered one propeller. The vessels of this original design, which entered service as the "Flower" class, proved unsatisfactory in Atlantic winter weather because of their tendency to a severe roll, but they were succeeded by the units of new and improved design, the "Castle" class, in relatively large numbers from the middle of the war even though the swelling numbers of frigates offered greater capabilities. Smaller than the anti-submarine frigate and armed with one 4-in (102-mm) gun and up to 72 depth charges, later augmented by a Squid projector, the "Modified flower" class corvette had a full-load displacement of 1,370 tons and reached 16.5 kt on its one triple expansion steam engine. The corvettes were the core of British anti-submarine escort capability up to 1944, and in their later forms were very successful in U-boat hunter/killers.

Two key elements in the design, construction and operation of warships between the middle of the 19th century and the middle of the 20th century were armour protection and guns. Although proposals for the protection of warships by the addition of armour plates along their sides dates from 1805, it was only after the Battle of Sinope in 1853 that serious consideration was given to the large-scale adoption of armour. In 1854 France, Great Britain and the USA started to build floating batteries with protection provided by 4.5 in (114 mm) of wrought iron over teak 18 in (457 mm) thick. The success of the new protection was attested by the invulnerability of the French batteries as they bombarded the Russian forts at Kinburn in 1855, when the batteries took many hits but suffered only very modest casualties.

This spurred further development, and the first armour used for ships was of wrought iron in either one layer or in several layers including wood or concrete. Naval gunnery improved rapidly between 1860 and 1885, and in response iron armour grew to thicknesses up to 24 in (610 mm). Cast iron was trialled as an alternative to wrought iron, but was too brittle to withstand the impact of heavy shells without fracturing or shattering. The next turning point was therefore the introduction of steel by the Schneider company of France in 1876. Steel soon began to replace wrought iron as the primary material for protection, for 1876 trials in Italy confirmed that steel possessed much greater resistance to shellfire than wrought iron, even though it had a tendency toward fracturing, at least in its early forms. This tendency to fracture was combated initially by the 1877 adoption of compound armour in which a hard steel face was cemented with molten steel to a resilient wrought iron base.

The evolution of steel technology up to 1890 created steel plate without a tendency to fracture, but more important was the creation of ways to harden the face of the steel, achieved by chilling the heated surface of the steel with pressurized jets of water. It was almost immediately after this development's introduction that in 1891 the American H. A. Harvey pioneered the case hardening of steel plate without any need for a wrought iron backing. The elimination of the wrought iron base was decisive, for its allowed the weight of the protection to be reduced significantly without loss of resistance to penetration. In 1892 this all-steel armour was further improved by the addition of small quantities of nickel and chromium.

In 1893 the German Alfred Krupp introduced a new process, based on heat treatment, to give steel armour a hard face significantly thicker than that which could be achieved by case hardening and a back which was also considerably stronger. This process came into general use and, though improved in a number of respects, remained definitive type of steel armour plate so long as the material was used. However, with the disappearance of the battleship as the arbiter of naval warfare, the significance of armour protection, up to 26 in (660 mm) thick, has disappeared. Modern warships are

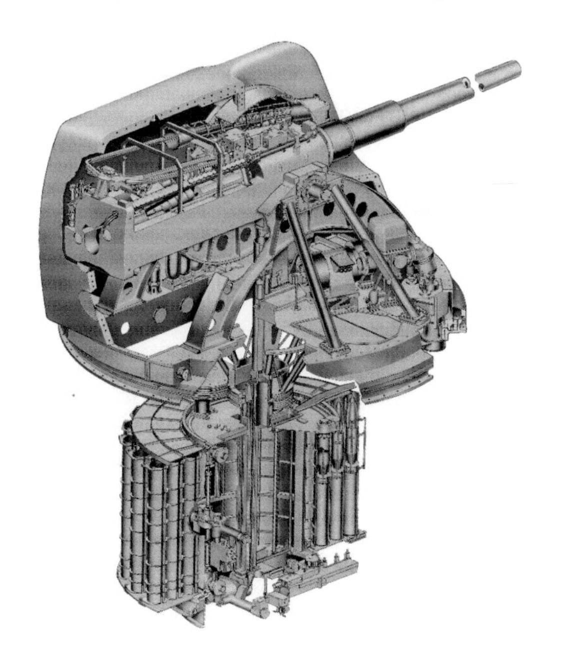

smaller and are not faced with the prospect of receiving heavy shell impacts, but on the other hand face the threat of penetration effects of shaped-charge warheads and the like, and therefore derive their protection from spaced layers of metals and also materials such as Kevlar.

It was the introduction of explosive shells in combination with the development of armour in the mid-19th century which paved the way for a complete revolution in naval gunnery, the first since the middle of the 16th century. What emerged was a capability race between the shell's ability to penetrate armour and armour's ability to resist the penetration of the shell. This meant that by the middle of the 1870s armour had reached a thickness of 20 in (508 mm) and gun calibre 17.7 in (450 mm) in rifled weapons turning the scales at 110 tons.

The escalation of size and weight was then reversed, albeit for only a short time, by the introduction of face-hardened armour on the defensive side and nitrocellulose-based propellants, higher muzzle velocities and armour-piercing projectiles on the offensive side. Then the see-saw battle between armour and the gun started once again after the implications of the new technologies had been digested, continuing to the effective replacement of the gun by the guided missile in the 1950s. By this time guns had peaked with the 18.1-in (460-mm) weapon of the "Yamato" class battleships: this gun fired a 3,220-lb (1460-kg) shell to a maximum range of 45,275 yards (41400 m), or 25.73 statute miles, at the rate of 1.5 rounds per minute.

The large naval gun was changed not only in calibre and weight of projectile from the middle of the 19th century, however. The rifling of barrels and the introduction of nitrocellulose propellants boosted accuracy and range to a remarkable degree. The replacement of muzzle loading by breech-loading mechanisms, using the sliding wedge or interrupted-thread breech block concepts, improved the rate of fire, especially after the invention of quick-firing breech mechanisms which allowed the breech to be opened or shut by the single motion of one lever. Guns of large calibre (12 in/305 mm and upward), medium calibre (between 12 and 6 in/305 and 152 mm) and even small calibre (6 in/152 mm downward) were mounted in turrets or gun houses which were hydraulically or electrically operated. The final developments have included guided projectiles and fully automated guns of up to 8-in (203-mm) calibre.

French Windmill Powered Warship (1798)

Vast scientific advances were made in the later 18th century, a period also marked by a fascination with all types of what we would today call technological marvels, most of them wholly impractical, The majority of the technologies demanded for these schemes were at only the earliest stages of human understanding, and this combined with the absence of any effective and self-contained powerplant to allow the creation of workable vehicles of any size.

None of these factors was any hindrance to the more "visionary" designers of the period. For such men there was very little that could not be dreamed and, they believed, turned into workable hardware. In conditions such as those when revolutionary France was ruled by the so-called Directory in 1798, there was great scope for the dreamer with a greater grasp of concept than reality.

France needed modern ships, and currently there was a vogue for wind power to operate mechanisms of all types. The led to the "design" of a number of weird warships such as that seen here. Based on a saucer-shaped hull of wooden construction and shallow draft with fore-and-aft loading by means of drawbridges, the vessel was to be propelled by eight paddle wheels driven, in a wholly unspecified manner, by the rotation of windmill sails. Other features of this nightmare vessel were furnaces for heating shot, and a central "keep" surmounted by a semaphore machine for signalling.

French windmill-powered warship

Type:	gun-armed "warship"
Tonnage:	not known
Dimensions:	length 200 ft (61 m); beam 120 ft (36.6 m); draft not known
Propulsion:	windmill-powered paddle wheels for an unknown speed
Armour:	none
Armament:	68 muzzle-loading smooth-bore guns and four muzzle loading smooth-bore mortars
Complement:	not known

Demologos (1813)

The world's first steam-powered warship, the *Demologos* or *Fulton the First*, was built for the US Navy and was the last ship designed by Robert Fulton, a pioneer of steam-powered ship design. In December 1813 Fulton suggested his concept of a "floating battery" to break the British blockade of New York during the War of 1812. Funding for this "frigate" was provided by the Congress, and in October 1814 a large crowd saw the launch into the East River before the vessel was towed to Fulton's New Jersey workshops. The two pontoon hulls were joined by a gun deck containing a centerline opening for a paddle wheel with a diameter of 16 ft (4.9 m), an armoured upper cover, and driven by machinery in one hull using steam generated by a boiler in the other hull. The hulls were doubled-ended, the engine was reversible, and there were two sets of rudders so that the ship could be steamed in either direction. Even the auxiliary sailing rig was double ended, consisting of a lateen sail and jib at each end, although this was later replaced by a conventional twin-masted fore-and-aft rig on each hull.

In February 1815 Fulton died of pneumonia but work on the ship went on, and trials in the summer showed that the principle of a steam-powered warship was technically valid. The *Demologos* was then laid up, except for use in a brief tour of New York harbour by President Madison in 1818. With her engines and armament removed in 1821, the *Demologos* was used as a receiving ship at the Brooklyn Navy Yard until June 1829, when she accidentally blew up.

Demologos

Type:	paddle-wheel steam frigate
Tonnage:	2,475 tons displacement
Dimensions:	length 156 ft (47.5 m); beam 56 ft (17.1 m); draft 11 ft (3.35 m)
Propulsion:	one single-cylinder engine delivering 120 hp (89.5 kW) to one paddle wheel for 6 kt
Armament:	24 32-pdr guns
Complement:	200

The Demologos marked the advent of steam power into the world's navies.

HMS *Salamander* (1832)

In the early 1830s the Royal Navy ordered the design and construction of five steam-powered warship "prototypes." These differed in size and power, and were early efforts by four shipwrights to create a paddle-wheel warship more formidable than a gun vessel. Designed by Joseph Seaton, master shipwright of the Sheerness Dockyard in which she was built, HMS *Salamander* was launched in May 1832 and was at first armed with two 10-in (254-mm) pivot guns and two 32-pdr carronades on truck carriages, two more carronades being added later. Like all the Royal Navy's early paddle-wheel ships, the Salamander had side-lever engines, and her barque rig offset the engines' high fuel consumption.

The *Salamander* saw service off Spain in 1836/37 on the side of Queen Isabella against her uncle, Don Carlos, and often carried troops or provided gunfire support. Though the screw made paddle-wheelers obsolescent as major war vessels in the later 1840s, many continued to give years of useful service in other roles. The *Salamander* took part in the 2nd Burma War (1852) and in 1865 surveyed the Queensland coast. The vessel was paid off in 1875 and sold in 1883 after 50 years of service.

The Salamander was a prototype paving the way for the adoption of steam power into the Royal Navy.

HMS *Salamander*

Type:	second-class paddle-wheel sloop
Tonnage:	1,014 tons displacement
Dimensions:	175 ft 5 in 82.9 m); beam 32 ft 2 in (9.8 m); draft 13 ft 6 in (4.1 m)
Propulsion:	two side-lever engines delivering 506 ihp (377 kW) to two paddle wheels for 7.2 kt
Armament:	two 10-in (254-mm) guns and four 32-pdr carronades
Complement:	135

USS *Mississippi* (1841)

One of the first side-wheel steam frigates ordered for the US Navy, the wooden-hulled USS *Mississippi* was built by the Philadelphia Navy Yard as a barque-rigged which was extensively used for evaluation of steam power. The *Mississippi* was flagship of Commodore Matthew Perry's West Indian Squadron in the Mexican War of 1845/47, and in 1849/51 was in the Mediterranean. In 1852 she sailed for the Far East in Perry's mission to open trade with Japan. Except for a US visit in 1855/56, the *Mississippi* remained in the Far East to 1860, supporting British and French ships during the bombardment of Taku in June 1859 and landed US Marines to protect US interests at Shanghai in August.

The *Mississippi* returned to Boston in 1860, and was assigned to blockade duty off Key West in June 1861. When a Federal fleet entered the *Mississippi* in April 1863, as the fleet passed the forts below New Orleans, the *Mississippi* destroyed the CSS *Manassas*. The Mississippi remained at New Orleans until 1863, when she took part in the run past Port Hudson, the largest Confederate fort below Vicksburg. The vessel ran aground, and after losing 64 men killed by the fire of shore batteries, her captain ordered the vessel to be set on fire and abandoned.

The paddle wheels of the USS Mississippi, 28 ft (8.5 m) in diameter, were very vulnerable to battle damage.

USS *Mississippi*

Type:	side-wheel frigate
Tonnage:	3,220 tons displacement
Dimensions:	length 229 ft (69.8 m); beam 66 ft 6 in (20.25 m); draft 21 ft 8 in (6.6 m)
Propulsion:	two side-lever steam engines delivering 700 notional hp (522 kW) for 11 kt
Armament:	two 10-in (254-mm) and 19 8-in (203-mm) smooth-bore guns
Complement:	257

La Gloire (1860)

The first real test of the ironclad warship, created by the attachment of plates of wrought iron to the outer sides of a conventional primary hull structure of wood, was that provided under what were then "modern" operational conditions in the course of the Crimean War (1853/56) between Russia on the one side, and France, Turkey and the UK on the other. Impressed by the success of early ironclad ships, most particularly against the Russian shore batteries at Fort Kinburn, at the mouth of the River Dniepr, the French navy began a program of ironclad warship construction. This effort had the wholehearted support of the Emperor Napoléon III in the awareness of the rivalry emerging between France and the UK.

Becoming naval constructor of the French navy in 1857, Stanislas Dupuy de Lôme completed the design of six broadside ironclad warships, with conventional broadside gun batteries, in the course of 1858. The first of these were the units of the "La Gloire" class, and as the lead vessel on this class *La Gloire* was in essence a development de Lôme's design for what had emerged as the world's first steam warship with propeller propulsion, *Le Napoléon* of 1850. Lacking the industrial base for the construction of a wholly iron-hulled warship, the French were compelled to compromise, and as a result *La Gloire*, when completed by the Arsenal de Toulon in August 1860, was seen to be an ironclad vessel in which the sides of the wooden hull, between 24 and 26 in (610 and 660 mm) thick, carried wrought iron plates between 4.7 and 4.3 in (120 and 110 mm) thick and heavily reinforced

As completed in 1860, La Gloire had a barquentine rig of 11,840 sq ft (1100 m²), but this was later changed to a ship rig of 26,910 sq ft (2500 m²).

with iron fastenings. *La Gloire* had a single iron deck, and was completed with a relatively small three-masted barquentine rig later replaced, for better sailing performance under peacetime conditions, with a full ship rig carrying a larger area of canvas. The single propeller was driven by a horizontal return connecting rod engine supplied with steam by eight oval boilers. Intended to operate within the context of the traditional battle line, *La Gloire* carried the broadside armament of 36 6.4-in (163-mm) rifled muzzle-loading guns disposed as 18 on each side of the gun deck. This scheme was soon changed to 12 or 16 6.4-in (163-mm) guns, 12 55-pdr smooth-bore guns and four 8.8-in (346-mm) rifled muzzle-loading howitzers.

The other two ships of the class were *L'Invincible* and *La Normandie*, the first built at the Arsenal de Toulon and completed in March 1862 and the second at the Arsenal de Cherbourg and completed in May 1862. These three ships were partnered by the iron-hulled *La Couronne* and the 10 ships of the "Flandre" class, of which *La Heroïne* had an iron hull, as well as the 50-gun broadside ironclads *Magenta* and *Solferino*.

La Gloire remained in service for eight years before being taken in hand for an extensive upgrade, re-emerging with eight 9.4-in (239-mm) and six 7.6-in (193-mm) rifled guns, which marked the French navy switch to breech-loading weapons. In 1879, *La Gloire* was stricken, and four years later she was broken up. Though not notably successful, *La Gloire* led the British to build HMS *Warrior*, a much larger iron-hulled warship which wholly eclipsed *La Gloire* and gave birth to a new type of warship.

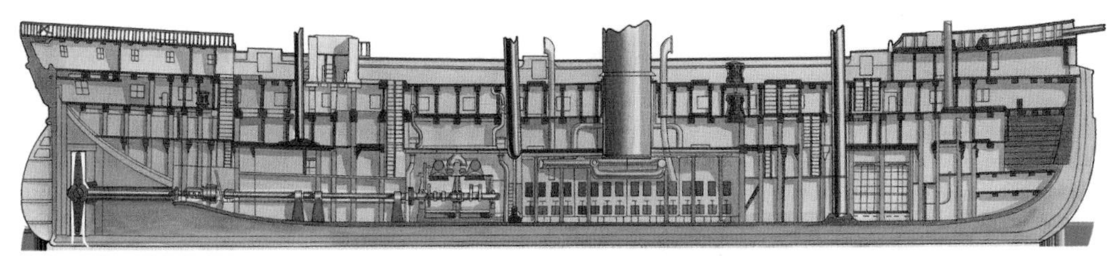

A cut-away illustration highlights the internal arrangements, including the large-diameter smoke stack, of La Gloire's hull. The layout of the steam plant meant that the main and mizzen masts could not be stepped on the keelson.

***La Gloire* (as completed)**

Type:	broadside ironclad warship
Tonnage:	5,630 tons displacement
Dimensions:	length 255 ft 6 in (778 m); beam 55 ft 9 in (17 m); draft 27 ft 10 in (8.5 m)
Propulsion:	one HRCR steam engine delivering 2,500 ihp (1864 kW) to one propeller for 13 kt
Armour:	4.3- to 4.7-in (110- to 120-mm) belt and 4-in (100-mm) conning tower
Armament:	36 6.4-in (163-mm) modèle 1858/60 rifled muzzle-loading guns
Complement:	570

HMS *Warrior* (1861)

The response to the threat implied to British maritime supremacy by *La Gloire* and other French ironclad warships designed in the later 1850s, the revolutionary HMS *Warrior* was a superb warship resulting from the initiative of the First Sea Lord, Admiral Sir John Pakington, who ordered Admiral Sir Baldwin Wake Walker, the Surveyor of the Navy, to create the world's most powerful and heavily protected warship.

The greatest innovation in the *Warrior* was the hull, for this was the world's first ocean-going warship based on an iron rather than ironclad wooden hull. As a result, the *Warrior* was the largest warship of the day, with a length some 140 ft (42.7 m) greater than that of the 120-gun line-of-battle sailing ship HMS *Howe* completed in 1860. La Gloire and her two sisters were only 255 ft 6 in (77.9 m) long. Less quantifiable but no less telling was the elegance of the *Warrior's* hull lines and notably slender 6.5/1 length/beam ratio. Despite her great length, the Warrior had only a modest primary armament in the form of 26 68-pdr breech-loading guns. Twenty-two of these were located on the main deck within a central citadel, which was in effect an armour-protected box in the middle of the ship. The citadel also accommodated four 110-pdr breech-loading guns. Just forward of the citadel were two more 110-pdr guns, and just abaft the citadel two further 110-pdr guns as well as four more 68-pdr weapons. The upper-deck guns comprised single 110-pdr bow and stern chasers and, working aft, one 6-pdr, one 12-pdr, two 20-pdr and four 40-pdr weapons. With only the heaviest guns featuring in the calculation system, the *Warrior* was classified as a 40-gun ship.

The *Warrior* was designed to use her greater speed and superior agility to outrun and outmaneuver any steam battleship. Yet even though it was now relatively advanced in the technical sense, steam machinery was still known to lack reliability and to be so demanding in coal that long steam-powered voyages were impossible.

HMS Warrior is seen ready to steam, with her propeller lowered and her funnels raised.

Thus the *Warrior* was designed to fighter under steam, but to cruise as a three-masted ship, in which circumstances the two-blade propeller was lifted clear of the water. Similarly, the two funnels, which extended through the deck between the fore and main masts, could be lowered.

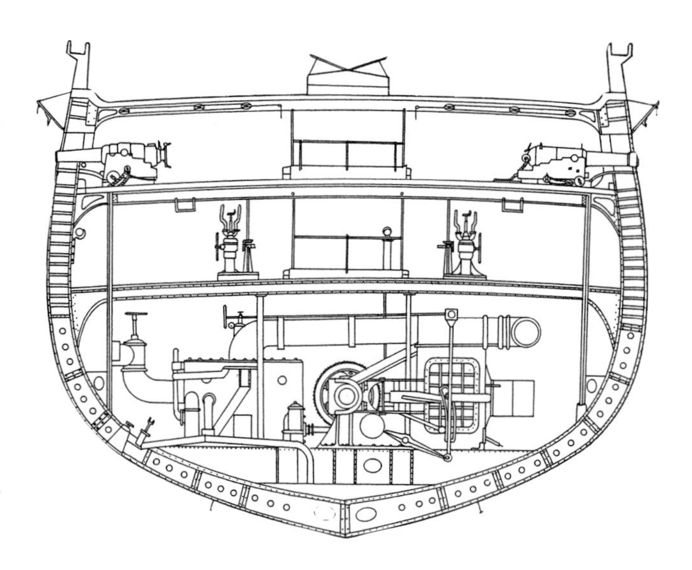

Cross section of HMS Warrior's hull showing the machinery space and three decks above it.

Built by the Ditchburn and Mare yard in Blackwall, London, the *Warrior* was commissioned as part of the Channel Fleet in August 1861, and spent the whole of her active life with this fleet as a primary asset in the event of the emergence of any threat from the great French port of Cherbourg. The *Warrior's* first refit lasted from 1964 to 1867, but by this time the ship had been overtaken, in technical terms, by the ironclads of the next British generation, which included the four-masted HMS *Achilles* and the five-masted "Minotaur" class broadside ships. The *Warrior's* most remarkable achievement came in 1869, when she and her sister ship, HMS *Black Prince,* were used to tow a floating dry-dock across the north Atlantic to Bermuda. The *Warrior* was taken in hand during 1871 for a four-year upgrade and refit in which her bowsprit was cut back, a poop deck was added and her boilers were replaced. The ship then became an element of the First Reserve Fleet for the next eight years, making eight summer cruises usually in home waters or to Gibraltar and the western Mediterranean.

In 1883 the *Warrior* was reclassified as an armoured cruiser, and in 1900 was hulked as a torpedo depot vessel. Subsequently the ship was a floating oil jetty, minesweeper depot ship and oil hulk, In 1979 the hulk was towed to Hartlepool and refurbishment began. In 1987 she was towed to Portsmouth for permanent display.

HMS *Warrior* (1968 standard)

Type:	broadside ironclad frigate
Tonnage:	9,137 tons displacement
Dimensions:	length 420 ft (128 m); beam 58 ft 4 in (17.8 m); draft 26 ft (7.9 m)
Propulsion:	one Penn horizontal expansion single trunk engine delivering 5,267 ihp (3927 kW) to one propeller for 14.1 kt
Armour:	4,5-in (114-mm) belt with 18-in (457-mm) wood backing, and 4.5 in (114-mm) bulkheads
Armament:	four 8-in (203-mm) and 28 7-in (178-mm) rifled muzzle-loading guns
Complement:	707

Le Napoléon (1852)

Although steam-powered warships with paddle-wheel propulsion had been built in modest numbers, practical experimentation had confirmed by the mid-1840s that the screw propeller offered greater efficiency. It was also clear that such a propulsion device, buried in the water, would also be less vulnerable to an enemy's fire than side-mounted paddle wheels which were mostly out of the water. The French were as quick as any to appreciate the fact, and the first result of their efforts was the screw frigate *La Pomone*, which was revealed in 1844. An exhaustive series of experiments, undertaken for the French navy by MM. Bourgois in 1847/48 and then further proved in 1849, was used to find the relative efficiency of different types of screw propeller for use in ships of different hull forms and dimensions under a host of differing wind and sea conditions.

La Napoléon and her sister ships represented a far-sighted venture into screw propeller propulsion, but were soon obsolete.

This work paved the way for the creation, from 1847 by Dupuy de Lôme, of *Le Napoléon*, which was a two-deck three-masted line-of-battle ship, of wholly wooden construction, adapted on the stocks as the world's first battleship with screw propeller propulsion. The ship was launched at the Arsenal de Toulon in May 1850, at Toulon, with her interior revised for the 550-ton Indret two-cylinder geared steam engine, which drove a propeller with four parallel-chord blades and a diameter of 19 ft 0.33 in (5.8 m) in diameter. Some 927 tons of coal were carried, and this provided for a steaming endurance of 40 days. *Le Napoléon* had eight boilers, each having five furnaces, with a full-speed consumption of 143 tons of coal per day, reducing steaming endurance to just five days. The boilers and engines occupied a length of 82 ft (25 m).

Le Napoléon was notably fast, on occasion exceeding 13 kt, but her machinery was unreliable. Such was the pace of development, however, that the ship's successors were completed with somewhat lighter machinery whose higher revolutions allowed the omission of the first ship's geared transmission, which was both heavy and cumbersome. After trials had revealed the capabilities of *Le Napoléon*, there followed in 1855/56 four sister ships, namely *L'Algésiras*, *L'Arcole*, *L'Impérial*, and *La Redoutable*, and then in 1858/60 three marginally heavier ships, *La Ville de Bordeaux*, *La Ville de Lyon* and *La Ville de Nantes*. These eight ships provided the renascent French navy with a core of heavily armed ships independent of the vagaries of the wind and tide.

Le Napoléon confirmed the practicability of using a screw propeller even for large warships, but also revealed that the utility of current screw propeller propulsion was limited. The propulsion plant and its fuel were notably heavy, and required considerable volume in the hull, so reducing the volume for other supplies. Something else which had to be factored into the equation was the fact that the exhaustion of the coal supply left *Le Napoléon* with the sail area of a 60-gun ship. The ships were soon obsolete, and by 1883 had been stricken, hulked or adapted as transports.

Le Napoléon

Type:	steam-powered two-deck battleship
Tonnage:	5,120 tons
Dimensions:	length 255 ft 3 in (77.8 m); beam 55 ft 9 in (17 m); draft 27 ft 7 in (8.4 m)
Propulsion:	one geared steam engine delivering 574 ihp (428 kW) to one propeller for 12.1 kt
Armour:	none
Armament:	(typically) 58 30-pdr guns, eight 8.66-in (220-mm) guns, and 14 6.3-in (160-mm) guns
Complement:	not available

CSS *Alabama* (1862)

In the history of commerce warfare, the CSS *Alabama* must be reckoned as one of the most successful raiders ever when measured in terms of the number of vessels she took: in her relatively short career the *Alabama* captured and burned 55 ships, and seized and sent in another 10. The origins of the *Alabama* can be found in the work of Commander James Dunwoody Bulloch, the naval agent in Europe of the Confederate States of America in the American Civil War (1861/65). Bulloch had the extremely difficult task of creating, from absolutely nothing and from overseas sources, an effective ocean-going navy for the Confederacy. Bulloch ordered a hull, No. 290, from the Laird Brothers' yard of Birkenhead on the southern shore of the River Mersey, and this was subsequently launched as the supposedly mercantile *Enrica*, a three-masted wooden vessel of the barque-rigged type with auxiliary steam machinery characterized by a single funnel and a propeller which could be lifted from the water to reduce drag when the vessel was under sail. The *Enrica* sailed from the river Mersey on July 29, 1862

The CSS Alabama was a simple vessel with her two heaviest guns on pivoted centerline mounts and her six 32-pdr weapons (three on each beam) on carriages.

despite the fact that Charles Francis Adams, the US minister in London, had claimed steadfastly that the construction and delivery of the vessel violated the UK's 1861 declaration of neutrality: the British government issued an order of detention, but the ship sailed (ostensibly for trials) on the day before this order was served. In purely legal terms, the vessel did not break the type of neutrality which the UK had declared, for it was not until she had been fitted with armament that the vessel actually became a warship. This happened well after the vessel's departure from British waters when, off the Azores Islands, the vessel received her guns, ammunition and powder from the supply ships *Agrippina* and *Bahama*, so making it possible for Captain Raphael Semmes to commission the vessel into Confederate service on 24 August 1862 as the *Alabama*.

After taking on her comparatively light armament and other specifically naval equipment and supplies, the *Alabama* cruised initially from region of the Azores northwest to Newfoundland and thence south to the Caribbean Sea, In this part of her career, the *Alabama* sank 27 ships

The fight of the USS Kearsarge and CSS Alabama off Cherbourg.

between September and December 1862. On January 11, 1863, the *Alabama* encountered the USS *Hatteras*, a schooner converted into an auxiliary paddle-wheel gunboat, of the US Navy's Gulf Coast Blockading Squadron about 20 miles (32 km) south of Galveston in Texas. After sinking the *Hatteras*, the *Alabama* rescued the survivors of the Federal ship and put them ashore in Jamaica. The *Alabama* then continued on her raiding cruise. On June 20, 1863 she was cruising off the coast of Brazil when she spotted and overhauled the mercantile barque *Conrad*, which was registered in the Philadelphia in the state of Pennsylvania. The *Conrad* surrendered to the *Alabama*, and Semmes armed his prize for service as the CSS *Tuscaloosa* under the command of Lieutenant John Low. The *Tuscaloosa* cruised in the South Atlantic for six months before being seized by the British in Simon's Bay, South Africa, on the 26th of December. Semmes, meanwhile decided to change his hunting ground, and visiting South Africa during the autumn of 1863, sailed the *Alabama* into the Indian Ocean and indeed as far to the east as Singapore. With his ship's bottom foul with weed and barnacles, Semmes then returned to Europe for an extensive refit.

The *Alabama* dropped anchor off the northern French port of Cherbourg, in the English Channel, on June 11, 1864. Semmes intended to remain at Cherbourg for several months, but the Federal government of the USA had recently persuaded the French authorities to fix a 24-hour limit on the stay in French territorial waters of any vessel flying the flag of the Confederacy. In the meantime, the USS *Kearsarge*, a wooden-hulled screw sloop of some 1,490 tons under the command of Captain John A. Winslow, arrived at Cherbourg from Flushing in Belgium, during the course of June 14th. While trying to take on board US sailors landed from the *Alabama*, Winslow was informed that this would be a violation of French neutrality, and left.

Preferring that his ship succumb in honourable defeat rather than continue to deteriorate uselessly while blockaded on the French coast, Semmes apparently said to one of his officers, Lieutenant John M. Kell, "Although the Confederate government has ordered me to avoid engagement with the enemy cruisers, I am tired of running from that flaunting rag!" So on June 19th the *Alabama* set sail from Cherbourg and, while still in sight of the spectators lining the coast, opened fire on the waiting *Kearsarge* shortly before 11 o'clock in the morning. With a foul bottom and tired equipment, the *Alabama* was no match for the *Kearsarge* and in some 60 minutes was reduced to a sinking wreck. Semmes repeatedly struck his flag, but before the *Kearsarge* could rescue the survivors or try to save the *Alabama*, Semmes and some 40 of his men were rescued by the *Deerhound*, a British yacht. In the USA this was deemed illegal, and in December 1865 Semmes was arrested on the instruction of Gideon Welles, the Secretary of the Navy. The sinking of the *Alabama* had no material effect on the result of the American Civil War, but the vessel had become something of a legend in the Confederacy and her loss was a blow to morale.

It is to the depredations of the *Alabama* and other Confederate raiders, most notably the CSS *Florida* and CSS *Shenandoah*, to which the decline of US mercantile shipping in the second half of the 19th century had often been ascribed. Certainly, an immediate result of the raiders' endeavours was a 900 percent rise in insurance rates for US-flagged ships, and the resulting transfer of large numbers of ships to the registry of other nations. After the war, the USA insisted that the UK was liable for the destruction wrought by British-built commerce raiders, and the resulting process became known as the "*Alabama* claims." A international tribunal finally awarded the USA some $15.5 million in damages.

CSS *Alabama*

Type:	barque-rigged auxiliary raider
Tonnage:	1,050 tons
Dimensions:	length 220 ft (67.1 m); beam 31 ft 8 in (9.65 m); draft 14 ft (4.25 m)
Propulsion:	one direct-acting steam engine delivering 600 hp (447.5 kW) to one propeller for 13 kt
Armour:	none
Armament:	one 6.4-in (163-mm) 100-pdr Blakeley rifled muzzle-loading gun, one 68-pdr smooth-bore gun, and six 32-pdr smooth-bore guns
Complement:	145

American Civil War monitors (1864)

The monitor is a mobile battery of heavy artillery, designed with a shallow draft to operate in rivers as well as coastal waters. The type derives its designation from the USS *Monitor* created by John Ericsson for service in the American Civil War (1861/65). Built by the Continental Iron Works by February 1862, the *Monitor* was based on an armoured "raft" of wood and iron construction 5 ft (1.5 m) deep, with a slab-sided iron lower hull overhung by the "raft" to the extent of 14 ft (4.25 m) forward, 32 ft (9.75 m) aft and 3 ft 9 in (1.15 m) on each side amidships. This protected the lower hull, rudder and propeller from ram attack. The fully-laden freeboard was just 1 ft 2 in (0.35 m). Ericsson's original plan featured wrought iron side and deck plating 6 and 2 in (152 and 51 mm) thick respectively, but the weight of such protection would have sunk the ship and thinner armour, fabricated from 1-in (25-mm) or thinner plates riveted or bolted together, was used. The turret had an internal diameter of 20 ft (6.1 m) and was 9 ft (2.75 m) tall with a latticed roof of railway rails. The turret's lower edge was of bronze and rested on a bronze deck ring, and the turret was traversed by steam power. Forward there was a small pilot house fabricated of iron blocks 9 in (229 mm) thick, and a 3-in (76-mm) glacis was later added round this.

The *Monitor* fought her famous action with the Confederate monitor CSS *Virginia* in Hampton Roads on 9 March 1862, neither vessel being able to inflict serious damage on the other. The *Virginia* offered to take up the fight again in April 1862 after she had been improved, but the *Monitor* refused. The *Monitor* foundered on December 31, 1862 while under tow.

The 10 monitors of the following "Passaic" class, which were completed in 1862/65, were of an improved and

The CSS Virginia (left and below) was based on a shallow but basically conventional hull which floats with its deck awash, and above this was an armoured barbette with the 7-in (178-mm) guns fore and aft and each firing through any one of three ports, the 6.4- and 9-in (163- and 229-mm) weapons in the side of the casemate, and provision for two 12-pdr howitzers on the roof.

The USS Monitor (above and right) was of metal construction and carried two 11-in (279-mm) guns in her traversing central turret.

enlarged "Monitor" class design with a displacement of 1,875 tons, overall length of 200 ft (61 m), speed of 7 kt and, in most, an armament of one 15-in (381-mm) and one 11-in (279-mm) smooth-bore guns. The armament was improved later in the war. The following USS *Roanoke*, completed in June 1863 with a displacement of 4,395 tons, was the world's first warship with more than two turrets. The forward turret carried one 15-in (381-mm) smooth-bore gun, and of the two after turrets the forward unit carried single 15- and 11-in (381- and 279-mm) smooth-bore guns, and the after unit one 11-in (279-mm) smooth-bore and one 8-in (203-mm) rifled guns. The USS *Onondaga* and USS *Dictator* were another two one-off designs, and next came the four units of the 3,400-ton "Miantonomoh" class. Only one was completed in time for Civil War service, and was considered that war's best monitor. Built in four Federal navy yards, the ships had a maximum speed of 10 kt, and their two turrets each carried two 15-in (381-mm) smooth-bore guns.

The nine monitors of the "Canonicus" class, of which only seven were commissioned in 1864/71, were built to an improved "Passaic" class design with a displacement of 2,100 tons, a speed of 8 kt and one turret carrying two 15-in (381-mm) smooth-bore guns. The vessels incorporated the lessons of the US Navy's considerable experience in monitor operations in the first two years of the Civil War, and some of the units survived to the end of the 19th century. The largest class of monitors was the "Casco" class of shallow-draft vessels intended for riverine service with a displacement of 1,175 tons, a draft of 6 ft 4 in (1.9 m) and an armament of

The most important type of gun used by the US Navy was the so-called Dahlgren gun, introduced by Commander J. A. Dahlgren in 1859 as a development of the French Paixhan gun. One of the first weapons designed after experimental determination of gas pressure at various points along the bore, the gun had a distinctive "ginger beer bottle" shape.

American Civil War monitors *continued*

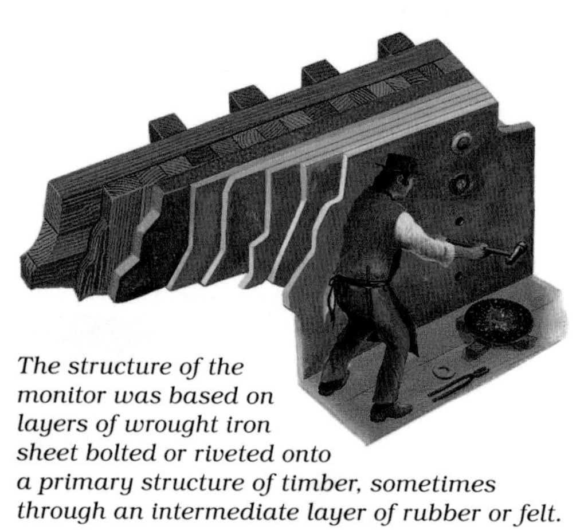

The structure of the monitor was based on layers of wrought iron sheet bolted or riveted onto a primary structure of timber, sometimes through an intermediate layer of rubber or felt.

two 11-in (279-mm) smooth-bore guns in a single turret. Some 20 units were completed in 1864/65, but of these just nine were commissioned into US service, the last of them surviving only into the mid-1870s.

With their scantier industrial resources, the Confederates could not hope to match the Federals in the creation of advanced weapons, and built no turreted monitors, instead concentrating of a small number of ironclad vessels offering similar capabilities. The first of these was the initial *Virginia*, built out of the recovered wreckage of the USS *Merrimack*, which had been partially burned as the Federal forces retired from Norfolk, Virginia, and completed in February 1862. This set the mold for Confederate armoured ships: the forward and after ends of the hull were awash except for a low coaming at the bows, and amidships was a casemate with inclined sides. The lower edge of the casemate was only 6 in (150 mm) above water, 12 in (305 mm) less than intended. On their withdrawal from Norfolk in May 1862, the Confederates burnt the *Virginia* as she drew too much water to escape up the James river.

The best of the Confederate ironclads was a second CSS *Virginia*, completed at Richmond, Virginia, in 1864 and scuttled at the end of the war. She was smaller than the first ship of the name, and her casemate carried four rifled and smooth-bore guns of various calibres, and 12-pdr smooth-bore howitzers on the casemate roof. There were another 15 Confederate ironclads, the best known of them the CSS *Tennessee* completed in 1864 at Selma, Alabama. This was 209 ft (63.7 m) long, could achieve 5 kt using machinery stripped from the paddle-wheeler *Alonzo Child*, and was armed with two 7-in (178-mm) and six 6,4-in (163-mm) rifled muzzle-loading guns, these all being Brooke weapons.

Pictures Courtesy National Park Service,
U.S. Department of the Interior,
artist John Batchelor.

A cut-away illustration reveals the interior of the USS Monadnock, the "Miantonomoh" class monitor built at Boston Navy Yard. The turrets (detailed left) were installed fore and aft of the crew quarter's, boilers and bunkers, with the officers' quarters and stores forward of the fore turret, and the machinery abaft the after turret. The turret had an internal diameter of 23 ft (7 m) and trained round a fixed central spindle carrying the pilot house. Each turret carried two 15-in (381-mm) Dahlgren smooth-bore guns.

USS *Monitor*

Type:	ironclad monitor
Tonnage:	987 tons displacement
Dimensions:	length 172 ft (52.4 m); beam 41 ft 6 in (12.6 m); draft 10 ft 6 in (3.2 m)
Propulsion:	one Ericsson vibrating lever steam engine delivering 320 ihp (238.5 kW) to one propeller for 6 kt
Armour:	2/4.5-in (51/114-mm) sides, 8/9-in (203/229-mm) turret, and 1-in (25-mm) deck
Armament:	two 11-in (279-mm) smooth-bore guns
Complement:	49

CSS *Virginia*

Type:	ironclad warship
Tonnage:	not known
Dimensions:	275 ft (83.8 m); beam 38 ft 6 in (11.75 m); draft 22 ft (6.7 m)
Propulsion:	one return connecting rod steam engine delivering unknown power to one propeller for 7.5 kt
Armour:	4-in (102-mm) casemate, 1- or later 3-in (25- or later 76-mm) sides
Armament:	two 7-in (178-mm) Brookes rifled muzzle-loading guns, two 6.4-in (163-mm) Brookes rifled muzzled-loading guns, six 9-in (229-mm) smooth-bore guns, and two 12-pdr smooth-bore howitzers
Complement:	320

HMS *Staunch* (1867)

The extent of the Royal Navy's commitment continued to grow on a global basis in the second half of the 19th century, reflecting the steadily increasing volume of British shipborne mercantile trade and the expansion of the British empire. So far as the Royal Navy was concerned, this meant ever larger numbers of warships, of all sizes, able to deploy to the farther reaches of the British sphere of interest. However, during the later 1860s and early 1870s there began to emerge, somewhat closer to home, the threat (or at least the perceived threat) of a return to hostilities with France. This perception was derived from a number of factors, one of them a resurgence in French naval strength through the construction of modern warships in steadily increasing numbers as the state of French industrial growth permitted.

The spectre of renewed French naval strength led the British public and also politicians to fear the possibility of a French invasion. Thus there was public and political pressure for a general improvement in the capabilities of the British coastal defences and also for the construction of gunboats intended solely for short-range work in British coastal waters. Working on the basis of gunboats he had designed for export sales, George Rendel, the senior naval architect of the Armstrongs armament company,

HMS Staunch was one of the two prototypes for the highly novel "flatiron" approach to coastal gunboat design for British service.

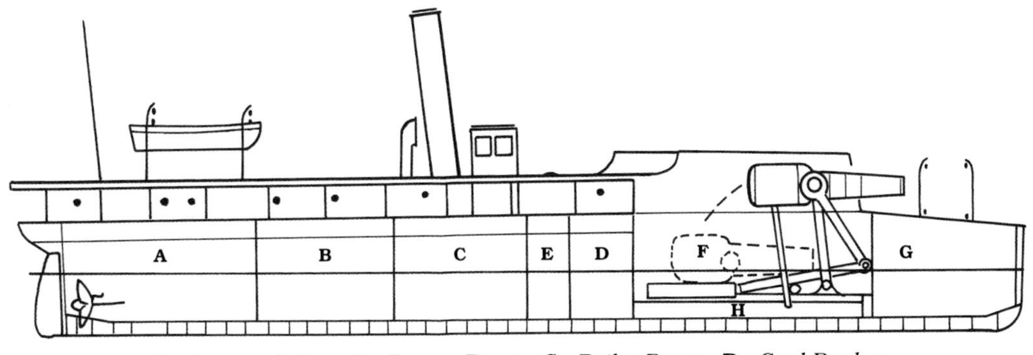

A - *Accomodation* **B** - *Engine Room* **C** - *Boiler Room* **D** - *Coal Bunker*
E - *Boiler Room working space* **F** - *Gun House* **G** - *Muzzle Loading Space* **H** - *Ammunition*

Cut-away illustration of HMS Staunch showing the hydraulically operated lowering/lifting mounting for the single gun.

created the concept of the "Rendel gunboat," which was a mastless type characterized by slow speed and poor seaworthiness, but mounting one 9- or 10-in (229- or 254-mm) rifled muzzle-loading gun.

Generally known as "flatiron gunboats" for their strange appearance at a time when masts and yards were still standard, even in vessels with steam machinery, some 30 of these gunboats were laid down between 1867 and 1881. The first of the genuine "flatiron gunboats," lacking even the most rudimentary sailing rig for the first time in any British warship, was HMS *Plucky,* which was launched in December 1867 with a displacement of 193 tons, a speed of 7.5 kt, and the armament of one 9-in (229-mm) gun. The *Plucky* was essentially a prototype, and was followed by another, HMS *Staunch* launched in December 1867 from the yard of Charles Mitchell & Co. Like the *Plucky*, the *Staunch* was of iron construction and revealed herself to be very maneuvrable, and among her features were a 9-in (229-mm gun on a hydraulic mounting that allowed the weapon to be lowered into the vessel's hold for enhanced seaworthiness on longer passages, but then raised for action.

In 1870/74 there followed the 20 units of the "Ant" class, in 1879 the four units of the "Gadfly" class, and in 1991 the two units of the "Bouncer" class, all of them with one 10-in (254-mm) gun.

HMS *Staunch*

Type:	"flatiron" coastal gunboat
Tonnage:	164 tons displacement
Dimensions:	length 75 ft (22.9 m); beam 25 ft (7.6 m); draft 56 ft 6 in (2 m)
Propulsion:	two Walter/Stephenson horizontal single expansion steam engines delivering 134 ihp (100 kW) to two propellers for 7.7 kt
Armour:	none
Armament:	one 9-in (229-mm) rifled muzzle-loading gun
Complement:	31

Le Redoutable (1873)

Laid down in August 1873 after being ordered as part of the 1872 French construction program, which included 28 ironclads, 34 cruisers and more than 100 smaller warships, *Le Redoutable* was an example of the "central battery" ship, in which the boilers and much of the armament were grouped into a central position.

Designed by L. de Bussy, the ship was of a design quite different to that of preceding central battery warships: beam was increased, draft reduced and the central battery shortened with only four 10.8-in (274-mm) guns mounted at its corners. The ship was notable for her pronounced tumblehome, and the central battery was extended right out to the full beam of the hull, which provided all-round fire at the price of limited broadside arcs. Of the other four main-calibre guns, two were mounted in semi-barbettes above the battery, one under the forecastle and one aft in unprotected positions.

For the first time steel was used extensively for the hull. This was mild steel developed by the Creusot works and up to 30 percent stronger than iron. Wrought iron was retained for the armour. This latter included a full-length belt extending from 5 ft (1.52 m) below to 4 ft 10 in (1.47 m) above the waterline with a thickness of 14 in (355 mm) amidships thinning to 8.7 in (220 mm) forward and 9 in (230 mm) aft. The upper edge of the battery armour was 19 ft (5.8 m) above the waterline, and there was a 2,4-in (60-mm) armour deck at the upper edge of the belt outside the battery, which lacked any armoured roof. There was a double bottom, but the protection this offered was reduced by the lack of any watertight longitudinal bulkheads, and another failing was the location of the steam steering engine above water.

The four 10.8-in (274-mm) battery guns were of a lower velocity, lighter type than the four unarmoured upper-

Like most of the larger French warships of her era Le Redoutable was a notably unattractive vessel.

deck guns. The secondary armament comprised six 5.5-in (140-mm guns later replaced by 3.9-in (100-mm) weapons, and these were located on the upper deck. The battery guns' magazines were susceptible to overheating as they were close to the machinery spaces. A first rearmament saw the introduction of improved main armament, while a second upgrade saw the replacement of the four battery guns by 9.4-in (240-mm) weapons.

As completed by the Arsenal de Lorient in December 1878, *Le Redoutable* was fully ship-rigged with 24,000 sq ft (2230 m^2) of canvas, but she was later re-rigged as a barquentine and, finally, she had two military masts which, with the large funnel, gave her an imposing appearance. The ship was re-engined and reboilered in 1894, and was stricken in 1910.

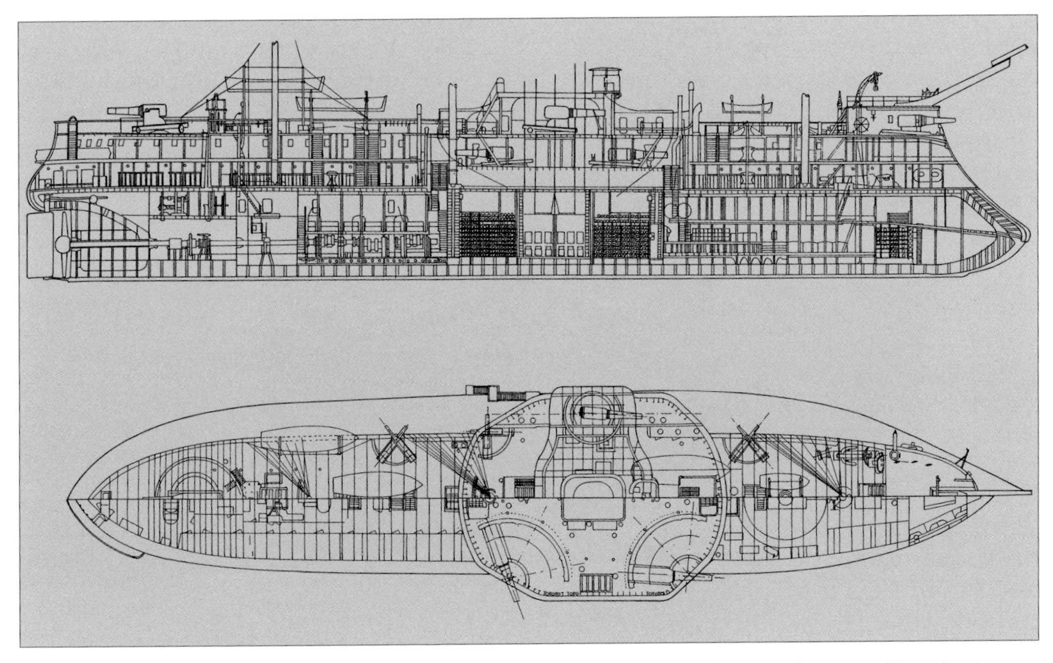

Plan and section drawing of Le Redoutable highlight the central battery feature of her design.

Le Redoutable

Type:	central battery ironclad
Tonnage:	9,244 tons displacement
Dimensions:	318 ft 8 in (97.1 m); beam 64 ft 6 in (19.7 m); draft 25 ft 7 in (7.80 m)
Propulsion:	horizontal return connecting rod compound steam engines delivering 6,200 ihp (4623 kW) to one propeller for 14.7 kt
Armour:	8.7/14-in (220/355-mm) belt, and 9.5-in (240-mm) belt
Armament:	eight 10.8-in (274-mm guns, six 5.5-in (140-mm gun, 12 1-pdr revolver guns, and two 14-in (356-mm) torpedo tubes
Complement:	705

USS *Alarm* (1873)

The so-called "spar torpedo" was an explosive charge (initiated by a contact pistol) attached to the outboard end of a pole rigged over the bow or beam of a small vessel for stand-off detonation against the outside of the target vessel's hull. The weapon was developed in the American Civil War (1861/65), and its most notable exploit was the October 1864 sinking of the Confederate ram CSS *Albemarle* at Plymouth, North Carolina. The spar torpedo was a weapon often as dangerous to its user as its enemy, and was rendered wholly obsolete by Robert Whitehead's development of the locomotive torpedo between 1870 and 1890.

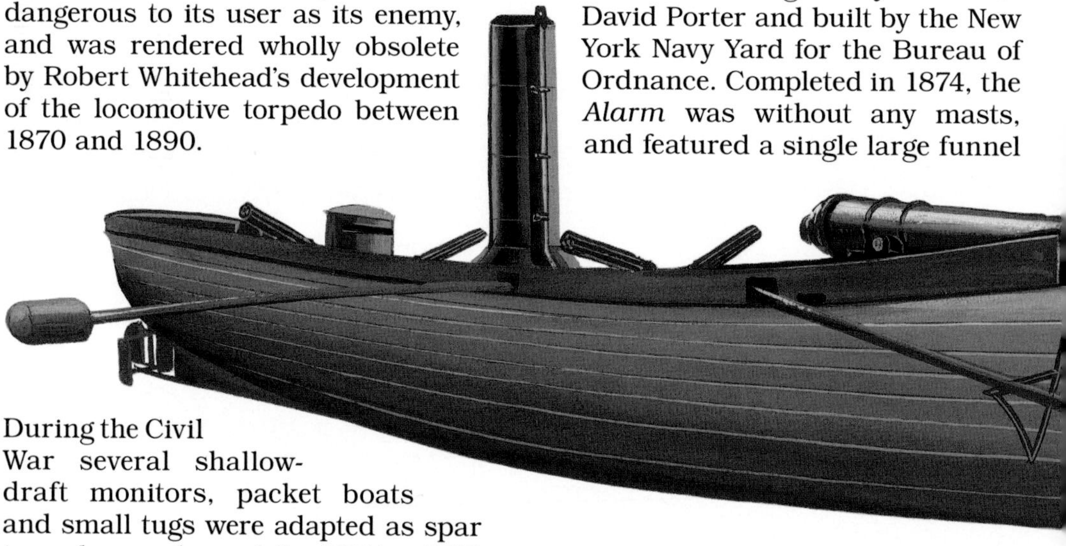

During the Civil War several shallow-draft monitors, packet boats and small tugs were adapted as spar torpedo vessels, and the 207-ton USS *Spuyten Duyvil* (originally *Stromboli*) was completed in 1864 as the US Navy's first purpose-designed spar torpedo vessel. Its torpedo pole was extended through a watertight box in the bows, the charge was detached and fired automatically at the spar's extreme reach, and at the same time the spar's return was begun. The watertight box was pumped out quickly, allowing another of the 12 stowed charges to be attached. The torpedo handling gear turned the scales at some 10 tons, The wooden hull was partially armoured with wrought iron 5 in (127 mm) thick on its sides and on the pilot house and 3 in (76 mm) thick on its deck. The draft was increased from 7 ft 5 in (2.25 m) to some 9 ft (2.75 m) in action, The *Spuyten Duyvil* was later employed to clear obstructions on the James river, and after the end of the Civil War she was used for experimental and development work.

The US Navy's second experimental torpedo ram was the iron-hulled USS Alarm designed by Admiral David Porter and built by the New York Navy Yard for the Bureau of Ordnance. Completed in 1874, the *Alarm* was without any masts, and featured a single large funnel and a tapered "snout" bow some 15 ft (4.6 m) long. The torpedo spar mounted in the bows was 30 ft (9.15 m) long and controlled by means of a steam winch and tackles. There were also two beam spars each 18 ft (5.5 m) long.

Propulsion and steering were entrusted to a Fowler horizontal feathering paddle wheel, the conceptual progenitor of the Voith Schneider system often used in ferries and tugs, and was later replaced by a steering propeller. The *Alarm* was said to handle well, but lacked

The USS Alarm had a compartmented double bottom and watertight bulkheads every 25 ft (7.6 m).

the speed for any operational role. Only the bow had protection, in this instance 1.5 in (38 mm) thick, and the draft aft was 15 ft 9 in (4.80 m) as the skeg framework for the Fowler wheel extended 3 ft 6 in (1.07 m) below the keel.

The *Alarm* was laid up in 1885 and fitted out as a gunnery training ship in 1890/91, but appears to have been little used.

USS *Alarm*

Type:	spar torpedo ram
Tonnage:	800 tons displacement
Dimensions:	length 173 ft 52.7 m); beam 28 ft (8.5 m); draft 10 ft 6 in (3.2 m) mean
Propulsion:	two compound steam engines delivering 600 ihp (447.5 kW) to one Fowler propulsion and steering paddle for 10 kt
Armour:	1.5-in (38-mm) bow
Armament:	one 15-in (381 mm) smooth-bore gun in a fixed bow mounting, four Gatling guns, and bow and beam spar torpedoes
Complement:	40

Novgorod (1874) & *Vice-Admiral Popov* (1877)

Given her naval defeats in the Crimean War (1853/56), which offered the British and French great scope to exploit their naval advantage for tactical flexibility in the land campaign, Russia decided from the late 1850s to improve her navy in terms of quality and quantity. The nature of the Russian empire, with access to the all-important Black Sea controlled by Turkish possession of the narrows between the Dardanelles and the Bosporus, meant that vessels for the Black Sea Fleet had to be built and maintained locally.

Along its Russian shores, the Black Sea is characterized by very shallow coastal waters, demanding a draft of no more than 13 ft (3.95 m). Coastal defence based on large-calibre naval guns thus presented special problems which the Black Sea Fleet's commander, Vice-Admiral Popov, addressed most eccentrically as he sought to protect Nikolayev and the estuary of the Dniepr river.

Basing his work on the pioneer thinking of the Glaswegian John Elder, who believed that a ship of circular plan would be very stable and have only a shallow draft, Popov laid out a saucer-like coastal defence ship, the *Novgorod*, which was built in sections at St Petersburg and then assembled at Nikolayev by 1874. The side armour extended from the edge of the strongly cambered deck, 1 ft 6 in (0.46 m) above the waterline, to a point 4 ft 6 in (1.3 m) below it: this armour was 9 in (230 mm) thick over its upper 3 ft (0.9 m), and 7 in (180 mm) thick below this. The deck rose to 5 ft 3 in (1.6 m) above the waterline in the center and was 2.75 in (190 mm) thick, and the barbette rose 7 ft (2.15 m) above this deck. The hull was covered with wood up to 2 ft 3 in (0.7 m) thick outside the armour, and was

The Novgorod and Vice-Admiral Popov were among the most unusual warships ever created. They were each steered by one rudder, and propelled by a bank of propellers extended to the rear of the trailing edge of the inverted saucer-like ship.

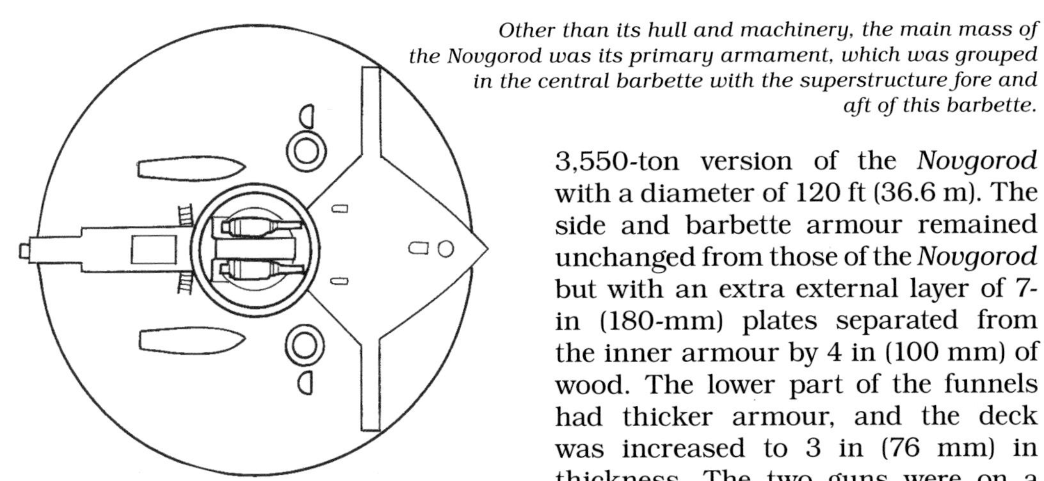
Other than its hull and machinery, the main mass of the Novgorod was its primary armament, which was grouped in the central barbette with the superstructure fore and aft of this barbette.

sheathed with copper. The machinery at first drove six propellers, but the two outer pairs were later removed, reducing speed to 5 kt.

Originally named *Kiev*, the *Vice-Admiral Popov* was completed at Nikolayev in 1877 as an enlarged 3,550-ton version of the *Novgorod* with a diameter of 120 ft (36.6 m). The side and barbette armour remained unchanged from those of the *Novgorod* but with an extra external layer of 7-in (180-mm) plates separated from the inner armour by 4 in (100 mm) of wood. The lower part of the funnels had thicker armour, and the deck was increased to 3 in (76 mm) in thickness. The two guns were on a hydraulically lowering/lifting mount and, like the *Novgorod*, the *Popov* later had her two outboard pairs of engines and propellers removed, trimming the speed from 8 to 6 kt. The ships were not successful, and were both stricken in about 1900.

Novgorod

Type:	coast defence ship
Tonnage:	2,491 tons displacement
Dimensions:	diameter 101 ft (30.8 m); draft 13 ft 6 in (4.1 m)
Propulsion:	six horizontal compound steam engines delivering 3,000 ihp (2237 kW) to six propellers for 7 kt
Armour:	7/9-in (180/230-mm) sides, 9-in (230-mm) barbette, 2,75-in (70-mm) deck, and 4.5-in (115-mm) funnels
Armament:	two 11-in (280-mm) guns, two 3.4-in (86-mm) guns, two 2.5-pdr guns, and spar torpedoes
Complement:	149

Vice-Admiral Popov

Type:	coast defence ship
Tonnage:	3,550 tons displacement
Dimensions:	diameter 120 ft (36.6 m); draft 13 ft 6 in (4.1 m)
Propulsion:	six horizontal compound steam engines delivering 4,500 ihp (3355 kW) to six propellers for 8 kt
Armour:	14/16-in (355/405-mm) sides, 16-in (405-mm) barbette, 3-in (76-mm) deck, and 7-in (175-mm) funnels
Armament:	two 12-in (305-mm) guns, eight 3.4-in (86-mm) guns later reduced to six, two 1-pdr revolver guns, and spar torpedoes
Complement:	203

HMS *Victoria* (1880)

The six ships of the "Admiral" class, were built in three subvariants as barbette ships in an effort to create first-class warships with good firepower, speed and endurance on a modest, and therefore affordable, hull. Through they had excellent points, the ships received public as well as professional criticism for the lack of protection they afforded. In the "Victoria" class the Admiralty thus reverted to the turret ship. Designed by Nathaniel Barnaby as the British counter to the French "Hoche" and "Marceau" class ships, the two "Admiral" class ships were comparatively well protected, and although the use of a turret rather than barbettes provided the main armament with better protection, the hull protection of the new ships was in fact little better than that of the barbette ships. In its basic design the "Victoria" class was essentially an improved "Conqueror" class turret ram of the late 1870s, but with the hull size increased to ensure that the ships were truly first-class vessels. The two 16.25-in (413-mm) breech-loading guns of the primary armament were mounted in a single turret forward, this arrangement being considered more weight-economical than a pair of guns in single turrets fore and aft of the superstructure. As in HMS *Benbow*, the last "Admiral," 16.25-in (413-mm) guns were used main to reduce the pressure on manufacture of the 13.5-in (343-mm) gun which was otherwise standard.

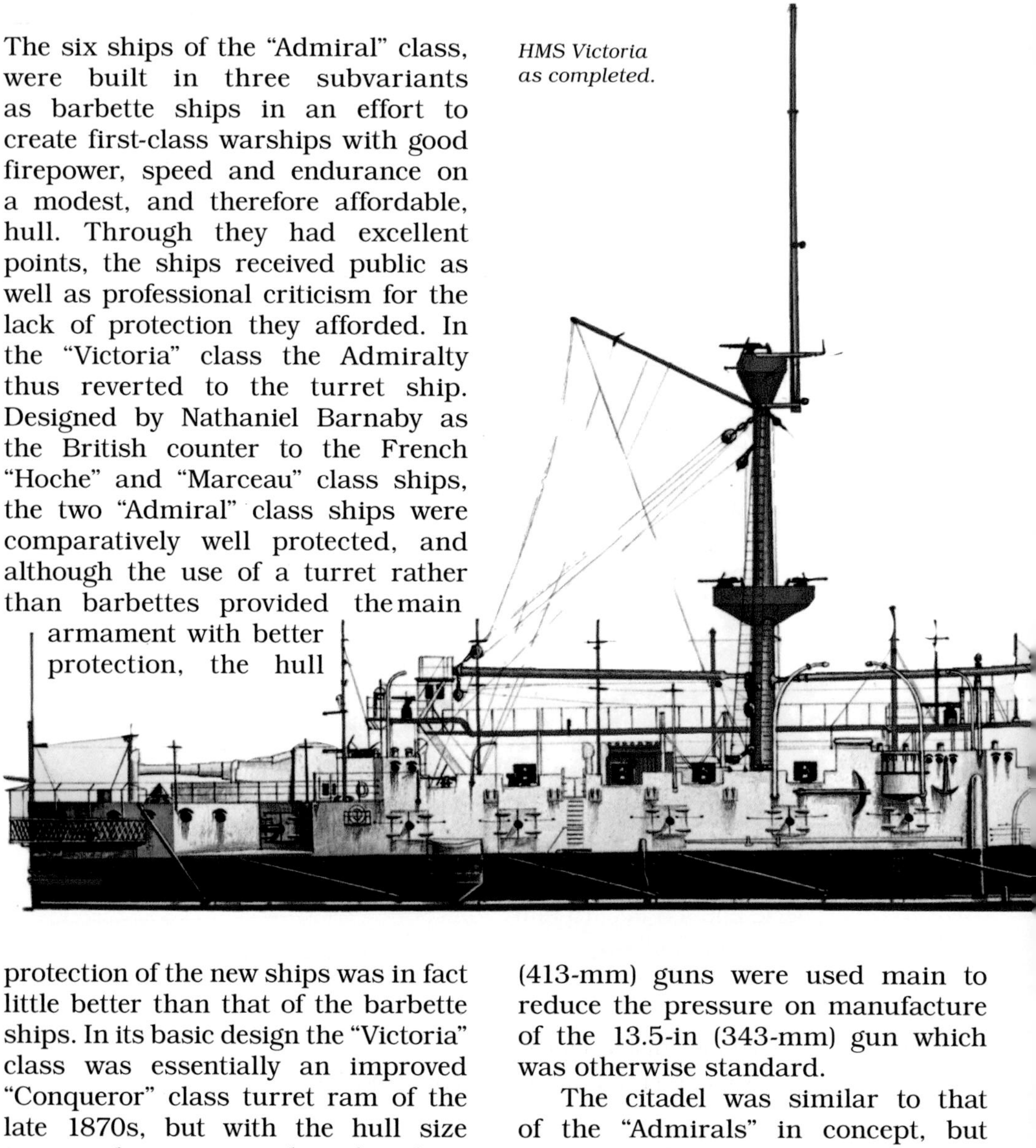

HMS Victoria as completed.

The citadel was similar to that of the "Admirals" in concept, but was somewhat larger with a length of 162 ft (49.4 m), The main deck over the citadel and the lower deck fore and aft of the citadel were 3 in (76 mm) thick. The base of the main armament turret was protected by a pear-shaped redoubt extending down to the citadel's forward end. The secondary armament comprised 12 6-in (152-mm) single guns split into fore and aft groups by a 3-in (76-mm) athwartships bulkhead, and was protected against raking fire by 6-in (152-mm) bulkheads at its ends. One 10-in (254-mm) gun was mounted without protection on the spar deck aft to provide fire astern, the main armament's fire being limited to the forward arc.

The "Victoria" class ships were the first battleships with triple-expansion steam engines, and the eight coal-fired boilers, working at a pressure half as high again as those of the "Admiral" class ships, were located in four compartments. For the first time in a British warship, the two funnels were side-by-side. HMS *Victoria*, built by Armstrongs of Elswick (its first battleship) and completed in March 1890, initially had short funnels, but these were heightened by 17 ft (5.2 m) later in 1890, and HMS *Sans Pareil*, built by Thames Iron Works of Blackwall, was completed in July 1891 with the taller funnels. Each ship had been delayed some 16 months by the late delivery of its main armament. The ships steamed well, and their engines proved to be more powerful than had been designed. Better seaboats to a modest degree than the "Admiral" class ships, the "Victoria" class vessels were stable and better able to hold their speed in a seaway, but they had a low freeboard and this rendered them wet forward, a hindrance to the effectiveness of the forward turret.

On June 22, 1893 the *Victoria*, flagship of the Mediterranean Fleet was lost during fleet maneuvers off Tripoli as a result of a collision with HMS *Camperdown*. The *Sans Pareil* was sold for breaking in 1907.

HMS *Victoria*

Type:	turret battleship
Tonnage:	10,470 tons displacement
Dimensions:	length 363 ft (110.6 m); beam 70 ft (21.3 m); draft 26 ft 9 in (8.15 m)
Propulsion:	two Humphreys triple-expansion steam engines delivering 14,244 ihp (10605 kW) to two propellers for 17.3 kt
Armour:	18-in (457-mm) belt, 16-in (406-mm) bulkheads, 17-in (432-mm) turret, 18-in (457-mm) redoubt, 3/6-in (76/152-mm) battery screens, 3-in (76-mm) decks, and 2/14-in (51-356-mm) conning tower
Armament:	two 16.25-in (413-mm) guns, one 10-in (254-mm) gun, 12 6-in (152 mm) guns, 12 6-pdr QF guns, nine 3-pdr QF guns, four 14-in (356-mm) torpedo tubes, and two 14-in (356-mm) torpedo launching carriages
Complement:	550

La Fusée (1884)

In common with many other technically capable and militarily concerned nations of the period between 1860 and 1900, France was highly worried with the possibility of an attack on her coast. This led to the diversion of funding, production effort and manpower resources to the creation and maintenance of what was seen as a potent coastal defence capability. Intended to operate from well protected harbours on short-range sorties to defeat any attack, coast-defence ships were not required to possess good seagoing capability, protracted endurance or good habitability, but rather to mount the heaviest possible offensive armament and to be moderately well protected.

When developing its coastal defence capability, the French navy started with three classes of floating battery, totalling 11 ships carrying 6.4- or 7.6-in (163- or 193-mm) guns. There followed two classes of armoured ram totalling five ships armed with 9.4-in (239-mm) guns, then two classes of somewhat larger breastwork monitor totalling four ships armed with two 10.8- or 13.4-in (274- or 340-mm) guns in a single centerline turret and also numbers of smaller-calibre guns, and two classes of barbette ship totalling two ships armed with two 13.4-in (340-mm) guns as well as numbers of smaller-calibre guns. All of these types were of low freeboard and very modest speed, and in the breastwork monitors and barbette ships there was clear evidence of the current French ship designers' penchant for a substantial superstructure that in many respects appeared to overwhelm the hull on which it was placed.

At this stage, in the early 1880s, a more practical approach to coastal defense started to make itself apparent in the design and construction of two classes of armoured gunboat, totalling eight ships, The first four of these, laid down between October 1882 and 1884 for completion between December 1885 and 1889, were *La Fusée*, *La Flamme*, *La Grenade* and *La Mitraille* of the "Fusée" class. The first and third units were built by the

In her final form, La Fusée had a very lean and hungry aspect with only vestigial upper works.

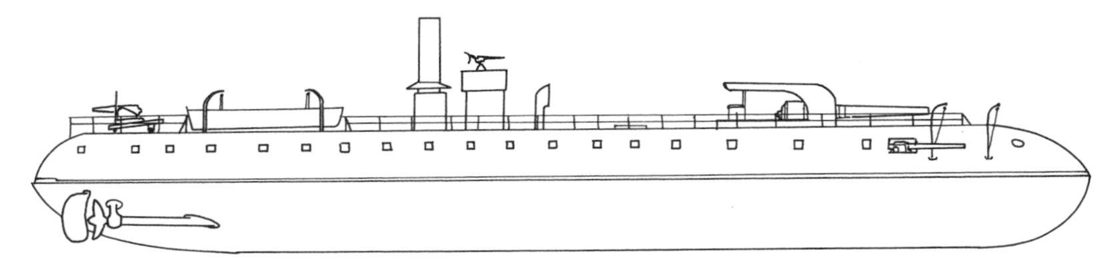

La Fusée's 9.4-in (239-mm) main gun was originally faired into the forward end of a long, narrow superstructure which was later removed, together with two masts.

Arsenal de Lorient, the second at the Arsenal de Cherbourg and the last at the Arsenal de Rochefort. "Fusée" is the French word for "rocket," and the name was certainly apposite for the design of these vessels if not their performance in any objective manner.

The design of the "Fusée" class armoured gunboat was the work of M. Albout, a naval architect on the staff of the Arsenal de Lorient. The vessel was of built of iron and steel between 0.75 and 1 in (20 and 25 mm) thick, and the her hull was basically cylindrical over most of its length with the rounded bow and stern typical of French naval architecture at this time. The waterline was very slightly above the mid-line of the cylindrical section and, as completed, *La Fusée* had a long but comparatively narrow superstructure extending along mist of the length of her hull. From this superstructure rose two masts with fighting tops, and the tall, cylindrical funnel. The two Lorient-built units, *La Fusée* and *La Grenade*, had steel armour, while *La Flamme* and *La Mitraille* had compound armour, in each case comprising a belt 2 ft 9 in (0.7 m) wide increasing to 4 ft 1 in (1.25 m) at the ram bow. The upper edge of this belt was 9.5 in (240 mm) thick forward, 8 in (200 mm) thick amidships and 4.7 in (120 mm) thick aft, the equivalent figures for the lower edge being 7, 4.7 and 4 in (180, 120 and 100 mm) respectively. The upper edges of the belt were connected by an armoured deck 2 in (50 mm) thick, and the main armament of one 9.4-in (239-mm) gun was located inside a barbette between 4.7 and 8 in (120 and 200 mm) thick. The superstructure and masts were removed, leaving the gun semi-exposed behind a splinter shield. The vessels were stricken in pairs during 1906 and 1910.

La Fusée

Type:	coastal defense armoured gunboat
Tonnage:	1,073 tons displacement
Dimensions:	length 165 ft (50.3 m); beam 32 ft 6 in (9.9 m); draft 10 ft 4 in (3.15 m)
Propulsion:	two vertical compound steam engines delivering 1,500 ihp (1118.5 kW) to two propellers for 12.5 kt
Armour:	4/9.5-in (100/240-mm) belt and 4.7/8-in (120/200-mm) barbette
Armament:	one 9,4-in (239-mm) gun, one 3,5-in (89-mm) gun and between four and seven 1-pdr revolver guns
Complement:	89

HMS *Archer* (1888)

The Royal Navy's third-class cruisers, laid down in 1884/1903, were intended for worldwide service in several roles and were typified by the maximization of speed at the expense of firepower and protection. Within the designation "third-class cruiser," a particular subtype was the torpedo cruiser as typified by the two "Scout" class units of 1884 and the eight "Archer" class units of 1885. Intended for the seagoing role, the torpedo cruiser had the speed and endurance to operate with the fleet in the task of defeating any enemy torpedo craft while itself making torpedo attacks on the enemy fleet. Such a cruiser had thus to be larger and more seaworthy than torpedo boats, but also cheap enough to be built in useful numbers. This compromise meant that the torpedo cruiser had inadequate speed and poor seaworthiness. The vessels were therefore used mainly for commerce protection, scouting and other independent tasks with the designation third-class cruiser.

The "Archer" class was based on the "Scout" class with an increase in size to carry six 6-in (152-mm) rather than four 5-in (127-mm) guns. Four of these weapons were disposed as in the earlier class, with pairs of weapons on the sides of the forecastle and poop, and the other two as one on each side on the upper deck amidships. The other weapons and the protection were those of the "Scout" class: eight 3-pdr guns on the upper deck as two on each side amidships and one

The "Archer" class torpedo cruisers were elegant ships, but were of little practical value except for imperial policing.

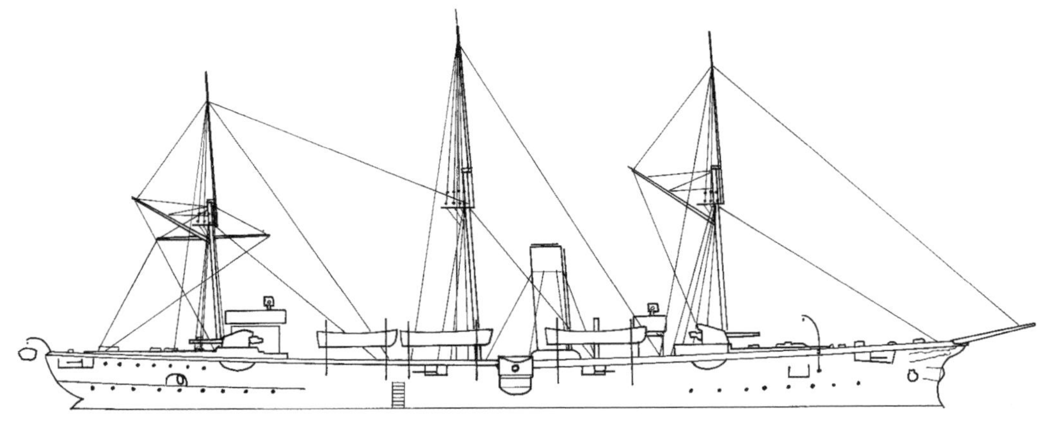

The "Archer" class cruisers had a somewhat anachronistic appearance as a result of their three masts and long bowsprit.

on each side forward and aft, one submerged torpedo tube in the bows and two centreline torpedo launcher carriages each able to launch though two above-water ports. The steam machinery was increased in forced-draft power by 300 ihp (224 kW), but the greater beam and displacement of the "Archer" class meant that all but the two cruisers built in royal dockyards, with 4,500-ihp (3355-kW) machinery, were 0.5 kt slower than the "Scouts."

The machinery was arranged as in the "Scout" (with four boilers in two rooms) except that the two engines were in separate engine rooms. Power was comparatively high for the size of ship, the engine and boiler rooms were cramped, but the power plant proved reliable. The "Archers" were the last British cruisers with horizontal engines. The "Archers" differed from the "Scouts" in having three rather than two masts. They were adequate sea boats but overgunned, resulting in a severe rolling tendency and making them very wet in adverse conditions. The class comprised HMS *Archer*, *Brisk*, *Cossack*, *Mohawk*, *Porpoise*, *Racoon*, *Serpent* and *Tartar*, the sixth and seventh built by Devonport Dock Yard and the others by Thompson of Glasgow for completion in 1881/91. The *Serpent* was wrecked in November 1890, and the other seven were sold out of the service in 1905/06.

HMS *Archer*

Type:	torpedo cruiser
Tonnage:	1,950 tons full load
Dimensions:	length 240 ft (73.15 m); beam 36 ft (11 m); draft 14 ft 6 in (4.4 m)
Propulsion:	two horizontal direct acting compound steam engines delivering 3,500 ihp (2610 kW) to two propellers for 16.5 kt
Armour:	0.375-in (10-mm) deck, 1-in (25-mm) gun and torpedo shields, and 3-in (76-mm) conning tower
Armament:	six 6-in (152-mm) guns, eight 3-pdr QF guns, two machine guns, one 14-in (356-mm) torpedo tube, and two 14-in (356-mm) torpedo launcher carriages
Complement:	176

USS *Chicago* (1889)

The US Navy remained essentially unaltered in basic concept and equipment in the period after the end of the American Civil War (1861/65). The service thus wallowed in the technical doldrums, the various administrations having little interest in military and naval matters, and the country being more concerned with reconstruction after the Civil War. By the early 1880s the USA was starting to look farther abroad as its economy boomed, trade swelled, and population burgeoned. It became impossible to ignore the US Navy's obsolescence and inadequacy. These factors combined in 1882/83 to mark the transition of the US Navy from the "Old Navy" to the "New Navy."

One of the first fruits of this process was the introduction of modern cruisers, and one of the first of these was the USS *Chicago*, a protected cruiser laid down by John Roach in December 1883 for completion in April 1889 by Roach's successor, Delaware River. The *Chicago* was only poorly protected, with a deck only 1.5 in (38 mm) thick and 136 ft (41.45 m) long over the machinery spaces but only 0.75 in (19 mm) thick over the magazines. The four 8-in (203-mm) guns of the main armament were fitted in four upper-deck sponsons, while the secondary armament of eight 6-in (152-mm) and two 5-in (127-mm) guns, was installed on the main deck with the smaller-calibre weapons right aft. All of these guns were short L/30 weapons. The five cylindrical boilers of the steam plant were somewhat unusual inasmuch as they were externally fired, and the vessel was also sail-rigged as a barque.

The *Chicago* was rebuilt in 1895/98. The changes were centered primarily on protection, armament

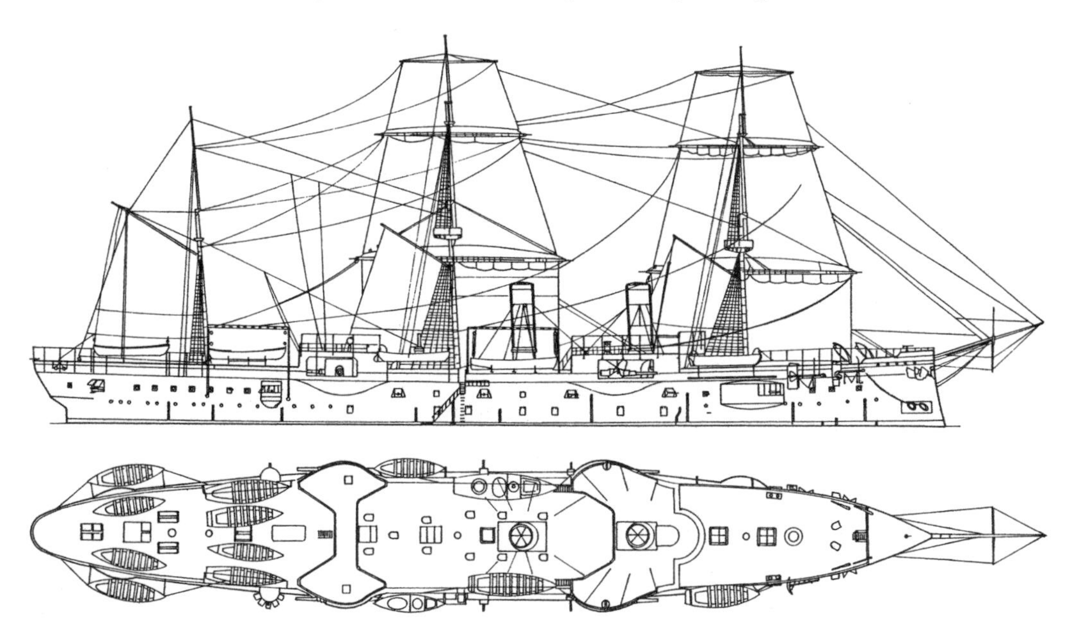

As completed, the USS Chicago was barque rigged with main, top and topgallant sails on her fore and main masts.

The USS Chicago was obsolescent even as she was completed,

and machinery. The first saw the addition of 1.5-in (38-mm) deck plating over the steering gear, a strip of 1-in (25-mm) side armour to protect the gun crews, 70 ft (21.3 m) of 1.125-in (28.5-mm) bow amour for greater strength in ramming, and 3-in (76-mm) armour for the conning tower. The second saw the introduction of 8-in (203-mm) L/35 guns and replacement of the secondary battery by 14 5-in (127-mm) L/40 guns. The third saw the use of six Babcock & Wilcox and four cylindrical boilers to feed horizontal triple expansion engines delivering 9,000 ihp (6710 kW) to two propellers for 18 kt, as well as the removal of the sails.

From 1910 to 1917 the *Chicago* served with two state naval militias, and in 1917/23 served mostly with submarines with just four 5-in (127-mm) L/51 guns. The ship was an accommodation vessel at Pearl Harbor in 1923/35, being renamed USS Alton in July 1928, and in 1936 was sold but foundered in tow to San Francisco.

USS *Chicago* (as completed)

Type:	protected cruiser
Tonnage:	4,864 tons full load
Dimensions:	length 342 ft 2 in (104.3 m); beam 48 ft 3 in (14.7 m); draft 19 ft (5.8 m)
Propulsion:	two compound overhead beam steam engines delivering 5,000 ihp (3728 kW) to two propellers for 14 kt
Armour:	1.5-in (38-mm) deck ad 0.75-in (19-mm) magazines
Armament:	four 8-in (203-mm) guns, eight 6-in (152-mm) guns, two 5-in (127-mm) guns, two 6-pdr guns and two 1-pdr guns
Complement:	470

Tatsuta (1894)

The Imperial Japanese navy came into existence in 1869 at the end of the civil war that saw the restoration of imperial power in place of the shogunate which had long ruled Japan. The emperor wanted to transform Japan into a technically modern state, and as finances permitted his government contracted for foreign construction as well as buying in foreign expertise to develop an industrial and military capability in Japan. The 1st Naval Expansion Act, passed in 1882, authorized the construction of 48 new ships, although in the event only 46 were ordered: 14 of these, including two cruisers, were built in the newly upgraded Japanese yards, while the other 32, mainly cruisers, were ordered from British and French yards. This gave the Japanese what they believed was the correctly balanced mix of cruisers, gunboats and torpedo boats, but then the worsening of Japan's relations with China led to a change as the Japanese navy's three armoured vessels were clearly inferior to the latest Chinese vessels from Germany. Japan therefore ordered two battleships and one cruiser from the UK, but none of these had been completed before the outbreak of the Sino-Japanese War (1894/95).

Japanese also ordered other vessels, and in 1892 Armstrongs of Elswick contracted for the design and construction of an unprotected cruiser, the *Tatsuta* which was intended as a replacement for the French-built *Chishima*, The new cruiser was laid down in April 1893 and completed in July 1894. Intended as a "torpedo catcher," the new cruiser reached 20.5 kt on trials. Armstrongs had agreed to delivery the new cruiser to Yokohama, and the *Tatsuta* sailed at the end of August 1894. The Sino-Japanese War started while the ship was still in European waters, and as a result the British authorities in Aden detained the ship until the end of November 1894, when the British government decided to allow the delivery of the ship to be completed, though with a Japanese crew. The *Tatsuta* finally reached Yokohama early in 1895. The war was not yet over, but there is no evidence that the new cruiser played any active role. Reclassified as a despatch vessel in 1898, the *Tatsuta* was part of

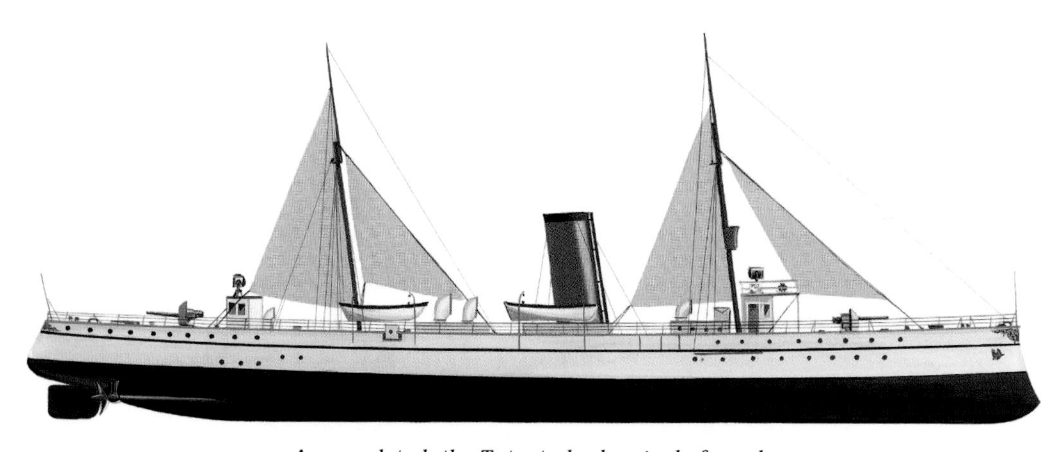

As completed, the Tatsuta had a single funnel.

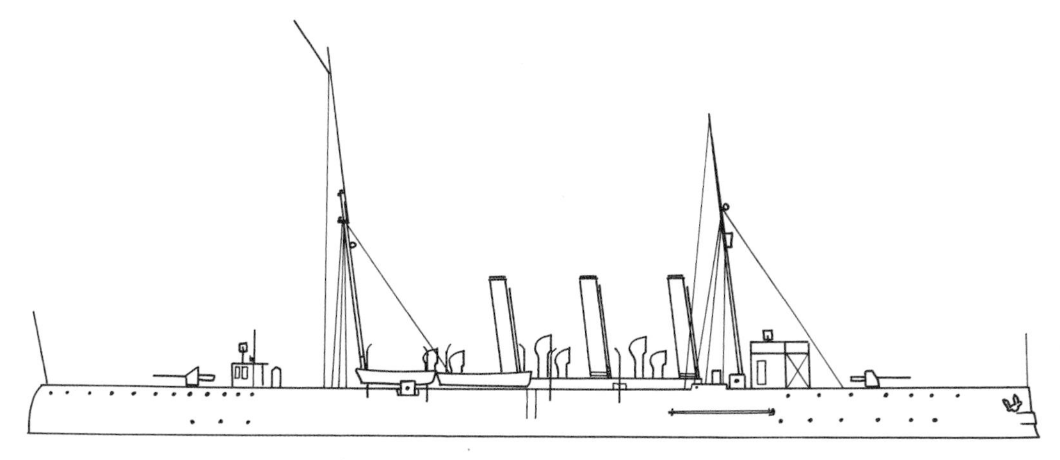

As revised and reboilered, the Tatsuta had three funnels.

Admiral Heihachiro Togo's squadron off Taku during the Boxer rebellion of 1900 in China.

At some time, probably 1903, the *Tatsuta* was reboilered with four Miyabara (Kanpon) small-tube boilers, and three slim funnels replaced the original single wide funnel. By the start of the Russo-Japanese War (1904/05) the Tatsuta was part of the 1st Division of the 1st Squadron, itself an element of the Japanese fleet blockading Port Arthur. On May 15th, three months after the outbreak of war, the Japanese battleships *Yashima* and *Hatsuse* succumbed to Russian mines 10 miles (16 km) outside the harbour, and Rear Admiral Natsuba then transferred his flag from the *Hatsuse* to the *Tatsuta* which, later in the same day, ran into fog and went ashore on the westernmost of the Elliott Islands, where she remained for a month before being refloated and repaired. She rejoined the fleet in September and in November captured a German steamer. At the Battle of Tsushima in May 1905, the *Tatsuta* was the despatch vessel of Togo's 1st Squadron. In 1905 the four 3-pdr QF guns and 14-in (356-mm) torpedo tubes were replaced by 12-pdr QF guns and 18-in (457-mm) tubes respectively. In 1918 she became the *Nagaura*, a submarine tender, and was scrapped in 1926.

Tatsuta (as completed)

Type:	unprotected cruiser
Tonnage:	850 tons normal
Dimensions:	length 240 ft (73.1 m) between perpendiculars; beam 27 ft 6 in (8.4 m); draft 9 ft 6 in (2.9 m)
Propulsion:	two vertical triple expansion steam engines delivering 5,500 ihp (4101 kW) to two propellers for 21 kt
Armour:	none
Armament:	two 4.7-in (120-mm) QF guns, four 3-pdr QF guns, five 2.5-pdr QF guns, and five 14-in (356-mm) torpedo tubes
Complement:	100

USS *Katahdin* (1896)

The American-Civil War (1861/65) spurred a revival of the concept of the ram warship as a significant "weapon." The Confederacy started to build some ram-equipped armoured vessels, and one of these, the CSS *Manassas*, actually used her ram in action. Then the apparent success of the ram at the Battle of Lissa (1866) and in the sinking of several ships in the course of accidents spurred a further resurgence in the popularity of the ram during the 1870s and 1880s. Many naval officers, including the US Navy's Rear Admiral Daniel Ammen, the Chief of the Bureau of Navigation, continued to press for the construction of small, fast and maneuvrable vessels, with acutely sloping armoured sides and a very low silhouette, with a strong ram bow as their primary weapon. The French had already produced ram vessels for the harbor-defence role, but these were completely unsuccessful. The ship generally held to be the prime example of the ram vessel was the 2,640-ton HMS *Polyphemus*, which was completed for Royal Navy service in 1882. This was not the case, however, for the *Polyphemus* was principally a seagoing torpedo ship, and though she was classified as a torpedo ram, her ram was most definitely a secondary weapon.

After long debate, the US Navy finally reached the decision in 1891 to order its own armoured ram. By this time the concept was not just obsolescent but wholly obsolete. Firstly, by this time it had been established beyond reasonable doubt that it was extremely difficult to ram an enemy vessel which was still capable of steering and steaming; and secondly, the warships of the world's more advanced navies were equipped with quick-firing guns of that type specifically designed to counter any close approach with a hail of fire. Thus what may have appeared to have possessed some validity in the time when guns were very slow-firing, inaccurate and short-ranged weapons, certainly no longer did so by the 1890s.

The USS Katahdin is depicted at what passed for high speed.

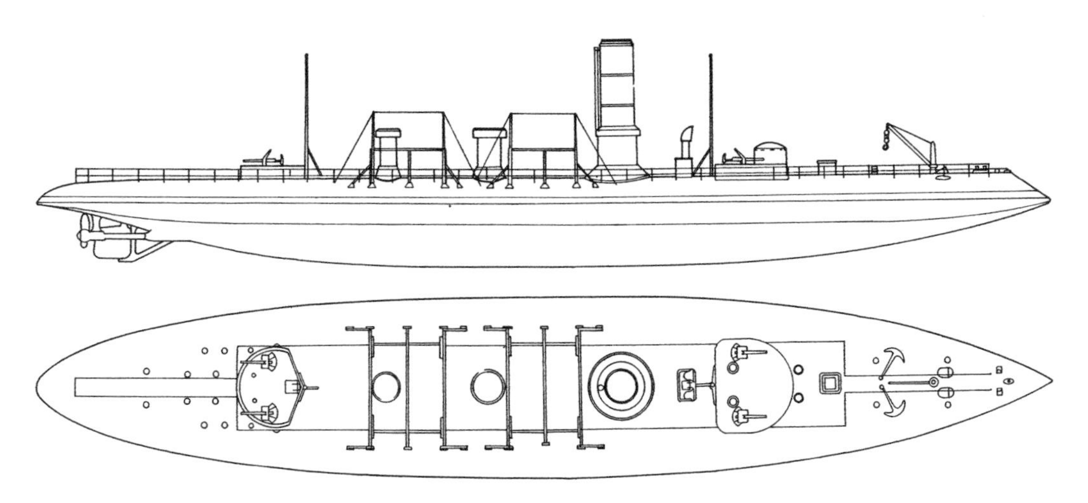

The USS Katahdin was wholly obsolete in concept even as she was designed.

Designed by Ammen, the USS *Katahdin* was built by the Bath Iron Works but not launched until 1893 and then completed only in 1895. The American vessel was decidedly inferior to the *Polyphemus* in design and capability. She had no torpedo armament and therefore relied entirely on her ram for offensive capability, and her four 6-pdr defensive guns were mounted not high on a flying deck, as in the British vessel, but on the hull. The design speed was only 17 kt despite the enormous funnel designed to give the best possible natural draft. Perhaps even worse was the fact that the *Katahdin* combined very limited agility with difficult steering, making it all but inevitable that she would be unable to close and ram any maneuvering target. The vessel was also very uncomfortable for a crew inside a hull low in the water, hot, poorly ventilated and badly laid out.

It was not until the outbreak of the Spanish-American War (1898) that the *Katahdin* was used operationally as part of the force patrolling the USA's eastern seaboard. Despite pressure from the press, the *Katahdin* was not sent to engage the Spanish fleet. This was a decided blessing for her hapless crew, for seldom has any warship been so patently useless. It was therefore no surprise when the *Katahdin* was sunk as a target in 1909.

USS *Katahdin*

Type:	armoured ram
Tonnage:	2,383 tons full load
Dimensions:	length 250 ft 9 in (76.4 m); beam 43 ft 5 in (13.2 m); draft 15 ft 1 in (4.6 m)
Propulsion:	two horizontal triple expansion steam engines delivering 5,068 ihp (3779 kW) to two propellers for 16 kt
Armour:	3/6-in (76/152-mm) sides, 6-in (152-mm) uptakes, 2/6-in (51/152-mm) deck, and 18-in (457-mm) conning tower
Armament:	four 6-pdr guns
Complement:	97

Turbinia (1896)

Though in no way a warship in her own right, the *Turbinia* should be included in any discussion of warships as the craft in which the advantages of the steam turbine, as developed by the Hon. Charles A. Parsons, over the reciprocating steam engine were clearly shown. Though the turbine is conceptually simpler than that of the reciprocating engine, the latter is simpler to design and build, and was therefore earlier to enter service. Even compound- and triple-expansion engines are less efficient than any turbine, however, and their heavy cylinders, pistons and bearings are subject to enormous stresses and cannot be driven at high speeds for long periods. Parsons' first working steam turbine was a 6-hp (4.5-kW) unit developed in 1884, and the technology was quickly adopted for electricity generation on land. However, it was not until 1897, when Parsons' phenomenal *Turbinia* raced through the Spithead Naval Review, that the capabilities of the turbine were publicly revealed.

Confident of the advantages of the turbine for shipboard service, Parsons had created the Marine Steam Turbine Company to build and test a turbine-driven vessel. The advantages which Parsons believed would be offered by a practical steam turbine propulsion arrangement included greater speed, increased carrying power, superior economy in steam consumption, reduced purchase and maintenance costs, reduced machinery mass, very radically reduced vibration levels, and reduced size and weight of the shaft and propeller.

Parsons had a problem selecting the best propulsion layout, and went through seven different propulsion designs, including three propellers on one shaft. Because the turbine turned the shaft faster than an expansion engine would, the screws were not as efficient as predicted due to cavitation. This phenomenon, the result of a vacuum forming around a screw turning at high speed, was first observed in early trials of the *Turbinia*. When the vessel failed to attain her design speed, Parsons replaced the single shaft with three separate shafts (at first there were three propellers on each shaft) and at the same time replaced the centrifugal-flow turbine with a more efficient axial-flow unit. The results were scarcely credible, and in supervised trials the steel-hulled *Turbinia*, built by the Turbinia Works (Brown & Hood) of Wallsend-on-Tyne in 1894, reached 34 kt.

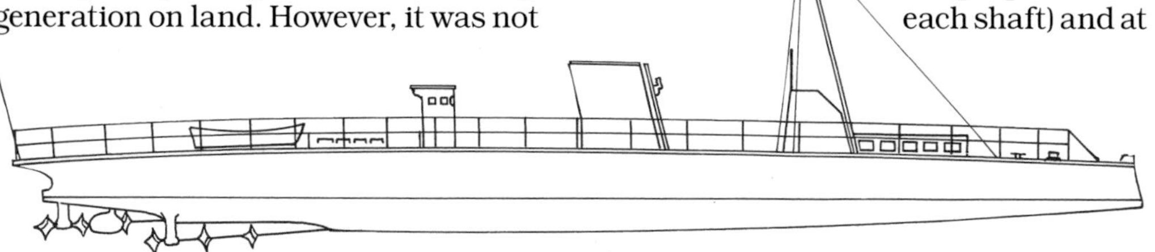

The Turbinia was built to validate Parsons' steam turbine propulsion concept, and was also used for development work

On June 26, 1897, during the international naval review to celebrate the 60th year of Queen Victoria's reign and after the queen had inspected the assembled vessels from the royal yacht *Victoria and Albert*, the *Turbinia*

The Turbinia races through the lines of warships assembled for the Spithead Naval Review of 1897.

tore through the anchored fleet in a demonstration of unimagined speed and agility. Soon after this the Parsons Marine Steam Turbine Company was formed, and in 1899 the Admiralty, which had been kept informed of Parsons' work, ordered its first turbine-powered vessel, the 36-kt destroyer HMS Viper.

The *Turbinia* last ran in 1907, and was removed from the water in 1927. She was cut in two and the after part was put on exhibit at the Science Museum in London. In 1944, about 15 ft ft (4.6 m) of the fore section was displayed at the Museum of Science and Engineering in Newcastle. In 1959 the Parsons company arranged for the reassembly of the vessel, which has been exhibited at Turbinia Hall in the Tyne & Wear County Council Museum in Newcastle since 1960.

Turbinia

Type:	steam-turbine propulsion test bed launch
Tonnage:	44.5 tons displacement
Dimensions:	length 103 ft 9 in (31.6 m); beam 9 ft (2.7 m); draft 3 ft (0.9 m)
Propulsion:	one Parsons three-stage steam turbine delivering 2,100 shp (1566 kW) to three shafts for 34.5 kt
Armour:	none
Armament:	none
Complement:	not known

USS *Brooklyn* (1896)

A ship which reflected the growing industrial maturity of the USA as well as the increasing sophistication of the US Navy, the USS *Brooklyn* was a one-off armoured cruiser designed as an improved version of the USS *New York*. Authorized in July 1892, the *Brooklyn* was the first US Navy vessel whose contract specified that all of her major components must be made in the USA rather than imported.

Characterized by pronounced tumblehome, three tall wire-stayed funnels and a ram bow, the *Brooklyn* was innovative in several respects. She was more heavily armed than virtually every other cruiser, with eight rather than four 8-in (203-mm) L/35 guns. These were mounted in turrets forward, aft and the two wing positions amidships in a layout which allowed the training of six guns forward, aft and on each broadside. The forward turret was at forecastle deck level, and the other turrets at upper deck level, the supports for the wing turrets rising from the inward-sloping sides. Originally the forward and starboard wing turrets were electrically trained and the other two steam trained, but the electrical training was so successful that the other two turrets were changed and the system became standard for the turrets of US Navy ships. Eight of the secondary battery's 12 5-in (127-mm) L/40 guns were in main deck sponsons and the other four at upper deck level, the foremost pair sponsoned under the forecastle.

The armour was of the Harvey and nickel steel types, and the 3-in (76-mm) belt covered only the machinery spaces. Protection therefore depended largely on the armour deck, which was 3 in (76 mm) thick on the flat, 6 in (152 mm) thick on the slopes by the belt, and 2,5 in (63.5 mm) thick fore and aft. The barbettes were shallow rings 4 to 8 in (102 to 203 mm) thick with 3-in (76-mm) ammunition tubes. The *Brooklyn* was built by Cramp and was completed in December 1896, on trials reaching 21.9 kt on 18,770 ihp (13995 kW) at the light displacement of 8,150 tons.

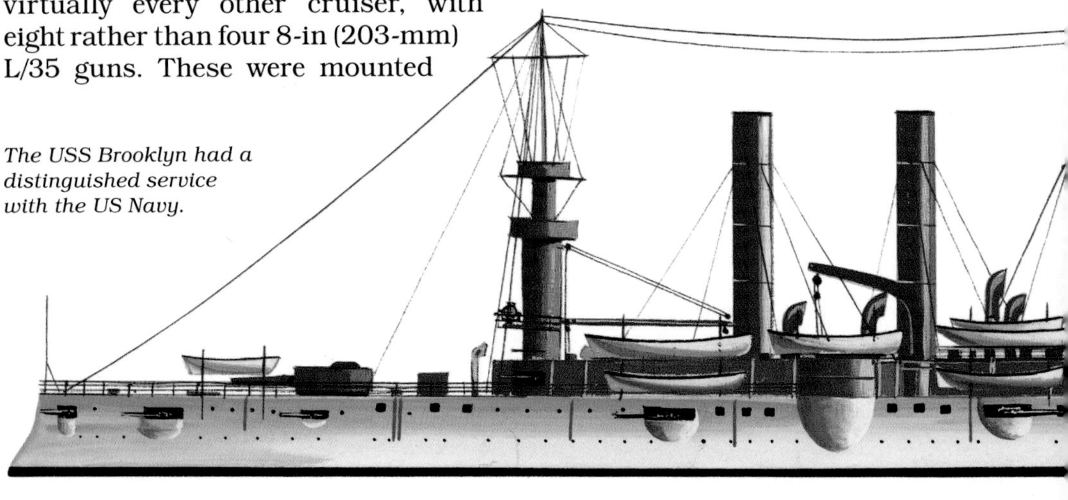

The USS Brooklyn had a distinguished service with the US Navy.

The *Brooklyn* represented the US Navy at Queen Victoria's diamond jubilee naval review and, on returning home, patrolled on the Atlantic coast

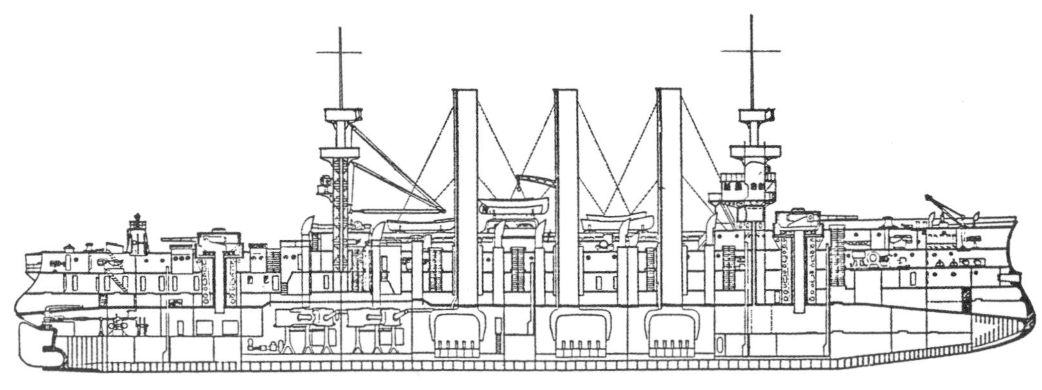

Cut-away of the USS Brooklyn.

and West Indies until 1898, when she became flagship to Commodore W. S. Schley's Flying Squadron during the Spanish-American War. At the end of May, Schley began the US blockades of Cienfuegos and Santiago, where the bulk of Admiral Pascual Cervera's fleet of antiquated cruisers lay. On July third, Cervera tried to break out and, after almost ramming the USS *Texas*, the *Brooklyn* led the chase and action which sank four Spanish armoured cruisers. In 1902 she returned to Havana for ceremonies marking the transfer of government from the US to a Cuban government, and thereafter served with the North Atlantic Fleet and the European Squadron. The *Brooklyn* was in and out of commission from 1908 to 1914, receiving improved turret hoists and a fire-control system, but having her torpedo tubes removed. In 1914 the cruiser joined the Neutrality Patrol off Boston before becoming flagship of the Asiatic Fleet. She remained in the Pacific until 1921, when she was sold out of the US Navy.

USS *Brooklyn*

Type:	armoured cruiser
Tonnage:	10,068 tons full load
Dimensions:	length 402 ft 7 in (122.7 m); beam 64 ft 8 in (19.1); draft 24 ft (7.3 m)
Propulsion:	two vertical triple expansion steam engines delivering 16,000 ihp (11930 kW) to two propellers for 20 kt
Armour:	3-in (76-mm) belt, 3/8-in (76/203-mm) barbettes, 5.5 in (140-mm) turrets, 4-in (102-mm) secondary battery, and 8.5 in (216-mm) conning tower
Armament:	eight 8-in (203-mm) guns, 12 5-in (127-mm) guns, 12 6-pdr guns, four 1-pdr guns, and five 18-in (457-mm) torpedo tubes
Complement:	581

Henri IV (1899)

The French coast-defense battleship *Henri IV*, designed by Emile Bertin and built by the Arsenal de Cherbourg for completion in September 1903, was a remarkable ship probably to be regarded more as a prototype for some of the ideas of her design than as a mainstay of the French fleet. The freeboard was a mere 4 ft (1.2 m), extended upward over the forward portion of the ship to the standard upper deck height in a process that was continued into a very narrow superstructure.

The protection was based on a belt which ended just short of the stern in a 4-in (100-mm) bulkhead and extended from 4 ft (1.2 m) above the waterline to 4 ft 3 in (1.3 m) below it: this belt was 11 in (280 mm) thick amidships with a 7-in (180-mm) lower edge, and declined in thickness to 7-in (180-mm) ends with 3-in (76-mm) lower edges. The upper belt was generally of 4-in (100-mm) thickness and extended right from the bows to a point 30 ft (9.15 m) abaft the middle section along the superstructure sides. This upper belt was 6 ft 7 in (2 m) wide increasing to 13 ft 1.5 in (4 m) forward, and its end was closed by a 3-in (76-mm) bulkhead. At the upper edges of the main belt was an armoured deck 2.4 in (60 mm) thick reducing to 1.2 in (30 mm) at its ends. Below this was another deck 0.8 in (20 mm) thick along its centreline increasing to 1.3 in (35 mm) near its edges and curved down about 3 ft (0.9 m) inboard to form a torpedo bulkhead before joining the inner bottom. Other protection was provided by cellular layers between the armoured decks and by a large number of small compartments inboard of the torpedo bulkhead. This arrangement was derived from experiments at Lorient in 1894. It was not tested under wartime conditions, but there is no doubt that the torpedo bulkhead was too close to the side.

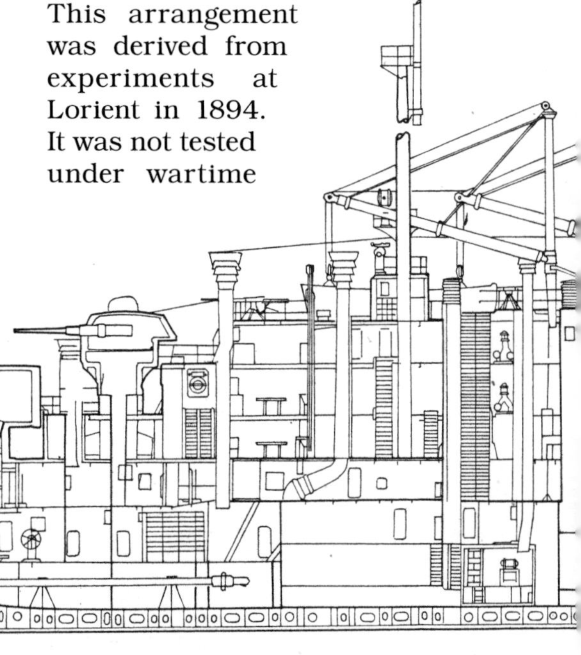

The turreted forward 10.8-in (275-mm) gun had an axis height of 29 ft 6 in (9 m) and the after gun of 13 ft 8 in (4.15 m), while of the seven 5.5-in (140-mm) guns of the secondary battery four were mounted in main-deck casemates, two in shields on the upper deck and one in a superfiring turret above the after 10.8-in (275-mm) turret. This was the first time that superfiring turrets had been

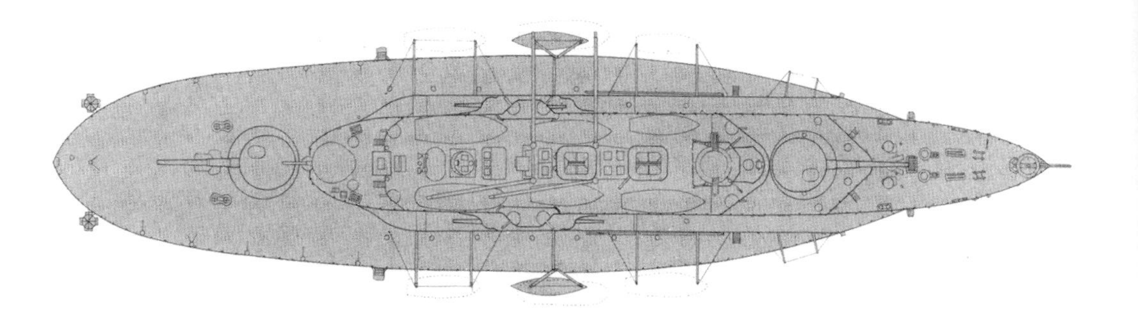

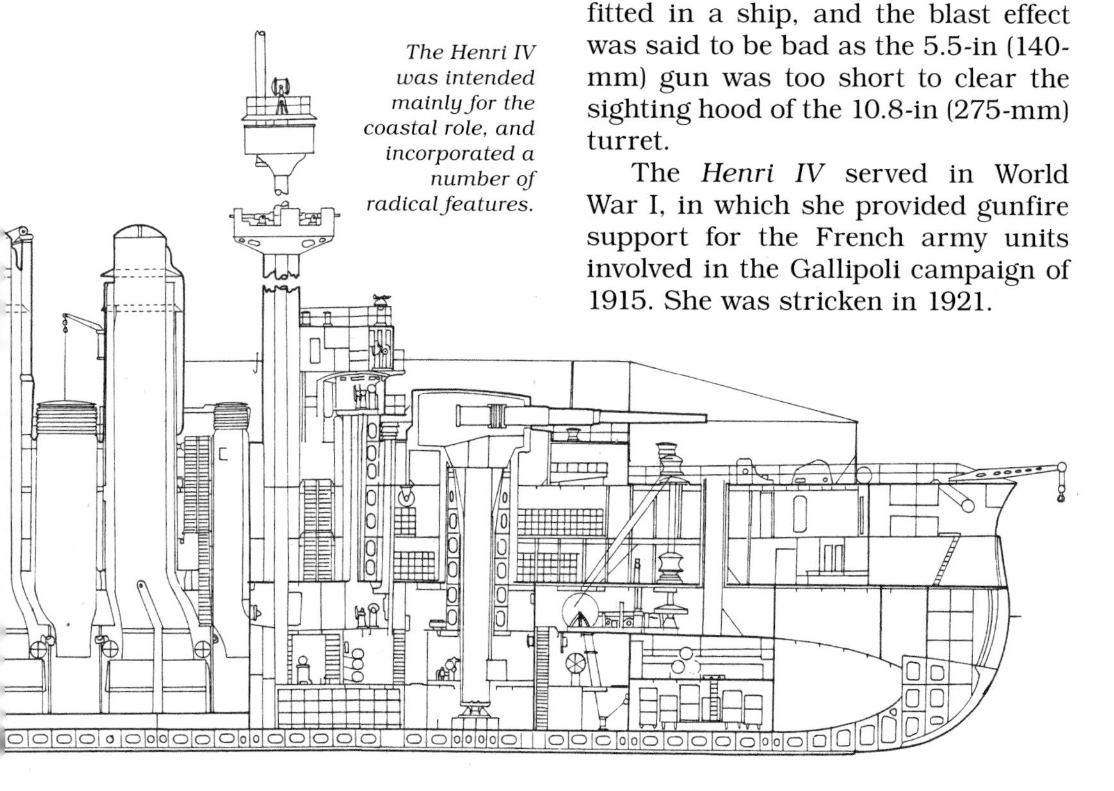

The Henri IV was intended mainly for the coastal role, and incorporated a number of radical features.

fitted in a ship, and the blast effect was said to be bad as the 5.5-in (140-mm) gun was too short to clear the sighting hood of the 10.8-in (275-mm) turret.

The *Henri IV* served in World War I, in which she provided gunfire support for the French army units involved in the Gallipoli campaign of 1915. She was stricken in 1921.

Henri IV

Type:	battleship
Tonnage:	8,807 tons displacement
Dimensions:	length 354 ft 4 in (108 m); beam 72 ft 10 in (22.2 m); draft 22 ft 11 in (7 m)
Propulsion:	three vertical triple expansion steam engines delivering 11,000 ihp (8202 kW) to three shafts for 17 kt
Armour:	3/11-in (75/280-mm) belt, 3/4-in (75/100-mm) upper belt, 12-in (305-mm) turrets, 9.5-in (240-mm) barbettes, 3/6.4-in (75/160-mm) secondary armament, and 9.5-in (240-mm) coming tower
Armament:	two 10.8-in (274-mm) guns, seven 5.5-in (140-mm) QF guns, 12 3-pdr QF guns, two 1-pdr guns, and two 18-in (457-mm) torpedo tubes
Complement:	464

USS *Kearsarge* (1900)

Authorized in March 1895, the two "Kearsarge" class battleships were only the second class-built battleships, after the three "Indiana" class units, to serve with the US Navy. The primary point of interest in these ships is that they marked a step in the change from the "big and small gun" to the "all big gun" battleship: earlier battleships had carried perhaps four main and 12 secondary guns, but the "Kearsarge" class ships had a much more powerful but numerically smaller secondary battery in addition to a numerous tertiary battery. Another interesting feature was the location of the primary and secondary armament in a superfiring layout which was supposed to offer the secondary battery greater arcs of fire, freedom from main battery blast interference, and the combination of good base and ammunition feed protection as a result of the shared barbette. Another claimed improvement was control of the pairs of primary and secondary turrets by a single officer. On the other side of the coin were factors such as the lack of independent fire capabilities for the primary and secondary guns, the possibility of one hit disabling both a primary and a secondary battery turret, and stability and structural problems.

The ships were the USS *Kearsarge* and USS *Kentucky*, both built by Newport News for completion in February and May 1900 respectively. These were flush-decked ships with a ram bow. Their protection was based on Harvey steel armour, and centered on a thick belt extending from 3 ft 6 in (1.1 m) above to 4 ft (1.2 m) below the waterline.

The 8-in (203-mm) gun turrets were fixed on the roofs of the 13-in (330-mm) gun turrets, the two turrets training together as a single unit. The 13-in (330-mm) turret crowns were 3.5 in (89 mm) thick, and those of the 8 in (203 mm) turrets 2 in (51 mm) thick. The 5-in (127-mm) guns were located in an upper-deck battery with 6-in (152-mm) armour. Turret training was electrical, and the "Kearsarge" class ships were the

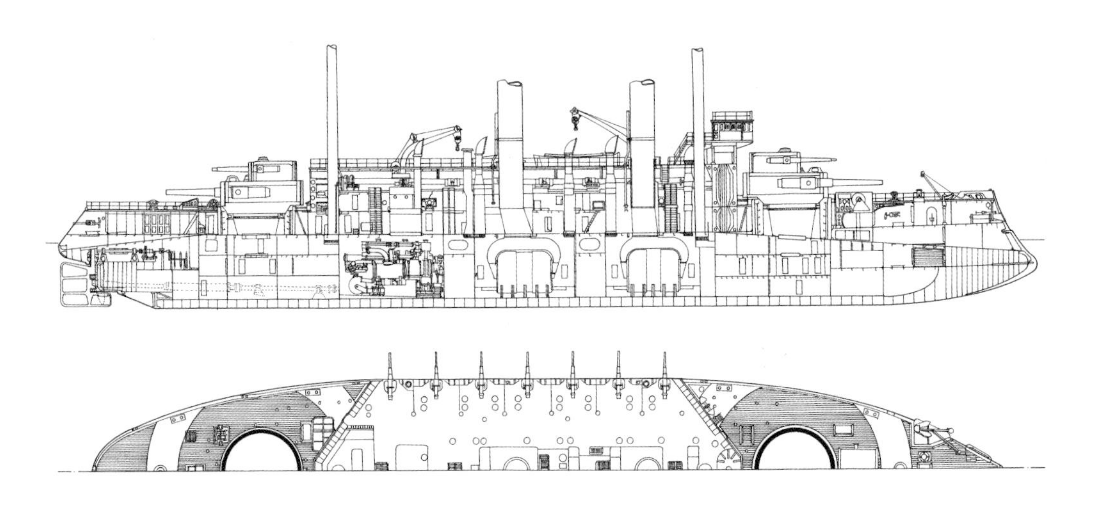

The "Kearsarge" class battleship.

The USS Kearsarge is caught by the camera at low speed.

first US Navy battleships to make extensive use of electrical auxiliary machinery.

The ships were apparently very poor gun platforms. The torpedo tubes were soon removed, and in 1909/11 the turrets were modified, most of the 6-pdr guns removed, four more 5-in (127-mm) guns added on the super-structure, cage-type fore and main masts fitted, and the five cylindrical boilers replaced by eight Mosher boilers. By 1919 the 5-in (127-mm) guns had been reduced to eight in number, and two 3-in (76-mm) AA guns added. The *Kearsarge* was converted to a crane ship in 1920, stability being increased by bulges to permit the installation of a large 250-ton revolving crane. She was sold in 1955, the *Kentucky* having been sold in 1923.

USS *Kearsarge*

Type:	battleship
Tonnage:	12,850 tons full load
Dimensions:	length 375 ft 4 in (114.4 m); beam 72 ft 3 in (22 m); draft 23 ft 6 in (7.16 m)
Propulsion:	two vertical triple expansion steam engines delivering 10,000 ihp to two propellers for 16 kt
Armour:	4/16.5-in (102/419-mm) belt, 12/5/15-in (318/381-mm) barbettes, 15/17-in (381/432-mm) turrets, 6/11-in (152/281-mm) tertiary armament, 10-in (254-mm) conning tower
Armament:	four 13-in (330-mm) guns, four 8-in (203-mm) guns, 14 5-in (127-mm) guns, 20-6pdr QF guns, eight 1-pdr guns, and four 18-in (457-mm) torpedo tubes
Complement:	553 in peace and 868 in war

Potemkin (1905)

The Russian battleship *Kniaz Potemkin Tavritchevski* was built at Nikolayev for service with the Black Sea Fleet. The ship was laid down in February 1898, launched in October 1900 and completed in November 1903, and was in essence an improved version of the preceding *Peresviet*, though with her upper rather than forecastle deck extending to a position abaft the main mast. The ship was the scene in June 1905 of a celebrated mutiny which led in Odessa to serious rioting in which many thousands of people lost their lives. The mutinous crew then cruised round the Black Sea in the hope that others ships' crews would mutiny, but when this did not happen they scuttled the ship in shallow water off Constanza. After being raised and refitted, the ship was renamed as the *Pantelimon*, but this was changed to *Potemkin* in April 1917 and finally to Boretz za Svobodu only one month later.

There was a decidedly French-influenced flavor to this three-funnelled design, especially in the French type of turrets for the main armament, and the ship had French Belleville boilers, no fewer than 22 of these being employed to deliver steam to the vertical triple expansion engines which produced power for 16.6 kt. The main armament of four 12-in (305-mm) L/40 guns was installed in centerline twin-gun turrets of the French types forward and aft. The secondary armament comprised 16 6-in (152-mm) L/45 guns, and these were installed as four in upper-deck casemates and the other 12 in a main-deck battery. The armour was of the Krupp cemented type, and was based on a main belt 237 ft (72.25 m) long and 7 ft 6 in (2.3 m) wide: this was 8/9-in (203/229-mm) thick tapering to a lower edge 5 in (127 mm) thick. The 6-in (152-mm) upper belt was taken to the main deck over a length of 156 ft (47.5 m), a figure some 14 ft (4.25 m) less than the length of the battery armour. The bulkheads were 5/7 in (127/178 mm) thick, figures which were significantly highly than those for the preceding Peresviet and reflecting a greater appreciation of the effects of raking fire, and the alloy

The Potemkin had a tall, slab-sided combination of hull and superstructure.

Renamed as the Pantelimon, the Potemkin was a key element of Russian naval power in the Black Sea during World War I.

steel armour deck 2 in (51 mm) thick on the flat with 2.5 in (63.5 mm) thick slope sections outside the area of the battery, increased to 3 in (76 mm) at the ends. The battery roof was 1.5 in (38 mm) thick, and the crowns of the turrets were 3 in (76 mm) thick.

The *Pantelimon* was involved in many of the Black Sea Fleet's forays and operations, largely against the Turkish navy, during the course of World War I. In this war the first intimations of a new type of warfare became at least marginally evident through the addition of two specialized 11-pdr anti-aircraft guns. Even though they were strapped for modern weapons, the ship's new Soviet masters had to concede by the early 1920s that the *Boretz za Svobodu* was obsolete and also virtually impossible to maintain with the reduced capabilities now available in the Black Sea area, and the ship was scrapped in 1922.

Kniaz Potemkin Tavritchevski

Type:	battleship
Tonnage:	12,582 tons
Dimensions:	length 378 ft 6 in (115.4 m); beam 73 ft (22.25 m); draft 27 ft (8.25 m)
Propulsion:	two vertical triple expansion steam engines delivering 10,600 ihp (7903 kW) to two propellers for 16.6 kt
Armour:	5/9-in (127/229-mm) belt, 5/7-in (127/178-mm) upper belt, 5/7-in (127/178-mm) bulkheads, 5/10-in (127/254-mm) turrets, 5-in (127-mm) battery, 6-in (152-mm) casemates, and 9-in (229-mm) conning tower
Armament:	four 12-in (305-mm) guns, 16 6-in (152-mm) guns, 14 11-pdr QF guns, six 3-pdr QF guns, and five 15-in (381-mm) torpedo tubes
Complement:	750

La République (1906)

Though they had appreciated the limitations of their capital ships for some time, it was not until the advent of the two-ship "République" class designed from the late 1890s, that they were permitted the greater displacement and beam that allowed the creation of a much improved battleship type. Even so, it took so long to build these ships that they were essentially obsolete even as they were completed. The ships' looks were distinctive, with a high forecastle deck extending as far to the rear as the main mast, much reduced tumblehome and an arrangement of three funnels as two forward and one well aft for the 24 Niclausse boilers.

The armour was of the Krupp cemented type, and based on a belt reaching from the bows to a point close to the stern and from the main deck, some 7 ft 7 in (2.3 m) above the waterline, to a depth of 4 ft 11 in (1.50 m) below it. Amidships the belt was 11 in (280 mm) thick on the waterline tapering to 9.5 and 3.2 in (240 and 80 mm) at its upper and lower edges: the equivalent figures fore and aft were 7, 5.5 and 3.2 in (180, 140 and 125 mm). Above the belt, between the bows and

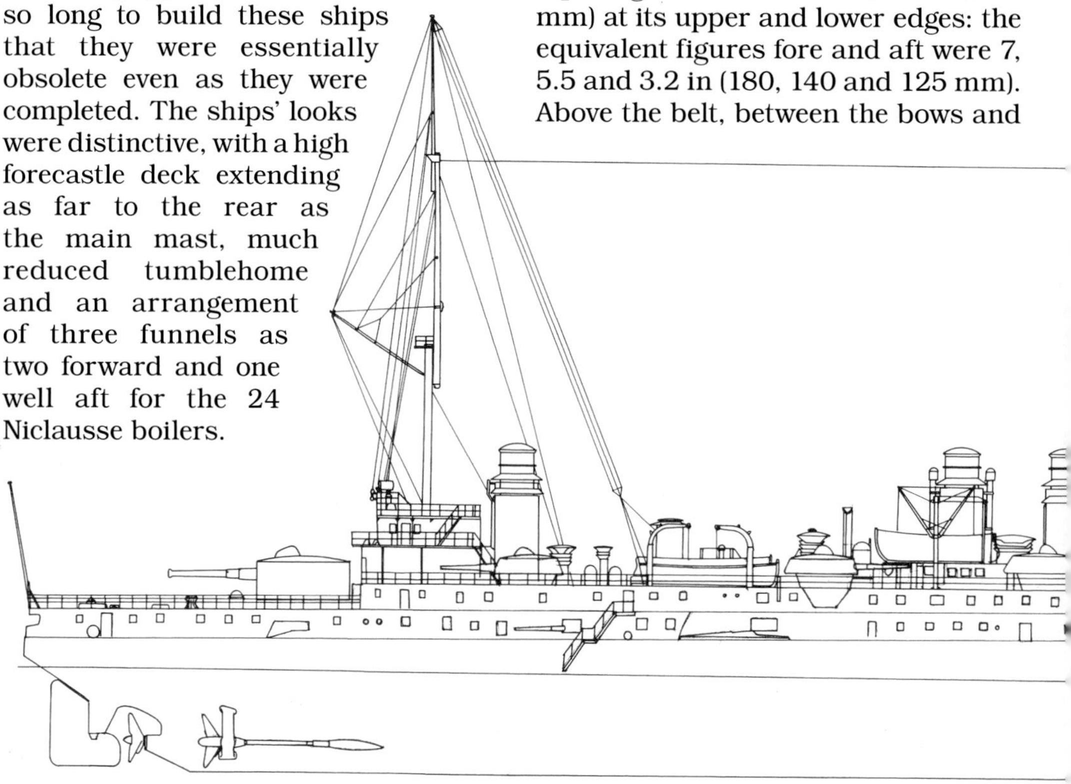

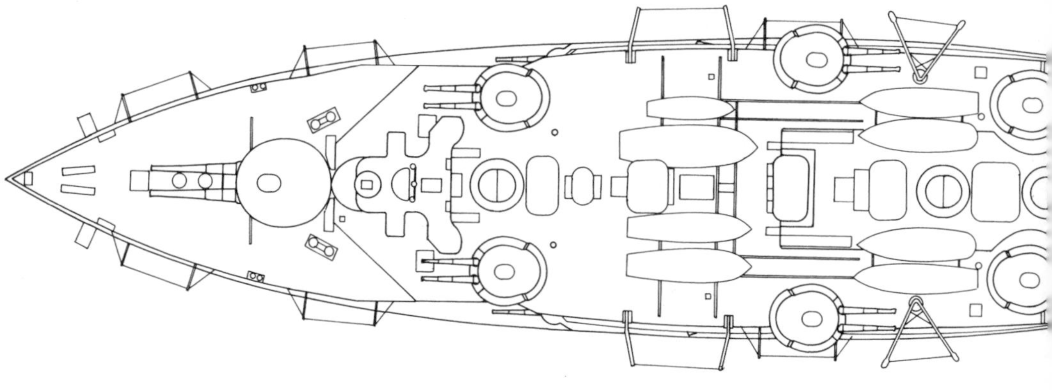

La République

Type:	battleship
Tonnage:	14,605 tons displacement
Dimensions:	length 439 ft (133.8 m) between perpendicular; beam 79 ft 7 in (24.25 m); draft 27 ft 7 in (8.4 m)
Propulsion:	three vertical triple expansion steam engines delivering 18,000 ihp (13420 kW) to three propellers for 19 kt
Armour:	3.2/11-in (80/280-mm) belt, 2/2.75-in (50/70-mm) decks, 11/14-in (280/355-mm) main turrets, 10-in (255-mm) main turret bases, 3.5/6-in (90/150-mm) secondary guns, and 12-in (305-mm) conning tower
Armament:	four 12-in (305-mm) guns, 18 6.4-in (160-mm) guns, 25 3-pdr QF guns, and two 18-in (457-mm) torpedo tubes
Complement:	766 in peace and 825 in war

the fore mast, there was 3.2-in (80-mm) armour to a height of 16 ft 5 in (5 m). The main deck amidships was a 2.1-in (55-mm) sandwich of alloy steel between two mild steel layers, and the lower deck was similar but only 2 in (50 mm) thick increasing to 2.75 in (70 mm) on the sides sloping to the lower edge of the belt. The cellular layer between the armour decks comprised a cofferdam, passage, three coal bunkers and then a central passage.

The main armament was four 12-in (305-mm) L/40 guns in fore and aft twin turrets, and the secondary armament 18 6.4-in (160-mm) L/50 guns in six twin turrets at forecastle deck level, two guns in upper-deck casemates forward and four in main-deck casemates aft of amidships.

La République and La Patrie were built respectively by the Arsenal de Brest and the Forges et Chantiers de la Mediterranée (La Seyne), and both served in the Mediterranean during World War I. The vessels were stricken in 1921 and 1928.

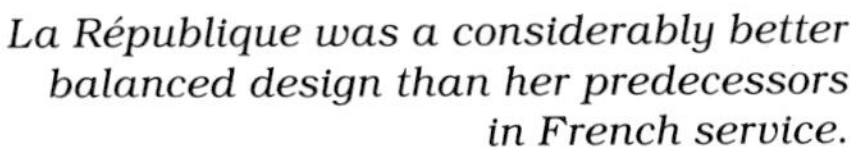

La République was a considerably better balanced design than her predecessors in French service.

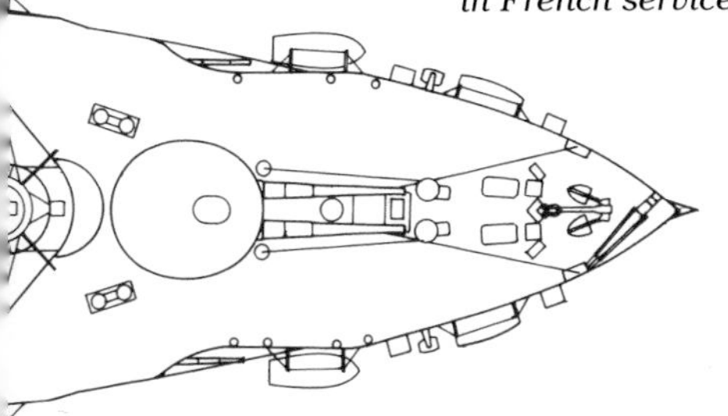

Model of La République

HMS *Velox* (1904)

By the end of the 19th century a high level of development had been reached in the destroyer, or more properly the torpedo boat destroyer as its primary task was the interception and destruction of the small, fast and nimble torpedo boats which were deemed to represent the major surface threat to battle fleets. They were armed with quick-firing guns and powered reciprocating steam engines for speeds in the order of 30 kt. The rate of coal consumption by these vessels at high speed was a severe restraint on their endurance, and their machinery required long and therefore comparatively expensive hulls. In 1896/97 the Admiralty ordered three "33-kt special" destroyers from different yards, but these were technically unsuccessful and failed to achieve the specified speed.

By the time the "33-kt specials" were running their trials early in the 20th century, there had appeared the new type of machinery which would make the reciprocating steam engine obsolete for high-speed warships. In 1897 the Hon. Charles A. Parsons' *Turbinia* had made her spectacular appearance at the Jubilee Review at Spithead, and shown that the steam turbine was fully practical. The Director of Naval Construction had been kept informed about Parsons' trials for some time, moreover, and had followed them with interest. It was not therefore surprising that a turbine-powered destroyer should be ordered from Parsons on March 4, 1898. Soon after this the Armstrongs company began work on a turbine-powered destroyer at a private venture by its Elswick yard, and this was taken over by the Admiralty before completion. The first results with these vessels, HMS *Viper* and HMS *Cobra*, were encouraging, but both were lost in 1901: the first was stranded in the Channel Islands and the second foundered. In neither case was the turbine machinery relevant to the loss, though, and to provide another turbine-powered vessel for operational evaluation Admiralty purchased the *Velox*, which Parsons had started as a private venture on the basis of a hull constructed by Hawthorn Leslie. All three of these turbine-powered destroyers were in effect "30-kt special" warships in all respects except their machinery.

Parsons had contracted the hull of its *Viper* to Hawthorn Leslie, and the type emerged as a three-funnel warship and, to allow the power of the turbines to be fully used two propellers were fitted on each shaft. One of the great advantages of the steam turbine over the reciprocating engine was its lack of vibration, and this became

HMS Velox was a destroyer built as a private venture.

HMS Velox's turtledeck forecastle was typical of destroyer design at the end of the 19th century.

fully evident during trials, as did the steam turbines' much greater ability to sustain high speed. The *Cobra* was completed with four funnels, and was purchased from Armstrongs in 1900. The destroyer had run her first trials as early as July 1899, but had then suffered damage in a collision. Three propellers were fitted on each shaft The vessel's construction was lighter than was normal for Royal Navy destroyers, which may help to explain her loss on her delivery voyage; the *Cobra* suddenly broke in two and sank in heavy weather off the Yorkshire coast

Parsons began the *Velox*, initially to have been named *Python*, as a private venture, again with a Hawthorn Leslie hull, for the evaluation of a mixed machinery arrangement. The vessel was bought by the Admiralty in 1901. Turbines optimized for high speeds were not fuel-economical at ordinary cruising speeds, so a separate pair of triple expansion engines was coupled to the low-pressure turbine shafts The problem would eventually be solved by fitting separate cruising turbines, as was effected in the *Velox* during 1906. The *Velox* had three funnels, that in the middle thicker than the other two, and two propellers on each shaft. Completed in February 1904, the *Velox* was lost in 1915 when she hit a mine.

HMS *Velox*

Type:	torpedo boat destroyer
Tonnage:	445 tons full load
Dimensions:	length 215 ft (65.5 m); beam 20 ft 6 in (6.25 m); draft 7 ft (2.1 m)
Propulsion:	four steam turbines delivering unspecified power to four propellers for 27 kt
Armour:	none
Armament:	one 12-pdr QF gun, five 6-pdr QF guns and two 18-in (457-mm) torpedo tubes
Complement:	63

HMS *Blanche* (1910)

The nature of the battle fleets which characterized the world's navies by the beginning of the 20th century combined with the steadily evolving capabilities of the torpedo boat destroyer (soon shortened to just destroyer) to suggest a wider role for the latter in the naval operations posited for the battle fleets. The expanded role saw the destroyer not just as a defense against an enemy's torpedo boats, but as a potent offensive/defensive weapons that could use its speed and endurance to scout for the battle fleet and also attack the enemy's fleet. This paved the way for small cruisers possessing basically the same performance as the destroyer flotillas they were to lead.

This demand created the light "scout cruiser" from 1906 onward. For British service, these scout cruisers were built in three series totalling seven ships (two ships of the "Boadicea" class in the 1907 program, two ships of the "Blonde" class in the 1909 program and three ships of the "Active" class in the 1910 and 1911 programs). All seven of the ships were built by Pembroke Dockyard and, as might be imagined, each of the two later classes showed a slight improvement over its predecessor. Experience soon revealed that the scout cruisers were too small for oceanic operations but useful for the more confined waters of the North Sea, and also that they lacked the speed to operate with the newer generations of oil-fired destroyers, which were capable of 27-29 kt. The scout cruisers' armour was limited in effect to partial protection over the machinery spaces.

The first two ships were HMS *Boadicea* and HMS *Bellona* with a deep-load displacement of 3,800 tons and a primary armament of six 4-in (102-mm) guns mounted as two (port and starboard) on a platform forward of the bridge, two (port and starboard) at the break of the forecastle and two on the centerline aft. By 1916 additions included four more 4-in (102-mm) guns in the waist and one 3-in (76-mm) AA guns replaced in 1918 by one 4-in (102-mm) AA gun. The *Boadicea* and *Bellona* led the 1st and 2nd Destroyers flotillas respectively in 1909/12, and in World War I were attached directly to the

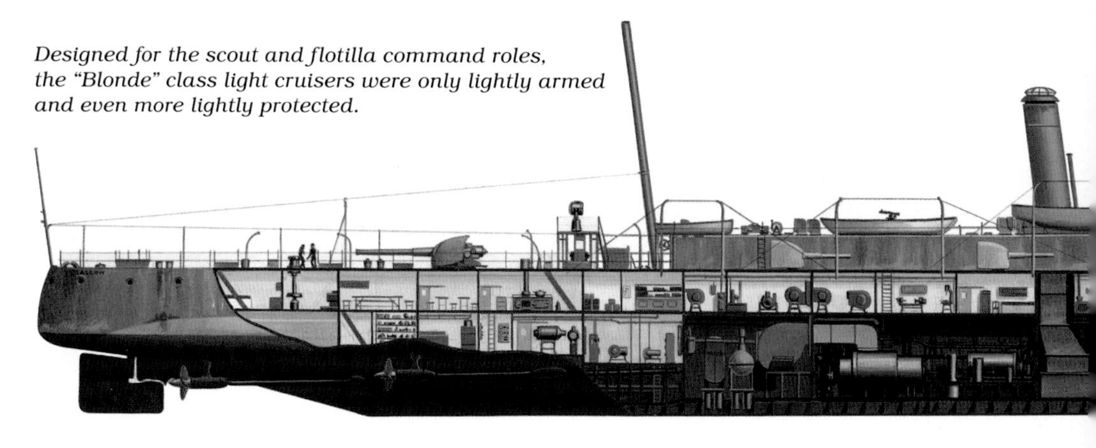

Designed for the scout and flotilla command roles, the "Blonde" class light cruisers were only lightly armed and even more lightly protected.

Grand Fleet before being adapted as minelayers. Both ships were paid off after World War I and scrapped in 1926 and 1921 respectively.

HMS *Blonde* and HMS *Blanche*, which were completed during May 1911 and November 1910 respectively, differed from their two predecessor ships in having 21- not 18-in (533- not 457-mm) torpedo tubes as well as four more 4-in (102-mm) guns, these latter being mounted in the waist. The deck armour was also slightly thicker over the machinery spaces. The ships were therefore of a fairly "racy" appearance with the forecastle break in line with the bridge structure, two tall pole masts, and four slightly angled-back funnels. The *Blanche* was attached to the 1st Destroyer Flotilla in 1911/12, and operated with the Grand Fleet's battle squadrons from August 1914, being present at the Battle of Jutland in 1916. In March 1917 she was adapted to lay 66 mines, and in this form laid 1,238 mines in 16 missions. She was paid off in 1919 and sold for breaking in 1921. The *Blonde* led the 7th Destroyer Flotilla in the Mediterranean during 1911/12, served with the Grand Fleet battle squadrons from August 1914 to 1919 but was not present at Jutland. She was adapted for minelaying in September 1917 but not used in this role, and was sold for breaking in 1920.

It is worth noting that the two "Blonde" class ships were followed by the five "Bristol" class units, which were in effect the first true cruisers as the current and considerably larger armoured cruisers were in reality second-class battleships. The "Bristol" class cruisers were somewhat larger than the "Blonde" class ships, and were better protected and more heavily armed.

HMS *Blanche*

Type:	scout cruiser
Tonnage:	3,850 tons deep load
Dimensions:	length 405 ft (123.4 m); beam 41 ft 6 in (12.6 m); draft 15 ft 6 in (4.6 m)
Propulsion:	four steam turbines delivering 18,000 shp (13420 kW) to four propellers for 24.5 kt
Armour:	1.5-in (38-mm) deck and 4-in (102-mm) conning tower
Armament:	10 4-in (102-mm) guns, four 3-pdr QF guns and two 21-in (533-mm) torpedo tubes
Complement:	314

SMS *Baden* (1916)

Naval warfare was transformed in 1906 by the completion of HMS *Dreadnought* as the world's first battleship with steam turbine propulsion and the "all big gun" armament of 10 12-in (305-mm) guns in three centreline and two wing turrets. Further development in dreadnought battleship design was rapid as the 13.5-in (343-mm) gun replaced the 12-in (305-mm) weapon, centreline turrets became standard, director firing was adopted for more effective fire at longer ranges, superfiring turrets were introduced to help keep down hull length and weight without sacrifice of protection and finally, in the period before World War I, the 15-in (381-mm) gun superseded the 13,5-in (343-mm) weapon.

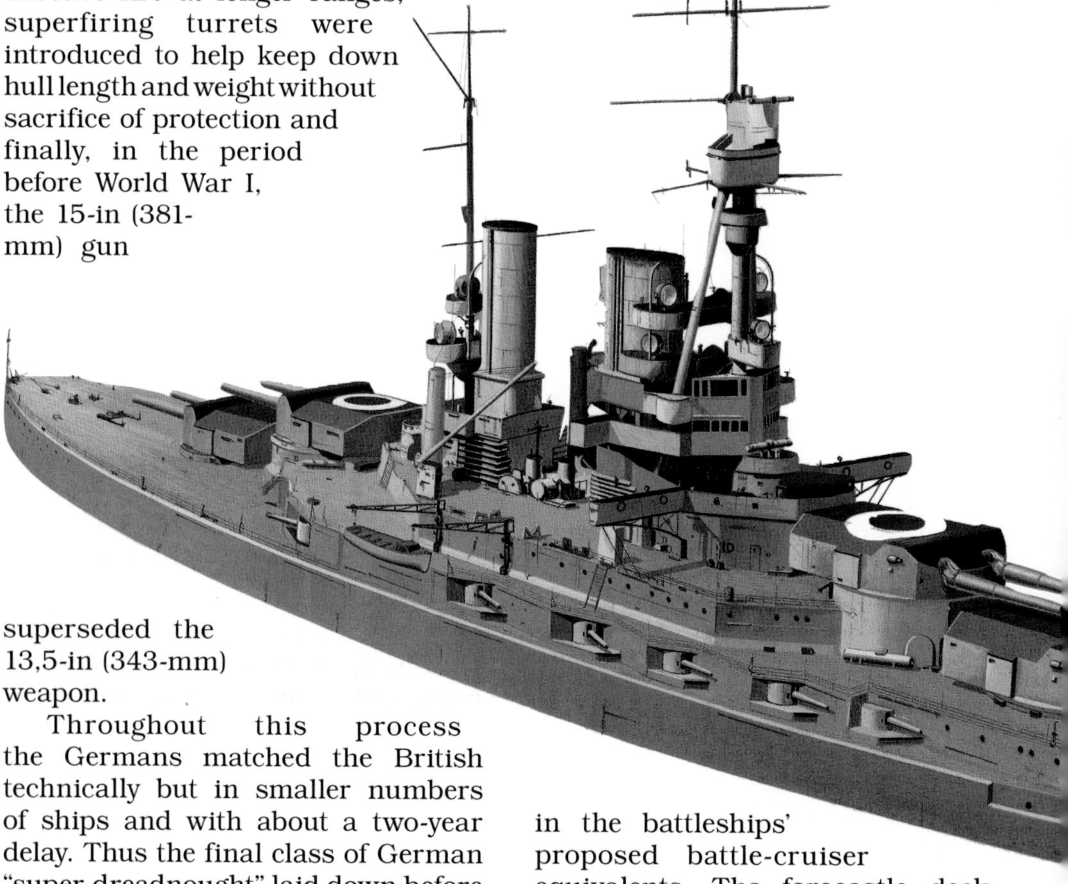

Throughout this process the Germans matched the British technically but in smaller numbers of ships and with about a two-year delay. Thus the final class of German "super-dreadnought" laid down before the outbreak of war in 1914, and the last to be completed in World War I, was the "Bayern" class, comprising SMS *Bayern* and SMS *Baden* built by Howaldtswerke of Kiel and Schichau of Danzig for completion in June 1916 and February 1917.

In the "Bayern" class the calibre of the main armament was increased from 12 in (305 mm) to 15 in (380 mm) without any intervening 13.8 in (350 mm) as was to have been the case in the battleships' proposed battle-cruiser equivalents. The forecastle deck stretched back to the after superfiring turret, and the normal-load freeboard was 23 ft 8 in (7.2 m) forward and 15 ft 1 in (4.6 m) aft. The funnels were comparatively closely spaced, and the

SMS *Baden*

Type:	super-dreadnought battleship
Tonnage:	31,690 tons deep load
Dimensions:	length 589 ft 1 in (179.8 m); beam 98 ft 5 in (30 m); draft 30 ft 9 in (9.4 m)
Propulsion:	three steam turbines delivering 48,000 shp (35790 kW) to three shafts for 21 kt
Armour:	4.7/14-in (120/350-mm) belt, 5.5/12-in (140/300-mm) bulkheads, 4/14-in (100/350-mm) turrets, 1/14-in (25/350-mm) barbettes, 6.7-in (170-mm) battery, 6.7/14-in (170/350-mm) conning tower
Armament:	eight 15-in (380-mm) guns, 16 5.9-in (150-mm) guns, eight 3.45-in (88-mm) AA guns, and five 23.6-in (600-mm) torpedo tubes
Complement:	1,271

design included a tripod foremast as well as a small main mast close abaft the after funnel, this mast not initially being fitted in the *Bayern*. The main armament's four turrets were superfiring pairs fore and aft, and the gun mountings permitted elevation to +16°, later increased to +20° in the *Bayern*. Each turret had a rangefinder with a base length of 26 ft 9 in (8.15 m). The propellant magazines were located above the shell rooms, and their crowns were provided by the armour deck. The casemated secondary battery was mounted on the upper deck, and the full complement of eight 3.45-in (88-mm) AA guns specified was not shipped, the number of such guns being two or four. The torpedo tubes were arranged as one in the bows and two on each beam, but after the *Bayern* had been mined the two forward beam tubes were removed from both ships.

The 14-in (350-mm) belt ran from 5 ft 10 in (1.8 m) above to 1 ft 2 in (0.35 m) below the waterline over the length between the end barbettes, then tapered in thickness to 6.7 in (170 mm) at its lower edge 5 ft 7 in (1.7 m) below the water. Between the main and upper decks the armour was 10 in (250 mm) thick. Forward of this it was 8 declining to 6 in (200 declining to 150 mm) thick, ending 49 ft 2.5 in (15 m) from the bows, and aft 8 declining to 4,7 in (200 declining to 120 mm) thick. The turrets had 14-in (350-mm) faces, 10-in (250-mm) sides, 11.5-in (290-mm) rears and 4/8-in (100/200-mm) roofs. There were three oil- and 11 coal-fired boilers in nine rooms, and three sets of steam turbines were in six rooms.

The *Bayern* was mined on October 12, 1917 in the Gulf of Riga, suffering serious flooding and not reaching Kiel for 19 days. The *Bayern* was scuttled in Scapa Flow in June 1919, but raised in 1934 and broken up. The *Baden* was sunk in trials during August 1921.

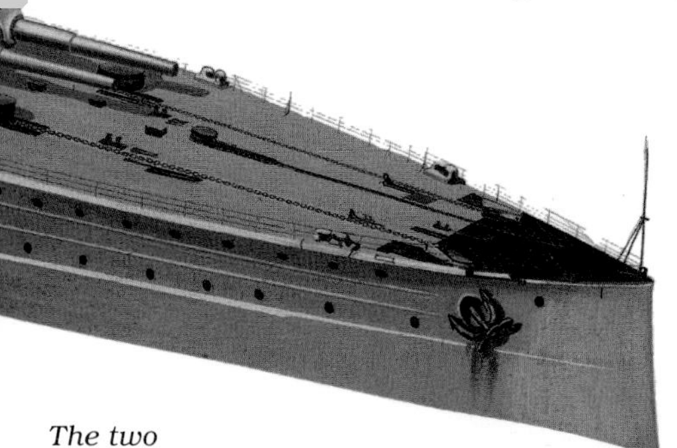

The two Bayern' class battleships were designed to rival the Royal Navy's six "Queen Elizabeth" class battleships.

Dazzle Painting (1914/18)

From the beginning of World War I, the Admiralty was bombarded with schemes for the painting of British ships in camouflage so that they would become "invisible" to their opponents. From the bridge or look-out position of another surface ship the camouflage might seem to be effective as the target melded into the background. But to the captain of a U-boat the camouflage was not effective for, with the head of his periscope only just above the level of the sea, he was scanning for a target silhouetted against the skyline. Moreover, whereas the look-outs on a surface vessel were relying for optical detection of a target, the captain of a U-boat also received the acoustic reports of his hydrophone operator, which were often far more revelatory in detection of possible victim's presence.

It was a British artist, Norman Wilkinson, who suggested that attempts should be made not to make ships invisible but rather riotously visible to the extent that the information received by the look-out or U-boat captain confused him. It was Wilkinson's clever notion that ships should be painted in a fashion which would produce in the mind of the look-out or U-boat captain an optical illusion and so mislead him as to the proposed target's real size, course and speed. Wilkinson rightly appreciated that this would greatly complicate the finalization of a realistic fire-control solution for gun fire or torpedo launch.

The concept was adopted in World War I and became generally known as dazzle painting as it was intended to dazzle the enemy with skewed data (suggesting, for instance, that the ship was farther away than it really was, or sailing more rapidly, or steering a different course) and so make it difficult for him to mount an effective attack.

The shape of the ship and the camouflage could be used, in vessel such as the "Kil" class patrol vessels, to confuse the viewer as to the direction in which the vessel was moving.

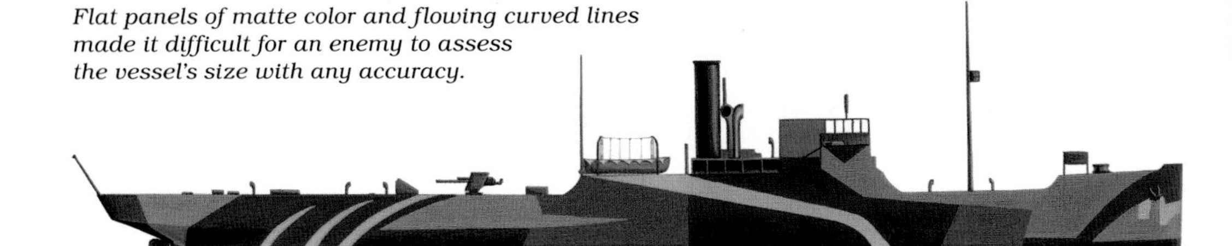

Flat panels of matte color and flowing curved lines made it difficult for an enemy to assess the vessel's size with any accuracy.

A dazzle-painted ocean liner, a ex-German vessel completed in 1914 and operated by the United States Lines as the Leviathan.

Further developing the concept embodied in Wilkinson's idea, the Admiralty discovered that by painting a ship in different

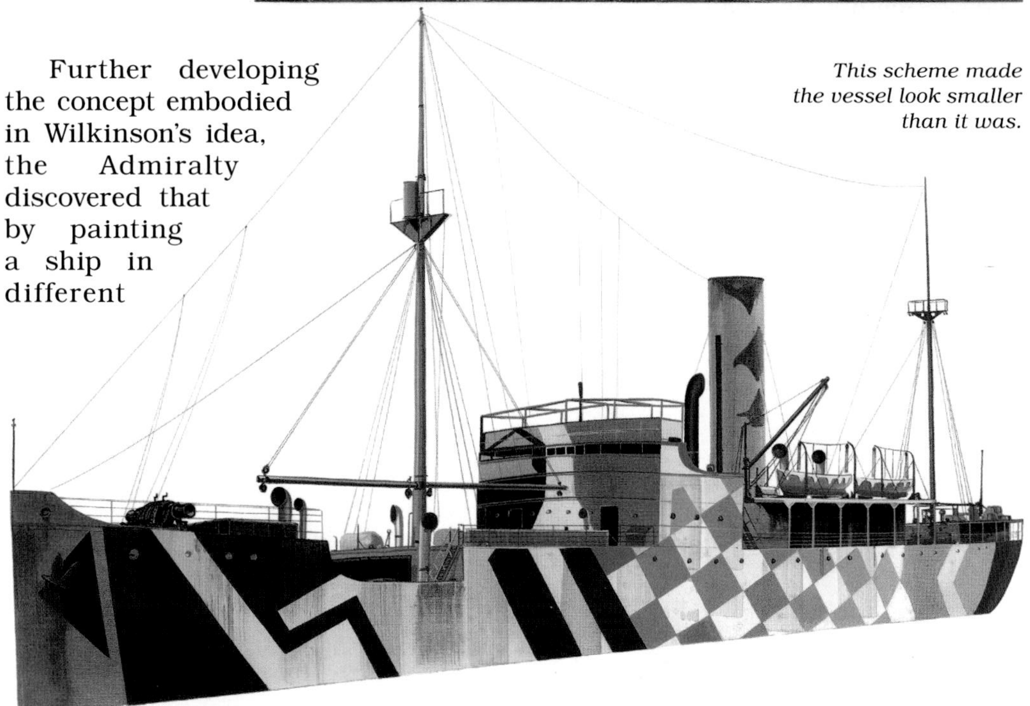

This scheme made the vessel look smaller than it was.

colours certain parts of it could be made to seem invisible. The use of large simple areas of flat contrasting colours broke up the form and outline of a ship, and the design was continued over the superstructure, as the bridge and funnels were important stadiametric points for submarine fire-control purposes. By October 1917 the Admiralty had begun to paint the whole of the mercantile marine and a number of warships. The designing of the dazzle patterns was carried out at the Royal Academy in Piccadilly and dazzle officers supervised the painting of the ships at port. There is no conclusive proof that dazzle-painting saved any ships from destruction, but its success at confusing the observer is well attested.

Courbet (1913)

Authorized in 1910 (*Courbet* and *Jean Bart* both built by the Arsenal de Brest) and 1911 (*France* and *Paris* built by AC de la Loire and FC de la Mediterranée), the "Courbet" class units were the first French "dreadnought" battleships. Although the protection was increased in comparison with that of the "Danton" class final pre-dreadnoughts, it was still thin by contemporary standards but, reflecting French fears about underwater attack, the side armour was extended deep below the waterline. At 5.46 in (138.6 mm), the calibre of the secondary battery was comparatively small, but was adopted to gain a higher rate of fire, an important factor in current thinking on defence against torpedo boats. The 12-in (305 mm) main guns were mounted in two superfiring pairs of twin turrets fore and aft and two twin turrets on the sides on the same frames.

During World War I all four ships were based in the Mediterranean, the lead vessel being revised with searchlights on a platform astern of her second funnel and her main mast removed to facilitate the towing of a kite balloon. All of the class had triple 12-ft (3.6-m) rangefinders installed above their conning towers. The *Jean Bart* was hit by a torpedo from the Austro-Hungarian submarine U-12 in the Adriatic Sea on December 21, 1914, but the explosion wrecked the wine store without detonating the adjacent forward magazine. The *Jean Bart* and the *France* ended

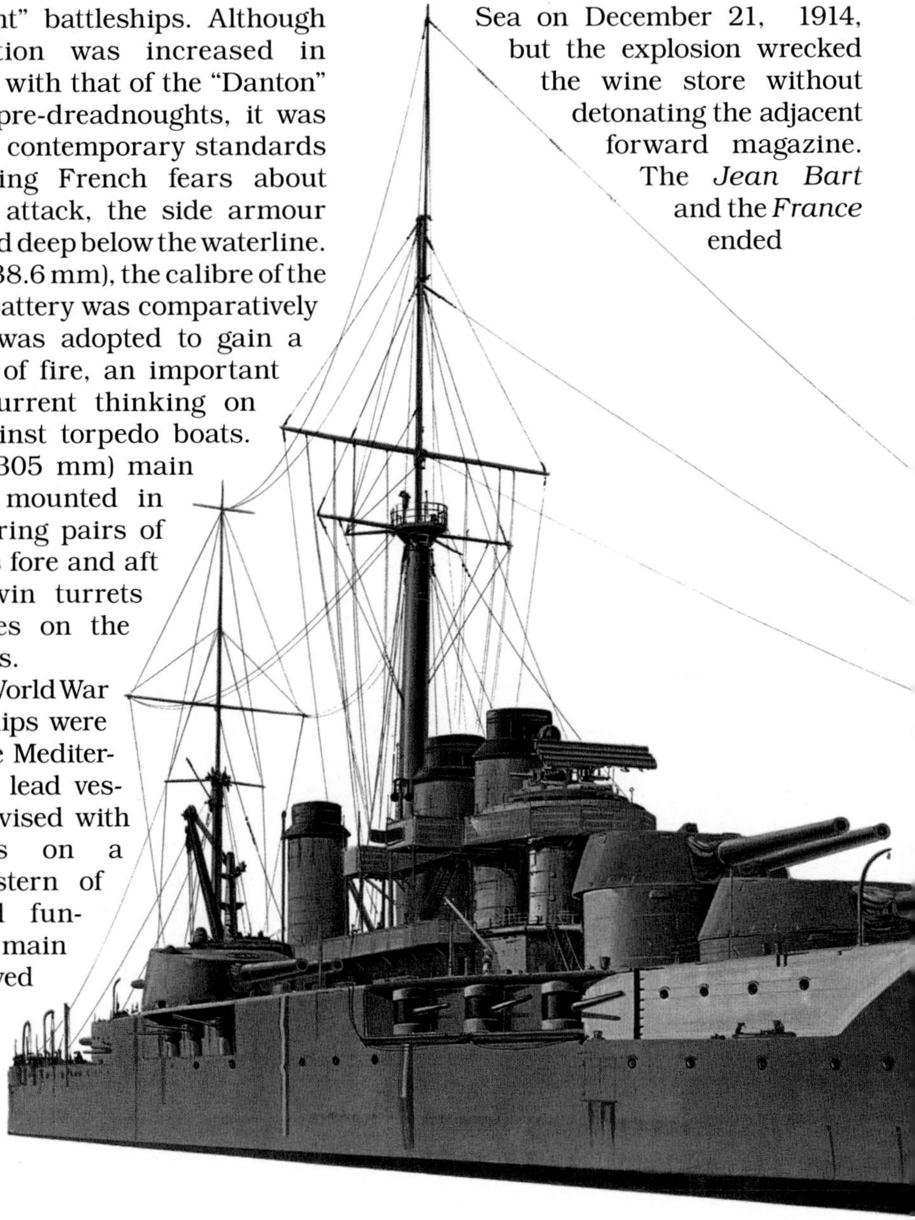

Courbet

Type:	dreadnought battleship
Tonnage:	26,000 tons full load
Dimensions:	length 551 ft 2 in (168 m); beam 91 ft 6 in (27.9 m); draft 29 ft 6 in (9 m)
Propulsion:	four steam turbine engines delivering 28,000 shp (20877 kW) to four propellers for 21 kt
Armour:	7.1/10.6-in (180/270-mm) belt, 1.2/2.76-in (30/70-mm) decks, 11-in (280-mm) barbettes, 3.9/11.4-in (100/290-mm) turrets, 7.1-in (180-mm) casemates, and 11.8-in (300-mm) conning tower
Armament:	10 12-in (305-mm) guns, 22 5.5-in (139-mm) guns, four 47-mm QF guns, and four 18-in (457-mm) torpedo tubes
Complement:	1,108

With two pairs of superfiring turrets, the "Courbet" class battleships were very compact.

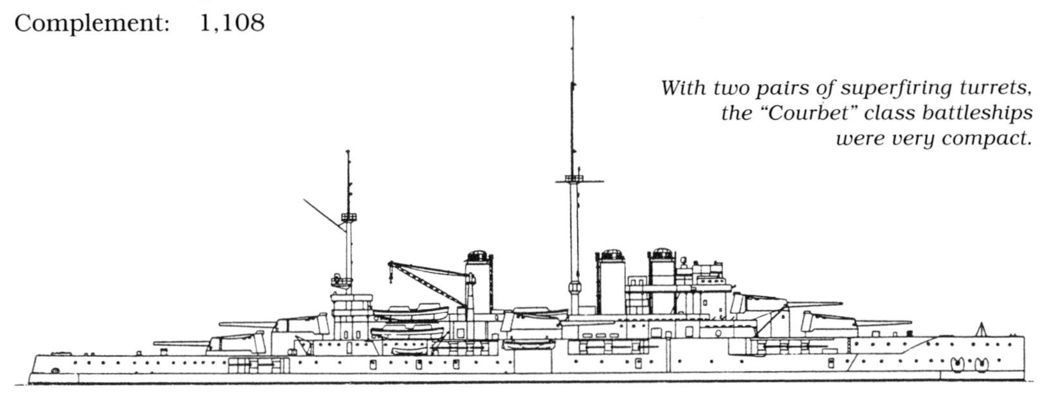

their active service in and after World War I in the Allied operations against the Bolsheviks in the Crimea during 1919.

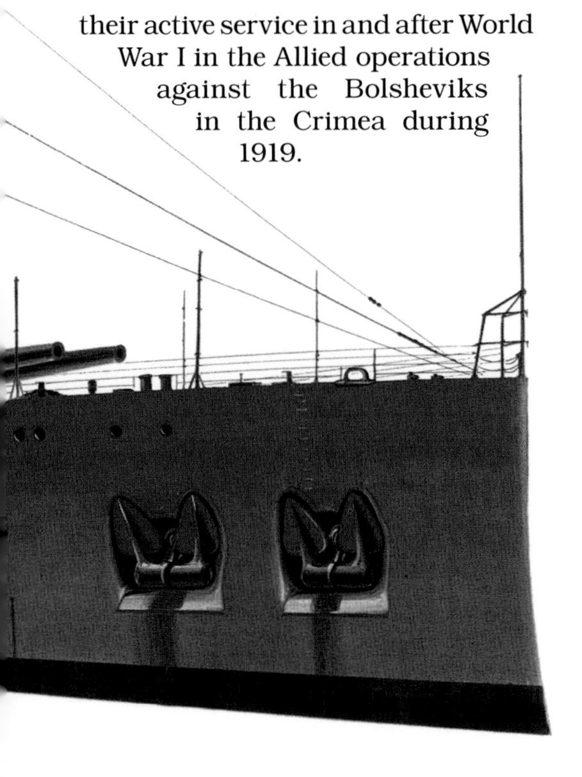

Although the "Courbet" class ships were generally thought to have been excellently constructed and were well finished in all their details, these battleships rapidly became obsolete after 1918 as France lacked the financial resources and the will to implement any thorough-going modernization program, and another limitation was the wetness of the forecastle in any sort of sea, this latter resulting from the mass of the forward turrets, each of which turned the scales at some 560 tons. Moreover, France lacked a dry dock long enough to allow the ships to be lengthened. The *France* foundered in 1922, and of the others two survived into the mid-1940s and the *Paris* to 1955.

The Courbet and her sisters had too much weight forward and therefore had wet forecastles.

Ikazuchi (1899)

Ordered from Yarrow's Poplar yard on the Thames under the 1896 and 1897 estimates, and completed between February 1899 and January 1900, the *Akebono*, *Ikazuchi*, *Inazuma*, *Niji*, *Oboro* and *Sazanami* were the six torpedo boat destroyers of the Imperial Japanese navy's "Ikazuchi" class. These vessels were the first genuine destroyers ordered by the Japanese navy, and the design was in essence an improved version of Yarrow's "Corrientes" class destroyer for the Argentine navy. The six destroyers of the basically contemporaneous "Murakumo" class ordered from Thornycroft were basically similar but slightly smaller with reduced bunkerage (80 rather than 100 tons of coal). The "Ikazuchis" also had slightly greater power than the "Murakumos," and their machinery therefore required greater volume, as provided in their 9 ft (2.7-m) greater length. The power was increased from 5,800 to 6,000 ihp (4324 to 4474 kW), to give 1 kt greater speed at the normal displacement of 307 tons.

The 12-pdr gun was sited right aft, while the two single 18-in (457-mm) trainable torpedo tubes were mounted in the centerline fore and aft of the main mast. The deck was fitted with rails to aid the handling of torpedoes to the tubes. At some time in their career the forward 6-pdr gun was replaced by an additional 12-pdr weapon.

The *Ikazuchi* and *Oboro* were both damaged during the Russo-Japanese War (1904/05), the former by gun fire at the Battle of Tsushima on 27 May 1905, and the latter by a mine off Port Arthur on November 2, 1904.

The destroyer Ikazuchi of the Imperial Japanese navy.

Ikazuchi

Type:	torpedo boat destroyer
Tonnage:	410 tons full load
Dimensions:	length 220 ft 9 in (67.25 m); beam 20 ft 6 in (6.25 m); draft 5 ft 3 in (1.6 m)
Propulsion:	two vertical triple expansion steam engines delivering 6,000 ihp (4474 kW) to two propellers for 31 kt
Armour:	none
Armament:	one 12-pdr QF gun, five 6-pdr QF guns, and two 18-in (457-mm) torpedo tubes
Complement:	55

Mimi and *Toutou* (1915)

In the first period of World War I, the Germans controlled Lake Tanganyika, between the present-day Tanzania and Democratic Republic of Congo, with three vessels, namely the 200-ft steamer *Graf von Götzen* armed with two 4-in (100-mm) and two smaller guns, the 70-ft steamer *Hedwig von Wissmann* armed with two 6-pdr and one 37-mm guns, and the 55-ft launch *Kingani* armed with one 37-mm gun. These were a decided thorn in the side of the allies forces trying to expel the Germans from German East Africa, and the British decided to mount a "naval" expedition from the UK.

Here two small launches, originally to have been named *Cat* and *Dog* but then christened *Mimi* and *Toutou*, were found and prepared for service on Lake Tanganyika. The two were shipped from Tilbury to Cape Town in south Africa, whence they were moved by rail some 2,300 miles (3700 km) north to Fungurume in the Belgian Congo. Loaded onto wheeled carriages, the launches were then towed 120 miles (195 km) by steam traction engines and then moved by water and rail to Lukuga on the western side of the lake, where the arrived late in October 1915. The German base was at Kigoma on the lake's eastern shoreline.

At the end of the year the British launches intercepted and captured the *Kingani*, which was placed in British service as the *Fifi*. In February 1916 the three British vessels collaborated to intercept, trap and sink the *Hedwig von Wissmann*. Thereafter personal problems interfered with the operations of the now mixed Belgian and British squadron, and the three launches went south to co-operate with the land forces. In the capture of Bismarckburg. The 800-ton *Graf von Götzen* survived to July 1916, when her captain scuttled her after realizing that the Germans were on the verge of losing the lake's shores. By this time the vessel had survived two bombing raids by Belgian seaplanes.

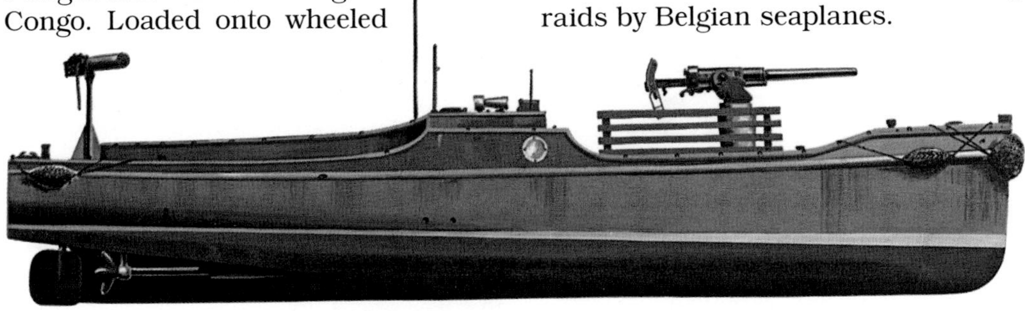

Mimi and _Toutou_

Type:	armed motor launch
Tonnage:	4.5 tons displacement
Dimensions:	length 40 ft (12.2 m); beam 8 ft (2,4 m); draft not available
Propulsion:	one petrol engine delivering power to one propeller for 15 kt
Armour:	none
Armament:	one 3-pdr QF gun, and one 0.303-in (7.7-mm) Vickers machine gun
Complement:	not available

HMS *Queen Elizabeth* (1915)

In its 1912 program the Admiralty planned three battleships and one battle-cruiser to an improved "Iron Duke" class design with 13.5-in (343-mm) guns. However, suggestions that the German navy was planning a calibre increase suggested a heavier armament for the new ships, namely the 15-in (381-mm) Mk I weapon designed by the Elswick company and firing a 1,920-lb (871-kg) shell. Because no such gun had yet been made, the ships had to be started without any certainty that the new gun would prove successful. The faith of the Admiralty was well founded, though, the 15-in (381-mm) Mk I gun proving to have greater hitting power and accuracy than the standard 13.5-in (343-mm) Mk V gun without an increase in barrel wear, and range was usefully lengthened.

New designs were prepared, at first for a 21-kt ship based on the "Iron Duke" class with five twin turrets. It was soon realised that a reduction of one turret would still yield a devastating broadside, and the volume saved could be used for more boilers to give 24-25 kt. The design also matured as the first for a capital ship with only oil-fired boilers. The new class of fast battleships removed the need for a battle-cruiser, which was therefore replaced by a fourth battleship. Then the Federated Malay States offered to fund a fifth ship, which became HMS *Malaya*. A sixth unit was ordered in the 1914 program, but was not laid down.

The "Queen Elizabeth" class in fact sought to incorporate too much on the displacement, and the ships were thus not as good as they could have been. All five were overweight, with a completion displacement of 33,500-34,000 tons, and the refusal to adopt small-tube boilers made 25 kt impossible. Other than the *Malaya*, built by Armstrongs, the other ships were HMS *Queen Elizabeth*, HMS *Warspite*, HMS *Valiant* and HMS *Barham* built by Portsmouth Dock Yard, Devonport Dock Yard, Fairfield and John Brown respectively, and all five ships were completed between January 1915 and February 1916.

The *Queen Elizabeth* was the only unit completed with the planned secondary battery of 16 6-in (152-mm) guns but, as in the "Iron Duke" class, the four guns under the quarterdeck were washed by the sea and removed, a single shielded gun being mounted port and starboard above the battery amidships. The other four ships were completed to this standard. The battery's forward guns were badly affected in any seaway, and the battery was revised with small walls inside the battery and rubber sealing joints. In 1916 two 6-in (152-mm) guns were replaced by 3-in (76-mm) AA guns. The

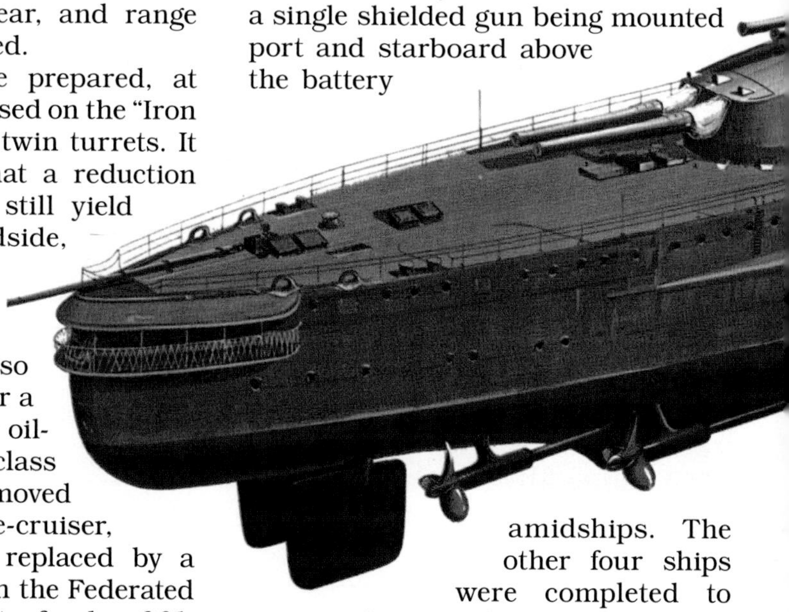

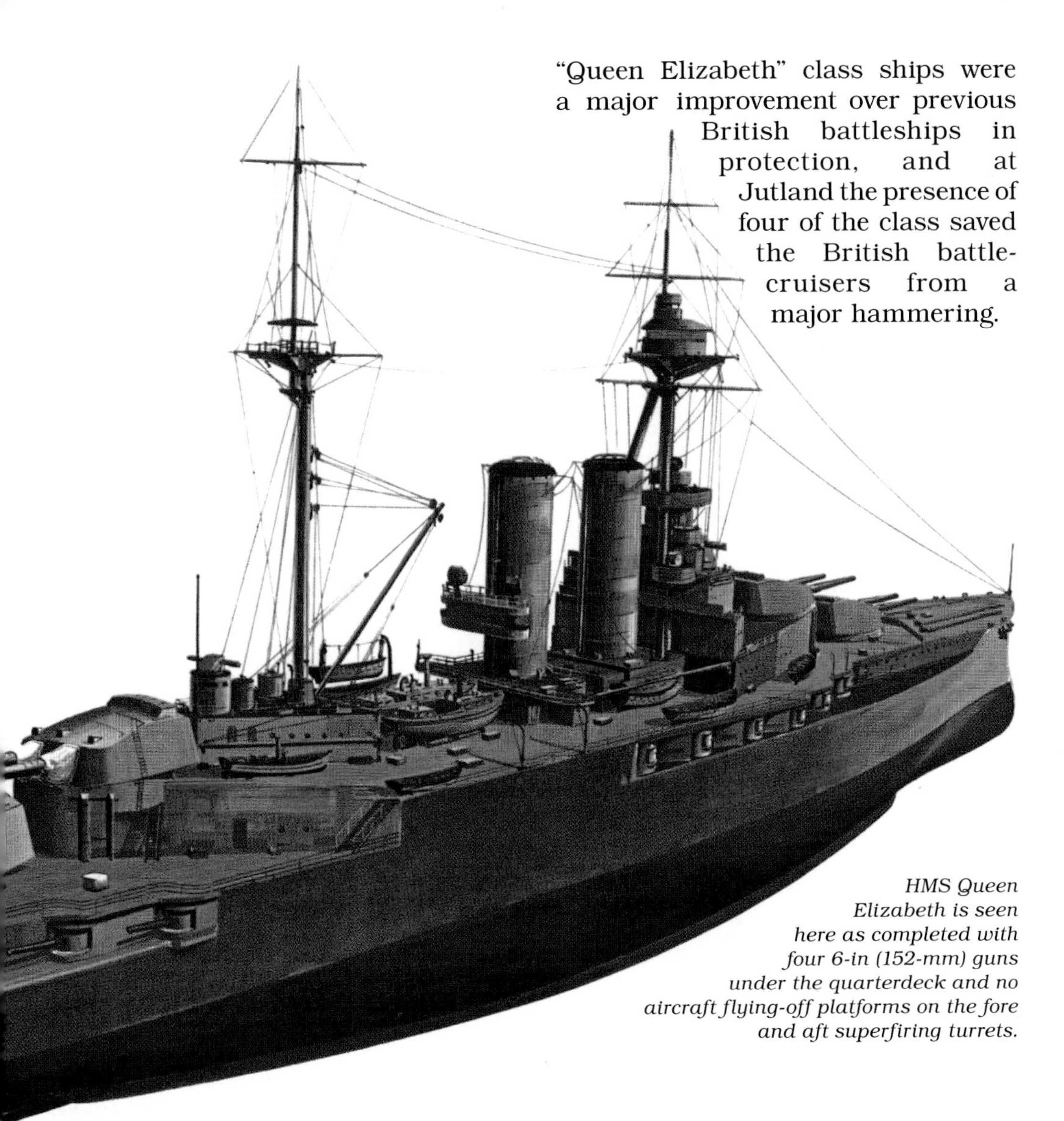

"Queen Elizabeth" class ships were a major improvement over previous British battleships in protection, and at Jutland the presence of four of the class saved the British battle-cruisers from a major hammering.

HMS Queen Elizabeth is seen here as completed with four 6-in (152-mm) guns under the quarterdeck and no aircraft flying-off platforms on the fore and aft superfiring turrets.

HMS *Queen Elizabeth*

Type:	super-dreadnought battleship
Tonnage:	31,500 tons deep load
Dimensions:	length 645 ft 9 in (196.8 m); beam 90 ft 6 in (27.6 m); draft 28 ft 9 in (8.8 m)
Propulsion:	four steam turbines delivering 56,000 shp (41764 kW) to four propellers for 23 kt
Armour:	6/13-in (152/330-mm) belt, 4/6-in (102/153-mm) bulkheads, 1/3-in (25/76-mm) decks, 13-in (330-mm) turrets, 4/10-in barbettes (102/254-mm), and 11-in (279-mm) conning tower
Armament:	eight 15-in (381-mm) guns, 16 6-in (152-mm) guns, two 3-in (76-mm) AA guns, and four 21-in (533-mm) torpedo tubes
Complement:	951

Early Aircraft Carriers (1914)

British experiments in the carriage of aircraft by warships began in 1911/12 with the temporary installation on "runways" on the forecastles of three pre-dreadnought battleships. The first airplane take-off from a British warship was made from HMS *Hibernia* in January 1912, and the first take-off from a ship under way was from her sister ship HMS *Africa* in May of the same year. In 1913 the old cruiser HMS *Hermes* was also given a forward launching platform and carried two floatplanes which could be fitted on wheeled trolleys for take-off. All this equipment had been removed from the ships by the outbreak of World War I in August 1914. The practical development of the aircraft carrier therefore started in the war, and was governed both by the evolution of aircraft types and by the availability of suitable ships which could be spared for conversion. The Royal Naval Air Service came into existence on July 1st, 1914, and was amalgamated with the Royal Flying Corps, so creating the Royal Air Force, on April 1st, 1918. By this time the RNAS was operating some 2,950 aircraft as well as shore-based airships.

The first aircraft carriers were seaplane tenders rather than examples of the "true" aircraft carrier with a flight deck. The first vessel to be completed as an aircraft carrier was the 7,750-ton HMS *Ark Royal*, which had been laid down as a collier and was adapted while still building. Five seaplanes carried in the holds were lifted by cranes, lowered on to the water for take-off and subsequently brought inboard again, which was a somewhat dangerous undertaking even in good weather conditions and with a calm sea. She also had an early form of launching trolley on deck for the two landplanes which could be embarked. The *Ark Royal* later did good service as an aircraft transport and repair ship. However, ships capable of a speed considerably higher than the *Ark Royal*'s 11-kt figure were needed for fleet service on scouting duties and, later, to reach sufficient speed for aircraft take-off.

The 2,500-ton HMS Riviera is seen in her original form after conversion as a seaplane carrier with canvas hangars fore and aft.

In 1914/17, therefore, the Royal Navy took over eight fast cross-Channel steamers, with a displacement in the order of 1,800 to 3,300 tons and a speed in the order of 20 kt, as well as the considerably larger Cunard liner *Campania*. The fast ferries were

HMS Ark Royal was the first British "aircraft carrier," her floatplanes being craned onto and off the water by a pair of steam-powered cranes.

adapted as the seaplane carriers HMS *Empress*, *Engadine*, *Riviera*, *Ben-my-Chree*, *Manxman*, *Vindex*, *Pegasus* and *Nairana*.

Typical of the fast ferry conversions was the *Ben-my-Chree*, which had been built by Vickers and completed in 1908 for the Isle of Man Steam Packet Company. Possessing a normal displacement of 3,888 tons and a speed of 24.5 kt on the 14,000 shp (10438 kW) delivered by her three sets of steam turbines, the ship was converted by Cammell Laird from January 1915, and on completion was based for a short time at Harwich before being transferred to the Dardanelles, and then Aden and finally back to the Aegean. The ship carried four Short Type 184 floatplanes, and was hit by Turkish artillery fire off Castelorizo, near Rhodes, in January 1917, finally catching fire and blowing up.

In August 1915 there took place the first successful take-off, from the *Campania*, by an airplane with wheeled floats, and the first effective attack with an air-launched torpedo was made by a floatplane from the *Ben-my-Chree* against a Turkish ship in the Dardanelles. Three months later a landplane lifted off from the *Vindex*, and from this time onward floatplanes were replaced steadily for operational tasks by more capable landplanes.

HMS *Campania*

Type:	seaplane carrier
Tonnage:	18,000 tons normal
Dimensions:	length 622 ft (189.6 m); beam 65 ft (19.8 m); draft 26 ft (7.9 m)
Propulsion:	two triple expansion steam engines delivering 28,000 ihp (20877 kW) to two propellers for 21 kt
Armour:	none
Armament:	six 4.7-in (119-mm) QF guns, 1 3-in (76 mm) AA gun, and 10 floatplanes
Complement:	600

First Carrier Take-Offs (1910)

It is perhaps ironic that very shortly after the modern battleship reached its definitive form as an "all big gun" warship, in the form of HMS *Dreadnought* commissioned in 1906, the first inklings of the weapon that was to render it obsolete was making themselves evident: the first powered airplane. The Wright Flyer I, had flown in December 1903, and the airplane had become an increasingly realistic vehicle from 1905, the year in which the Wright brothers tested their Flyer III. There followed what was, in real terms, a gap of three years when the Wrights did not fly and their competitors achieved little more than indifferent teeterings into the air, but from 1908 the pace of aeronautical development gathered pace rapidly. By 1910 the airplane was seen as a practical vehicle which might, with development, be used for military and naval purposes.

For naval purposes the seaplane, in both its flying boat and floatplane forms, seemed to offer the greater short-term capabilities, but was still at an earlier stage of development than the landplane. Moreover, it was recognized at an early stage that fleets operating far from land, or without a tender able to launch and recover seaplanes, might nonetheless benefit from the availability of an organic air component. The problem which now had to be overcome was how best to launch and recover an airplane, either of the landplane type with wheeled landing gear or a seaplane on a wheeled trolley.

The launch of an airplane was the easier of the two tasks to accomplish, and on November 14, 1910 a Curtiss

Flying a Curtiss Model D, the Curtiss exhibition pilot Eugene B. Ely passes over the bow of the light cruiser USS Birmingham just getting under way in Hampton Roads on November 14, 1910.

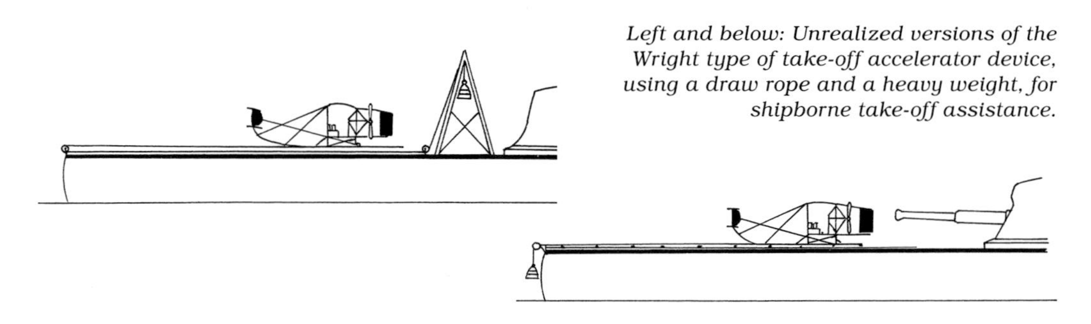

Left and below: Unrealized versions of the Wright type of take-off accelerator device, using a draw rope and a heavy weight, for shipborne take-off assistance.

Below: The take-off system adopted for experimental purposes by the Americans and British (here the latter) was an inclined platform.

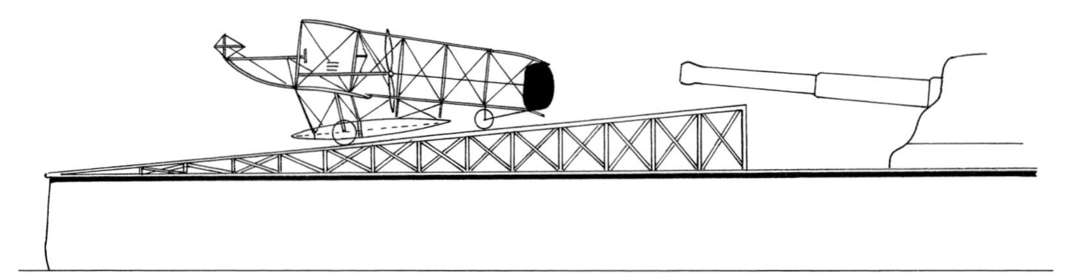

exhibition pilot, Eugene B. Ely, made the world's first take-off from a ship at Hampton Roads, Virginia. The vessel was the US Navy's light cruiser USS *Birmingham*, which had been fitted with an inclined ramp over her bows. It had been intended that the ship should steam into the wind and therefore ease Ely's task in lifting off his Curtiss Model D biplane, but the pilot was impatient and ordered his airplane to be released after the ship had weighed anchor but before she was properly under way. The ramp was only 83 ft (25 m) long, and the Model D had not reached flying speed as it passed over the ramp's forward edge 37 ft (11.25 m) above the water, descending toward the sea and actually touching its surface just as Ely found he had reached flying speed. The touch had damaged the propeller, but Ely managed to fly the Model D 2.5 miles (4 km) to a safe landing at Willoughby Spit.

This was one half of what was necessary, and thought was now turned toward the recovery of an airplane. Late in 1910 the US Navy armoured cruiser USS *Pennsylvania* was taken in hand for modification for use in landing experiments. A raided wooden platform, some 120 ft (36.6 m) long and 32 ft (9.75 m) wide, was built over the ship's after deck and turrets. This platform had a downward-angled rear edge and itself sloped upward toward the superstructure and after mast. The platform was also fitted with an improved arrester system based on ropes stretched between 100-lb (45-kg) sandbags. With the ship anchored in San Francisco Bay on January 18, 1911, Ely lifted off from the Presidio Field near San Francisco in a Curtiss Model D IV Military biplane and approached the anchored *Pennsylvania* from astern. Ely landed downwind on the stern platform and came to a halt, after a run of only about 30 ft (9.1 m), when he snagged the 12th and later arrester lines. After lunching with the ship's officers, Ely then took off from the armoured cruiser and returned

Flying a Curtiss Model D IV Military, Eugene B. Ely approaches the stern platform of the USS Pennsylvania anchored in San Francisco Bay on January 18, 1911.

to the field from which had set off earlier that morning.

The next evolutionary step in the development of shipborne naval aviation was the first take-off from a moving ship, and here the torch of development crossed the Atlantic Ocean to the UK. Lieutenant Charles R. Samson, who had been the first Royal Navy officer to take-off from a ship, in a Short S.27 biplane from the pre-dreadnought battleship HMS *Africa* unofficially in December 1911 and officially on January 10, 1912, was the officer responsible. Embarked in a Short biplane amphibian, Samson lifted off from the platform over the bow of another pre-dreadnought battleship, HMS *Hibernia*, while the vessel steamed at 10.5 kt during the royal naval review of May 4, 1912 off Portland. In October 1912, Samson became the commanding officer of the Naval Wing of the Royal Flying Corps which, on the eve of World War I's outbreak in August 1914, became the separate Royal Naval Air Service.

The last and most difficult conceptual problem now to be overcome was the landing of an airplane on a moving ship, and here again it was the British who took the lead. The world's first true aircraft carrier was the light battle-cruiser HMS *Furious*, which was adapted from May 1917 as an aircraft carrier by the replacement of her forward 18-in (457-mm) single gun turret by a light platform and hangar.

This allowed the vessel to embark four seaplanes and six Sopwith Pup landplanes, and her senior flying officer was Squadron Commander E. H. Dunning. On August 2nd, 1917 Dunning cruised alongside the *Furious*, which was steaming at 26 kt into a 21-kt headwind, in a Pup adapted with handling straps. Once he had matched speed with the *Furious*, Dunning sideslipped toward the deck, when the awaiting team seized the straps and hauled down the airplane. Only five days later Dunning was killed as he made a similar effort but his airplane stalled and went over the side.

There were still many hurdles to cross, but practical carrierborne operations became feasible with the advent of HMS *Argus* as the world's first flushdecked carrier in 1918, allowing landing aircraft to approach from astern and touch down on an unrestricted flight deck 565 ft (172.2 m) long.

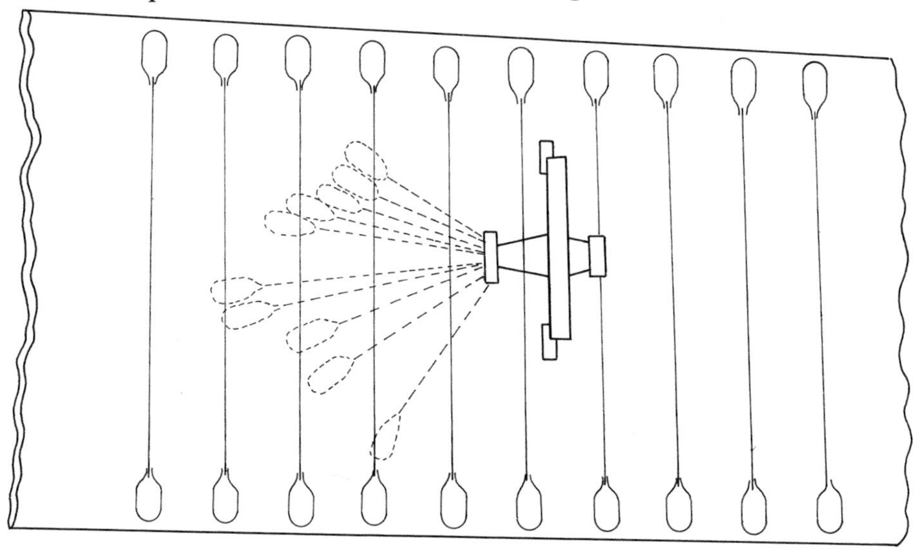

The first "arrester gear" comprised a series of lines stretched between sandbags. The landing airplane's strengthened tailskid caught the lines and the drag of the sandbags brought the machine to a swift halt.

HMS *Hibernia*

Type:	pre-dreadnought battleship
Tonnage:	17,009 tons deep load
Dimensions:	length 453 ft 9 on (138.3 m); beam 78 ft (23.8 m); draft 25 ft 8 in (7.7 m)
Propulsion:	two vertical triple expansion steam engines delivering 18,000 ihp (13421 kW) to two propellers for 18.5 kt
Armour:	8/9-in (203/229-mm) belt, 8/12-in (203/305-mm) bulkheads, 1/2.5-in (25/64-mm) decks, 12-in (305-mm) barbettes, 8/12-in (203/305-mm) main turrets, 5/9-in (127/229-mm) secondary turrets, 7-in (178-mm) battery, and 12-in (305-mm) conning tower
Armament:	four 12-in (305-mm) guns, four 9.2-in (234-mm) guns, 10 6-in (152-mm) guns, 14 12-pdr QF guns, 14 3-pdr QF guns, and four 18-in (457-mm) torpedo tubes
Complement:	777

SMS *König* (1915)

The "König" class dreadnoughts were improved versions of the "Kaiser" class ships, which had introduced a forecastle deck to German battleship practice, but with five twin centerline turrets in place of three centerline and two echeloned wing turrets. The first three were SMS *König*, *Grosser Kurfürst* and *Markgraf* built under the 1911/12 program by three different yards and completed in 1914/15, and SMS *Kronprinz* (renamed *Kronprinz Wilhelm* in January 1918) under the 1912/13 program by Germania and completed in 1915.

The turrets were disposed as superfiring pairs fore and aft, with the fifth located between the funnels at the after superfiring turret's height. The turrets allowed 13.5° gun elevation, later increased to 16°. The guns were served by magazines below the shell rooms. The secondary battery's 5.9-in (150-mm) guns were casemated on the upper deck, and later the 3,45-in (88-mm) tertiary guns were removed and the 3.45-in (88-mm) AA guns reduced to just two.

The armour was essentially similar to that of the "Kaiser" class, but with slightly greater maximum thickness in the tapered fore and aft ends. The upper deck amidships was 1.2 in (30 mm) thick outside the battery and 0.8 in (20 mm) thick where it was the battery's floor, while the torpedo bulkhead was 2 in (50 mm) thick and continued as a splinter bulkhead 1.2 in (30 mm) thick to the upper deck.

The boilers comprised 12 coal- and three oil-fired units, the latter in the three forward boiler rooms and the former comprising six in the next three boiler rooms and six in the three boiler rooms. The three sets of turbines were located in six engine rooms. In service the ships were generally reckoned to be faster than the "Kaiser" class units. At 24 kt the *Grosser Kurfürst* was apparently the fastest, but was outpaced at the Battle of Jutland in June 1916 by the *König*. On November 5, 1916, both the *Grosser Kurfürst* and the *Kronprinz* were hit by torpedoes from the British submarine HMS *J-1*, the former right aft and suffering a jammed port rudder, and the latter in line with

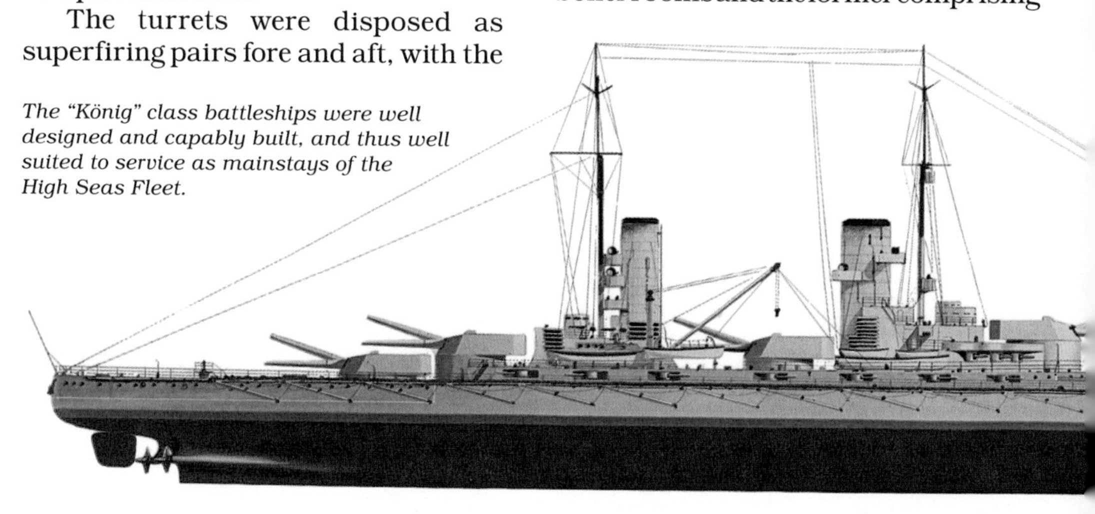

The "König" class battleships were well designed and capably built, and thus well suited to service as mainstays of the High Seas Fleet.

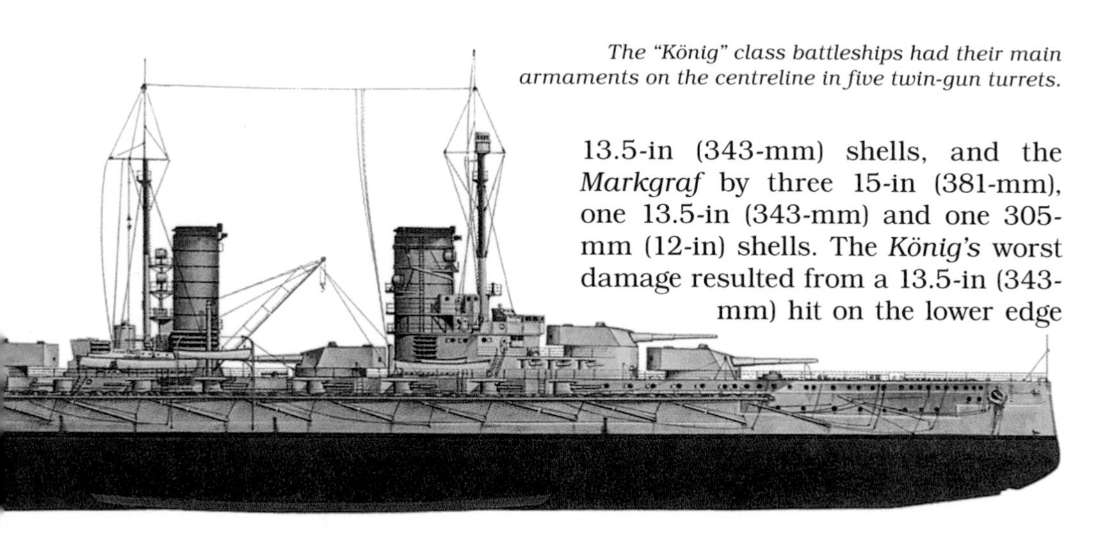

The "König" class battleships had their main armaments on the centreline in five twin-gun turrets.

the bridge. Even so, both ships maintained 17-19 kt. In operations against the Russians in the Gulf of Riga, the *Grosser Kurfürst* was mined on October 12, 1917 and the *Markgraf* on October 29, 1917, but the torpedo bulkhead limited flooding in both to 260-280 tons.

At the Battle of Jutland the *König* was hit by one 15-in (381-mm) and nine 13.5-in (343-mm) shells, the *Grosser Kurfürst* by five 15-in (381-mm) and three 13.5-in (343-mm) shells, and the *Markgraf* by three 15-in (381-mm), one 13.5-in (343-mm) and one 305-mm (12-in) shells. The *König's* worst damage resulted from a 13.5-in (343-mm) hit on the lower edge of the belt, which burst about 7 ft (2.1 m) inboard sending many fragments through 6 ft 6 in (2 m) of coal and the 2-in (50-mm) torpedo bulkhead into a 5.9-in (150-mm) ammunition room. Sea water flooding in limited the fire to 15 cartridges, but most of the 1,630 tons of water taken in was the result of this hit.

All survived World War I to be interned at Scapa Flow where, with the other ships of the High Seas Fleet, they were scuttled in June 1919. The *Grosser Kurfürst* was raised for scrap in 1936, but the salvage rights to the other three were not released until 1962.

SMS *König*

Type:	dreadnought battleship
Tonnage:	29,200 tons deep load
Dimensions:	length 575 ft 6 in (175.4 m); beam 96 ft 9 (29.5 m); draft 27 ft 3 in (8.3 m)
Propulsion:	three steam turbines delivering 31,000 shp (32114 kW) to three propellers for 21 kt
Armour:	3.2/14-in (80/350-mm) belt, 5/12-in (130/300-mm) bulkheads, 3.2/12-in (80/300-mm) turrets and barbettes, 6.7-in (170-mm) battery, and 6.7/14-in (170/350-mm) conning tower
Armament:	10 12-in (305-mm) guns, 14 5.9-in (150-mm) guns, six 3.45-in (88-mm) guns, four 3.45-in (88-mm) AA guns, and five 19.7-in (500-mm) torpedo tubes
Complement:	about 1,300

Viribus Unitis (1912)

Just as there was a naval race in the North Sea between the UK and Germany, in the Mediterranean there was a similar dreadnought-building race between Italy and Austria-Hungary. On learning that the Italians were about to start work on their first dreadnought battleship, the *Dante Alighieri* with novel features such as a main armament of 12 12-in (305-mm) guns carried in four triple turrets and a secondary armament of 20 4.7-in (120-mm) guns including eight carried in four twin turrets, the Austro-Hungarians embarked in 1910 on the construction of their first and, as it turned out, only class of dreadnought battleships.

These were the "Tegetthoff" class *Viribus Unitis*, *Tegetthoff*, *Prinz Eugen* and *Szent Istvan*, the first three built by Stabilimento Tecnico Triestino at Trieste and the last by Danubius at Fiume. The ships were completed between December 1912 and December 1915, and had been conceived in the light of Austria-Hungary's desire to counter Italy's naval strength and also to preserve the capabilities of STT. Admiral Count Montecuccoli, head of the Austrian naval department, in fact ordered the first two from STT without parliamentary approval, but in 1911 the legislature approved his action and added two more ships. To win Hungarian approval the fourth unit (and other warships) were ordered from the Danubius yard at Fiume, but this was poorly prepared for an order of such a size and the *Szent Istvan* was thus three years building while the *Viribus Unitis* was completed in 26 months.

The ships were based on the "Radetsky" class of pre-dreadnought battleships adapted with heavier firepower in a far superior layout. Firepower was increased and the length and displacement kept down by mounting the 12-in (305-mm) main guns in four Skoda triple turrets mounted on the centreline on superfiring pairs fore and aft. Thus six heavy guns fired ahead and astern, and all 12 in a broadside. Speed and endurance were adequate for Mediterranean purposes but, as war experience later confirmed, the underwater protection was poor: a 1.9-in (50-mm) anti-torpedo bulkhead shielded only the machinery spaces, and the compartmentation was poor. During World War I the number of 2.6-in (66-mm) QF guns singly mounted on the main turrets was reduced from 18 to 12, and two 3-in (76-mm) AA guns were added.

On June 10, 1918 the *Szent Istvan* was sunk in the southern Adriatic by two torpedoes from the Italian torpedo boat *MAS 15*. A mere few hours after being taken over by Yugoslavia after Austria-Hungary's collapse, on November 1st, 1918 the *Viribus Unitis* was sunk in Pola harbor by the 375-lb (170-kg) detachable warhead of an Italian manned-torpedo. *The Prinz Eugen*, ceded to France, was expended as a target in 1922, and the *Tegetthoff*, ceded to Italy, was scrapped in 1924/25.

The Viribus Unitis was one of only four Austro-Hungarian dreadnought battleships to be completed.

Viribus Unitis

Type:	dreadnought battleship
Tonnage:	21,225 tons full load
Dimensions:	length 499 ft 3 in (152.2 m); beam 89 ft 8 in (27.35 m); draft 27 ft (8.25 m)
Propulsion: propellers	four steam turbines delivering 25,000 shp (18640 kW) to four for 20 kt
Armour:	5.9/11-in (150/280-mm) belt, 11-in (280-mm) barbettes and turrets, 1.9-in (50-mm) decks, and 11-in (280-mm) conning tower
Armament:	12 12-in (305-mm) guns, 12 5.9-in (150-mm) QF guns, 18 2.6-in (66-mm) QF guns, and four 21-in (533-mm) torpedo tubes
Complement:	1,050

Troubridge torpedo launch (1914)

By the end of December 1914, only five months after World War I's start, the Serbs had twice driven the Austro-Hungarians out of their country, and once again held the southern bank of the River Danube, their northern border, and Belgrade, their capital. At this time the UK sent a naval mission to advise the Serbs on the best means of defending the Danube waterway. The mission's 75 men were led by Rear Admiral E. C. Troubridge, recently acquitted by court martial of the charges brought against him after the escape of the battle-cruiser SMS *Goeben* and light cruiser SMS *Breslau* to Turkey.

Troubridge's primary task was to deny the Austro-Hungarians the use of the Danube river as a means of communication and supply to Bulgaria and from bringing up their river monitors to bombard Belgrade. The first part of the mission was achieved by sealing the river at Semlin (Zemun) and Semendria (Smederevo) with guns, mines and torpedo tubes, so preventing the river monitors from moving downstream from Semlin after two of these craft had been sunk. These two had been sunk by Lieutenant Commander Kerr in a picket boat fitted with gear to carry and release two small torpedoes.

The motor launch used by Troubridge's little command was a simple yet effective adaptation.

Troubridge torpedo launch

Type:	torpedo launch
Tonnage:	not available
Dimensions:	length 56 ft (17.1 m); beam 11 ft (3.35 m); draft 2 ft 3 in (0.7 m)
Propulsion:	one reciprocating steam engine delivering 17 ihp (12.7 kW) to one propeller for 11 kt
Armour:	none
Armament:	two 14-in (356-mm) torpedoes and one 0.5-in (12.7-mm) Nordenfeldt machine gun

Grillo (1918)

In both world wars, the Italians showed great enterprise and ingenuity in the design and manufacture of weapons for special purposes, and also considerable dedication and bravery in the use of these pioneering weapons.

One of the major threats faced by the Italians in World War I was that of the Austro-Hungarian "fleet in being." Lying in the well-protected harbour of Pola, this fleet was a constant threat to the Italian navy in the Adriatic Sea, and also to the land forces on the northeastern front, where the Italian right flank could be vulnerable to assault supported by naval gun fire. The defenses of Pola were deemed to strong for conventional assault from the sea, so the Italian navy and an engineer named Attilio Bisio joined forces to create was in effect a tracked motor torpedo boat: this *barchino saltatore* (jumping boat) was a flat-bottomed type with spiked tracks running round the two sides of the hull just inboard of the two launchers for the torpedoes which were the primary weapons. The idea was for the craft, of which four were built as the *Cavalletta*, *Grillo*, *Locusta* and *Pulce*, to cruise slowly and quietly up to the Austro-Hungarian torpedo net defences and climb over them with their spiked tracks before closing on the targets, releasing their torpedoes and escaping.

Built in great secrecy at the Venice navy yard, the craft were very vulnerable to gunfire into their bellies as they climbed over the nets, and all but the *Locusta* were scuttled by their crews when they attacked Pola on 13/14 April 1918.

The "Grillo" class special attack boats were ingenious but operationally very dangerous to their crews.

Grillo

Type:	special torpedo attack vessel
Tonnage:	8 tons displacement
Dimensions:	length 52 ft 6 in (16 m); beam 10 ft 2 in (3.1 m); draft 2 ft 3 in (0.7 m)
Propulsion:	two electric motors delivering 10 hp (7.5 kW) to one propeller for 4 kt or to two tracks
Armour:	none
Armament:	two 17.7-in (450-mm) torpedoes
Complement:	four

Faà di Bruno (1917)

Given the fact that the southern edge of the eastern front between the Italians and Austro-Hungarians came down to the northern end of the Adriatic Sea, it is not surprising that the Italians made comparatively extensive use of monitors to support their ground forces as well as bombard Austro-Hungarian bases and protect their own.

Among the various Italian monitors, those with the heaviest armament were the basically conventional *Alfredo Cappellini* and the altogether radical *Faà di Bruno*, each of which was armed with two 15-in (380-mm) guns. These weapons had been designed for use on the "Caracciolo" class of super-dreadnought battleship, of which four were laid down in 1914/15, only one launched and none completed.

The *Faà di Bruno* was fitted with one of the twin-gun turrets fabricated for the *Cristoforo Colombo*. The vessel was designed by Engineer Rear Admiral Giuseppe Rota for construction by the Venice navy yard for launch in January 1916 and completion in July 1917 with a very low hull, a tripod mast, a tall turret that could be trained 30° left and right of the centerline, and engines stripped from old torpedo boats. The low-freeboard hull was of steel surrounded by a concrete cofferdam 9 ft 6 in (2.9 m) thick, The Faà di Bruno was discarded in 1924, but remained in existence and was used as a floating defense battery at Genoa in World War II.

The Faà di Bruno floated very low in the water, and with only two old engines was very slow.

Faà di Bruno

Type:	monitor
Tonnage:	2,809 tons displacement
Dimensions:	length 182 ft 1 in (55.5 m); beam 88 ft 7 in (27 m); draft 7 ft 3 in (2.2 m)
Propulsion:	two reciprocating steam engines delivering 465 ihp (347 kW) to two propellers for 3 kt
Armour:	9.5-ft (2.9-m) concrete cofferdam, 1.6-in (40-mm) deck, 2,4-in (60-mm) barbette, and 0.8+0.8+2.75-in (20+20+70-mm) turret
Armament:	two 15-in (380-mm) guns, four 3-in (75-mm) AA guns, and two 40-mm AA guns
Complement:	not available

SMS *Kaiser Barbarossa* (1900)

With the five "Kaiser" class battleships (SMS *Kaiser Friedrich III, Kaiser Wilhelm II, Kaiser Wilhelm der Grosse, Kaiser Karl der Grosse* and *Kaiser Barbarossa*) completed in the last years of the 19th century and first years of the 20th century, the Imperial German navy set the mould for its battleships until the construction of the "Westfalen" class as its first dreadnought battleships in 1907/10. Compared with those of most other naval powers, the German pre-dreadnoughts had a lighter but faster-firing main armament (three rounds per minute as opposed to one round per minute for the 11-in/280-mm gun) and a heavier secondary armament. In the "Kaisers," the four 9.4-in (240-mm) main guns were mounted in twin turrets in barbettes fore and aft, six 5.9-in (150-mm) guns in small 5.9-in (150-mm) armoured single turrets and 12 5.9-in (150-mm) guns in 5.9-in (150-mm) armoured casemates.

With the exception of the *Karl der Grosse*, the "Kaiser" class ships were reconstructed in 1907/10, four 5.9-in (150-mm) guns and the above-water torpedo tube at the stern being removed, two 3.45-in (88-mm) guns added to the rearranged tertiary armament, the superstructure cut down, and the funnels heightened None of the ships played an active role in World War I, and all of the ships were scrapped in 1920/21.

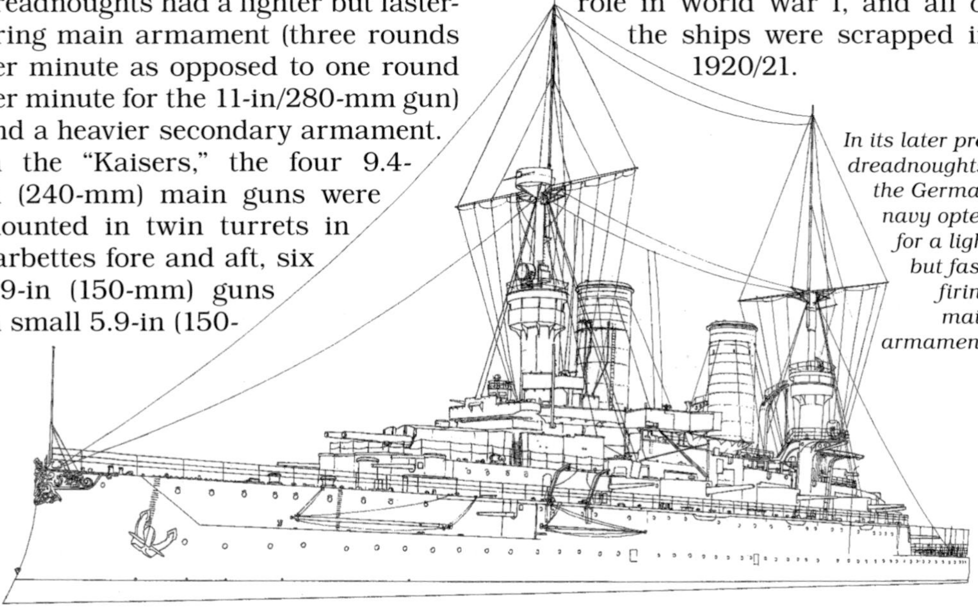

In its later pre-dreadnoughts, the German navy opted for a light but fast-firing main armament.

SMS *Kaiser Barbarossa*

Type:	pre-dreadnought battleship
Tonnage:	11,599 tons
Dimensions:	length 411 ft (125.3 m); beam 67 ft (20.4 m); draft 27 ft (8.25 m)
Propulsion:	three triple expansion steam engines delivering 14,000 ihp (10438 kW) to three propellers for 17 kt
Armour:	4/12-in (100/300-mm) belt, 10-in (250-mm) barbettes and turrets, 2.5-in (65-mm) decks, and 10-in (250-mm) conning tower
Armament:	four 9.4-in (240-mm) guns, 18 5.9-in (150-mm) guns, 12 3.45-in (88-mm) guns, 12 machine guns, and six 17.7-in (450-mm) torpedo tubes
Complement:	651

HMS *Good Hope* (1901)

Provided under the Admiralty's 1898/99 program, the four first-class armoured cruisers of the "Drake" class were in essence enlarged versions of the "Cressy" class cruisers. Compared with that of the "Cressy" class, the length and displacement were increased by 61 ft 6 in (18.75 m) and 3,000 tons respectively to provide the volume for more potent machinery providing a 2-kt speed increment, four more guns in the battery of 6-in (152-mm) secondary guns, and a number of individually small but, it was hoped, collectively useful protective enhancements. The 6-in (152-mm) side armour extended over a length of 257 ft (78.3 m) amidships, and then tapered in thickness to 4 in (102 mm) and finally 2 in (51 mm) at the bows, this thicker bow armour allowing the omission of the forward armoured bulkhead of the "Cressy" class. The protective deck was 2.5 in (64 mm) thick between the stern and the after bulkhead, and then 1 in (25 mm) thick forward to the bows. The rest of the protection was basically similar to that of the "Cressy" class. The four added battery guns were accommodated in the upper part of what were now double-storey casemates amidships and also at the ends in line with the fore funnel and the main mast. In an effort to limit the area vulnerable to incoming fire, most of the midship structure (the boat deck in earlier classes) was discarded, windsails replaced cowl ventilators, and other fittings and structures above the upper deck were trimmed to the minimum.

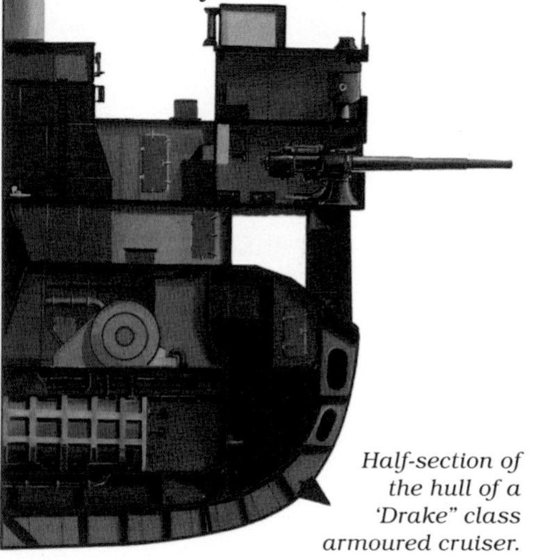

Half-section of the hull of a 'Drake" class armoured cruiser.

The ships were HMS *Drake*, HMS *Good Hope* (originally *Africa*), HMS *King Alfred* and HMS *Leviathan*, built by Pembroke Dock Yard, Fairfield, Vickers and John Brown respectively for completion between November 1902 and December 1903. At the time of their completion, the "Drake"

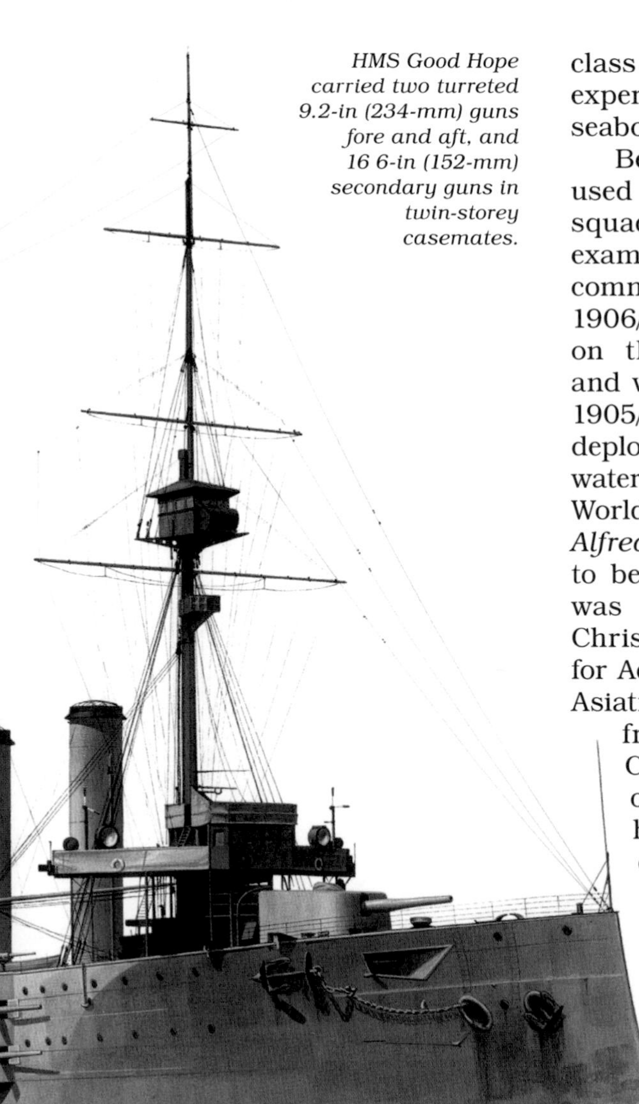

HMS Good Hope carried two turreted 9.2-in (234-mm) guns fore and aft, and 16 6-in (152-mm) secondary guns in twin-storey casemates.

class ships were notably fast, and experience revealed them to be good seaboats.

Before World War I the ships were used mainly as flagships of cruiser squadrons: the *King Alfred*, for example, was flagship of the admiral commanding the China Station in 1906/10, and the *Leviathan* served on the China station in 1903/04 and with the Mediterranean Fleet in 1905/06. The ships were otherwise deployed almost exclusively in home waters from completion to the start of World War I in 1914. While the *King Alfred* and the *Leviathan* survived to be sold in 1920, the *Good Hope* was the flagship of Admiral Sir Christopher Cradock as he searched for Admiral Graf von Spee's German Asiatic Squadron trying to return from China to Germany via Cape Horn, and was completely outclassed and sunk with all hands in the Battle of Coronel, off Chile, in November 1914, The *Drake* succumbed to U-boat attack in October 1917.

HMS *Good Hope*

Type:	first-class armoured cruiser
Tonnage:	14,150 tons load
Dimensions:	length 533 ft 6 in (162.6 m); beam 71 ft 4 in (21.75 m); draft 26 ft (7.9 m)
Propulsion:	two triple expansion steam engines delivering 30,000 ihp (22368 kW) to two propellers for 23 kt
Armour:	2/6-in (51/152-mm) belt, 1/2.5-in (25/64-mm) belt, 5-in (127-mm) bulkhead, 6-in (152-mm) turrets and barbettes, 2/5-in (51-127-mm) casemates, 3-in (76-mm) ammunition tubes, and 12-in (305-mm) conning tower
Armament:	two 9.2-in (234-mm) guns, 16 6-in (152-mm) guns, 14 12-pdr QF guns, three 3-pdr QF guns, and two 18-in (457-mm) torpedo tubes
Complement:	900

SMS *Dresden* (1909)

During the later part of the 19th century, the development of the cruiser in most nations diverged into two lines: one for protection and/or destruction of shipping, and the other for fleet duties such as scouting and the control of flotillas of lighter vessels. This was a practice eschewed by the Imperial German navy, which opted instead for dual-purpose cruisers of a compromise type possessing great endurance but also larger, slower and less agile than British cruisers. Another factor characteristic of the German cruiser was the overlong retention of a light primary armament based on the 4.1-in (105-mm) gun, well after other navies had switched to the 6-in (152-mm) gun.

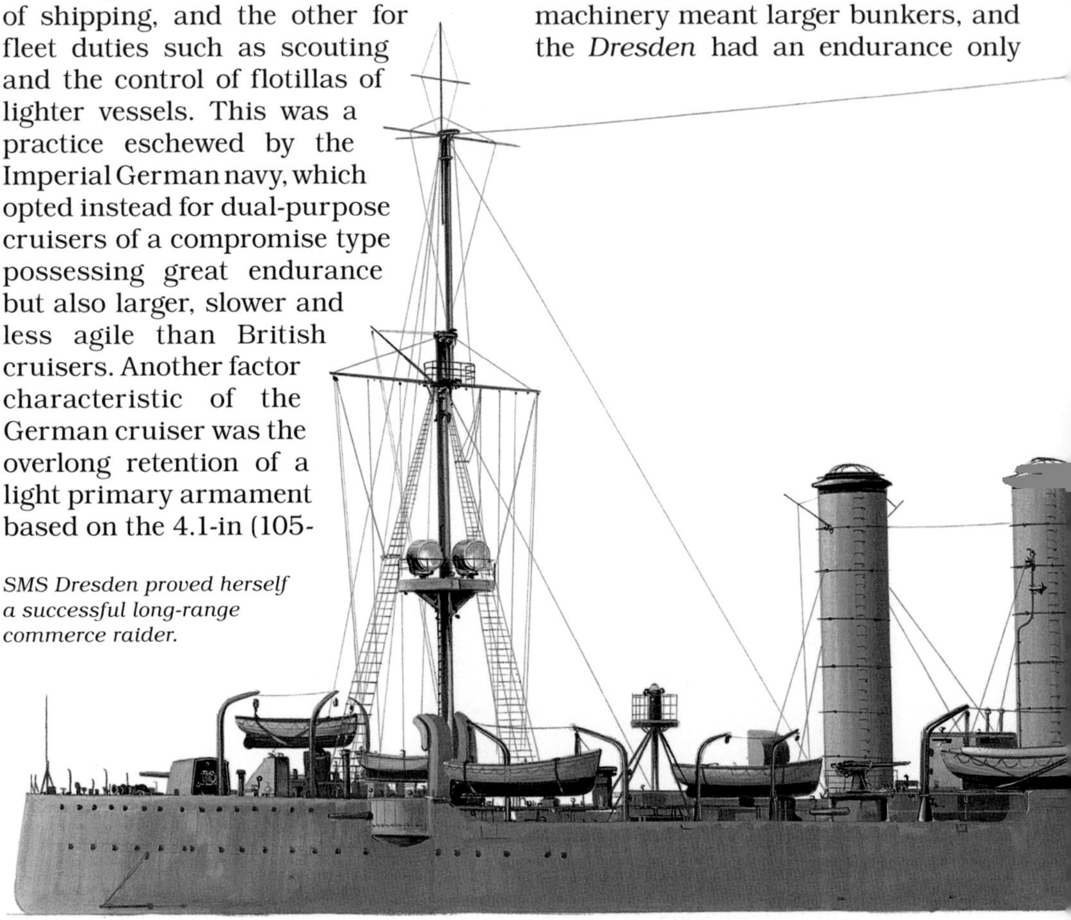

SMS Dresden proved herself a successful long-range commerce raider.

The two light cruisers ordered in the German 1905/06 naval program were SMS *Dresden* and *Emden* of the "Dresden" class. This was a logical development of the two ships of the preceding "Königsberg" class, but with different propulsion machinery: while the *Emden* retained vertical triple expansion steam engines delivering 13,500 ihp (10088 kW) for 23.5 kt, the *Dresden* had Parsons steam turbines (again with 12 boilers) delivering 15,000 shp (11184 kW) for 24 kt. The more compact nature of the turbine machinery meant larger bunkers, and the *Dresden* had an endurance only slightly less than that of the *Emden* but at a 2-kt greater cruising speed.

The *Dresden* was built by Blohm & Voss for completion in November 1908, while the *Emden* was constructed at the Danzig Navy Yard for completion in July 1909. The *Dresden* was in the West Indies on the outbreak of World War I in 1914. She then passed into the Pacific via the Straits of Magellan, joined forces with SMS *Leipzig*, and then linked up with Admiral Graf

von Spee's East Asia Squadron at Easter Island. The *Dresden* survived the Battle of the Falklands in which most of von Spee's squadron was sunk, escaped once more to the Pacific and was finally trapped by the British cruisers HMS *Kent* and *Glasgow*, as well as the armed merchant cruiser *Orama*, at the Chilean island of Mas a Fuera, and shelled into submission on March 14, 1915. Lying in neutral waters, the *Dresden* was scuttled to avoid capture.

The *Emden* had been in Chinese and Pacific waters since 1909, and in 1914 was at Tsingtao in China, a German treaty port from which she escaped as the Japanese attacked it. The *Emden* then embarked on a commerce-raiding cruise until caught by the cruiser HMAS *Sydney* in the Cocos Islands. Following an engagement on November 9, 1914 the *Emden* was beached on the reefs of North Keeling Island.

SMS *Dresden*

Type:	light cruiser
Tonnage:	4,201 tons deep load
Dimensions:	length 386 ft 10 in (117.9 m); beam 44 ft 4 in (13.5 m); draft 18 ft (5.5 m)
Propulsion:	four steam turbines delivering 15,000 shp (11184 kW) to two propellers for 24 kt
Armour:	0.8/1.2-in (20/30-mm) deck, 2-in (50-mm) gun shields, and 3.9-in (100-mm) conning tower
Armament:	10 4.1-in (105-mm) guns, eight 2-in (52-mm) QF guns and two 17.7-in (450-mm) torpedo tubes
Complement:	361

SMS *Prinzregent Luitpold* (1912)

Germany's third class of dreadnought battleships, following the four-strong "Nassau" and "Helgoland" classes, SMS Kaiser, SMS *Friedrich der Grosse*, SMS *Kaiserin*, SMS *König Albert* and SMS *Prinzregent Luitpold* were the "Kaiser" class battleships which marked a departure from Germany's previous dreadnought practice. The ships were built in five yards and, with the first two and last three authorized under the 19109/10 and 1910/11 programs respectively, were completed between December 1912

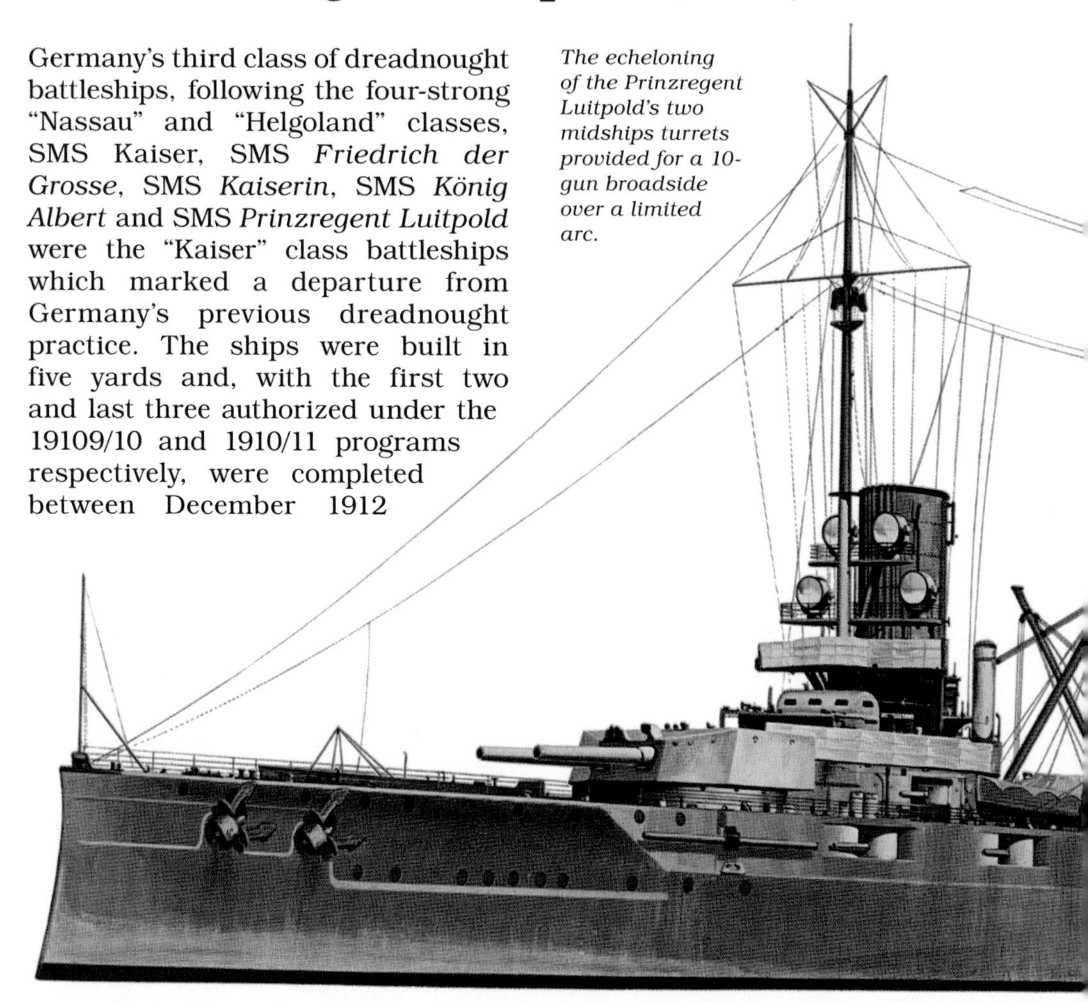

The echeloning of the Prinzregent Luitpold's two midships turrets provided for a 10-gun broadside over a limited arc.

and December 1913. The forecastle deck extended to a point abaft the main mast, and the boiler rooms and funnels were widely spaced. The arrangement of the main turrets, each mounting two 12-in (305-mm) guns, was altered to one forward, two in a superfiring layout aft, and two echeloned amidships: this made provided for a 10-gun broadside as the midships turrets each possessed a 120° arc on the opposite beam. The mountings initially possessed a maximum elevation of 13.5°, a figure later increased to 16°. The magazines were below the shell rooms. The secondary armament was 14 5.9-in (150-mm) guns located in an upper-deck battery. The tertiary armament of eight 3.45-in (88-mm) was later removed, and the number of 3.45-in (88mm) AA guns was later reduced in number from five to two.

The side armour was considerably superior to that of the preceding eight German dreadnought battleships, the belt between the end barbettes being 13.8 in (350 mm) thick from the main deck, some 5 ft 11 in (1.8 m) above the waterline to 1 ft 2 in (0.35 m) below it and then tapering to 7.1 in (180 mm) at 5 ft 7 in (1.70 m) below the waterline. The belt was 7.9 in (200 mm) thick between the main and upper decks. The belt tapered to 3.15 in (80 mm) forward and 5.1 in (130 mm) aft except in the *Kaiserin* and *Prinzregent Luitpold*, in which the equivalent figures were 3.15 in (80 mm) and 5.9 in (150 mm) The barbettes were 8.7/11.8 in (220/300 mm) thick reducing to 5.5 in (140 mm) behind the battery and upper belt, and to 3.15 in (80 mm) behind the main belt. The main turrets had 11.8-in (300-mm) faces, 9.85-in (250-mm) sides 11.4-in (290-mm) rears and 3.15/4.33-in (80/110-mm) roofs. The armour deck was 1.2 in (30 mm) thick amidships, 2.4 in (60 mm) thick forward and 2.4/4.7 in (60/120 mm) thick aft. Between the end barbettes the upper deck was 1/1.2 in (25/30 mm) thick outside the battery, and the forecastle deck was 1.2 in (30 mm) thick over the battery. The torpedo bulkhead was 1.6 in (40 mm) thick except in the *Kaiserin* and *Prinzregent Luitpold*, in which it was 2 in (50 mm) thick, and in all of the ships it was continued to the upper deck as a 1.2-in (30-mm) splinter bulkhead.

There were 10 boiler rooms and three sets of turbines in six engine rooms, delivering 31,000 shp (23114 kW) to three propellers for 21kt except in the *Prinzregent Luitpold*, which had two sets in four engine rooms. The boilers were coal-fired with provision for tar-oil spraying.

The five units of the class saw moderate service in World War I, none of them suffering significant damage. All were interned at Scapa Flow after World War I and scuttled by their crews in June 1919. The vessels were raised between 1929 and 1937, and sold for scrap.

SMS *Prinzregent Luitpold*

Type:	dreadnought battleship
Tonnage:	27,400 tons deep load
Dimensions:	length 565 ft 7 in (172.4 m); beam 95 ft 2 in (29 m); draft 27 ft 3 in (8.3 m)
Propulsion:	two steam turbines delivering 26,000 shp (19386 kW) to two propellers for 22 kt
Armour:	3/15/14-in (80/350-mm) belt, 5.1/11.8-in (130/300-mm) bulkheads, 6.7-in (170-mm) battery, 3.15/11.8-in (80/300-mm) barbettes and turrets, and 4.9/13.8-in (80/350-mm) conning tower
Armament:	10 12-in (305-mm) guns, 14 4.9-in (150-mm) guns, eight 3.45-in (88-mm) guns, four 3.45-in (88mm) AA guns, and five 19.7-in (550-mm) torpedo tubes
Complement:	1,084 increasing to about 1,275 during World War I

Carlo Mirabello (1916)

In common with other navies, the Italian navy discovered that the overall utility of its torpedo boat and destroyer flotillas could be improved significantly if they were led by slightly larger ships possessing improved command and control facilities but also performance generally similar to that of their charges. Such flotilla leaders were initially classified by the Italian navy as *esploratori* (scouts) before being reclassified as *esploratori leggieri* (light scouts) in July 1921 and as destroyers during September 1938.

The first such vessels in Italian service were the three units of the "Poerio" class. The vessels of the next class to see the light of day were the *Carlo Mirabello*, *Carlo Alberto Racchia* and the *Augusto Riboty* of the "Mirabello" class. The design was drafted during 1913 as a 5,000-ton type based on the "Quarto" class scout cruiser with only very light protection, and was the work of Engineer Captain Nabor Soliani in collaboration with the Società Gio Ansaldo & C. of Genoa. For cost reasons the final design was for an altogether lighter type with an armament of eight 4-in (102-mm) guns, a full-load displacement of less than 2,000 tons and no protection at all. The three ships were laid down by Ansaldo at Genoa in 1914/15, and completed only in 1916/17 as a result of steel shortages. In 1917 the *Racchia*'s and *Riboty*'s forward 4-in (6-in) gun was replaced by one 6-in (152-mm) L/40 gun, making the vessels the world's first destroyers with a cruiser-standard gun, and in the next year the *Mirabello* was similarly converted but with a 6-in (152-mm) L/45 gun. The 6-in (152-mm) gun was too heavy and too slow-firing, and also caused damage to the structure when fired, so in 1919 it was removed from all three ships.

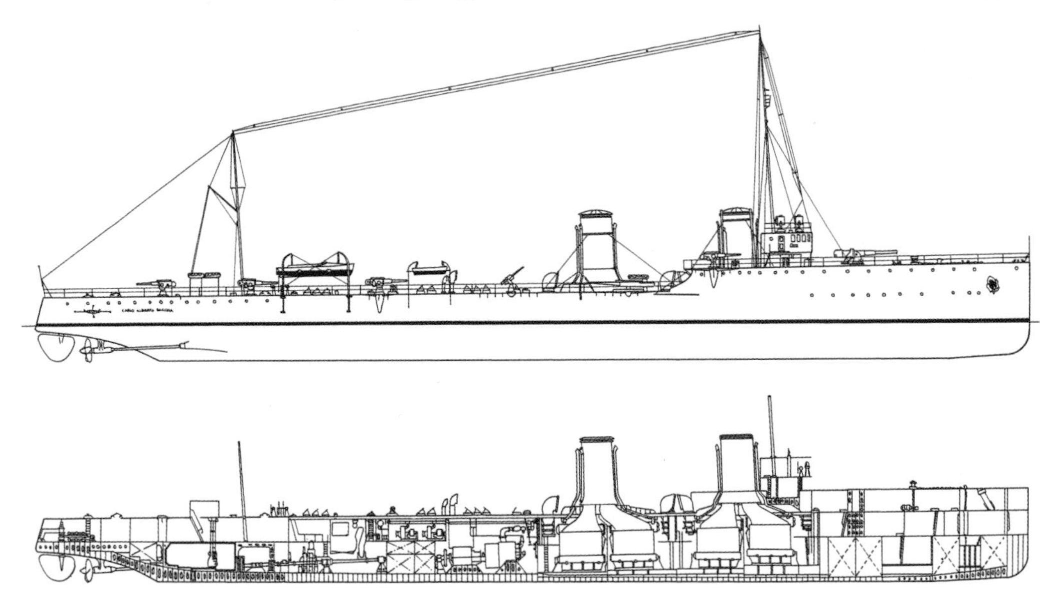

Exterior and interior details of the Italian flotilla leader Carlo Mirabello with a 6-in (152-mm) gun on her forecastle.

The ships of the "Mirabello" class were fast, but too lightly built to carry, or more importantly to fire, a 6-in (152-mm) gun.

In the period 1920/22 the armament of the class was 8 4-in (102-mm) L/45 guns, two 3-in (76-mm) AA guns replaced after only a few months by two 40-mm AA guns, and two 6.5-mm machine guns as well as four 17.7-in (450-mm) torpedo tubes. In 1925 the *Mirabello* was adapted to carry, for short-term experimental purposes, a floatplane.

The *Racchia* fell victim to a mine off Odessa in the Black Sea in July 1920, and the *Mirabello* also succumbed to a mine, although in this instance in World War II, off Cape Dukato in Albania, during May 1941. In 1942 the *Riboty* had two of her 4-in (102-mm) guns removed but another 40-mm AA gun added, and the light AA armament was changed to a pair of 8-mm machine guns. In 1943 her armament was again altered, becoming four 4-in (102-mm) guns, six 20-mm AA cannon, two 8-mm machine guns and no torpedo tubes. The vessel was allotted to the USSR after World War II, but remained in Italy because of her age and was scrapped in 1951.

Carlo Mirabello

Type:	flotilla leader
Tonnage:	1,972 tons full load
Dimensions:	length 339 ft 5 in (103.75 m); beam 31 ft 10 in (9.70 m); draft 10 ft 10 in (3.3 m)
Propulsion:	two steam turbines delivering 44,000 shp (32806 kW) to two propellers for 33.75 kt
Armour:	none
Armament:	eight 4-in (102-mm) guns, two 3-in (76-mm) AA guns, two 6.5-mm machine guns, four 17,7-in (450-mm) torpedo tubes, and provision for up to 100 mines
Complement:	169

SMS *Rheinland* (1910)

Whereas Germany's last pre-dreadnought battleships had been wholly indifferent, her first dreadnought battleships, the four "Nassau" class units, were qualitatively much better ships and, though later than the Royal Navy's first such battleships, marked a major jump in capability without any intervening classes. These four ships were SMS *Nassau* and SMS *Westfalen* built by Wilhelmshaven Navy Yard and Weser of Bremen under the 1906/07 program, and SMS *Rheinland* and *Posen* built by Vulkan of Stettin and Germaniawerft of Kiel under the 1907/08 program. The "Nassau" class ships were based on a flush-decked hull, and were readily identifiable by their pair of goose-neck cranes amidships. The ships were built without bilge keels, but these were retrofitted after it was discovered that the ships' rolling had the same period as the North Sea's swell.

The main armament comprised 12 11.1-in (28-mm) L/45 guns in six twin turrets. Two of these turrets were disposed fore and aft on the centreline, and the other four in fore and aft pairs on each beam, giving a broadside of only eight guns. All the guns had a maximum elevation angle of 20°. The magazines were located above the shell rooms except in the centreline turrets of the Nassau and Westfalen, where the situation was reversed. The secondary battery of 12 5.9-in (150-mm) L/45 guns was casemated on the main deck, and four 3.45-in (88-mm) AA guns eventually replaced the tertiary battery of 3.45-in (88-mm) guns intended to provide defence against torpedo craft but poorly sited for this task. The torpedo tubes were located at bow and stern and on either beam forward and abaft the torpedo bulkhead.

The propulsion arrangement was based on six boiler and three engine rooms, and through the boilers were coal-fired, 160 tons of tar oil were later carried for spraying on the coal. The ships' trials were lengthy, and the Nassau, Westfalen, Rheinland and Posen were entered full service during 1910 in pairs on May 3, and September 21.

The *Rheinland* ran aground at 15 kt on rocks off Lagskar on 11 April 1918, and more than 6,000 tons of mass, including the belt armour and all her guns, had to be removed before the vessel could be returned to Kiel, but she was not repaired and was broken up in 1921. The *Westfalen* was torpedoed amidships by HMS E-23 on August 19, 1916 and took on 800 tons of water, but though her bulkheads were sagging, she returned to harbor at 14 kt. The ship was scrapped in 1924. The Nassau was allocated to Japan in 1919 but scrapped in 1924, and like the other ships the *Posen* served with the High Seas Fleet before being scrapped in 1922.

On the outbreak of World War I in 1914, the British had 20 dreadnought battleships to the Germans' 13, and the comparable figures for battle-cruisers were eight and five, for pre-dreadnought battleships 40 and 22, for cruisers 102 and 41, for destroyers 301 and 144, and submarines 78 and 30. The British director firing, training, bases and industrial support were generally superior to those of the Germans, but the latter had a measure of like-for-like superiority in guns, projectiles, armour and other protective measures, and damage control.

The fact that SMS Westfalen and the other three units of the "Nassau" class had only two centerline turrets and four wing turrets meant that their broadsides were limited to eight guns, and end-on fire of six guns.

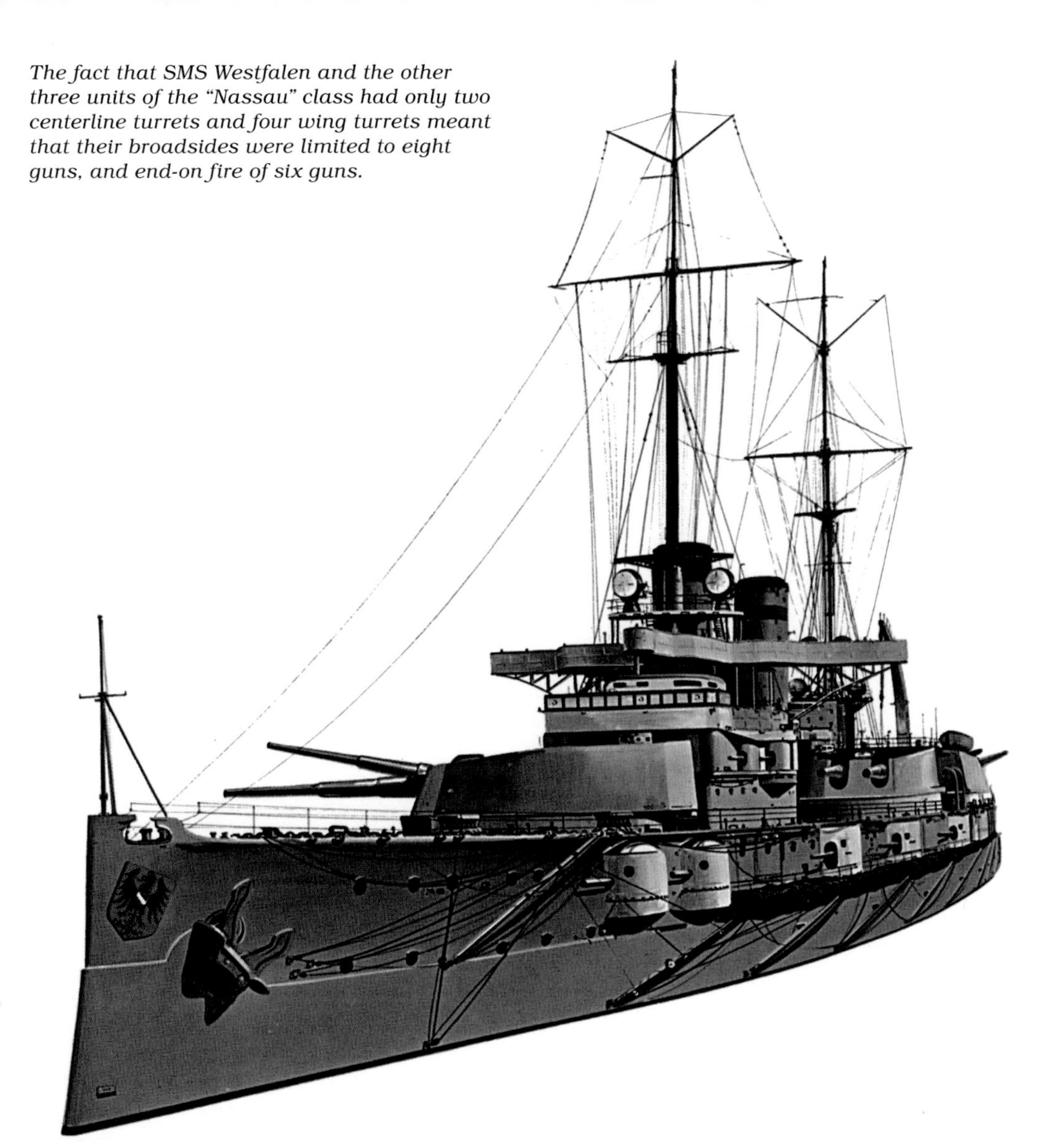

SMS *Rheinland*

Type:	dreadnought battleship
Tonnage:	21,000 tons deep load
Dimensions:	length 479 ft 4 in (146.1 m); beam 88 ft 5 in (26.9 m); draft 29 ft 3 in (8.9 m)
Propulsion:	three vertical triple expansion steam engines delivering 22,000 ihp (16403 kW) to three propellers for 19.5 kt
Armour:	3.15/11.8-in (80/300-mm) belt, 3.55/8.25-in (90/210-mm) bulkheads, 2.35/11-in (60/280-mm) turrets, 2/11-in (50/280-mm) barbettes, 6.3-in (160-mm) battery, and 3.15/11.8-in (80/300-mm) conning tower
Armament:	12 11.1-in (280-mm) guns, 12 5.9-in (150-mm) guns, 16 3.45-in (88-mm) guns, and six 17.7-in (450-mm) torpedo tubes
Complement:	1,139

SMS *Stettin* (1907)

The four light cruisers of the "Königsberg" class were ordered in the 1903/04 and 1904/05 programs for the Imperial German navy, and were completed with a number of differences. The four ships were SMS Königsberg and Nürnberg both built by the Kiel Navy Yard for completion in April 1907 and April 1908 respectively, Stuttgart built by Danzig Navy Yard for completion in February 1908, and Stettin built by Vulkan of Stettin for completion in October 1907. The waterline length was 383 ft 2 in (116.8 m) except for 376 ft 8 in (114.8 m) in the Königsberg, and the standard machinery was triple expansion steam engines delivering 12,000 ihp (8947 kW) to two propellers for 23 kt except in the Stettin, which had Parsons steam turbines delivering 13,500 shp (10066 kW) to four propellers for 24 kt. During World War I AA guns were added on the Stuttgart and Stettin.

The Königsberg was stationed at Dar-es-Salaam, in German East Africa, at the war's start and after a brief raiding career was blockaded in the River Rufiji during October 1914 and shelled by British monitors in July 1915 before being scuttled by her crew. The Nürnberg was part of the German East Asia Squadron, and was sunk during the Battle of the Falkland Islands on December 8, 1914. The Stuttgart was a gunnery training ship and also served with the High Seas Fleet before conversion, from

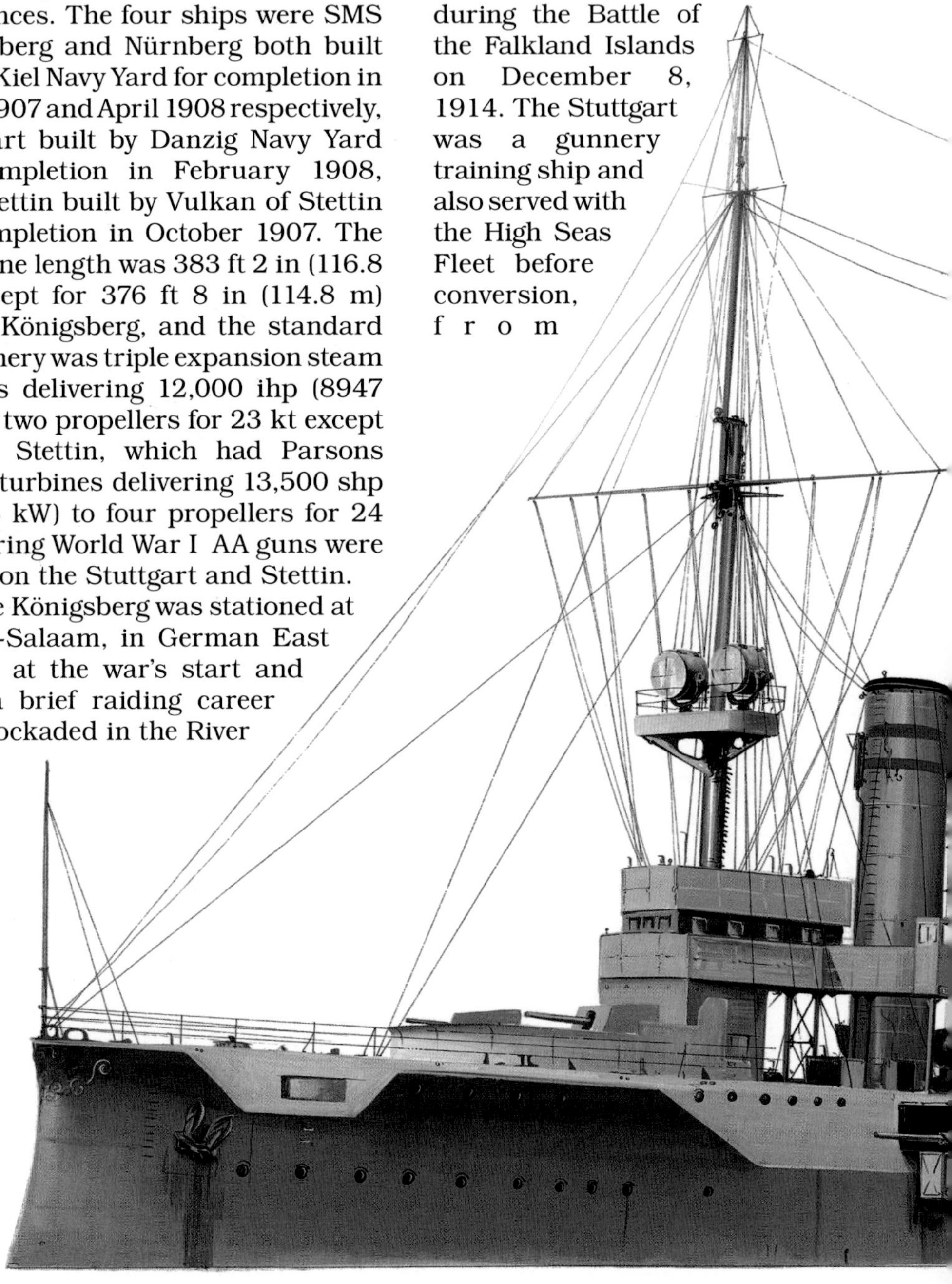

SMS *Stettin*

Type:	light cruiser
Tonnage:	3,762 tons deep load
Dimensions:	length 383 ft 2 in (116.8 m); beam 43 ft 8 in (13.3 m); draft 17 ft 5 in (5.3 m)
Propulsion:	two steam turbines delivering 13,500 shp (10066 kW) to four propellers for 24 kt
Armour:	0.8/1.2-in (20/30-mm) deck, 2-in (50-mm) gun shields, and 3.9-in (100-mm) conning tower
Armament:	10 4.1-in (105-mm) guns, eight 2-in (52-mm) QF guns and two 17.7-in (450-mm) torpedo tubes
Complement:	322

February 1918, to carry three seaplanes in a hangar abaft the after funnel. Her armament in this form was four 4.1-in (105-mm) and two 3.45-in (88-mm) AA guns as well as two 17.7-in (450-mm) torpedo tubes. The Stettin served with the High Seas Fleet from 1907, but her obsolescence and the decline of the High Seas Fleet led to her reallocation to the Submarine School in 1917. Both vessels were handed over to the UK after the war's end and scrapped in 1921/23.

SMS Stettin served with the High Seas Fleet for most of her life.

HMS *Argus* (1918)

Though the Royal Navy's plans for the conversion of the light battle-cruiser HMS *Furious* into an interim aircraft carrier with a flight deck in place of her forward main armament turret were formulated only in the spring of 1917, the fact that the ship was almost complete meant that the conversion could be effected easily and swiftly, and the ship was therefore completed in July 1917 as the first "real" British aircraft carrier. Before this, however, the Royal Navy had recognised that the vital importance of aircraft in naval warfare, a fact now no longer in any doubt, demanded the services of a fully optimised aircraft carrier. A short-term solution based on a large hull was the obvious solution, and was found in the *Conte Rosso*, a liner ordered in 1914 from Beardmore by the Italian Lloyd Sabaudo Line, but still resting incomplete on the stocks. The Admiralty bought the vessel in August 1916 and ordered her completion as an aircraft carrier.

The large hull was well suited for development and completion with a virtually full-length, uninterrupted flight deck and also a full-length enclosed hangar for aircraft accommodation and maintenance. The design and layout of several possible flight deck configurations were evaluated by use of wind-tunnel models, and as a direct result of this scientific endeavour a flush flight deck was selected, its only interruption being a small pilot house which could be lowered during flying operations to leave the flight deck wholly clear. The Admiralty was thinking of a more definitive layout for the future, however, and in October 1918, one month after the ship had been completed, HMS *Argus* was trialled in the Firth of Forth with a dummy "island" superstructure that was fixed but well offset from the centreline to leave the flight deck as unobstructed as possible.

The first aircraft embarked in the *Argus* were 18 examples of the Sopwith Cuckoo torpedo-bomber, and it was planned that this combination of carrier and

The flight deck of HMS Argus was built over the hull of the liner from which she was completed, and the ship is seen here in dazzle-painted form.

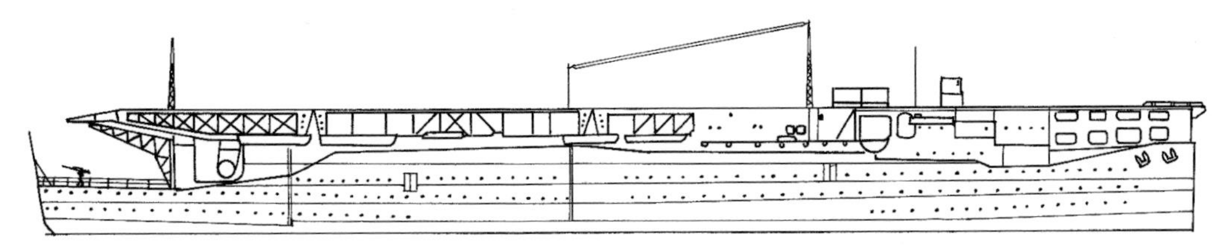
The lack of any real superstructure inevitably led to HMS Argus being nicknamed as the "Flatiron."

aircraft would form a central plank of the British plan for a major attack by the Grand Fleet on the German High Seas Fleet lurking in its North German harbors as a constant threat to British operations. The end of World War I in November 1918 put an end to all such plans, though, and in fact the *Argus* made no contribution to the British naval effort in World War I. In her first period of service with the Atlantic Fleet, up to 1923, the *Argus* proved very successful as her good turn of speed provided the high wind-over-deck factor conducive to effective carrierborne aircraft operations, and the ship carried, in succession, the Cuckoo, Sopwith Camel fighter, Sopwith 1½-Strutter general-purpose two-seater, Sopwith Pup light fighter, Parnall Panther fighter, Nieuport Nightjar fighter, and Fairey IIIB general-purpose floatplane.

As the 1920s progressed, however, it became clear that the *Argus* was limited by her lack of protection, considerable height, and the increasing weight and size of the aircraft she carried. In the middle of the decade, therefore, the ship was reconstructed with waterline bulges of the type which enhanced protection and also provided greater stability. The ship served on the China Station in 1927/28, and was placed in reserve during 1930. In 1937 the *Argus* was refitted, with the forward part of her flight deck made level rather than downward sloping, and with more modern aircraft carriers now being completed, the *Argus* was relegated in 1938 to the training role. By the outbreak of World War II in September 1939, the *Argus* was clearly inadequate, and so spent much of the war as an aircraft ferry, especially to Gibraltar, Malta and Takoradi, but was also used to escort Atlantic convoys and support the Allied landings of November 19421 in North-West Africa. The ship was paid off in 1944 and sold for breaking in December 1946.

HMS *Argus* (as completed)

Type:	aircraft carrier
Tonnage:	14,550 tons normal
Dimensions:	length 566 ft (172.5 m); beam 68 ft (20.7 m); draft 21 ft 6.4 m)
Propulsion:	four geared steam turbines delivering 20,000 shp (14912 kW) to four propellers for 20.5 kt
Armour:	none
Armament:	six 4-in (102-mm) AA guns and 20 aircraft
Complement:	401

HMS *Lion* (1912)

The battle-cruiser was an invention of Admiral Sir John Fisher, and reflected this dominant figure's desire for firepower and speed, the latter provided by a long hull, high-powered engines and only limited protection. As such the battle-cruiser was the successor to the armoured cruiser, itself the high-speed counterpart of the pre-dreadnought battleship. The battle-cruiser concept first took shape with the three "Invincible" class ships, which were high-speed counterparts of HMS *Dreadnought*, and the design and construction of battle-cruisers then proceeded in parallel with that of battleships.

HMS *Lion* and her sister ship HMS *Princess Royal* were the counterparts of the "Orion" class of super-dreadnought battleships with 13.5-in (343-mm) guns. However, whereas earlier British battle-cruisers had been slightly longer but of somewhat lighter displacement than their battleship counterparts, the ships of the "Lion" class were considerably longer and had a displacement increment of 4,000 tons over the "Orion" class ships. This was the direct result of the volume required for the heavier armament and massive machinery in a hull of the length/beam ratio necessary to produce the specified speed of 27 kt.

The primary armament was eight examples of the very capable 13.5-in (343-mm) Mk V L/45 gun, which could fire its 1,400-lb (635-kg) shell with a muzzle velocity of 2,700 ft (823 m) per second. This velocity was lower than that of the 12-in (305-mm) L/45 gun it succeeded, but reduced barrel wear and produced a more stable ballistic trajectory for accurate fire to 24,000 yards (21945 m). The guns were located in four twin turrets, all on the centerline, but instead of superfiring turrets aft as well as forward, W. T. Davis and E. L. Attwood chose to have one turret on the quarterdeck and one on the forecastle deck amidships, with limited firing arcs: this reduced

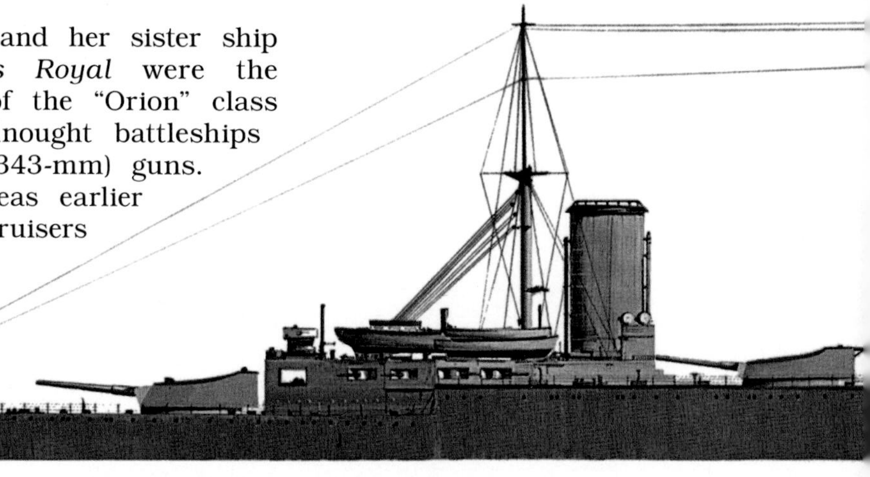

the bending moment imposed on the hull and so allowed savings in hull weight, but at the same time divided the boiler rooms into two groups. The 4-in (102-mm) secondary armament was mounted in casemate positions, all but two of the 16 such guns at forecastle deck level, four on each side of the two superstructure groupings. The protection was much criticised but was in reality adequate for the ships' role. The "Lion" class ships were the first British battle-cruisers in which the side armour was extended vertically to the main deck, but the ends and the sides of the ship between the upper and forecastle decks were unprotected: this reflected the design of earlier ships, which had been planned for engagements at no more than 9,000 yards (8230 m), a range at which horizontal rather than plunging fire might be expected. The "Lion" class ships had been planned round the concept of long-range engagements, where plunging fire was inevitable, so this design lapse was severe and exposed the ships' magazines and machinery spaces.

The *Lion* and *Princess Royal* were built by Devonport Dock Yard and Vickers for completion in May and November 1912 respectively. In 1914 the *Lion* became the flagship of Admiral Sir David Beatty's 1st Battle-Cruiser Squadron, and as such took part in the Battles of Heligoland Bight and of Dogger Bank In the latter she was hit by 18 heavy shells and disabled, having to be towed back to port by HMS *Indomitable*. Repaired, she became flagship of the Battle-Cruiser Force, and as such took part in the Battle of Jutland on May 31, 1916, when she was hit by 12 heavy shells but continued to function despite "Q" turret being burned out by a propellant fire. The *Lion* remained in service but was deleted in December 1922 and scrapped in 1924. The *Princess Royal's* career was very similar to that of the *Lion*, and she too was damaged at Jutland. She was discarded in 1922 and scrapped in 1926.

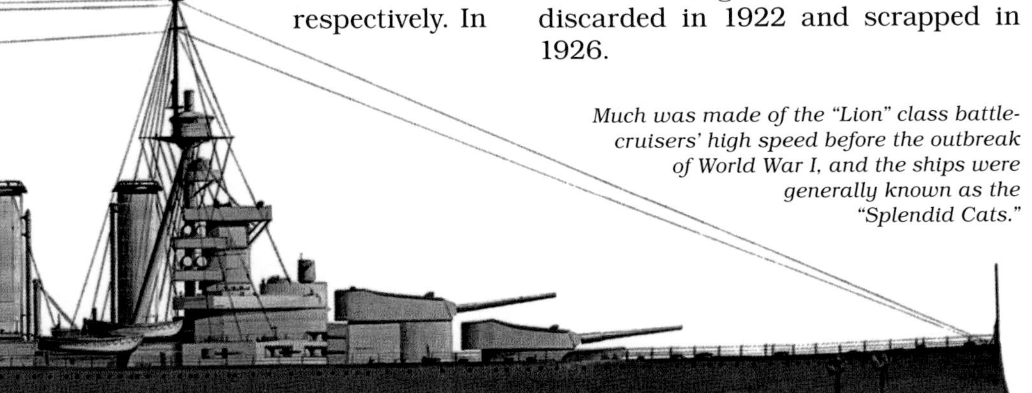

Much was made of the "Lion" class battle-cruisers' high speed before the outbreak of World War I, and the ships were generally known as the "Splendid Cats."

HMS *Lion*

Type:	super-dreadnought battle-cruiser
Tonnage:	29,680 tons full load
Dimensions:	length 700 ft 0 in (213.4 m); beam 88 ft 6 in (27 m); draft 28 ft 10 in (8.8 m)
Propulsion:	four steam turbines delivering 73,800 shp (55025 kW) to four propellers for 27 kt
Armour:	4/9-in (102/229-mm) belt, 4-in (102-mm) bulkheads, 1/2.5-in (25/64-mm) decks, 3/9-in (76/229-mm) barbettes, 9-in (229-mm) turret faces, and 10-in (254-mm) conning tower
Armament:	eight 13.5-in (343-mm) guns, 16 4-in (1-2-mm) guns, four 3-pdr QF guns, and two 21-in (533-mm) torpedo tubes
Complement:	997

SMS *Scharnhorst* (1907)

Given its late entry into an overseas empire and its development of an advanced navy only from the 1890s, it is hardly surprising that Germany did not make much of an impact with its navy's armoured cruisers. Like the Imperial German navy's battleships, these were typified by a primary armament of guns which were of smaller calibre but higher firing rate than those of other navies, and a heavier secondary armament. Another feature of Germany's armoured cruisers was the indifferent suiting of their guns. The last two such cruisers, classified by the Germans as heavy cruisers, were SMS *Scharnhorst* and SMS *Gneisenau*, completed in October 1907 and March 1908 by Blohm & Voss and Weser respectively.

The design was essentially a larger and faster version of the preceding two "Roon" class vessels with a similar protection scheme but double the number of main guns (four in two twin turrets on the centreline fore and aft, and the four additional guns mounted in casemates at the corners of the midships citadel at upper-deck level) and a scaled-down secondary armament. The two ships' British counterparts generally carried a smaller number of larger-calibre main guns or a similar but better disposed number of slightly smaller-calibre guns.

The two ships were the main strength of Admiral Graf von Spee's East Asia Squadron in China at the start of World War I, and von Spee headed across the Pacific to round Cape horn and get back to Germany. In the Battle of Coronel the German ships destroyed an ineffectual British force, and von Spee then led his squadron, comprising the *Scharnhorst* and *Gneisenau* and the three light cruisers SMS *Nürnberg*, SMS *Leipzig* and SMS *Dresden*, round Cape Horn and into the Atlantic. Meanwhile the British had despatched the battle-cruisers HMS *Invincible* and HMS *Inflexible* under Admiral Sir Doveton Sturdee to the Falkland Islands, where they were joined by the cruisers HMS *Kent*, HMS *Cornwall* and HMS *Glasgow*. The battle-cruisers reached the Falklands on December 7, and were coaling when the German squadron was sighted off the harbour. Realising

that he was confronted with an altogether superior force (the battle-cruisers each carried eight 12-in/305-mm guns), von Spee made off to the southeast at the highest speed his ships could manage after a long time in warm waters, but the British ships quickly got under way and set off in pursuit After a long-range action lasting four hours, the *Gneisenau* was sunk, followed 105 minutes later by the *Scharnhorst.*

Of the German squadron's remaining ships, the *Nürnberg* and the *Leipzig* were also sunk, but the *Dresden* escaped, only to blow herself up three months later when discovered by the cruisers *Kent* and *Glasgow* in the port of Mas a Fuera. The British losses during the Battle of the Falkland Islands were minimal, but the Germans suffered the loss of almost 2,000 men.

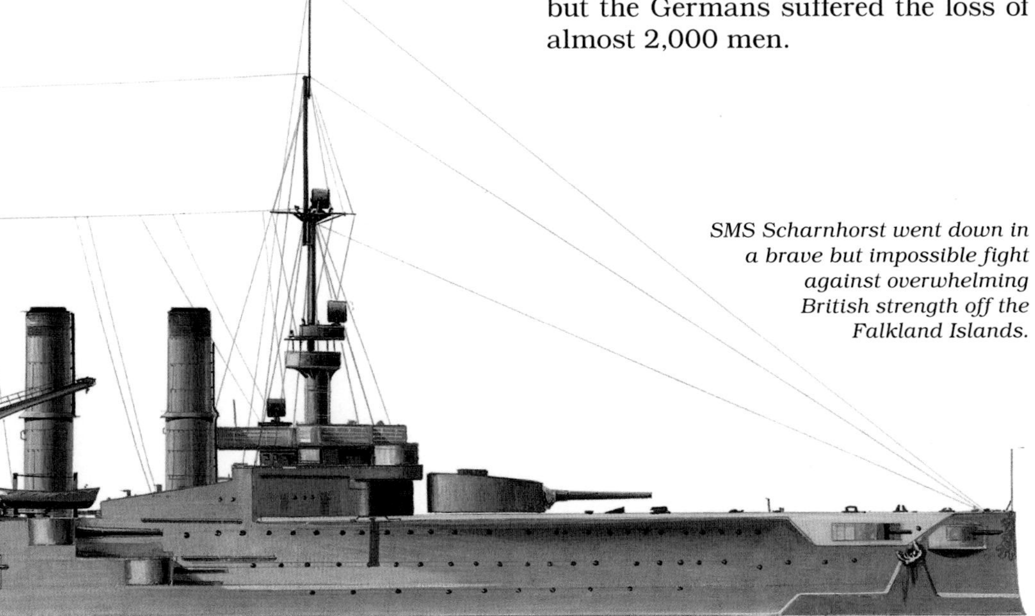

SMS Scharnhorst went down in a brave but impossible fight against overwhelming British strength off the Falkland Islands.

SMS *Scharnhorst*

Type:	armoured cruiser
Tonnage:	12,781 tons displacement
Dimensions:	length 474 ft 9 in (144.6 m); beam 71 ft (21.6 m); draft 27 ft 6 in (8.4 m)
Propulsion:	three triple expansion steam engines delivering 30,000 ihp (22368 kW) to three propellers for 23.5 kt
Armour:	5.9-in (150-mm) belt and 2-in (50-mm) deck
Armament:	eight 8.27-in (210-mm) guns, six 5.9-in (150-mm) guns, 18 3.45-in (88-mm) guns, four machine guns and four 17.7-in (450-mm) torpedo tubes
Complement:	764

Aurora (1903)

The Russian protected cruiser Aurora has a particular niche in world history as the vessel from which the first shot of the Bolshevik Revolution was fired in 1917. The Russian navy's earlier protected cruiser classes were the two-ship "Vitiaz" and one-ship "Admiral Kornilov" and "Svietlana" classes completed in 1886/97. Then came the "Pallada" class whose three units were the Pallada, Diana and Aurora completed in 1902/03 for Far Eastern service.

Though more modern than their predecessors, the "Pallada" class cruisers were still notable for a trio of tall, wire-stayed funnels in combination with a forecastle deck which extended as far back as the main mast. The main armament was eight 6-in (152-mm) guns. One of these was mounted forward of the bridge structure on the forecastle deck, another four in sponsons at upper-deck level near the bridge and fore funnel, and three aft as one centreline weapon and one on each beam abaft the main mast. Defense against light vessels was vested in quick-firing weapons, of which the most important were the 24 11-pdr guns on the main and upper decks. Two more 6-in (152-mm) guns were later added abreast the main mast, and in World War I the Aurora's main armament was further increased to 14 6-in (152-mm) guns, while the Diana had her 6-in (152-mm) guns replaced by 10 5.1-in (130-mm) guns.

All three ships served during the Russo-Japanese War (1904/05), the Pallada being torpedoed but not badly damaged in February 1904 before being sunk by land-based howitzer fire in December 1904. The ship was raised and placed in Imperial Japanese navy service as the Tsugaru, which was scrapped in 1923. The

The Aurora at sea.

The historic breech of one of the Aurora's 6-in (152-mm) guns.

Photos: J. Batchelor

The rebuilt Aurora as a memorial in the River Neva in St Petersburg.

Diana was interned in Saigon after the Battle of the Yellow Sea, but was then released, served in World War I and was scrapped in 1922. The Aurora was part of the Russian 2nd Pacific Squadron formed mostly from the Baltic Fleet and sent to the Pacific. On 27/28 May 1905, together with the rest of the Russian force, the Aurora was involved in the Battle of Tsushima, but managed to avoid being destroyed: with two other cruisers she broke through to internment in neutral Manila. In 1906 the Aurora returned to the Baltic and became a cadet training ship before serving in World War I.

At the end of 1916 the ship was moved to Petrograd (later Leningrad and now St Petersburg) for a major refit. The city was on the verge of revolution, and part of her crew joined the February 1917 rising. The ship's crew created a revolutionary committee, and most of the crewmen joined the Bolshevik faction preparing for a communist revolution. On October 25, (now November 7), a blank shot from her forecastle gun signalled the start of the attack on the Winter Palace and the outbreak of the Bolshevik revolution. In 1922 the Aurora was restored to service as a training ship, and in World War II the ship's guns were removed for the land defence of Leningrad. The ship was repeatedly shelled and bombed, being sunk in September 1941. After repairs in 1945/47, the Aurora was anchored as a monument.

Aurora (as completed)

Type:	protected cruiser
Tonnage:	6,731 tons displacement
Dimensions:	length 415 ft 8 in (126.7 m); beam 55 ft (16.75 m); draft 20 ft 10 in (6.35 m)
Propulsion:	three vertical triple expansion steam engines delivering 13,000 ihp (9693 kW) to three propellers for 19 kt
Armour:	2-in (50-mm) deck with 3-in (76-mm) slopes, 2.5-in (64-mm) funnel uptakes, 1.5-in (38-mm) ammunition hoists, and 6-in (152-mm) conning tower
Armament:	eight 6-in (152-mm) guns, 24 11-pdr guns, eight 1-pdr guns, and three 15-in (381-mm) torpedo tubes
Complement:	571

USS *California* (1921)

In 1913/14 the US Navy asked for new battleships with a displacement of some 35,500 tons and the primary armament of 10 16-in (406-mm) guns in five twin turrets. For financial reasons, the Secretary of the Navy refused this major increase in individual ship tonnage and decided that the two "New Mexico" class battleships now to be ordered would be repeats of the preceding pair of "Pennsylvania" class ships with 12 14-in (356-mm) guns in four triple turrets and also any low-cost improvements could be worked into the basic design. To counter earlier capital ships' tendency to wetness forward, the new design had a clipper bow, and 12 of the 22 5-in (127-mm) L/51 secondary guns were mounted in casemates one deck higher than in the preceding class. Only one of the ships, eventually three in number, was completed with all 22 guns, but the bow and after positions were soon plated in, reducing the number of guns to 14 including two above the deckhouse. The other major change was in the main armament, which was based on an L/50 rather than L/45 guns in mountings allowing fully independent elevation. Careful design allowed a thickening of some of the protection without any increase in displacement, and one of the ships, the USS *New Mexico*, tested a turbo-electric propulsion system proposed by General Electric as an alternative to geared steam turbines.

The three "New Mexicos" (two had been planned but the third was

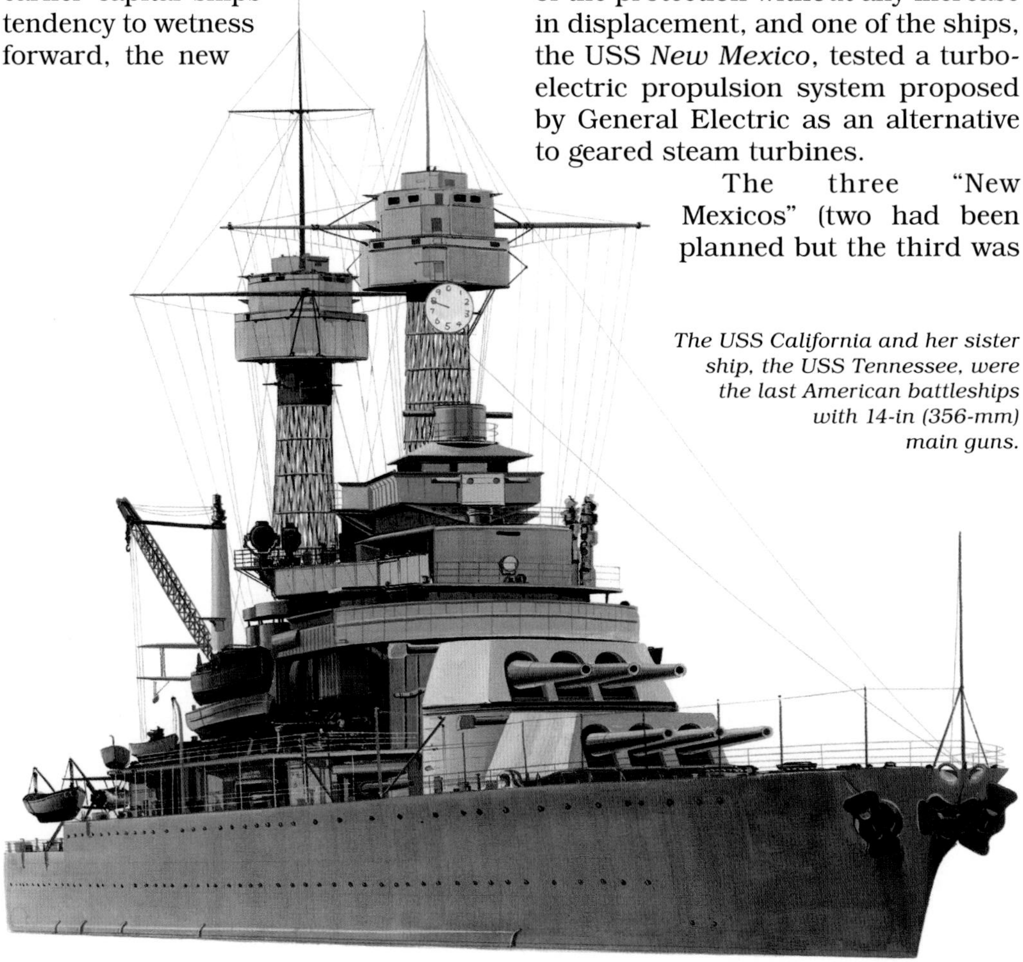

The USS California and her sister ship, the USS Tennessee, were the last American battleships with 14-in (356-mm) main guns.

added after two pre-dreadnoughts had been sold to Greece) were followed by the USS *Tennessee* and USS *California* of the "Tennessee" class, which was the last with 14-in (356-mm) guns. Developed from the "New Mexico" design, the primary change was a major enhancement of the underwater protection after the revelation that liquid- and air-filled compartments could better absorb the explosion of a torpedo warhead. Thus the ships had five bulkheads on each side to create air-filled outer and inner compartments round three liquid-filled compartments. Inboard of this torpedo protection, each boiler was in its own compartment, this constituting a type of inner protective layer. There were two large turbo-generators on the centreline.

The pilothouse and forward superstructure were considerably enlarged. The cage masts were of a new and heavier type less prone to the vibration that adversely affected fire control, and each carried a two-level enclosed top whose upper and lower levels were dedicated to main and secondary armament control respectively. The elevation of the main guns was increased from 15° to 30°.

The ships were completed, at New York and Mare Island Navy Yards during June 1920 and August 1921 respectively, in a slightly modified form with no hull-mounted secondary guns and the hulls faired over the casemates of the original design. The decision to use turbo-electric propulsion was bold as the machinery took up more space, was heavier and needed careful insulation, but its use obviated the need for separate reversing turbines, and allowed rapid change from ahead to astern drive. However, the ships were comparatively slow.

The AA defences were bolstered in 1928, but few other changes were made before World War II. Both ships were damaged at Pearl Harbor, and reconstructed with a revised dual-purpose secondary armament comprising, by 1945, 16 5-in (127-mm) L/38 guns, as well as a dedicated short-range AA armament comprising 40 40-mm and 50 20-mm guns.

Both ships served extensively in the Pacific until the end of World War II, and both survived kamikaze attacks early in 1945. They were then mothballed and sold for scrap in 1959.

USS *California*

Type:	battleship
Tonnage:	34,000 tons full load
Dimensions:	length 624 ft 6 in (190.7 m); beam 92 ft 3 in (29.7 m); draft 30 ft 3 in (9.2 m)
Propulsion:	two steam turbines and three electric motors delivering 30,908 shp (23045 kW) to four propellers for 21 kt
Armour:	8/14-in (203/356-mm) belt, 2.5/5-in (64/127-mm) decks, 13-in (330-mm) barbettes, 9/18-in (229/457-mm) turrets, and 16-in (406-mm) conning tower
Armament:	12 14-in (356-mm) guns, 14 5-in (127-mm) guns, four 3-in (76-mm) AA guns, four 6-pdr QF guns, two 1-pdr QF guns, and two 21-in (533-mm) torpedo tubes
Complement:	1,083

HMS *Dreadnought* (1906)

The completion of the battleship HMS *Dreadnought* in December 1906 was a decisive moment in warship design, for this British vessel was the world's first "all big gun ship" and also the first capital ship with all-turbine propulsion. There was nothing basically radical about the armament of 10 12-in (305-mm) guns in five twin turrets rather than a mixed battery of four 12-in (305-mm) and a powerful battery of secondary guns, for designers in Italy and the USA had already planned such ships. The concept had also been presaged by the introduction of intermediate-calibre guns in several battleship classes early in the 20th century, but all knew that the combination of large- and intermediate-calibre guns on the same ship raised the problems of fire control, armament layout, and ammunition stowage and handling.

The chief British advocate of the "all big gun" battleship was Admiral Sir John Fisher, who started to consider the matter in 1900 and then collaborated with W. H. Gard on the evolution of the type in several "Untakeable" designs. Fisher's thinking was based on a primary armament of 10-in (254-mm) guns as these offered a considerably higher rate of fire than the 12-in (305-mm) guns of the period. Several of the captains whose opinions Fisher valued said that they preferred the 12-in (305-mm) weapon for its much greater "kill" capability, however, and by the time Fisher became First Sea Lord in October 1904 the "Untakeable" had evolved into Design B with eight 12-in (305-mm) guns. The interest sparked by this design was largely responsible for the establishment in December 1904 of a Committee on Designs with Fisher as its chairman.

The committee considered new battleship and battle-cruiser designs: the former was planned round a speed of 21kt, adequate armour,

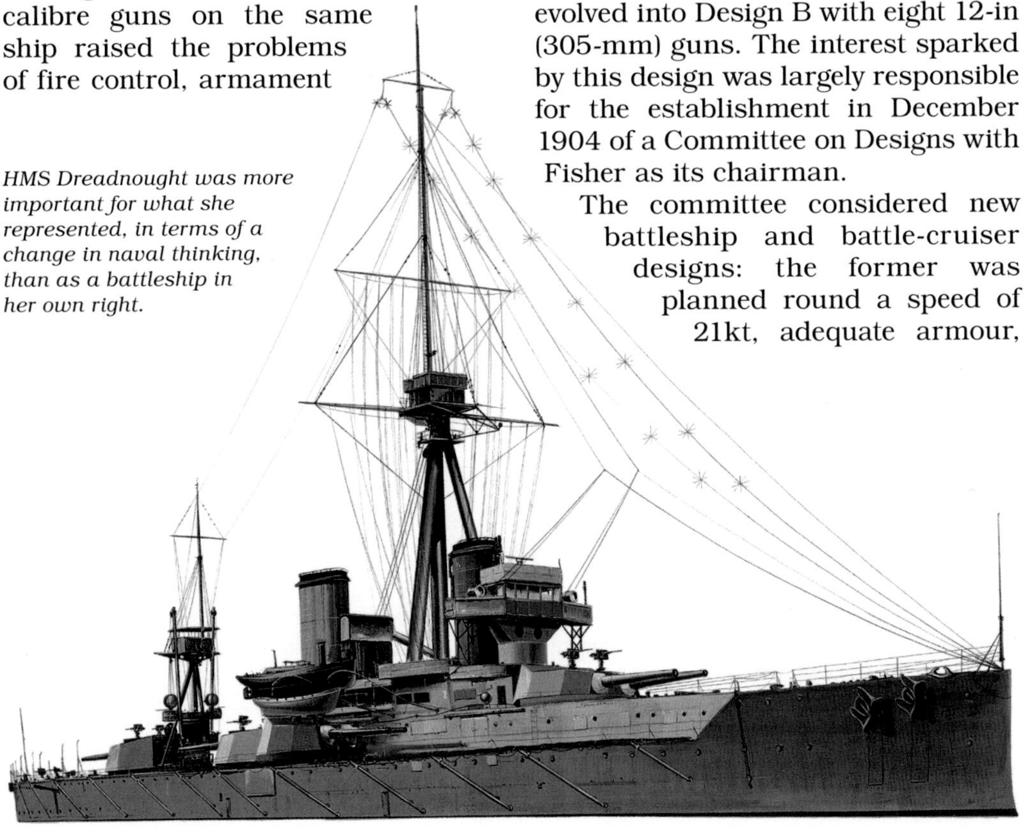

HMS Dreadnought was more important for what she represented, in terms of a change in naval thinking, than as a battleship in her own right.

and an armament of 12-in (305-mm) and anti-torpedo boat guns with nothing in the way of a conventional secondary battery. Several plans were considered, the primary difficulties being Fisher's demands for end-on rather than broadside fire capability and his demand for speed even at the expense of protection. Among the projects considered were three with reciprocating machinery and 12 12-in (305-mm) guns: "E" with two groups of three superfiring twin turrets, "D" with six twin turrets in two triangular groups before and abaft the superstructure, and "G" with six twin turrets located two on the centreline fore and aft and two on each beam. Finally came "H" with steam turbine machinery and 10 12-in (305-mm) guns in five twin turrets located as three on the centreline and one on each beam.

It was the last which emerged as the *Dreadnought*, which stunned the world not only with her power but with her completion in a mere 366 days, the latter attributable in part to the capabilities of Portsmouth Dock Yard and part to the use of turrets already built for the "Lord Nelson" class ships.

A widely spaced armament disposition was chosen to reduce the chance of a single hit knocking out more than one turret, and to reconcile an eight-gun broadside with Fisher's demand for end-on fire by at least four guns in a ship without superfiring turrets. The light armament of 27 12-pdr QF guns was later changed to 10 12-pdr guns, two 3-pdr AA guns and two 12-pdr AA guns. Fire control was at first inadequate, but improved by the fitting of director firing in 1915. The *Dreadnought* did not fire her guns in anger at a surface target in World War I, was sold for scrap in 1921 and broken up in 1923.

HMS *Dreadnought*

Type:	battleship
Tonnage:	21,845 tons full load
Dimensions:	length 527 ft (160.4 m); beam 82 ft 1 in (25 m); draft 26 ft 6 in (8.1 m)
Propulsion:	four steam turbines delivering 26,350 shp (19647 kW) to four propellers for 21.6 kt
Armour:	8/11-in (203/281-mm) belt, 4/6-in (102/153-mm) belt ends, 11-in (281-mm) bulkheads, 0.75/4-in (19/102-mm) decks, 4/11-in (102/281-mm) barbettes, 3/11-in (76/281-mm) turrets, and 8/11-in (203/281-mm) conning tower
Armament:	10 12-in (254-mm) guns, 27 12-pdr QF guns and five 18-in (457-mm) torpedo tubes
Complement:	773

HMS *Marshal Soult* (1915)

Although it had already ordered eight monitors each armed with two 12-in (305-mm) guns, the Royal Navy decided in January 1915 to order, from Palmer of Newcastle, two more heavy monitors each armed with two 15-in (381-mm) guns. This required a much enlarged hull, but the draft was still not to exceed 10 ft (3.05 m) and, to facilitate docking, the beam to be no more than 90 ft (27.4 m). The trickiest technical problem to be solved in this "Marshal Soult" class was how to provide room in a shallow hull for the ammunition trunk, and the solution was found in a 17-ft (5.2-m) extension of the barbette above the deck. Diesel propulsion was demanded, so the machinery of two fleet oilers was used.

Many of the errors typical of earlier monitors were perpetuated; power was so small that speed was very low and the ships almost impossible to steer. It had been hoped to use the turrets being fabricated as the proposed fourth turrets of the battle-cruisers HMS *Renown* and HMS *Repulse*, but these would not be available until 1916 so HMS *Marshal Ney* and HMS *Marshal Soult* were completed with turrets diverted from HMS *Ramillies*.

The results of the Ney's machinery trials were so dismal that serious consideration was given to stopping work on both ships and transferring the turrets to other vessels. As completed, the ships had very small funnels, which combined with the tall tripod mast and huge turret to offer a strange appearance. The *Ney* had her 15-in (381-mm) turret removed early in 1916 for use in HMS *Terror*, and was then towed to Portsmouth to be fitted with one 9.2-in (234-mm) and four 6-in (152-mm) guns. In March 1917 she received two more 6-in (152-mm) guns, and the *Soult* received one (and later another two) 6-in (152-mm) guns as well as one 3-in (76-mm) AA gun on the forecastle deck. More significantly, the 15-in (381-mm) gun turret

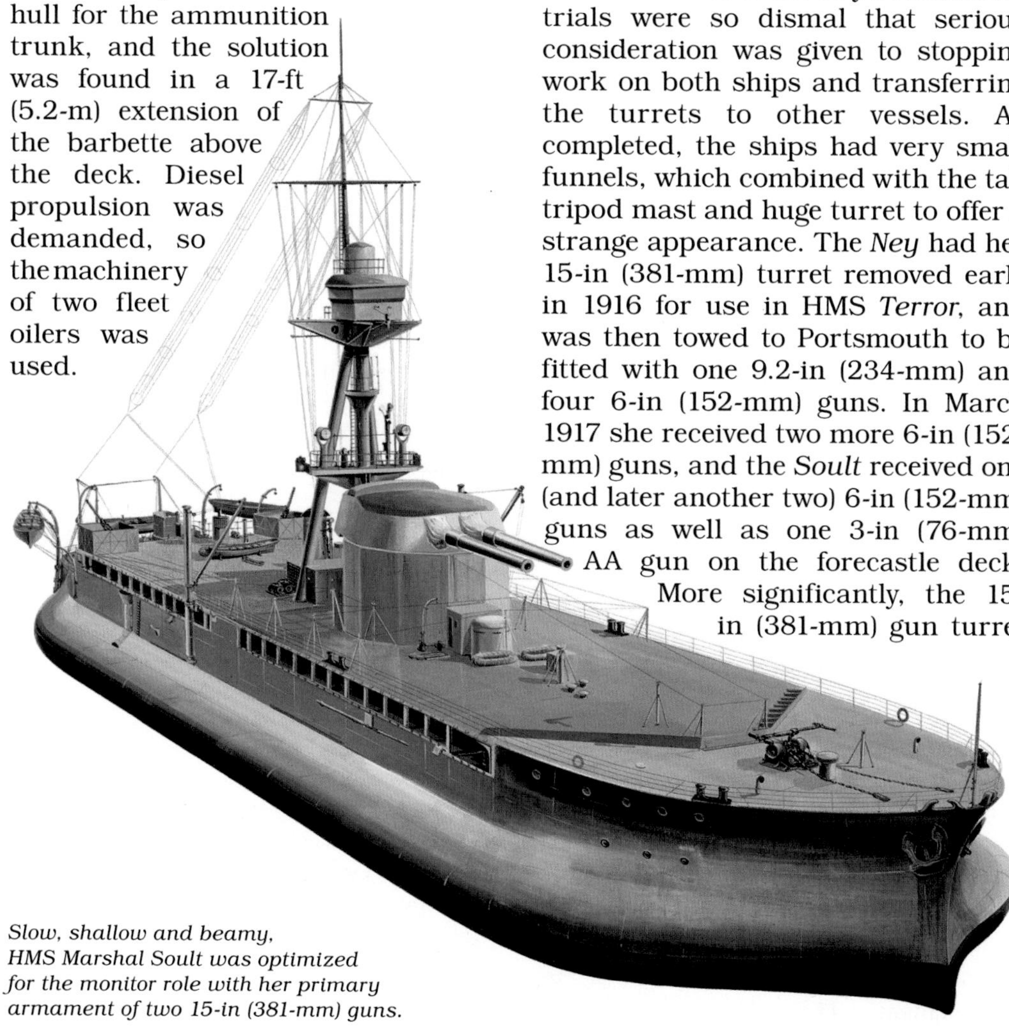

Slow, shallow and beamy, HMS Marshal Soult was optimized for the monitor role with her primary armament of two 15-in (381-mm) guns.

The monitor HMS Marshal Soult.

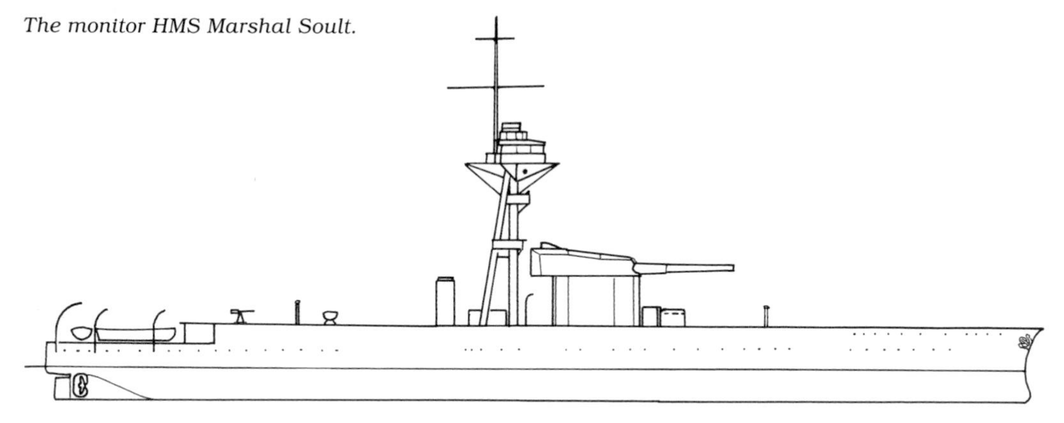

was modified to increase the guns' elevation angle to 30° and the range to 30,000 yards (27430 m). During 1918 the 6-in (152-mm) guns were replaced by eight 4-in (102-mm) guns, the funnel was made much taller, and a pair of 2-pdr AA guns was added aft. The *Ney* lost her armament in 1920, but the *Soult* remained essentially unaltered until she was disarmed in 1940.

The *Soult* joined the Dover Patrol in December 1915. After modification and refit, the monitor returned to Chatham late in October 1918 and was sent to Portsmouth as tender to HMS *Excellent*, the gunnery school She performed similar duties at Devonport in 1919/21, was then paid off before being brought back into service to relieve HMS *Glorious* as a gunnery training ship, refitted in 1924/25, and moved to Chatham in April 1926 to relieve HMS *Erebus*. She remained at Chatham for 14 years and was considered for a return to active service before the poor state of her hull was appreciated, and in March 1940 her turret was removed for use in the new monitor HMS *Roberts*. From December 1940 she served as a depot ship until paid off in March 1946 for breaking.

The *Ney* was completed in August 1915, but was plagued by problems with her diesel engines and steering, and was effectively withdrawn in December 1916, being stripped of her main armament and fitted with lighter weapons as a guardship. From December 1918 she was a base ship, and was sold for breaking in 1957.

HMS *Marshal Soult*

Type:	monitor
Tonnage:	6,900 tons deep load
Dimensions:	length 355 ft 8 in (108.4 m); beam 90 ft 3 in (27.5 m); draft 10 ft 5 in (3.2 m)
Propulsion:	two Vickers diesel engines delivering 1,500 bhp (1118.5 kW) to two propellers for 6 kt
Armour:	4-in (102-mm) internal belt and bulkheads, 1/4-in (25/102-mm) deck, 8-in (203-mm) barbette, 13-in (330mm) turret face, and 6-in (152-mm) conning tower
Armament:	two 15-in (381-mm) guns, two 12-pdr QF guns and one 3-pdr AA gun
Complement:	187

Georges Leygues (1936)

The French navy underwent as profound technical if not numerical revivification from the first half of the 1920s, the emphasis being in general an improved maritime capability and in detail the establishment and maintenance of a qualitative edge over the Italian navy. Within this effort the French created a number of impressive warship designs, most notably in the battleship, cruiser and destroyer categories. The single most important moment in the development of the French cruiser probably came with the authorization in the 1930 building program of the *Emile Benin*. This was originally envisaged as an improved version of the *Pluton* unarmoured minelaying cruiser, but in the design process gradually became more of a cruiser than a minelayer. This is reflected in the fact that the ship, completed in 1934, was used before World War II's outbreak in 1939 mainly as the flagship of a flotilla of 12 "Le Malin" and "Maillé Brézé" heavy destroyers. The most important development in the *Emile Bertin* was a new triple mounting for the 6-in (152-mm) modèle 1930 L/50 gun, which fired a 119.7-lb (54.3-kg) shell to a distance of 23,515 yards (21500 m).

The *Emile Bertin* was followed into service by the six units of the "La Galissonnière" class, namely *La Galissonnière*, *Jean de Vienne*, *La Marseillaise*, *La Gloire*, *Montcalm* and *Georges Leygues*. The design was a significantly improved version of that of the *Emile Bertin*, carrying much the same gun armament but with much improved protection. The design underwent considerable change during construction, and this inevitably delayed completion to the extent that the ships, which were built at different yards, entered service between December 1935 and December 1937 after being laid down between 1931 and 1933. The long gestation period also meant that the ships fell into two sub-classes comprising the first two and the last four units. A notable feature of the "La Galissonnière" class was the long and uncluttered quarterdeck, created to ease the launching of floatplanes, of which four could be accommodated in a hangar abaft the second funnel, by means of a single catapult on the after 6-in (152-mm) turret.

With the exception of *La Marseillaise* and *Montcalm*, all of the ships had their AA armament boosted in 1941 by the addition of one 37-mm and two 25-mm guns as well as four 13.2-mm machine guns. Three of the ships were scuttled by their crews in Toulon as the Germans seized

Georges Leygues

Type:	cruiser
Tonnage:	9,100 tons full load
Dimensions:	length 588 ft 11 in (179.5 m); beam 57 ft 4 in (17.5 m); draft 17 ft 7 in (5.35 m)
Propulsion:	two geared steam turbines delivering 84,000 shp (62630 kW) to two propellers for 31+ kt
Armour:	3.9-in (100-mm) belt, 2.5-in (65-mm) bulkheads, 0.75-in (20-mm) longitudinal bulkheads, 1.6-in (40-mm) main deck, 3.9-in (100-mm) main turret faces, 2-in (50-mm) main turret sides, backs and roofs, and 3.75-in (95-mm) conning tower
Armament:	nine 6-in (152-mm) guns, eight 3.5-in (90-mm) AA guns, eight 37-mm AA guns, 12 13.2-mm AA machine guns, four 21,7-in (550-mm) torpedo tubes, and four aircraft
Complement:	764

Vichy France in the aftermath of the Allied landings in French North-West Africa during November 1942. The *Georges Leygues*, last unit of the class and completed in December 1937 after construction by the Aciers et Chantiers de St Nazaire-Penhoët, was one of the three "La Galissonnière" class cruisers not in France at this time. When the British attacked Dakar in French West Africa during 1940, the ship sailed with *La Gloire* and *Montcalm* to intervene, reaching Dakar with the *Montcalm* and then being blockaded there until French West Africa went over to the Allies in November 1942. together with *La Gloire*, which had got only as far as Casablanca in 1940, the three cruisers were refitted in the USA during 1943. All floatplane provision was removed, and the light AA armament was changed to six quadruple 40-mm guns and 16 single 20-mm cannon. Radar was also fitted. A further refit was carried out in 1945 when the ships acquired a lattice fore topmast to carry new radar. Even so, the ships could still make 32 kt at a full-load displacement increased to 10,850 tons. The ships had active careers after World War II, and the *Georges Leygues* was sold for breaking only in 1959.

La Galissonnière (1931)

From the mid-1920s France came to see her potential enemies as German in a land campaign, and Italy in a naval campaign in the Mediterranean. During his period the Italian navy was much enlarged and modernized with new and impressive warship classes typified by great design flair and an effective combination of speed and firepower. The revival of Germany as a naval power from the late 1920s opened the possibility of a two-front naval war, and France responded to the threat of the "Deutschland" class pocket battleships with the 29.5-kt fast battleships *Dunkerque* and *Strasbourg*.

The effective use of these two units demanded capable screening and scouting forces based on light cruisers and large destroyers capable of notably high speeds. The cruisers were the six units of the "La

Galissonnière" class based ultimately on the Emile Bertin with considerable freeboard for oceanic capability and upgraded protection for improved survivability against 6-in (152-mm) fire. The design was notably attractive, and came to be generally regarded as the most successful French cruiser design comparing favorably with the best of current types in service with other nations' navies in terms of speed and seaworthiness. However, the pace of the whole program was badly affected by the decision, taken as the ships were being built, to modify the design: as well as delayed completion, this decision meant that the ships were completed as two sub-classes comprising the first two units (built by the Arsenals de Brest and Lorient) and the last four units (built by four different private yards). The ships were *La Galissonnière*, *Jean de Vienne*, *La Marseillaise*, *La Gloire*, *Montcalm* and *George Leygues*, which were completed between December 31, 1935 and December 4, 1937, the latter day seeing the completion of the last three ships simultaneously.

The ships were designed on the basis of a rated power of 97,600 shp (72771kW) for a speed of 32.5 kt< but on trials each of the ships exceeded this rated figure with a recorded power of more than 100,000 shp (74560 kW) for 35/36 kt maintained over a period of up to eight hours. The primary armament was nine 6-in (152-mm) guns, which were mounted in triple turrets disposed as a superfiring pair forward and a singleton aft. This last carried a catapult, and a hangar abaft the second funnel housed four aircraft. Except for *La Marseillaise* and *Montcalm*, the ships had one 37-mm, two 25-mm and four 13.2-mm AA guns added in 1941. After being scuttled, The first three ships were scuttled in Toulon on November 27,

The Montcalm was one of the four units of the second sub-class.

La Galissonnière and her sister ships were impressive and capable light cruisers.

1942 so that they would not fall into German hands. *La Galissonnière* was refloated by the Italians in 1943 but was bombed by Allied aircraft in August 1944 before being refitted, and *Jean de Vienne* suffered the same fate in November 1943. The remaining three were refitted in the USA in 1943, the hangar and aircraft equipment being removed, radar being added, and the light AA armament replaced by six quadruple 40-mm and 16 single 20-mm guns. Radar was also fitted. A further refit was carried out in 1945 when the ships acquired a lattice fore topmast to carry new radar. The ships had active careers after World War II: *La Gloire* and *Georges Leygues* were sold for breaking in the later 1950s, and the Montcalm was finally an accommodation ship 1970.

La Galissonnière

Type:	light cruiser
Tonnage:	9,100 tons full load
Dimensions:	length 588 ft 11 in (179.5 m); beam 57 ft 4 in (17.5 m); draft 17 ft 7 in (5.35 m)
Propulsion:	two geared steam turbines delivering 84,000 shp (62630 kW) to two propellers for 31 kt
Armour:	3.9-in (100-mm) belt, 2.5-in (55-mm) bulkheads, 0.75-in (20-mm) longitudinal bulkheads, 1.5-in (40-mm) main deck, 2/3.9-in (50/100-mm) turrets, and 2/3.75-in (50/95-mm) conning tower
Armament:	nine 6-in (152-mm) guns, eight 90-mm (3.5-in) AA guns, eight 37-mm AA guns, 12 13.2-mm) AA guns, four 21.7-in (550-mm) torpedo tubes, and four aircraft
Complement:	764

Myoko (1929)

In the early 1920s Vice Admiral Yuzuru Hiraga started work on the design of a new class of heavy cruisers right to the displacement limit of 10,000 tons fixed by the Washington Naval Treaty of 1922. The design was based on a main armament of 10 7.9-in (200-mm) guns, and was intended to provide the Imperial Japanese navy with an altogether superior heavy cruiser. Hiraga certainly achieved his objective, but the "Nachi" class cruisers considerably exceeded the treaty's displacement limit.

The protection of the "Nachi" class ships was notably impressive by contemporary standards, and based on the use of inclined armour, whose thickness was 1 in (25 mm) greater than that of the preceding "Aoba" class ships. The belt and main deck armour were 410 ft (125 m) long and covered the machinery and boiler spaces. Protection against torpedo attack also featured prominently in the form of an arched protective bulkhead inside the armour belt and a triple hull.

The ships of this class were the *Myoko, Nachi, Haguro* and *Ashigara*, which were laid down in 1924/25 at Yokosuka Navy Yard, Kure Navy Yard, Mitsubishi at Nagasaki and Kawasaki at Kobe within the context of the 1923 New Reinforcement effort and completed between November 1928 and August 1929 with a primary armament of 10 7.9-in (200-mm) guns in five twin turrets (three forward with "B" turret above "A" and "C" turrets, and a superfiring pair aft). The rest of the armament comprised six 4.7-in (120-mm) single AA guns and four sets of triple fixed 24-in (610-mm) torpedo tubes on the main deck. The notional tonnage had risen from the designed 10,000 tons to 10,940 tons, and the trials tonnage was 12,178 tons.

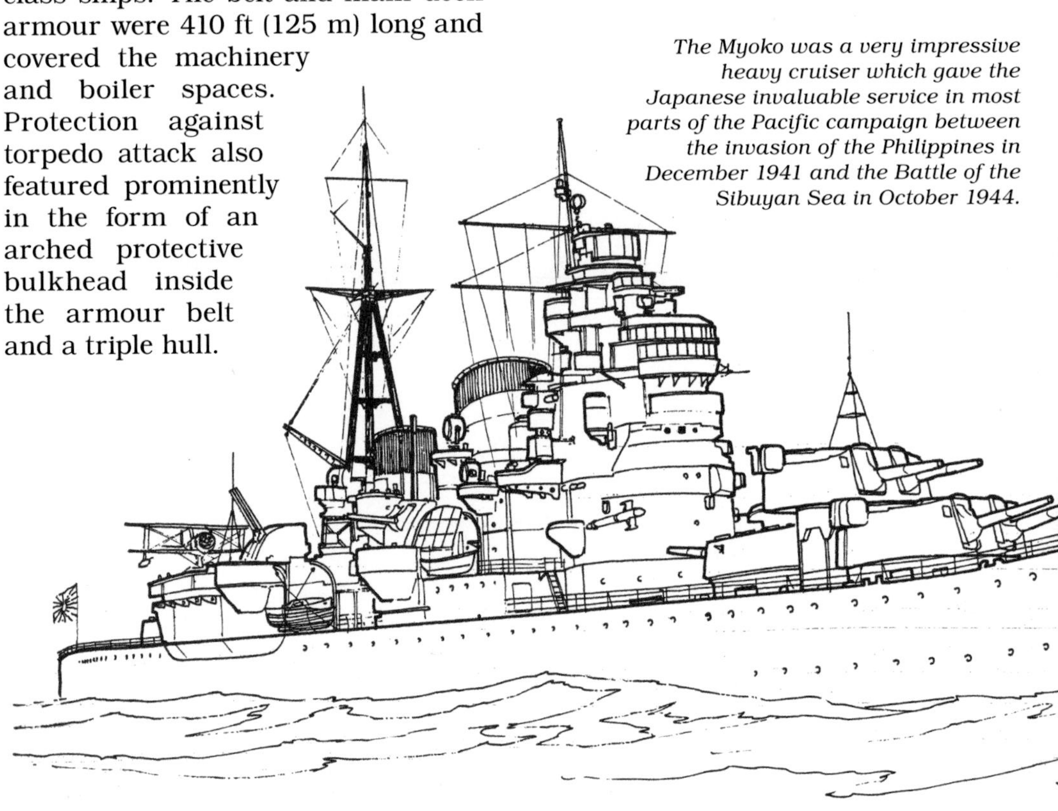

The Myoko was a very impressive heavy cruiser which gave the Japanese invaluable service in most parts of the Pacific campaign between the invasion of the Philippines in December 1941 and the Battle of the Sibuyan Sea in October 1944.

Myoko (after 1940 modernization)

Type:	heavy cruiser
Tonnage:	13,380 tons
Dimensions:	length 661 ft 9 in (201.7 m); beam 68 ft (20.7 m); draft 20 ft 9 in (6.3 m)
Propulsion:	four geared steam turbines delivering 130,000 shp (96928 kW) to four propellers for 33.75 kt
Armour:	3.9-in (100-mm) belt, 1.5-in (40-mm) decks and turrets. And 3-in (75-mm) turret bases
Armament:	10 8-in (203-mm) guns, eight 5-in (127-mm) AA guns, eight 25-mm AA guns, four 13-mm AA machine guns, 16 24-in (610-mm) torpedo tubes, and two aircraft
Complement:	more than 773

In 1934/36 the four cruisers were taken in hand for a major refit in which the 4.7-in (120-mm) guns were removed and waterline bulges were added, the latter increasing the beam from 56 ft 9 in (17.3 m) to 68 ft (20.7 m). The latter made it possible for the superstructure to be extended from the fore funnel to "X" turret, in turn permitting the addition of the 5-in (127-mm) AA twin mountings on either beam abreast the funnels. The single centreline catapult was replaced by two deck-edge catapults, and the fixed torpedo tubes were replaced by two quadruple 24-in (610-mm) mountings abaft the catapults on the upper deck. New directors for the 5-in (127-mm) guns were also shipped, and the floatplane complement was increased to two.

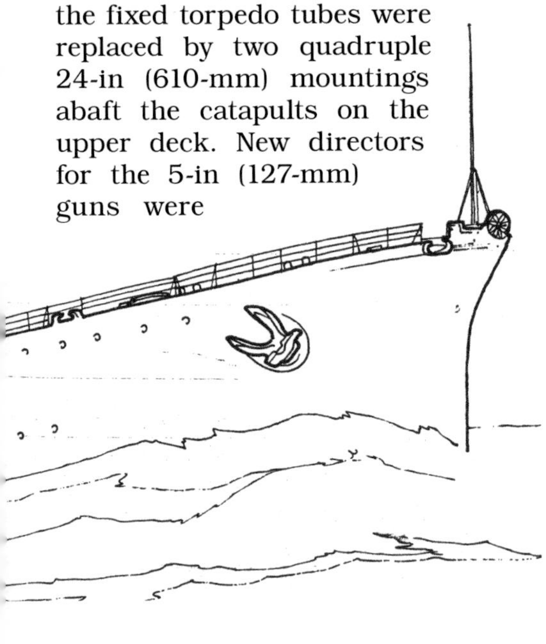

In 1938/41 the ships were subjected to a major modernization whose core was the replacement of the 7.9-in (200-mm) guns by 8-in (203-mm) weapons characterized by a higher muzzle velocity and greater range. Other major changes were the modernization of the bridge and all the control centers and the addition of two more quadruple torpedo tube mounts forward of each catapult on the upper deck. Four twin 25-mm AA guns were added round the funnels and two twin 13-mm AA machine guns in the bridge. The *Myoko* also received four triple 25-mm AA guns. These changes boosted the *Myoko's* displacement to 13,380 tons with 24 torpedoes and lattice fore mast in place of the original pole mast.

The ships had very full careers in World War II, the light AA armament being significantly boosted in May 1944 24 and by June 1944 to 52 25-mm guns. The *Nachi* was lost to air attack in November 1944, the *Myoko* survived to be scuttled after the war, the *Haguro* was sunk by gun fire and torpedoes in May 1945, and the *Ashigara* was sunk by torpedo in June 1945.

S-boote (1939)

It was not made completely clear in 1919 by the Treaty of Versailles, which ended the involvement of Germany in World War I, whether or not the small navy still permitted to Germany was allowed the type of vessels now known as fast attack craft. Thus the German navy initially undertook studies into such coastal craft in great secrecy. During 1923/26 the service bought six ex-imperial German navy "LM" type boats, and in the course of 1926 the Abeking & Rasmussen firm completed the experimental 40-kt *K* based on a British type, the Thornycroft 55-ft (16.75-ft) CMB (Coastal Motor Boat) type, while for competitive trials purposes Lürssen and the Caspar Werft at Travemünde delivered the 33.5-kt *Lux* and 34.8-kt *Narwal* respectively. In 1929 the boats were all reclassified as U-Bootszerstörern (submarine destroyers) and renamed *UZ11* to *UZ18*. Most advances came from Lürssen, all successful S-boot (Schnellboot, or fast boat) designs coming from this firm in close collaboration with the navy's own design department.

Based on the successful design of the fast yacht *Oheka II* and the *Lux*, Lürssen built the first German MTB (motor torpedo boat) in 1930: this was originally named as the *UZ16*, but later became the *W1* and in 1932 the *S1*. Further designs show a steady class-by-class improvement. All the S-boote had two fixed bow torpedo tubes and two reload torpedoes, but in the "S700" group all four torpedoes were ready to fire, with two fixed stern tubes as well as two bow tubes.

In overall terms the navy of Nazi Germany commissioned 249 S-boote excluding ex-Italian, "LS," coastal and experimental boats. Of these, 157 were lost or scuttled and the 92 which survived were allocated as 30, 34 and 28 to the USA, UK and USSR respectively, the USA and UK pooling their craft for onward sale to countries such as Norway (15) and Denmark (14). The British know the S-boot as the E-boat.

The S-boot was based on a round-bilge hull with wooden planking on light alloy frames. This hull form was slower than the hard-chine hull of British equivalents, but was very much more seaworthy and therefore allowed the S-boot to sustain its maximum speed in sea states that

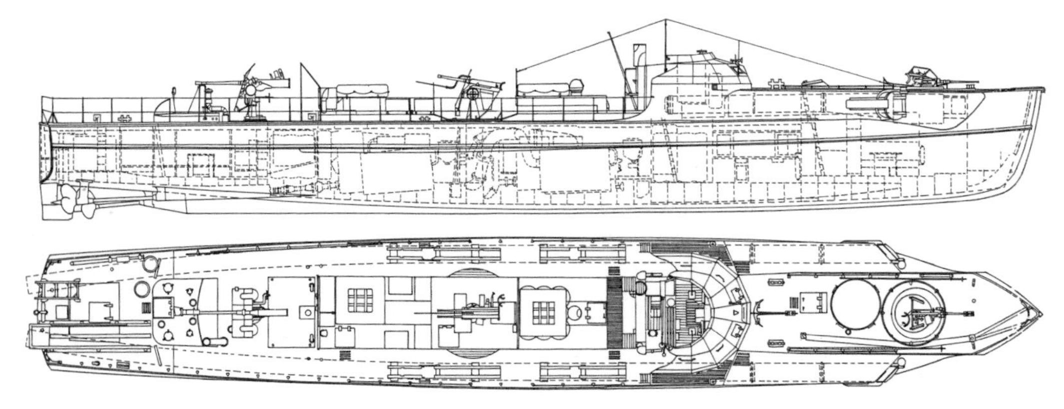

The German S-boote were larger and slower than British motor torpedo boats, but also quieter and better sea boats.

Being better sea boats, the S-boote could maintain speed more effectively than British motor torpedo boats in any sort of sea.

forced the British to throttle back to avoid excessive pounding. Diesel rather than gasoline engines were demanded from the beginning of the program, though the *S1* prototype of 1930 and the follow-on *S2-S5* of 1931/32 had to take gasoline engines while MAN and Daimler-Benz created suitable engines. Thus it was with the *S6-S13* of 1934/35 that three-shaft diesel propulsion became standard. These boats 106 ft 3 in (32.4 m) long and capable of 35 kt. This speed was thought too low, and in the next group the seven-cylinder diesels were succeeded by 11-cylinder units. Speed was increased but the hull length had to rise to 113 ft 8 in (34.7 m), and remained virtually constant to 1945.

The tubes were fitted forward of the wheelhouse, with space for two reloads abaft them. It was then standard from *S26* to raise the forecastle by 3 ft 3 in (1 m), so enclosing the tubes but leaving between them a gun pit and, just as importantly, providing greater freeboard. The gun armament was constantly increased to match that of Allied opponents, the extra weight being partially offset by improved weight-saving in the construction of the hull and by higher-powered engines. Protection was improved by the adoption of an armoured bridge.

"S100" class (1943-45)

Type:	fast attack craft (torpedo)
Tonnage:	100 tons displacement
Dimensions:	length 114 ft 8 in (34.9 m); beam 16 ft 9 in (5.1 m); draft 5 ft (1.5 m)
Propulsion:	three Daimler-Benz diesel engines delivering 7,500 bhp (5592 kW) to three propellers for 45 kt
Armour:	none
Armament:	two 21-in (533-mm) torpedo tubers with four torpedoes, one 40-mm gun and one 20-mm cannon
Complement:	21

HMS *Queen Elizabeth* (1939)

The "Queen Elizabeth" class of five battleships was designed to provide the Grand Fleet with a high-speed battleship capability in which protection would not be sacrificed to the demands of speed and firepower, and so remove the need for battle-cruisers as the new battleships could outgun as well as outspeed Germany's latest battleships. As such, the ships were the first in the world with 15-in (381-mm) guns, and also the first with oil-fired boilers having no provision for coal burning. As completed, these handsome ships had a distinctive appearance with two massive funnels, a heavy tripod fore mast and a lighter pole main mast.

HMS *Queen Elizabeth* was commissioned into Royal Navy service at Portsmouth in December 1914 and actually completed only on 19 January. In the next month the ship was dispatched to Mediterranean for service in Dardanelles, where she bombarded the Turkish coastal forts in the Narrows and offered gun fire support for the landings between February 25 and May 14, firing 86 15-in (381-mm) and 71 6-in (152-mm) shells. Lack of adequate 15-in (381-mm) shell supplies limited her role in the shore bombardment role, and the Admiralty had also issued strict instructions that the ship's main armament was not to be worn out. The ship departed for Gibraltar on May 14, reaching Scapa Flow on May 26 to join the Grand Fleet's 5th Battle Squadron. The ship was refitted at Rosyth between May 22 and June 4, 1916, and so missed the Battle of Jutland. In June 1916 the *Queen Elizabeth* became temporary flagship of the 5th BS, and between July 1916 and February 1917 she was refitted once again before being recommissioned as the flagship of the Grand Fleet, a position she held for the rest of World War I. The surrender of the German High Seas Fleet was signed on board the *Queen Elizabeth* on November 15, 1918, and she was the flagship of the Atlantic Fleet between July 1919 and July 1924, when she became the flagship of the Mediterranean Fleet.

All of the "Queen Elizabeth" class ships were retained after World War I, when financial limitations, treaty obligations and a strong national belief that World War I had indeed been the "war to end all wars" prevented much in the way of new construction. However, analysis of World War I operations, the manifest capabilities of the submarine and the mine, and the growing importance of air power combined with technical improvements to persuade the Admiralty to rebuild the ships to a more modern standard. The *Queen Elizabeth* was partially modernized in 1926/27 with long external bulges that increased her beam to 104 ft (31.7 m) and improved her protection against underwater weapons, her fore funnel trunked into the second funnel, her bridge remodelled, and her AA armament increased by the replacement of the 3-in (76-mm) weapons by four 4-in (102-mm) guns. In 1937/40 the ship was taken in hand, again by Portsmouth Dock Yard with completion at Rosyth, for a second reconstruction with new machinery (included four Parsons geared turbines working on steam delivered by eight Admiralty three-drum boilers), improved horizontal protection, a tower superstructure and pole mast, new weapons including higher-elevation main guns and a DP secondary armament of 20 4.5-in (114-mm) guns in twin turrets, and provision for a catapult and up to four aircraft.

Recommissioned on January 31, 1941, the ship saw widespread service in World War II in the Mediterranean (1941), home waters (1943/44) and Indian Ocean (1944/45). The ship was damaged by Italian frogmen in Alexandria in December 1941 and repaired in the USA before being recommissioned again in June 1943. The elderly battleship was paid off in July 1945 and sold in March 1948 for breaking.

HMS Queen Elizabeth in World War II.

HMS *Queen Elizabeth* (World War II after second reconstruction)

Type:	battleship
Tonnage:	35,000 tons full load
Dimensions:	length 640 ft (195.1 m); beam 90 ft 6 in (27.6 m); draft 34 ft 1 in (10.4 m)
Propulsion:	four geared steam turbines delivering 80,000 shp (59648 kW) to four propellers for 24 kt
Armour:	6/13-in (152/330-mm) belt, 4/6-in (102/152-mm) bulkheads, 1/4-in (25/102-mm) decks, 11/13-in (279/330-mm) turrets, 4/10-in (102/254-mm) barbettes, and 11-in (279-mm) conning tower
Armament:	eight 15-in (381-mm) guns, 20 4.5-in (114-mm) DP guns, 16 2-pdr AA guns, and 16 0.5-in (12.7-mm) AA machine guns
Complement:	1,124

Ise (1917)

Japan produced no dreadnought battleships with 12-in (305-mm) guns, but moved directly to the super-dreadnought type, with 14-in (356-mm) guns, in the "Fuso" class. This comprised two units completed in 1915 and 1917, and was followed by an improved version, the A-92 design that emerged in the form of the "Ise" class *Ise* and *Hyuga*. These were built by Kawasaki at Kobe and Mitsubishi at Nagasaki, and were completed in December 1917 and April 1918 respectively. By comparison with the "Fuso" class, the "Ise" class had slightly greater length and a rearrangement of the six main armament turrets. These latter were now concentrated in three superfiring pairs for improved fire control and protection. The secondary battery was initially planned on the basis of 6-in (152-mm) weapons, but was finalized on the basis of a new 5.5-in (140-mm) weapon. The protection of the casemates in which these weapons were mounted was reduced, and four of the guns had no protection whatsoever.

The protection was based on that of the "Fuso" with the important change of the middle deck being sloped down to meet the lower edges of the belt over the boiler rooms and magazines. The extent and capability of the splinter protection were significantly enhanced, though this added 1,000 tons of weight. The machinery was also improved, small-tube boilers being introduced for greater efficiency, and on trials in September 1917 the *Ise* was recorded at 23.6 kt.

In the early 1920s both ships received four 3.1-in (80-mm) AA guns. The ships were equipped with several fore mast platforms, and then in 1926/27 with smoke hoods on their fore funnels. Provision was also added for three floatplanes, which operated from a platform atop the "X" aft superfiring turret. Both ships were extensively reconstructed during the mid-1930s (*Ise* by March 1937 and *Hyuga* by September 1936) with features such as greater main armament elevation and quarterdeck catapults.

After the Battle of Midway in mid-1942, when the Japanese navy suffered the catastrophic loss of four fleet aircraft carriers as well as their aircraft and highly trained and all-but-irreplaceable aircrews, the two battleships were again taken in hand for a reconstruction, in this instance to a hybrid standard combining

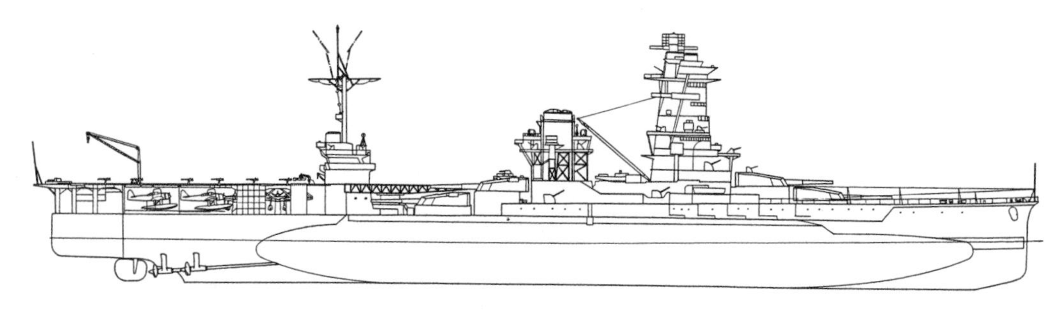

The Ise in her final form with an aircraft hangar and operating platform in place of her two after main armament turrets.

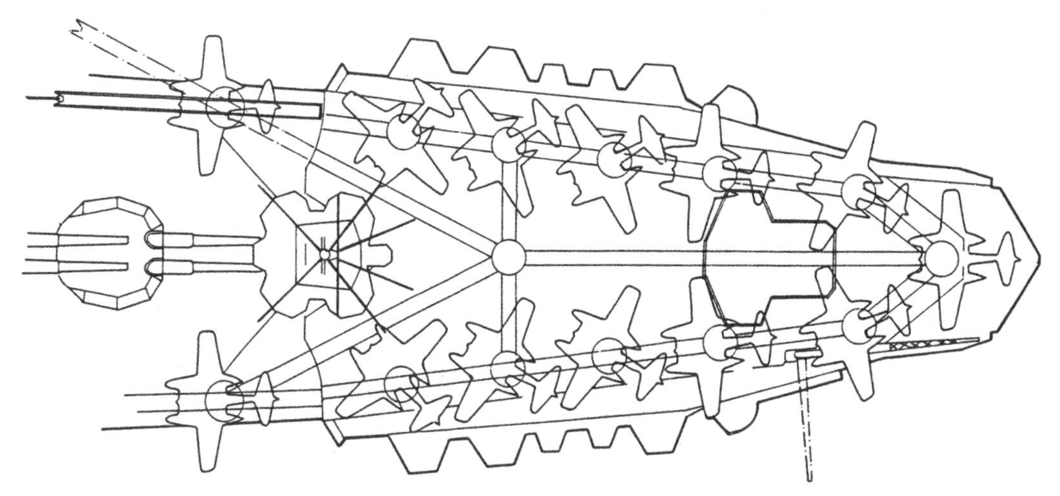

Ise's aircraft installation included two catapults, a centreline lift, and spots for 13 of her proposed complement of 22 aircraft.

battleship and aircraft carrier features. The *Ise* was modified at Kure between July and September 1943, and the *Hyuga* at Sasebo between July and November 1943. In this reconstruction the aftermost pair of turrets was replaced by a raised and enclosed flight deck, which was really a short aircraft-handling deck as the aircraft were launched from powerful catapults. The other major change was the removal of the entire secondary gun armament, leaving the ships with eight 14-in (356-mm) guns, 16 5-in (127-mm) AA guns and six 4.7-in (120-mm) rocket launchers. The aircraft complement was initially to have comprised 22 Yokosuka D4Y Suisei dive-bombers, but this scheme was later changed to the same number of Aichi E16A Zuiun floatplane dive-bombers. It seems, though, that no aircraft were ever in fact shipped. It was planned at one time for the two "Fuso" class ships to be converted in a similar fashion.

In this hybrid form the ships were used as decoys in the Battle of Leyte Gulf during October 1944. The ships were deactivated in March 1945, and

Ise (final form)

Type:	hybrid super-dreadnought battleship and aircraft carrier
Tonnage:	35,350 tons displacement
Dimensions:	length 720 ft 6 in (219.6 m); beam 111 ft 33.8 m); draft 29 ft 6 in (9 m)
Propulsion:	four steam turbines delivering 80,000 shp (59648 kW) to four propellers for 25.33 kt
Armour:	3/12-in (75/300-mm) belt, 1.25/6.75-in (30/170-mm) decks, 8/12-in (200/300-mm) turrets, 12-in (300-mm) barbettes, 5.9-in (150-mm) casemates, and 6/12-in (150/300-mm) conning tower
Armament:	eight 14-in (356-mm) guns, 16 5-in (127-mm) AA guns, 57 25-mm AA guns, and provision for 22 aircraft
Complement:	1,463

Kongo (1913)

In the years leading up to World War I's beginning, the Imperial Japanese navy was preparing to switch its whole capital ship building effort to Japanese yards, but nonetheless desired to exploit the latest concepts in British capital ship design. Japan therefore ordered its final foreign-built capital ship from the UK. This was the battle-cruiser *Kongo*, to be designed and built by Vickers as the name ship of a class whose other three units were to be built in Japan. The design by Sir George Thurston was derived from the ship designed and built as the Turkish *Reshadieh* but placed in service as HMS *Erin*. The design of the *Kongo* was so impressive that the Royal Navy ordered HMS *Tiger*, last of the four "Lion" class battle-cruisers, to be adapted while building to a standard as close as possible to that of the *Kongo*.

It seems that earlier versions of the design, drafted in the summer of 1910, were based on a main armament of eight (or in another form 10) 12-in (305-mm) guns supplemented by 16 6-in (152-mm) secondary guns and eight 21-in (533-mm) torpedo tubes, but were otherwise very close to the *Kongo* as completed. Signed in November 1910, the Japanese contract with Vickers demanded protection against 14-in (356-mm) fire at ranges between 22,000 and 27,250 yards (20115 and 24915 m) between 20,000 and 25,000 metres. The protection was notably better than that of the first "Lion" class ships, featured a large central citadel (sides belts, bulkheads and decks) including the secondary battery, and included considerable internal subdivision. The armament layout was also notably good, with the main armament located in a superfiring turrets forward, and the two after turrets well spaced with the third turret carried on a rearward extension of the forecastle deck.

The "Kongo" class units were the world's first capital ships armed with the new 14-in (356-mm) gun, which was an L/45 weapon, and at a full-load displacement of some 32,200 tons (of which slightly more than 23 per cent was allocated to protection) the ships were large for the time. The *Kongo* was completed in August 1913. The second ship was the *Hiei* built by the Yokosuka Navy Yard and completed in August 1914, but for lack of navy yard slips the other two units, the *Haruna* and *Kirishima* were ordered from Kawasaki of Kobe and Mitsubishi of Nagasaki, both of these ships being completed in April 1915 as the first Japanese capital ships built in private yards. Even so, much of the material for the new ships was supplied by Vickers from the UK.

The *Kongo* was the only unit completed with pairs of 12-pdr QF guns atop her turrets, and she and the Hiei were the only two units with "knuckled" 14-in (356-mm) turrets. The *Kongo* also differed from her sister ships in having her fore funnel closer to the fore mast, whereas in the other ships the fore funnel was much closer to the second funnel, and in *Haruna* and *Kirishima* it was also taller. Except in the *Kongo*, the second funnel was also markedly thinner than the other two. The *Hiei* was completed with machinery delivered by Vickers, and she was the first ship fitted with Japanese Kanpon water-tube boilers. The *Haruna* was unique in the class in having a three-shaft propulsion arrangement with a trio of Brown-Curtis turbines rather than the four-shaft arrangement with four Parsons turbines as in the other three ships. On trials in May 1913, the *Kongo* recorded 27.54 kt on 78,275 shp (58362 kW) at a displacement of 27,580 tons. The ships had comparatively uneventful careers in World War I, but in September 1917 the *Kongo* tested the prototype of an airplane flying-off platform, and in the same year the *Haruna* was damaged by a mine laid in the South Pacific by the German auxiliary cruiser *Wolf*.

In common with the other more modern units of the Imperial Japanese navy's capital ship force, in the period following World War I the "Kongo" class ships received massive new tops incorporating director fire controls, as well as fore funnel smoke hoods to reduce smoke interference. The ships then underwent two separate series of reconstructions to become battleships. In the first, which added 3,915 tons and reduced the speed to 25,95 kt, all but the *Hiei* had their boilers reduced in number from 36 to 16 in the form of six oil-burning and 10 mixed-firing units, the coal bunkerage reduced to allow greater oil storage, deck armour and lateral bulges added, the fore funnel removed and the bridge structure built up, half of the torpedo tubes removed, the

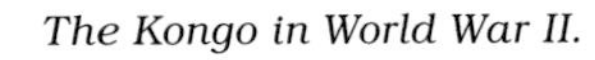

The Kongo in World War II.

Kongo (1913) *continued*

elevation of the 14-in (356-mm) guns increased from 33° to 43° raising the range of the main armament from 21,875 to 27,340 yards (20000 to 25000 m), and provision made for three aircraft (but no catapult) between the third and fourth turrets. The three ships so reconstructed were the *Haruna* at Yokosuka (March 1924 to July 1928), *Kirishima* at Kure (March 1927 to March 1930), and *Kongo* at Yokosuka (September 1929 to March 1931). At this time the AA battery was increased from four to seven 3.1-in (78-mm) guns.

During this period the *Hiei* (like HMS *Iron Duke* and the USS *Wyoming*) was demilitarised under the London Treaty of 1930 for use as a training ship, but was later restored to service as a battleship. All four ships were then cycled through a second reconstruction to re-emerge as fast battleships. Like the battleships that were similarly upgraded, the ships were lengthened, in this instance to 728 ft 3 in (222 m), and were also re-engined, the new arrangement of four Kanpon geared turbines and eight (11 in *Haruna*) boilers delivering 136,000 shp (101402 kW) for a speed of 30.5 kt and an endurance raised by some 20 per cent to 11,515 miles (18530 km) at 18 kt. The stern was remodelled, and the protection was usefully upgraded

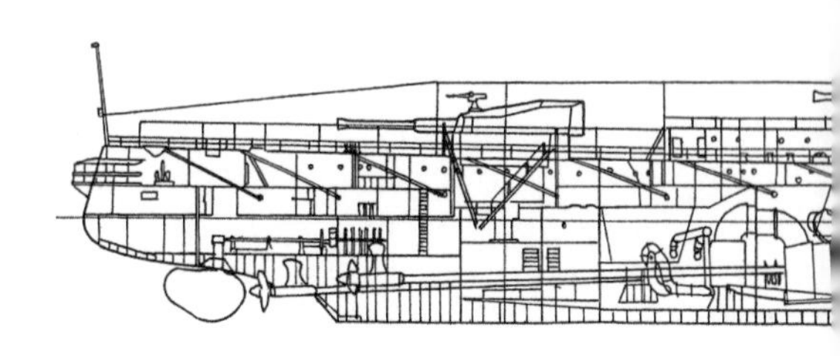

In her final form the Kongo carried reconnaissance/spotter floatplanes launched by catapult, but had no hangar.

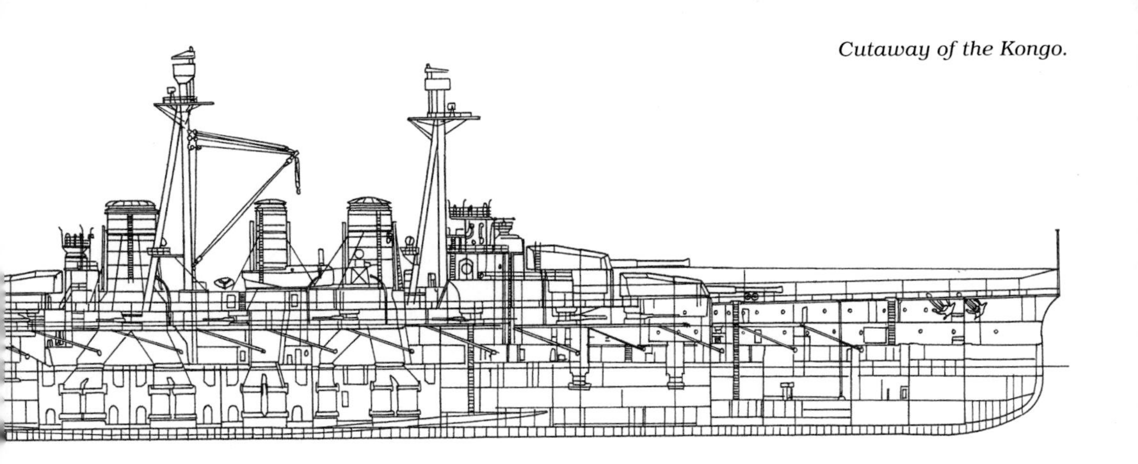

Cutaway of the Kongo.

to include 4.7-in (120-mm) deck and 11-in (280-mm) turret armour. The ships were also fitted with a new fire-control system and a catapult was installed between the third and fourth turrets. The secondary battery was reduced to 14 6-in (152-mm) guns with their elevation angles doubled from 15° to 30°, and defense against air attack was increased to eight 5-in (127-mm), four 40-mm and eight 13-mm weapons, the latter two soon being replaced by 20 25-mm weapons. The *Hiei* was the test bed for the "pagoda" type bridge structure designed for the forthcoming *Yamato*. The programr of reconstruction was effected on the *Haruna* and *Hiei* at Kure (August 1933 to September 1934 and November 1936 to January 1940), the *Kirishima* at Sasebo (June 1934 to June 1936) and the *Kongo* at Yokosuka (June 1935 to January 1937).

All of the ships saw extensive use in World War II until they were sunk, the *Hiei* and *Kirishima* within three days of each other in November 1942, the *Haruna* in July 1945, and the *Kongo* on November 21, 1944 to submarine attack. By this time the *Kongo* had seen service in the Malaya landings, the Dutch East Indies landings, in support of carrier operations against Darwin and Ceylon, and in the naval battles of Midway, Guadalcanal, Santa Cruz, the Philippine Sea and Leyte Gulf.

Kongo (as completed)

Type:	battle-cruiser
Tonnage:	32,200 tons full load
Dimensions:	length 704 ft (214.5 m); beam 92 ft (28 m); draft 27 ft 7 in (8.4 m)
Propulsion:	four steam turbines delivering 64,000 shp (47718 kW) to four propellers for 27.5 kt
Armour:	3/8-in (76/203-mm) belt, 5/9-in (127/229-mm) bulkheads, 1.625/2.25-in (41/57-mm) decks, 9-in (229-mm) turrets, 10-in (254-mm) barbettes, and 10-in (254-mm) conning tower
Armament:	eight 14-in (356-mm) guns, 16 6-in (152-mm) guns, 16 3-in (76-mm) guns, four 3.1-in (78-mm) guns, and eight 21-in (533-mm) torpedo tubes
Complement:	1,201

KMS *Scharnhorst* (1939)

KMS *Scharnhorst* was conceived as the Ersatz Elsass, an improved "Deutschland" class Panzerschiff ("pocket battleship") planned by the German navy. By 1933 the deficiencies of the "pocket battleship" were so clear, however, that Adolf Hitler authorized an enlargement from 19,000 to 26,000 tons (finally more than 32,000 tons) as a reply to France's fast battleships *Dunkerque* and *Strasbourg*, and then the building of two such battle-cruisers. It had been hoped to arm the ship with three twin 15-in (380-mm) turrets, but to save time the ships were completed with three triple 11-in (280-mm) turrets ordered for the improved "Deutschland" class ships.

For most of her life the *Scharnhorst*, built at Wilhelmshaven and completed in January 1939, operated in conjunction with her sister KMS *Gneisenau*, completed at Kiel in May 1938. The *Scharnhorst* was badly damaged by a torpedo fired by the destroyer HMS *Acasta* while attacking the carrier HMS *Glorious* in June 1940, and both ships made forays into the North Atlantic during 1940/41. Although the ships posed a threat to British convoys as they lay at Brest in 1941, and several raids by the Royal Air Force had inflicted nothing but casual damage, Hitler ordered the ships back to Germany in an audacious daylight dash along the English Channel in February 1942. Accompanied

The battle-cruiser KMS Scharnhorst.

The battle-cruiser KMS Scharnhorst was sunk in the Battle of the North Cape when she was outmaneuvered by lighter Allied warships and outgunned by the battleship HMS Duke of York.

The battle-cruiser KMS Scharnhorst was an immensely impressive and well-built capital ship.

by the heavy cruiser KMS *Prinz Eugen* and destroyers, the battle-cruisers fought off ineffectual air and sea attacks. The *Scharnhorst* was damaged by a mine in the later stages of the dash, but had been repaired by August 1942.

The ship was sent to Norway in March 1943 to threaten Allied convoys to the USSR. She took part in a raid on Spitzbergen during September of that year, but otherwise lay in a remote fjord until ordered in December 1943 to attack a British convoy. This German effort was badly planned, and the *Scharnhorst* could not sweep away the convoy's escorts. More vitally, poor air reconnaissance had given the German navy no intimation that the battleship *HMS Duke of York* was in the offing, and the *Scharnhorst* was caught by surprise when the British ship's 14-in (356-mm) shells started to hit her. The German ship managed to break away, but destroyers succeeded in slowing her with torpedoes, allowing the *Duke of York* to pound her once more before she was dispatched by torpedoes from HMS *Sheffield* and HMS *Jamaica*, going down with the loss of all but 46 of her 1,840 men. The *Gneisenau* was disarmed late in 1942, and scuttled as a blockship in Gdynia during March 1945.

KMS *Scharnhorst*

Type:	battle-cruiser
Tonnage:	38,900 tons deep load
Dimensions:	length 753ft 11 in (229.8 m); beam 98 ft 5 in (30 m); draft 32 ft 6 in (9.9 m)
Propulsion:	three geared steam turbines delivering 165,000 shp (123024 kW) to three propellers for 32 kt
Armour:	6.75/13.75-in (170/350-mm) belt, 1.75-in (45-mm) torpedo bulkhead, 2/3-in (50/75-mm) decks, 5.9/14-in (150/355-mm) main turrets, 2/5.5-in (50/140-mm) secondary turrets, and 3.9/13.75-in (100/350-mm) conning tower
Armament:	nine 11-in (280-mm) guns, 12 4.9-in (150-mm) guns, 14 4.1-in (105-mm) guns, 16 37-mm AA guns, eight 20-mm AA cannon, and three or four aircraft
Complement:	1,840

Hiryu (1939)

The Imperial Japanese navy's fleet aircraft carrier *Soryu*, which was built by Kure Navy Yard within the concept of the 1931/32 Supplementary Programme, was the model for nearly all subsequent Japanese aircraft carriers. Completed in December 1937, the ship had a full-load displacement of 19,800 tons, attained a speed of 34.5 kt, and carried 71 aircraft including eight were disassembled spares to provide short-term replacement of operational losses. The ship was therefore fast, but was lightly built and as such designed to deliver long-range attacks rather than take the pounding of any enemy's aircraft or major warships. The flight deck was 711 ft 6 in (216.85 m) long with a maximum width of 85 ft 4 in (26 m), and the connection between this and the two hangars was provided by three lifts. The small island was located to starboard, and just abaft the island two funnels discharged their gases almost horizontally just below the level of the flight deck. The *Soryu* was hit by three bombs from US dive-bombers during the Battle of Midway in June 1942, burst into flames, and blew up when inadequate damage control allowed the flames to reach the poorly protected aviation fuel tanks.

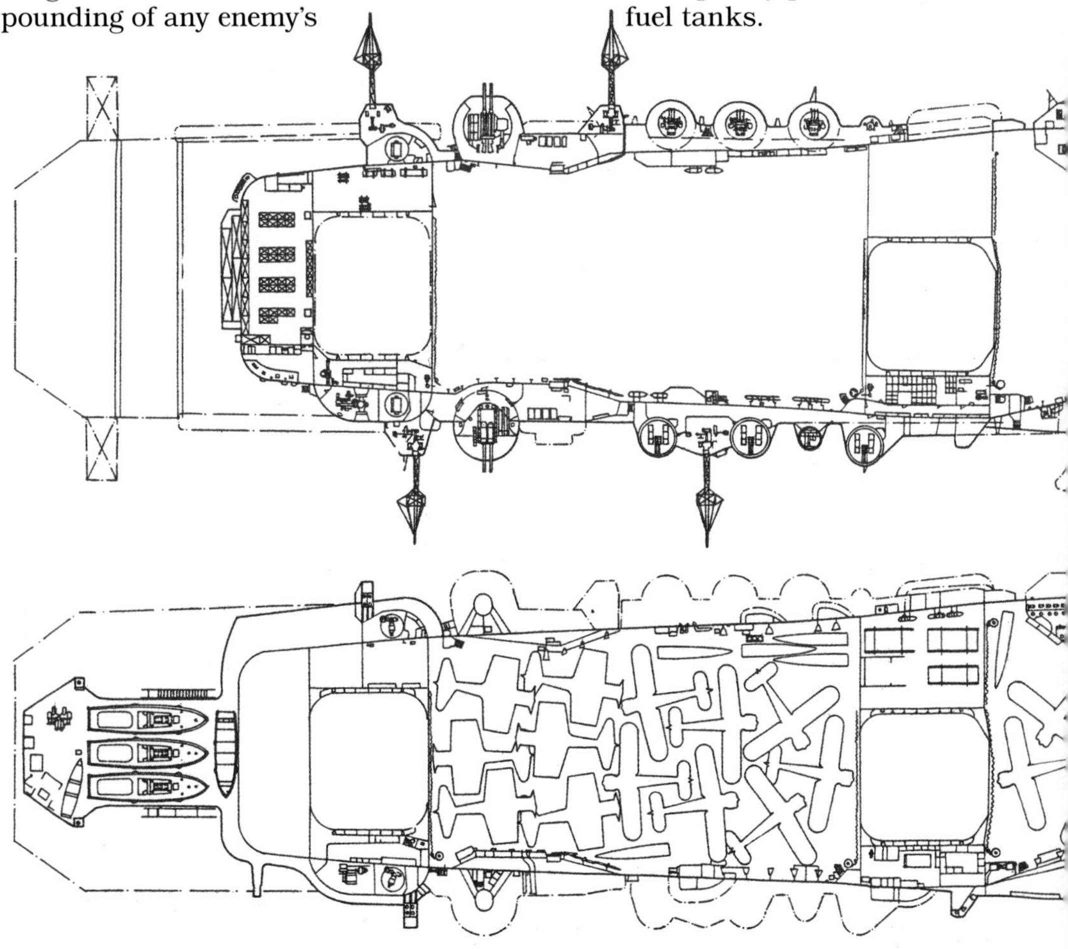

The *Soryu* was complemented in the 2nd Carrier Division of the Japanese navy's 1st Air Fleet by as half-sister, the *Hiryu*. Built by the Yokosuka Navy Yard within the context of the 1931/32 Supplementary Programme for completion in July 1939, the *Hiryu* reflected the lessons learned in the construction of the *Soryu* and also in the initial service period of the altogether smaller *Ryujo*, which had been completed in May 1933 and was clearly too lightly built and also unstable as a result of the decision to double her aircraft complement by adding another hangar.

By comparison with the *Soryu*, therefore, the *Hiryu* was both enlarged and modified. The beam was increased by 3 ft 3 in (1 m) to provide fuel bunkerage increased by 20 per cent to provide a 3,000-mile (4825-km) increase in range, the protection was improved although it was still light by comparison with that of Western nations' aircraft carriers, and the forecastle was raised by one deck level to reduce the amount of water that would be taken over the bows in adverse conditions. The flight deck had the same length as that of the *Soryu*, and was also connected with the two hangars by three lifts, but the ship's greater beam allowed an increase in width to 88 ft 6 in (27 m). The island was shifted to the port side (only the second and indeed the last time this was done on a Japanese carrier), and was considerably larger than that of the *Soryu* to provide more comprehensive command, control and communications facilities. This island was located almost amidships,

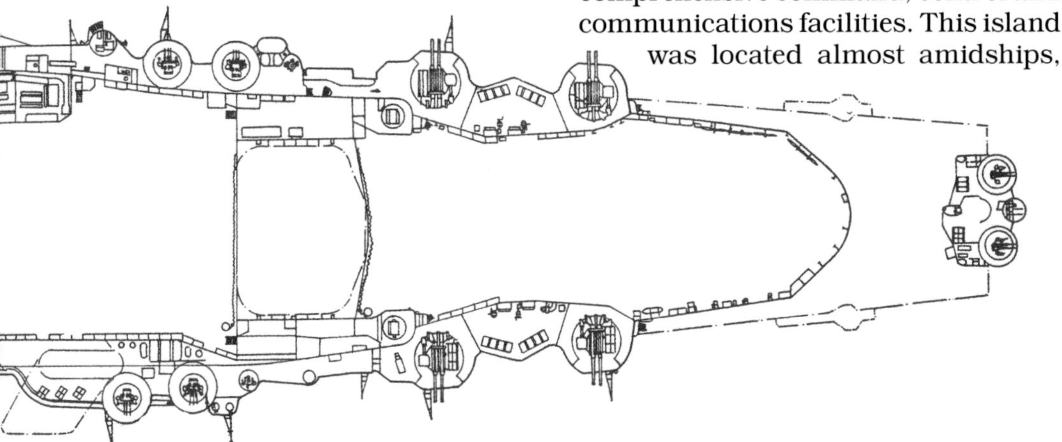

The flight deck (upper) and hangar deck (lower) layouts of the Hiryu.

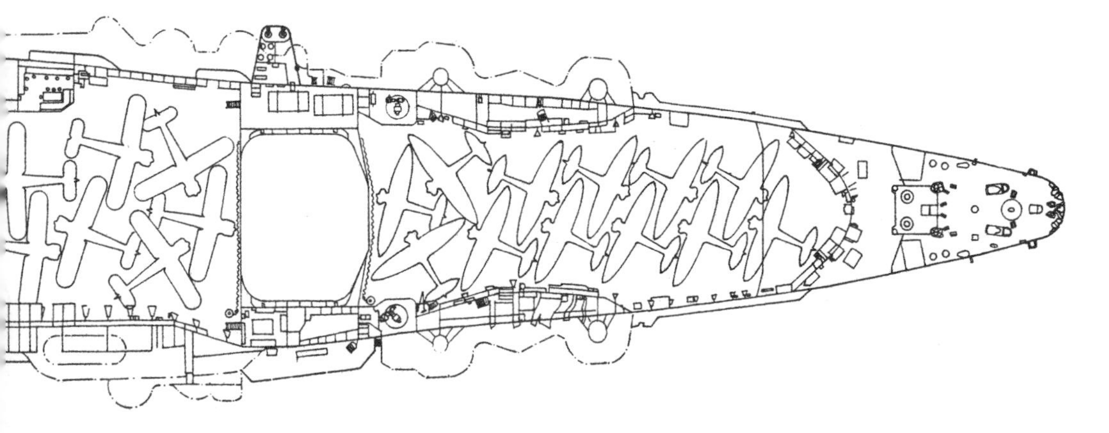

virtually in line with the two almost horizontal funnels on the starboard side. The port-side island was adopted in the knowledge that the *Hiryu* would be operated with the *Soryu*, the former's aircraft using a clockwise landing circuit and the latter's aircraft an anti-clockwise circuit. However, the turbulence associated with this island was so severe and unpredictable that the *Hiryu*'s aircraft suffered a disproportionately high level of landing accidents. And while the layout of the flight deck and island improved the facilities for aircraft taking off, it worsened those for aircraft coming in to land, as they had less deck length available to them, and also limited the space available on deck for the parking of aircraft.

Another limitation in the basis design of the *Hiryu* and other Japanese aircraft carriers of the time was the lack of any catapult suitable for a flush-fitting flight deck installation, and this limited the weight of the aircraft which could be operated by these carriers. The *Hiryu's* aircraft strength was 73, in the form of 64 operational and nine spare machines.

Throughout her active life the *Hiryu* served in partnership with the *Soryu* to constitute the 2nd Carrier Division of Vice Admiral Chuichi Nagumo's 1st Air Fleet. During the Pearl Harbor attack on December 7, 1941 the *Hiryu* launched 18 Nakajima B5N "Kate" torpedo-bombers and nine Mitsubishi A6M Reisen "Zero" fighters in the first strike, followed by 18 Aichi D3A "Val" dive-bombers and more "Zero" fighters in the second strike. The carrier's air group lost five aircraft in all. The 2nd Carrier Division was then diverted to support the stalled Japanese attempt to take Wake Island helped to destroy the US garrison's resistance. From January 1942 the two aircraft carriers supported the Japanese operations against the Dutch East Indies (including attacks on Ambon, Java and Tjilatjap), and on February 19 launched aircraft to attack the Australian port city of Darwin in the Northern Territory. With the Dutch East Indies readily falling to the Japanese, the 1st Air Fleet sortied into the Indian Ocean, and on April 1942, 5 and 9, the *Hiryu's* aircraft were among those which attacked Colombo and Trincomalee on the island of Ceylon.

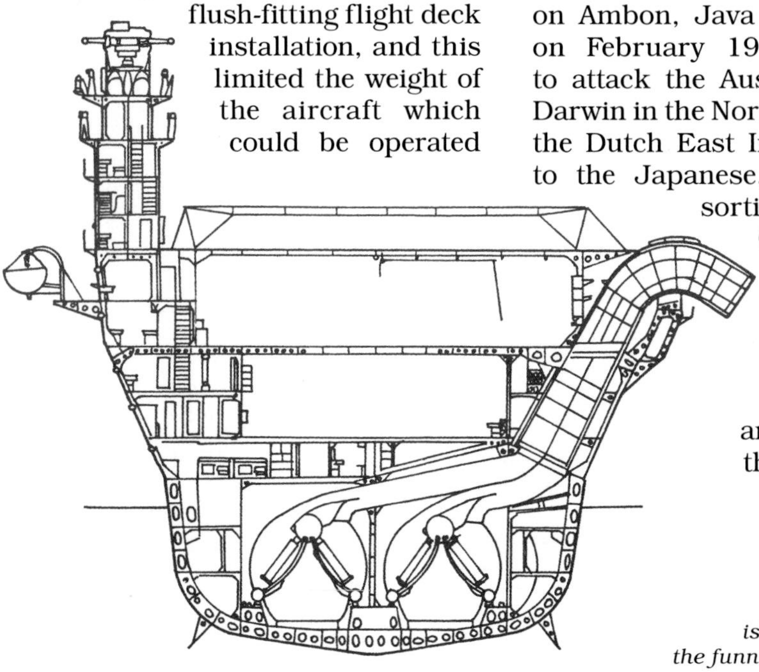

Hull section of the Hiryu looking forward with the island on the port side and the funnels on the starboard side.

The Hiryu at speed in action with AA shells bursting overhead.

After these operations in the Indian Ocean, the two carriers refitted and re-equipped for the Midway campaign. On June 4 the *Hiryu* launched 18 B5N torpedo-bombers and nine A6M fighters for a dawn strike on Midway Island, losing eight B5N and two A6M aircraft, but while this attack was taking place, dive-bombers of the US Marine Corps attacked the carrier, their best effort being a near miss which nonetheless caused considerable casualties. The *Hiryu* was not found by the American aircraft which struck the *Akagi* and *Kaga* (1st Carrier Division) as well as the *Soryu*, and about one hour later her 18 D3A found the USS *Yorktown* and scored three hits on this carrier, which eventually sank. Late in the afternoon 24 dive-bombers from the USS *Enterprise* eventually found the *Hiryu* and, taking her totally by surprise, dropped four bombs along the centerline of her flight deck. The carrier was still able to make 28 kt, but the fires quickly got completely out of control. After six hours of fruitless efforts to extinguish the flames, the carrier was abandoned. Two Japanese destroyer were called in to sink the crippled vessel with torpedoes, but the carrier remained afloat for another 12 hours before finally sinking on the next day with the loss of 416 men.

Hiryu

Type:	fleet aircraft carrier
Tonnage:	21,900 tons full load
Dimensions:	length 745 ft 11 in (227.4 m); beam 73 ft 3 in (22.3 m); draft 25 ft 9 in (7.85 m)
Propulsion:	four geared steam turbines delivering 153,000 shp (114076 kW) to four propellers for 34.3 kt
Armour:	3.5-in (90-mm) belt, 2,2/5.9-in (55/150-mm) magazines, and 1-in (25-mm) deck
Armament:	12 5-in (127-mm) DP guns, 31 25-mm AA guns, and 73 aircraft
Complement:	1,101

USS *PT-109* (1941)

The US Navy's interest in what are today called fast attack craft began properly in the mid-1930s, when it became clear that torpedo-armed coastal craft were being revived in a number of the world's navies as motor torpedo boats (UK) and Schnellboote (Germany). The US Navy had earlier imported Thornycroft CMBs (coastal motor boats) from the UK, and many high-speed craft of this basic type had been used as "rum-runners" during the USA's prohibition era of the 1920s and early 1930s. The US Navy then ordered prototypes, and among these were a Hall-Scott craft from the UK. This became *PT-9* and paved the way for subsequent "PT" (patrol torpedo) boat classes. In the shorter term it was the pattern for *PT-10* to *PT-19* and also for the anti-submarine *PTC-1* to *PTC-12*. All 23 of the craft were ultimately transferred to the Royal Navy. *PTC-13* to *PTC-60* were completed as *PT-33* to *PT-44* and *PT-57* to *PT-68*.

Of the low-numbered boats, *PT-1* to *PT-8* were experiments, and *PT-10* to *PT-19* were 70-ft (21.3-m) Electric Boat Company (Elco) craft. These first "PT" boats entered service in November 1940 with two 18-in (457-mm) torpedo tubes and, although they were basically satisfactory, it was recommended that further boats incorporate standard Packard gasoline engines and four 21-in (533-mm) torpedo tubes in a hull "stretched" to 77 ft (23.5 m). Elco built *PT-20* to *PT-68* to this enlarged size, and in a competition against other designs the Elco craft did well, revealing a high turn of speed and good maneuverability, but also a tendency to slam worse than the others. More length was suggested for improved seaworthiness and habitability: the maximum was put at 82 ft (25 m), but Elco opted for 80 ft (24.4 m).

This 80-ft Elco type became the US Navy's standard "PT" boat of World War II, and some 358 80-ft Elco craft were built, their three Packard

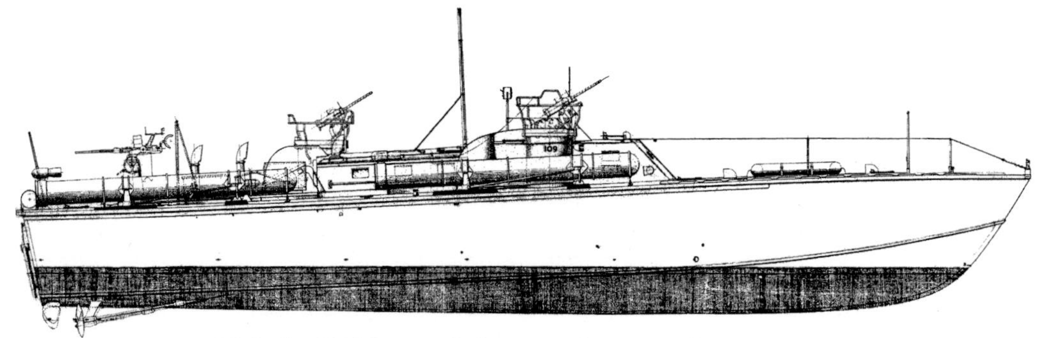

80-ft Elco "PT" boat with four torpedoes, one 20-mm cannon and four 0.5-in (12.7-mm) machine guns in two pairs.

PT-109 under way at low speed.

engines giving them a speed slightly greater than the similarly powered 78-ft (23.8-m) Higgins boats, of which more than 200 were delivered. Of the two the Elco type was preferred over the Higgins type, but suffered as its reserve displacement was used for extra gear. This was partially offset by upgrade of the engines' output.

The most famous of all 80-ft "PT" boats was *PT-109*, skippered by Lieutenant (jg) John F. Kennedy, later president of the USA. *PT-109* was rammed by the Japanese destroyer Amagiri on August 2, 1943 in the Blackett Strait between Kolombangara and Vella Lavella Islands in the Solomons chain. The boat was cut in half, and two members of the crew were killed. Kennedy led the survivors, clinging to the wreckage of the boat, to safety on the deserted Plum Pudding Island, and thence to their later rescue.

80-ft Elco "PT" boat (typical)

Type:	patrol torpedo boat
Tonnage:	38 tons displacement
Dimensions:	length 80 ft (24.4 m); beam 20 ft 9 in (6.3 m); draft 5 ft (1.5 m)
Propulsion:	three Packard petrol engines delivering 4,050 bhp (3020 kW) to three propellers for 40 kt
Armour:	none
Armament:	four 21-in (533-mm) torpedo tubes, one 40-mm gun, one 20-mm cannon, and four 0.5-in (12.7-mm) machine guns
Complement:	14

Giulio Cesare (1914)

The three "Conte di Cavour" class ships were Italy's first series of dreadnought battleships, and followed the *Dante Alighieri,* laid down in 1909 and completed in 1913 with a main battery of 12 12-in (305-mm) guns in four centerline triple turrets and a secondary armament of 20 4.7-in (120-mm) guns in 12 casemated mountings and four twin turrets: the triple main turrets and twin secondary turrets were the first of their type anywhere in the world.

There followed the *Conte di Cavour, Giulio Cesare* and *Leonardo da Vinci* of the "Conte di Cavour" class designed in 1908 by Engineer Vice Admiral Edoardo Masdea. Laid down between June and August 1910 by La Spezia Royal Navy Yard, Ansaldo of Genoa and Odero of Sesti Ponente, the three ships were completed only in April 1915 (first) and May 1914 (second pair), by which time they were obsolescent as most other navies had advanced to 13.5- or 14-in (343- or 356-mm) main guns.

The "Cavour" class ships improved on the firepower of the *Dante Alighieri* by mounting 13 12-in (305-mm) guns in five centerline turrets: triple and superfiring twin turrets forward and aft, and one triple turret amidships. The design did not readopt the turreted part of the *Dante Alighieri's* secondary armament, but of its 18 casemated guns the amidships section was located one deck higher. The guns' layout was an improvement over that of the *Dante Alighieri* but, as was common with Italian warships, the need for protection took a decidedly

Above:
The Giulio Cesare
as rebuilt in the 1930s.

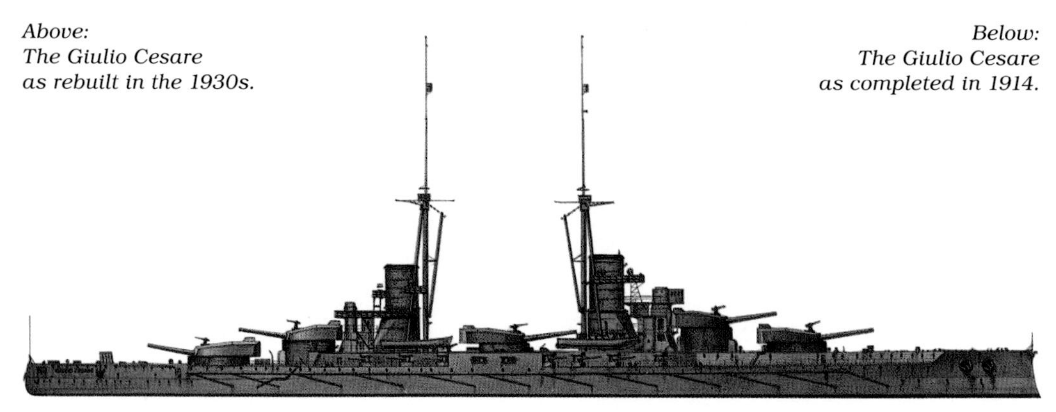

Below:
The Giulio Cesare
as completed in 1914.

second place in the design thinking behind the desire for firepower and speed. The design speed of 22 kt was rarely achieved.

In August 1916 the *Leonardo da Vinci* was sunk by a magazine explosion at Taranto, as a result of unstable cordite or an Austro-Hungarian sabotage effort, refloated upside down in 1919 and righted in 1921. The ship was not refitted, and was sold for breaking in 1923.

Like the two units of the following "Andrea Doria" class, the two surviving "Conte di Cavour" class ships were upgraded in the 1920s (with their tripod fore masts abaft the forward funnel replaced by four-legged units forward of the funnel, a seaplane and, in the case of the *Conte di Cavour*, a catapult), and then extensively rebuilt in 1933/37. The full-load displacement and length were increased by 4,015 tons and 33 ft 9 in (10.3 m) respectively, the original four-shaft propulsion arrangement with 20 boilers and Parsons turbines delivering 32,000 shp (23859 kW) to four propellers for 21.5 kt was replaced by eight boilers and Belluzzo geared turbines delivering greater power to two propellers for 27 kt, the superstructure remodelled, the central turret removed and the remaining guns bored out to a 12.6-in (320-mm) calibre, the secondary battery reduced and fitted in turrets, and the AA armament enhanced.

The *Conte di Cavour* was sunk by British air-launched torpedoes at Taranto in November 1940 and did not re-enter service despite being salvaged. The *Giulio Cesare*, renamed *Z 11* as a training ship from 1943, was transferred to the USSR as part of Italy's war reparations in 1948/49 and served in the Black Sea as the *Novorossiysk* up to 1955.

Giulio Cesare (as reconstructed in 1933/37)

Type:	battleship
Tonnage:	29,100 tons full load
Dimensions:	611 ft 6 in (186.4 m); beam 91 ft 9 in (28 m); draft 34 ft 2 in (10.4 m)
Propulsion:	two geared steam turbines delivering 75,000 shp (55920 kW) to two propellers for 27 kt
Armour:	9.8-in (250-mm) belt, 5.3-in (135-mm) deck, 11-in (280-mm) turrets, 9.45-in (240-mm) barbettes, and 10.25-in (260-mm) conning tower
Armament:	10 12.6-in (320-mm) guns, 12 4.7-in (120-mm) guns, eight 3.9-in (100-mm) AA guns, and eight 37-mm AA guns
Complement:	1,236

Andrea Doria (1915)

Built by La Spezia and Castellammare Royal Navy Yards respectively for completion in March 1916 and May 1915 respectively, the two "Andrea Doria" class battleships of the Italian navy were the *Andrea Doria* and *Caio Duilio*. The design was in essence an improvement of that used for the "Conte di Cavour" class, whose three units were Italy's first three series-built dreadnought battleships following the pioneering *Dante Alighieri*. The "Cavour" class introduced a centreline armament of 13 12-in (305-mm) guns in three triple turrets whose forward and after units were paired with superfiring twin turrets, but in the "Cavour" class the middle turret was lowered by one deck, the secondary armament was improved from 18 4.7-in (120-mm) to 16 6-in (152-mm) guns and disposed in a better arrangement (two groups forward and aft) to deal with destroyer and torpedo boat attacks, and the fore mast was relocated from abaft to ahead of the forward funnel.

A rebuilding program in the 1930s turned the obsolescent Andrea Doria into a ship useful for modern combat.

In this form the design had a full-load displacement of 24,720 tons, an overall length of 557 ft 5 in (176 m) and a speed of 21 kt on the 30,000 shp (22368 kW) delivered to four propellers. Limited anti-aircraft armament was added and then strengthened during World War I, and during the 1920s provision was made for a seaplane and then for a catapult for its shipboard launch.

By the mid-1930s both ships were wholly obsolete for fleet purposes, especially as their protection had always been indifferent if not actually poor, and they were therefore taken in hand for a radical reconstruction program. This lasted from April 1937 to October 1940 for the *Andrea Doria*, and to July 1940 for the *Caio Duilio*. After their reconstructions, the two vessels were in effect new ships, with their overall length increased by 35 ft 6 in (10.8 m) by the addition of a new and very attractive bow, the superstructure remodelled along the lines of the new "Vittorio Veneto" class of battleships, and wholly new two-shaft machinery with Belluzzo geared turbines in place of Parsons turbines and eight oil-fired boilers in place of 20 Yarrow boilers (eight oil- and 12 oil/coal-fired) for much greater power and also a higher speed despite the 3,800-ton increase in full-load displacement: the new boiler arrangement allowed the closer spacing of two shorter funnels. Other changes included the improvement of the protection over the machinery spaces and the magazines and the

The Andrea Doria in her original form.

addition of 1.6-in (40-mm) anti-torpedo bulkheads. The armament was also revised: the central turret was removed, the remaining 10 12-in (305-mm) guns were bored out to a 12.6-in (320-mm) calibre, and the secondary and AA armaments were now 12 5.3-in (135-mm) guns in four triple turrets and 10 3,5-in (90-mm) AA guns as well as about 30 smaller AA guns including 19 37-mm weapons.

In their reconstructed forms, both of these battleships were employed primarily for the convoy interception and convoy escort roles in World War II. The *Andrea Doria* was out of action for six months in 1941 after a torpedo hit at Taranto in November 1940, and both became training ships in 1944, surviving to 1957/58, when they broken up.

Andrea Doria (as reconstructed in 1937)

Type:	battleship
Tonnage:	29,000 tons full load
Dimensions:	length 613 ft 2 in (186.9 m); beam 91 ft 10 in (28 m); draft 29 ft 9 in (9.1 m)
Propulsion:	two geared steam turbines delivering 85,000 shp (63376 kW) to four propellers for 27 kt
Armour:	5/9.25-in (127/235-mm) belt, 6.7-in (170-mm) deck, 11-in (280-mm) turrets, 9.45-in (240-mm) barbettes, 6.7-in (170-mm) battery, and 11-in (280-mm) conning tower
Armament:	10 12.6-in (320-mm) guns, 12 5.3-in (135-mm) guns, 10 3.5-in (90-mm) AA guns, and 19 37-mm AA guns
Complement:	1,000

Kagero (1938)

The *Kagero* was the first of an 18-strong class of fleet destroyers for the Imperial Japanese navy, and this class was ordered as 15 ships of the "Type A" class in 1937 (3rd Reinforcement Programme) and the last three in 1939 (4th Reinforcement Programme). The ships were built in a number of yards, being laid down between 1937 and 1939, and completed between November 1939 and June 1941. In alphabetical order the ships were the *Amatsukaze, Arashi, Hagikaze, Hamakaze, Hatsukaze, Hayashio, Isokaze, Kagero, Kuroshio, Maikaze, Natsushio, Nowaki, Oyashio, Shiranui, Tanikaze, Tokitsukaze, Urakaze* and *Yukikaze.*

In overall appearance the new destroyers were to all intents and purposes identical with the 10 units of the earlier "Asashio" class ordered in 1934, but the "Kagero" class was notable for overcoming all of the problems associated with the "Asashio" class, which had been designed with no thought to Japan's treaty requirements but also revealed a number of steam turbine and steering problems. The dimensions of the "Kagero" class were the same as those of the "Asashio" class, but at 2,033 tons the displacement was 72 tons greater. The machinery used in the destroyers of the new class was further improved, with the three Kanpon boilers working at a higher pressure to provide the steam that allowed the pair of geared turbines to deliver 52,000 shp (38771 kW) for a speed of 35 kt. The *Amatsukaze* was fitted with a new type of experimental small boiler working at a higher temperature and a pressure 33.3% greater than those of the other ships, but on trials the best that the *Amatsukaze* could manage with the new boilers was a 34.55 kt 52,150 shp (38883 kW) at a 2,553-ton displacement.

The stability of the new destroyers was much improved through a careful program of reducing topweight as reflected in factors such as the location of the forward bank of torpedoes at a lower level and placing its complement of four reload torpedoes forward of the mount under the bridge instead of to one side of the forward funnel.

With the "Kagero" class the Japanese had created the design of a fleet destroyer which they felt was perfectly suited to their operational requirements. With high speed, the considerable endurance of 5,750 miles (9255 km) at 18 kt, and an effective armament based on dual-purpose guns and potent torpedoes, the "Kagero" class destroyers were superior to the British and US destroyers of the same period. Even when compared with the British "L" class, the only British destroyer design of the period before World War II with dual-purpose guns in enclosed turrets, the "Kagero" class ships possessed a decided advantage in torpedo armament and a slight advantage in range.

Early in the war the *Hamakaze* was fitted with a Type 22 radar and thus became the first Japanese destroyer to be equipped with radar. In 1943/44 many of the vessels had their "X" turrets replaced by two triple 25-mm mounts to provide a more capable anti-aircraft defensive suite centred on some 14 25-mm weapons. Four depth charge throwers and 36 depth charges replaced the stern-mounted mine equipment. After June 1944 the *Amatsukaze, Hamakaze, Isokaze, Nowaki, Shiranui, Urakaze* and *Yukikaze* had their AA defenses further boosted to between 18 and 28 25-mm guns, and four 13-mm weapons were added. Only the *Yukikaze* survived to the end of world War II, and was then transferred to China.

As completed, the Kagero had six 5-in (127-mm) dual-purpose guns in three twin turrets (one forward and two aft), and two quadruple launchers for 16 24-in (610-mm) torpedoes.

Kagero

Type:	fleet destroyer
Tonnage:	2,033 tons standard
Dimensions:	length 388 ft 6 in (118.4 m); beam 35 ft 6 in (10.8 m); draft 12 ft 4 in (3.7 m)
Propulsion:	two geared steam turbines delivering 52,000 shp (38771 kW) to two propellers for 35 kt
Armour:	none
Armament:	six 5-in (127-mm) DP guns, four 25-mm AA guns, and eight 24-in (610-mm) torpedo tubes
Complement:	240

Chokai (1932)

The *Chokai* was one of four "Takao" class heavy cruisers completed in the spring and early summer of 1932. The ships were built by two naval and two private yards, and saw extensive service in World War II, in which three (*Atago*, *Chokai* and Maya) were torpedoed and sunk in October 1944, only the *Takao* surviving the war to be scuttled in 1946.

After the four "Myoko" class heavy cruisers had been laid down, in 1927 the Japanese navy ordered four units of an improved design. The most significant change was in the bridge structure, which in the "Takao" class was notably massive but also well streamlined. Electric welding and light alloys were used to keep down the weight. The "Takao" class ships also had better magazine protection, and carried three rather than two floatplanes for launch by two catapults.

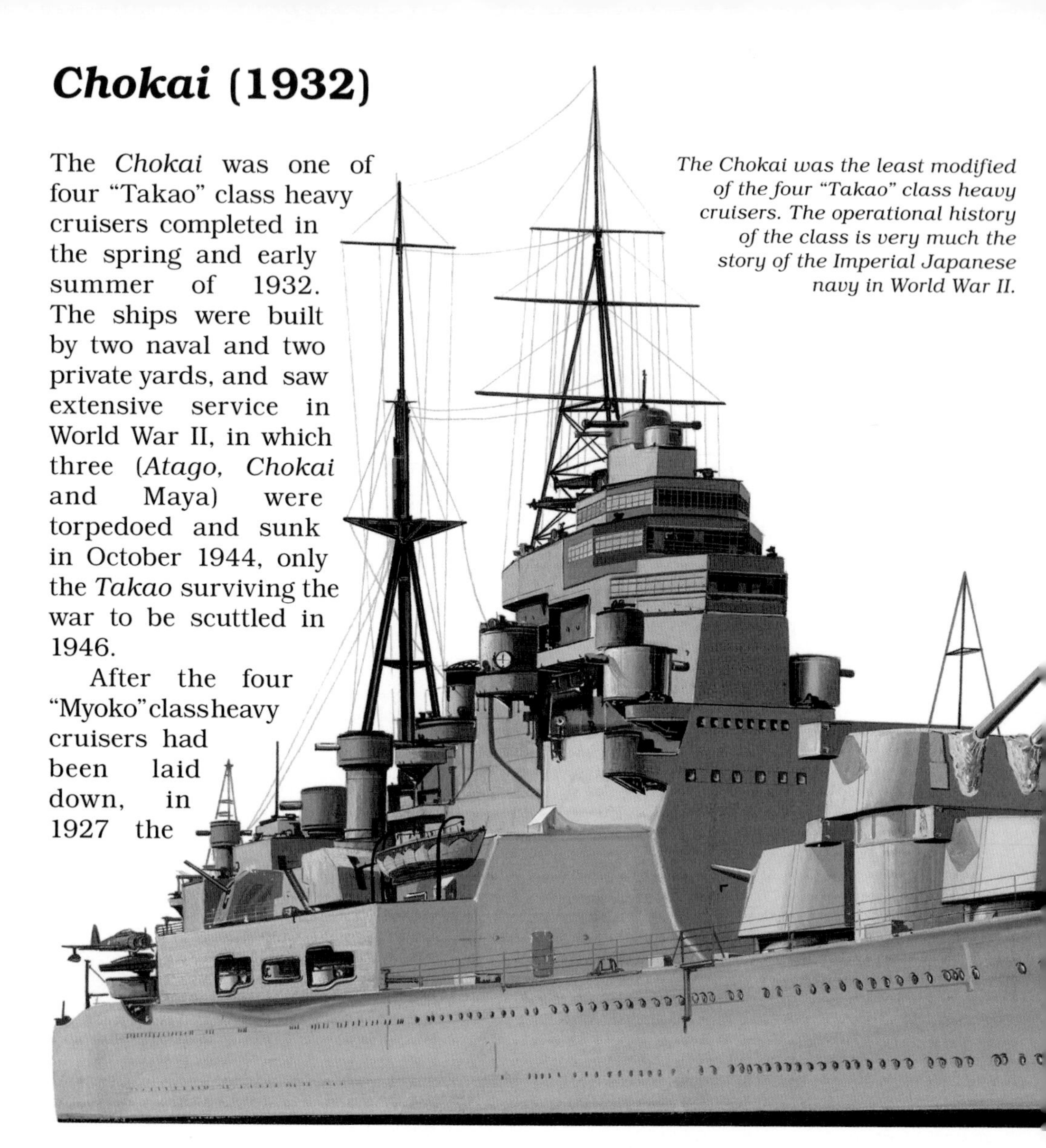

The Chokai was the least modified of the four "Takao" class heavy cruisers. The operational history of the class is very much the story of the Imperial Japanese navy in World War II.

The vessels were completed with four twin torpedo tube mountings on the upper deck, a location which added topweight but reduced the danger to the ship in any explosion: a well trained crew could fire and reload the tubes in only three minutes. The primary armament was 10 8-in (203-mm) guns in five twin turrets (three forward and two aft) in two superfiring groups. These guns could be elevated to 70°, the resulting AA capability allowing the medium battery to be trimmed to just four 4.7-in (120-mm) guns.

In August 1938 the *Atago* and *Takao* began a refit which lasted to October 1939. The main mast was shifted from just aft of the funnels to just forward of "X" turret, and a new superstructure was added just abaft the funnels. In the *Takao* the twin torpedo tube mounts were replaced by quadruple mounts and provision was made for 24 torpedoes. The 4.7-in (120-mm) guns were replaced by twin 5-in (127-mm) dual-purpose guns, and a new main director and rangefinder were fitted on the bridge. Eight 25-mm and four 13-mm guns were also added during this refit, and provision was made for one more floatplane. The beam was increased to 68 ft (20.75 m) and as a result of the alterations the displacement rose to 13,400 tons and the speed fell by 1 kt. The *Chokai* and *Maya* did not undergo a refit at this time, the former remaining essentially unaltered throughout the war. After the start of hostilities the *Maya* had her 4.7-in (120-mm) guns replaced by 5-in (127-mm) DP guns, and eight 13-mm guns were added. In November 1943 the *Maya* suffered severe damage in a bombing attack, and in a five-month refit had her "C" main turret replaced by two 5-in (127-mm) DP twin turrets, and her light AA armament boosted to 39 25-mm guns; one floatplane was also landed. In 1944 the *Atago*, *Maya* and *Takao* had the number of 25-mm weapons much enlarged to 60, 66 and 60 weapons respectively.

Chokai

Type:	heavy cruiser
Tonnage:	11,350 tons displacement
Dimensions:	length 668 ft 6 in (203.75 m); beam 59 ft 2 in (18 m); draft 20 ft 1 in (6.1 m)
Propulsion:	geared steam turbines delivering 130,000 shp (96928 kW) to four propellers for 35.5 kt
Armour:	3.9-in (100-mm) belt 4.9-in (125-mm) magazines, and 1.5-in (40-mm) decks and turrets
Armament:	10 8-in (203-mm) DP guns, four 4.7-in (120-mm) AA guns, two 40-mm AA guns, eight 24-in (610-mm) torpedo tubes, and three floatplanes
Complement:	773

KMS *Graf Zeppelin* (1940)

From 1933 the Germans started to consider the construction of its first aircraft carrier. The program had to be undertaken without any basis in experience, and was made more difficult by the fact that this was a time of rapid development of aircraft carrier concepts. In 1933/34 there emerged a draft for a 22,000-ton carrier with a speed of 35 kt and accommodation for 50 aircraft, but after the 1935 Anglo-German Naval Agreement Germany decided to build two 19,250-ton carriers, at first designated "A" and "B."

The studies were given to Deutsche Werke of Kiel, which established a special design bureau. Specifications for the ship were drawn up in close co-operation with the navy's construction department, but assistance from the air force was very limited. The consensus of the period was that a carrier should be able to defend itself against surface ships and should therefore have protection analogous to that of a heavy cruiser, and the threat of night destroyer attack was met with an armament of 16 5.9-in (150-mm) guns.

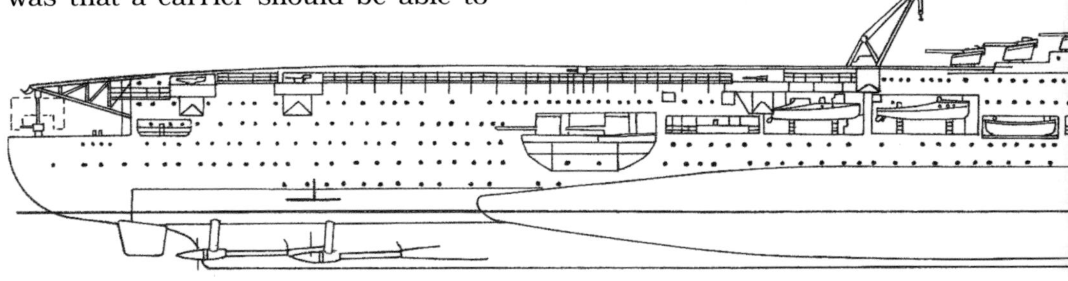

The keel of "A" was laid on the slip freed by the launch of the battle-cruiser KMS *Gneisenau*, and models of the electrically operated lifts were tested and trials of the arrester wire system were undertaken on land. The ship's survivability was emphasized by the filling with dry gas of all parts of the aviation fuel system not actually carrying fuel, all the gasoline pipes were enclosed in pipes loaded with a pressurised inert gas, and there was a sprinkler system in the hangars. The ship was designed with a straight stem, but in 1939 this was changed to a clipper bow.

Initial thoughts were based on an air group equipped with 10 Bf 109T and 13 Ju 87G (navalised versions of the Messerschmitt Bf 109 and Junkers Ju 87 land-based fighter and dive-bomber) as well as 20 Fieseler Fi 167 biplane torpedo bombers, but this was later changed to 12 Bf 109F and 30 Ju 87G machines.

KMS *Graf Zeppelin* was launched in December 1938, and by the start of World War II in September 1940 was some 85 to 90 percent complete, with commissioning anticipated by mid-1940. But then the need to redirect resources to the U-boat program meant that work on the carrier was suspended in about May 1940. In May 1942 it was ordered that work begin once again, despite the fact that the design was now obsolete. The

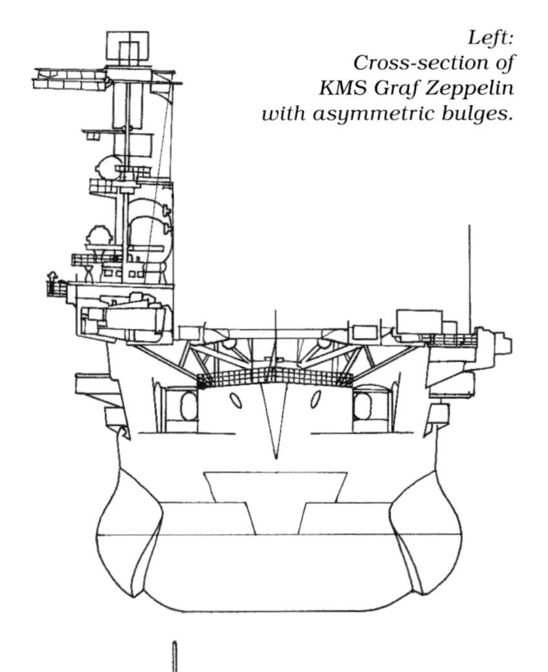

Left: Cross-section of KMS Graf Zeppelin with asymmetric bulges.

ship was revised with asymmetrical bulges to offset the additional weight of equipment on the island, thus reducing the speed to 33.8 kt. Work was stopped once more in January 1943, and the ship was soon towed to Stettin, where the Germans scuttled her in January 1945. The Soviets raised the vessel in 1946, and towed her toward Leningrad in September 1947 but did not arrive as she went down en route, probably after hitting a mine.

Germaniawerft's construction of "B" was very slow, and in March 1940 the hull was scrapped on the slip.

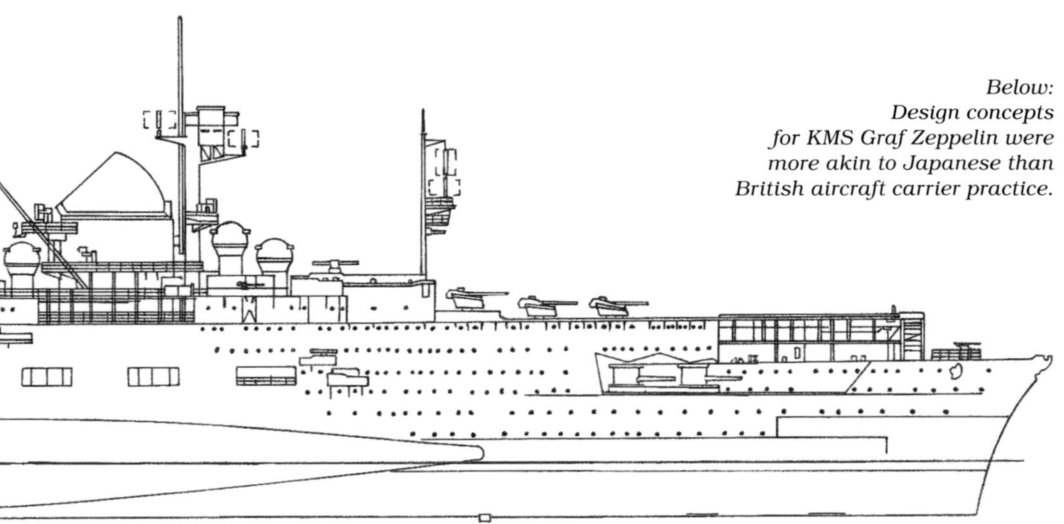

Below: Design concepts for KMS Graf Zeppelin were more akin to Japanese than British aircraft carrier practice.

KMS *Graf Zeppelin*

Type:	fleet aircraft carrier
Tonnage:	28,090 tons standard
Dimensions:	length 820 ft 2 in (250 m) on the waterline; beam 103 ft 4 in (31.5 m); draft 23 ft 7 in (7.2 m)
Propulsion:	four geared steam turbines delivering 200,000 shp (149120 kW) to four propellers for 35 kt
Armour:	3.5-in (90-mm) belt, 1.5-in (40-mm) deck, 0.75-in (20-mm) flight deck, and 1.25 in (30-mm) casemates
Armament:	16 5.9-in (150-mm) guns, 12 4.1-in (105-mm) AA guns, 22 37-mm AA guns, 28 20-mm AA guns, and up to 43 aircraft
Complement:	1,760 excluding flying personnel

Yamato (1941)

The *Yamato* and *Musashi* were the largest battleships ever designed and built, and also carried the heaviest main armament and the thickest armour ever installed on a modern capital ship. The ships, initially projected as a class of four such super battleships, represented an enormous investment by the Imperial Japanese empire and its navy, and as a result no fewer than 23 designs were prepared between 1934, the year in which there emerged the first thoughts for such super battleships, and 1937, when orders were placed for the initial pair of "Yamato" class ships with the Kure Navy Yard and the Mitsubishi yard at Nagasaki. The construction of the two ships was undertaken under the conditions of the greatest secrecy, this effort to conceal the real nature of the two ships including high fences, a protective roofing, and extensive arrays of camouflage netting: the netting which hid the Musashi weighed no less than 408 tons. The building dock at Kure was especially enlarged for the *Yamato*, while the *Musashi* was launched from a launchway 13 ft (4 m) wide at a weight of 35,737 tons, a figure exceeded at this time only by the liner *Queen Mary*. A special heavy-lift ship, the *Kashino*, was built to transport the 18.1-in (460-mm) guns and their mountings to the two yards.

Orders for two more units of the "Yamato" class were placed in 1939 with the Yokosuka and Kure Navy Yards. The first of these was the *Shinano* which, after the disastrous Japanese loss of four aircraft carriers in the Battle of Midway of June 1942, was revised as an aircraft carrier while building and was sunk by four torpedoes from a US Navy submarine, the USS *Archerfish*, on November 29, 1944. The second was hull no. 111, which had not yet received a name before being scrapped at Kure, when 30 percent complete, in 1941/42. Plans in 1942 for no. 797 to the same basic standard as the initial four ships, and for nos 798 and 799 to a revised standard with six 20-in and a belt probably 18.1 in (460 mm) thick, were abandoned before any of the ships had been formally ordered or allocated a name.

The design of the "Yamato" class ships was based on a long, very beamy but comparatively shallow hull with a bulbous bow, and the trading of draft for beam reflected the need of the Imperial Japanese navy to create a design which could operate safely in the shallow coastal waters surrounding the Japanese home islands. Protection was obviously a matter of signal importance, so the propulsion machinery was shoe-horned into a length representing

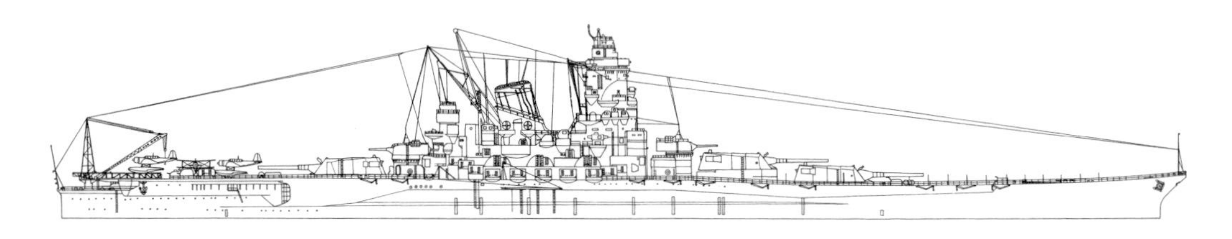

The Yamato and her sister ship had a tower superstructure rather than the "pagoda" arrangement of older Japanese capital ships.

The Yamato at sea.

only about 54 percent of the ships' waterline length. The main armoured deck was designed to withstand a 2,205-lb (1000-kg) armour-piercing bomb dropped from 9,845 ft (3000 m). Below this deck, the 16.1-in (410-mm) belt, which was angled out at 20° and designed to cope with the impact of an 18-in (457-mm) shell at any range between 22,965 and 32,040 yards (21000 and 29300 m), extended downward for some 63 ft (19.2 m) to a 3/7.9-in (75/200-mm) anti-torpedo bulkhead. This in turn sloped down at 14° to the outer plates of the triple bottom (only double under the machinery spaces) and extended fore and aft as a 2/3-in (50/75-mm) screen beneath the magazines. The armour was an integral part of the hull wherever possible, and during the building program extensive use was made of electric welding for the lowest possible weight consonant with the maximum possible strength. The main exception to this process was in the longitudinal members, which were made of an alloy which could not be welded satisfactorily.

The main armament of nine 18.1-in (460-mm) guns was installed in three triple turrets, themselves each weighing 2,774 tons and installed as a superfiring pair forward and a single unit aft. The 18.1-in (460-mm) gun fired a 3,241-lb (1470-kg) armour-piercing projectile at the rate of two rounds per minute to a maximum range of 45,275 yards (41400m) at a maximum elevation of 45°. Accurate fire-control in the widest sense of the phrase was the all-important tactical task of the "Yamato" class super-battleships, and was aided by the provision of three optical rangefinders, with a base length of 50 ft (15.25 m), and later ranging radars, above the tall and streamlined cylindrical tower that replaced the clumsy "pagoda" fore masts. The designed secondary armament was 12 6.1-in (155-mm) guns in four triple turrets (removed

Yamato (1941) *continued*

from "Mogami" class cruisers as these latter were rearmed) located as single units on tall barbettes above the superfiring forward main turret and the after main turret, and one on each beam abreast the single huge funnel amidships, The two latter were replaced on the *Yamato* in 1943 by an extra 12 5-in (127-mm) DP guns, thereby doubling the medium AA battery. The *Yamato's* light AA armament of 25-mm guns was increased to 36 in 1943, 98 in April 1944, 113 in July 1944 and finally 150 in 1945. The *Musashi's* 25-mm guns totalled 36 in 1943, 54 early in 1944, 115 in April 1944, and 130 in June 1944. As completed, each of the ships had two trainable catapults above the stern and provision for up to seven floatplanes for reconnaissance and spotting purposes.

The propulsion arrangement was based on four sets of Kanpon geared turbines working on the steam supplied from 12 Kanpon boilers, and the bunkers for 6,200 tons of oil provided a cruising radius of 8,295 miles (13350 km) at 16 kt. All the engines, boilers and ancillary equipment were located in separate watertight compartments, these latter totalling 1,147, of which 1,065 were located below the armoured deck. Apparently impressive, the watertight compartmentalization of the ships was in fact inadequate and, in combination with the Imperial Japanese navy's generally poor standards of damage control, meant that each of the ships took on some 3,000 tons of water when they were torpedoed by American submarines mid-way through their lives: the *Yamato* was torpedoed by the USS *Skate* in December 1943, and the *Musashi* by the USS *Tunny* in March 1944.

The *Yamato* was laid down on November 4, 1937, launched on August 8, 1940 and completed on December 16, 1941, while the *Musashi* was laid down on March 29, 1938, launched on November 1st, 1940 and completed on August 5, 1942. On trials the two super battleships proved to be excellent seaboats with enormous potential by a standard that was fast being rendered obsolete by the dominance of the US Navy's submarine and carrierborne air arms. Thus both the ships had relatively undistinguished careers as the Imperial Japanese navy was reluctant to commit either

The Yamato was a very impressive and attractive capital ship.

of its most powerful assets without the effective air cover which Japan increasingly lacked. The *Yamato* was involved in the Battles of Midway, the Philippine Sea and Leyte Gulf, while the *Musashi* was involved in the Battle of the Philippine Sea. Both ships were sunk by US naval air power; the *Musashi* took between 11 and 19 torpedoes and at least 17 bombs before sinking in the Sibuyan Sea on October 24, 1944. The *Yamato*, heading a task force on a one-way "suicide mission" to Okinawa, was intercepted in the East China Sea by US carrier planes and was sunk by 11 to 15 torpedoes and at least seven bombs on April 7, 1945.

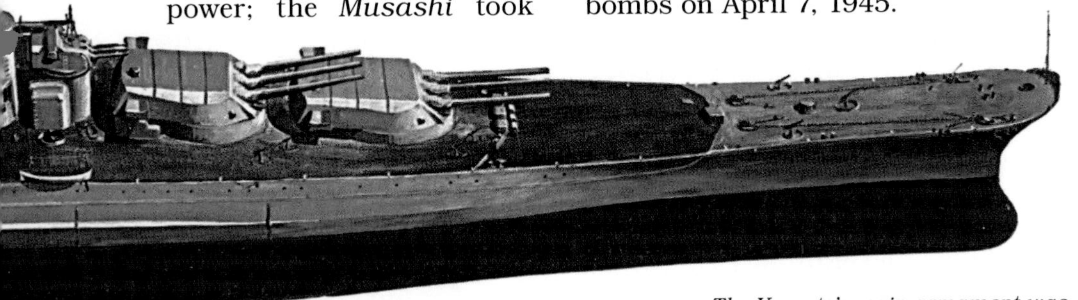

The Yamato's main armament was disposed forward of and abaft the superstructure, with her secondary and tertiary armaments grouped round the superstructure.

Yamato (as completed)

Type:	super battleship
Tonnage:	71,659 tons full load
Dimensions:	length 862 ft 9 in (263 m); beam 121 ft 1 in (36.9 m); draft 34 ft 1 in (10.4 m)
Propulsion:	four geared steam turbines delivering 150,000 shp (111840 kW) to four propellers for 27 kt
Armour:	16.1-in (410-mm) belt,7.9/9.1-in (200/230-mm) deck, 3/11.8-in (75/300-mm) torpedo bulkhead, 7.6/25.6-in (193/650-mm) turrets, 2/21.5-in (50/546-mm) barbettes, and 3/11.8-in (75/300-mm) conning tower
Armament:	nine 18.1-in (460-mm) guns, 12 6.1-in (155-mm) guns, 12 5-in (127-mm) DP guns, 24 25-mm AA guns, and four 13.2-mm AA guns
Complement:	2,500

"King George V" class (1940)

The Washington Naval Treaty of 1922, to last 15 years, fixed the maximum displacement and gun calibre of new warships at 35,000 tons and 16 in (406 mm) respectively. So far as the Royal Navy was concerned, this resulted in the design of the two somewhat unusual "Nelson" class capital ships with nine 16-in (406-mm) guns in three triple turrets forward. The British also kept themselves abreast of the latest in capital ship concepts with design exercises intended to determine how to create the best battleship possible within the limits of the Washington Naval Treaty.

In 1934 the Admiralty started to plan a class of battleships to be built after the expiration of the Washington Naval Treaty. The ships were schemed with a main armament of nine 16-in (406-mm) guns, a secondary armament of 6-in (152-mm) guns, and modest speed. By 1935 the 6-in (152-mm) weapons had been replaced by 4.7-in (120-mm) weapons, and later in the year these too fell by the wayside as the Admiralty opted for the 5.25-in (133-mm) DP gun in the type of twin mounting developed for the "Dido" class light cruiser.

Then the 2nd London Naval Treaty of 1935 limited main armament calibre to 14 in (356 mm) unless any of the Washington Naval Treaty's signatories opted out, and the design was revised for 14-in (356-mm) guns. Even though it seemed very likely that Japan would opt out of the 2nd London Naval Treaty and build ships with 16-in (406-mm) guns, the British wanted to have the new ships available from 1940, and thus had to order the weapons and mountings before any formal opt-out had removed the 14-in (356-mm) calibre limit. The Admiralty therefore retained the 14-in (456-mm) gun but with protection against 16-in (406-mm) fire.

The design was initially based on three quadruple main turrets (a superfiring pair forward and a single turret aft), but further consideration of the demands of protection against 16-in (406-mm) fire indicated the need for more horizontal protection, so the main armament

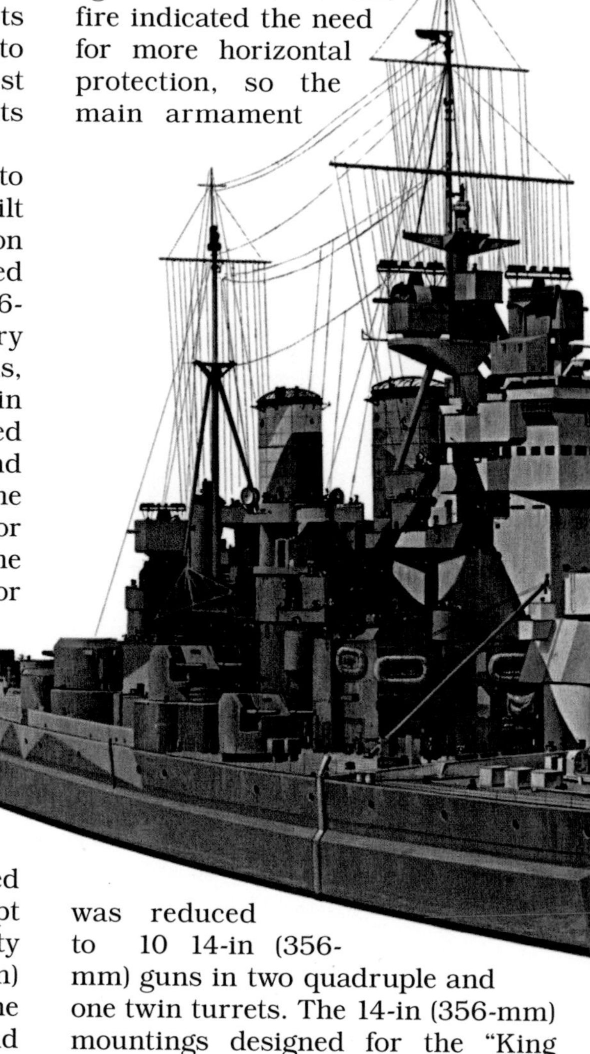

was reduced to 10 14-in (356-mm) guns in two quadruple and one twin turrets. The 14-in (356-mm) mountings designed for the "King George V" class allowed elevation up to 40°, providing a range of

36,000 yards (32,920 m). The 5.25-in (133-mm) secondary armament, which was grouped in two pairs on each beam abreast the forward and after superstructure blocks with each gun able to elevate to 70°, was designed to provide defense against destroyer attack and to offer heavy AA capability.

The design of the "King George V" class was more orthodox than that of the "Nelson" class, and featured a considerably larger area of side armour, reduced protection for the main armament which was now no longer concentrated forward, and much greater installed power as a result of major improvement in the power/weight ratio of the latest machinery.

The belt armour was vertical rather than inclined except where it followed the hull's sheer, and was external rather than internal as in the "Nelson" class and now seen to present repair problems. The belt extended upward to the level of the main deck between the barbettes and abreast the magazines had a maximum thickness of 15 in (381 mm) tapering to 5.5 in (140 mm) at its lower edge, and over the machinery spaces 14 in (356 mm) tapering to 4.5 in (114 mm). The two belt lengths between the barbettes were closed forward and aft respectively by 12 and 10 in (305 and 254 mm) bulkheads, and the lower strake of the belt continued some 40 ft (12.2 m) forward and aft of these bulkheads with an upper-edge thickness of 13 in (330 mm) tapering to 11 in (281 mm), reducing to a lower-edge thickness of 5 in (127 mm). Between the barbettes the belt was notably deep, and at deep-load draft stretched from 10 ft (3.05 m) above the waterline to 13 ft (4 m) below it. The protection was schemed on what was in effect an "all-or-nothing" basis, and was generally good. The protection against torpedo hits amidships was based on that of the "Nelson" class ships but the earlier ships' two outer longitudinal rows of compartments were replaced by central oil-filled compartments sandwiched between air-filled compartments.

The propulsion arrangement was based on four shafts each powered by an independent grouping of one set of turbines and two boilers, although the boilers could be cross-connected as and when required. This was designed to maximize survivability, and in furtherance of this aim the units driving the outer shafts were located ahead of those driving the inner shafts.

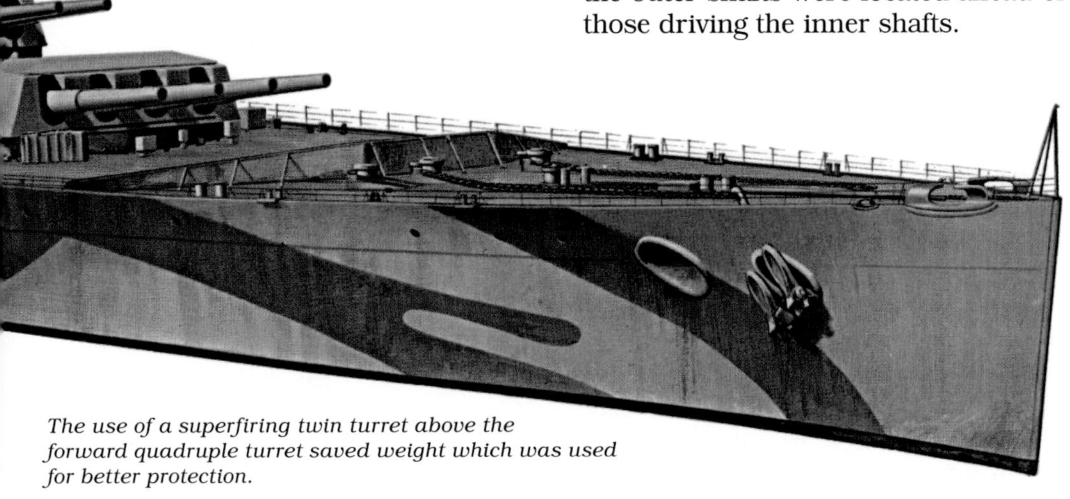

The use of a superfiring twin turret above the forward quadruple turret saved weight which was used for better protection.

"King George V" class (1940) *continued*

The 14-in (356-in) gun mountings were basically standard, but were nonetheless trouble-prone through much of the ships' lives. Another difficulty was the 5.25-in (133-mm) turrets, which were cramped and comparatively slow firing – hindsight suggests that the designers would probably have been sensible to opt for a secondary armament of 20 4-in (102-mm) despite their reduced capability in the anti-ship role.

Half-sections and plan views of HMS King George V reveal the location and relative thickness of the armour as well as the major internal subdivisions of the ship.

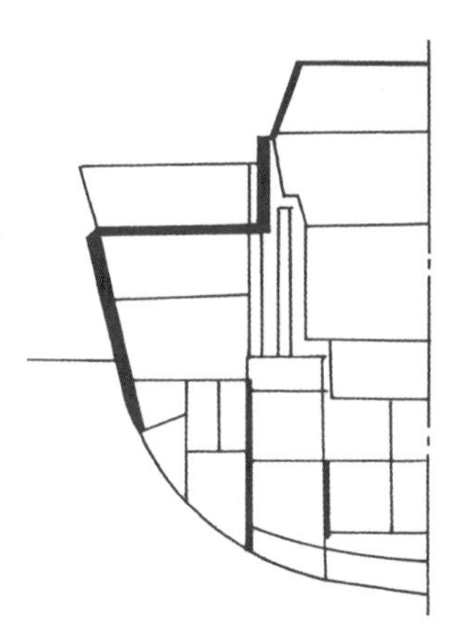

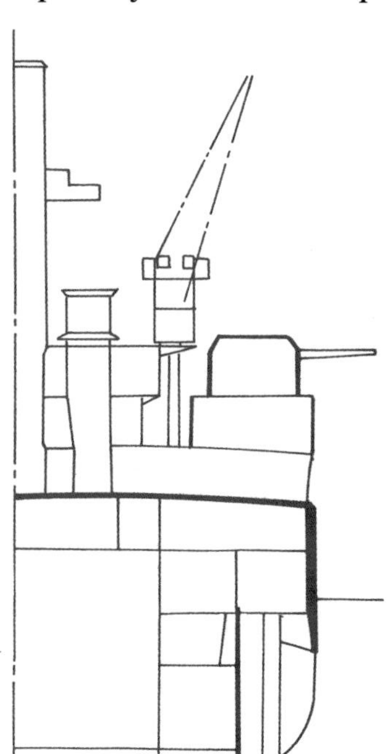

The ships were HMS *King George V*, HMS *Prince of Wales*, HMS *Duke of York* (ex-*Anson*), HMS *Anson* (ex-*Jellicoe*) and HMS *Howe* (ex-*Beatty*). These were laid down between January and July 1937 by Vickers-Armstrongs, Cammell Lair, John Brown, Swan Hunter and Fairfield respectively, and completed between December 1940 and August 1942. The ships proved to be good gun platforms with less tendency to rolls than the "Nelson" class ships, but their low freeboard forward meant that they were prone to taking water over the bows in any sort of a seaway. Moreover, as topweight increased during the ships' lives through the addition of more weapons and sensors, the displacement rose (eventually to 44,460 tons) and stability was adversely affected.

The only unit to be lost was the *Prince of Wales*, which succumbed to Japanese air attack off Malaya on December 12, 1941. The other ships saw considerable service in several theatres, and were steadily revised to the evolving dictates of operations. The aircraft catapult was stripped from the four surviving ships in 1943/45,

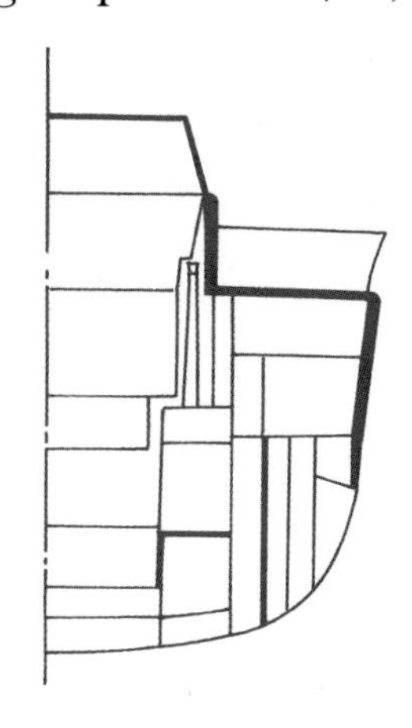

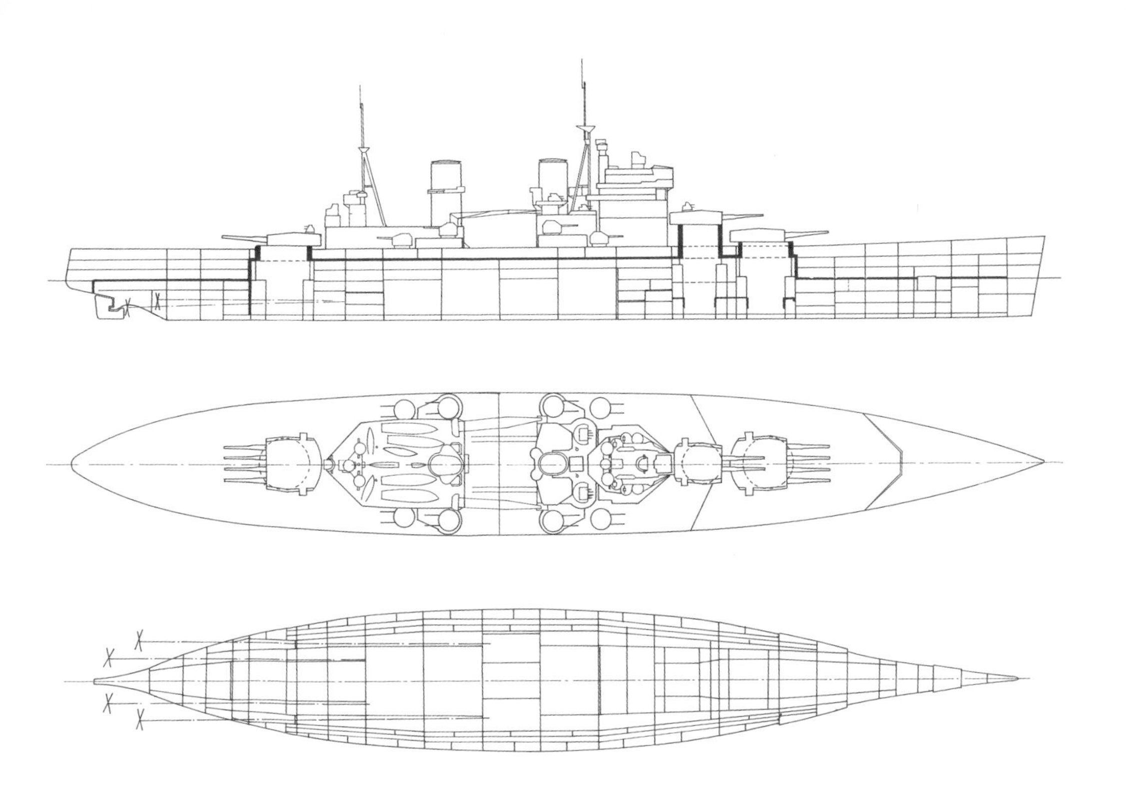

and there was a great increase in the light AA armament. Starting with four octuple 2-pdr pom-pom mountings in the *King George V* and *Prince of Wales*, this was increased to six such mountings in the last three ships, and eventually the four survivors each had eight of the octuple mountings as well as six quadruple mountings. As they became available, the 40-mm Bofors and 20-mm Oerlikon weapons were introduced (two quadruple 40-mm mountings in all and between two and 16 single mountings), and eventually there were also up to 65 20-mm AA cannon.

The surviving ships were scrapped in 1957/58.

HMS *King George V* (as completed)

Type:	battleship
Tonnage:	42,076 tons deep load
Dimensions:	length 745 ft (227.1 m); beam 103 ft (31.4 m); draft 32 ft 7 in (9.9 m)
Propulsion:	four geared steam turbines delivering 110,000 shp (82016 kW) to four propellers for 28 kt
Armour:	4.5/15-in 114/381-mm) belt, 4/12-in (102/305-mm) bulkheads, 5/6-in (127/152-mm) decks, 6/13-in (152/330-mm) main turrets, 11/13-in (279/330-mm) barbettes, 1/1.5-in (25/38-mm) secondary turrets, and 2/4.5-in (50/114-mm) conning tower
Armament:	10 14-in (356-in) guns, 16 5.25-in (133-mm) DP guns, 32 2-pdr pom-pom AA guns, and two aircraft
Complement:	1,422

British destroyers (World War II)

As the Royal Navy emerged from World War I with large numbers of modern destroyers, no further construction was authorized until 1924, when the 1,350-ton HMS *Amazon* and 1,175-ton HMS *Ambuscade* were ordered as prototypes. The builders, Thornycroft and Yarrow, were accorded the greatest possible design latitude within a basic Admiralty specification based on Thornycroft's "Modified W" class design. The two new destroyers were broadly similar with 2 kt more speed, greater range all-steel bridges and improved habitability. From these two there emerged a long line comprising the "A" to "I" classes totalling eight nine-ship flotillas one five-ship half flotilla and two ships for the Royal Canadian Navy.

The "A" class of 1927 (including the two Canadian units with strengthened hulls for ice navigation) pioneered quadruple torpedo tubes and had full shields for their 4.7-in (120-mm) guns; the "C" class of 1929 had one 3-in (76-mm) AA guns in place of the two single 2-pdr AA guns; the E" class of 1931 had two quadruple 0.5-in (12.7-mm) AA guns in place of the 3-in (76-mm) weapon and included two units which could be rapidly converted as minelayers (a feature adopted for the whole of the "G," "H" and "I" classes); "G" class of 1933 included one unit experimentally fitted with a quintuple torpedo launcher later adopted for the "I," "J," "K" and "N" classes; and the "H" class of 1934 included two units with the angled bridge front which became standard for all later classes, and another unit a 4.7-in (120-mm) twin mounting later adopted for the "Tribal," "J," "K" and "N" classes.
A temporary halt was now imposed as the Admiralty considered the implications of the larger destroyers being built abroad. The result was "Tribal" class in which the gun armament was doubled, the torpedo armament halved, the AA armament much improved, and minelaying and minesweeping capability foregone in favor of improved anti-submarine capability. The practice

of having a slightly larger and more heavily armed half-sister as the flotilla leader was now discontinued.

The "Tribal" class ships were so costly that there was no question of multiple repeats, so a reduced design was created with one twin gun mounting eliminated but the torpedo armament doubled to two quintuple launchers. These "J" and "K" class destroyers also introduced longitudinal framing and switched to just two boilers and a single funnel. The following "L" and "M" class units differed slightly in that their guns were fully enclosed in turrets and were DP weapons. The size and cost increased alarmingly, however, and the following "N" class vessels reverted to the earlier, simpler and cheaper design.

At the start of World War II the royal Navy was generally short of ships, especially for its destroyer and escort branches. Speed of construction was now vital, and this was facilitated by the adoption of a standard destroyer design with the longitudinal framing and two boilers of the "J" class in combination with the single guns of the "A" to "I" classes and, reflecting a belated appreciation of the AA armament's weakness, provision for four 20-mm cannon (port and starboard bridge wings and abreast the searchlight platform) with the quadruple 2-pdr mounting retained abaft the funnel. Twin 20-mm mountings were introduced when available, and single 40-mm mountings finally replaced those on the bridge wings and a twin 40-mm mounting replaced the 2-pdr weapon.

There were, of course, many detail differences and changes in the eight-ship classes which were built to this standard destroyer concept. The "O" class ships were fitted for minelaying and, as a result of a shortage of 4.7-in (120-mm) guns, half had old 4-in (102-mm) guns but had two banks of torpedo tubes, and the other half had a single 4-in (102-mm) AA gun in place of the after torpedo bank. The light AA armament comprised one quadruple 2-pdr and four 20-mm guns. The "P" class units were generally similar, but none initially had any 4.7-in (120-mm) guns and half had one 4-in (102-mm) AA gun in place of the after bank of torpedo tubes. In the "Q" class ships the light AA armament was increased to six 20-mm guns by the addition of two more weapons abreast the searchlight. In the "R" class ships the light AA armament was increased still further to eight 20-mm weapons (two twin and four single mountings), and in some the searchlight was replaced by surface search radar. One of the "S" class ships introduced the 4,5-in (114-mm) DP gun, and the class

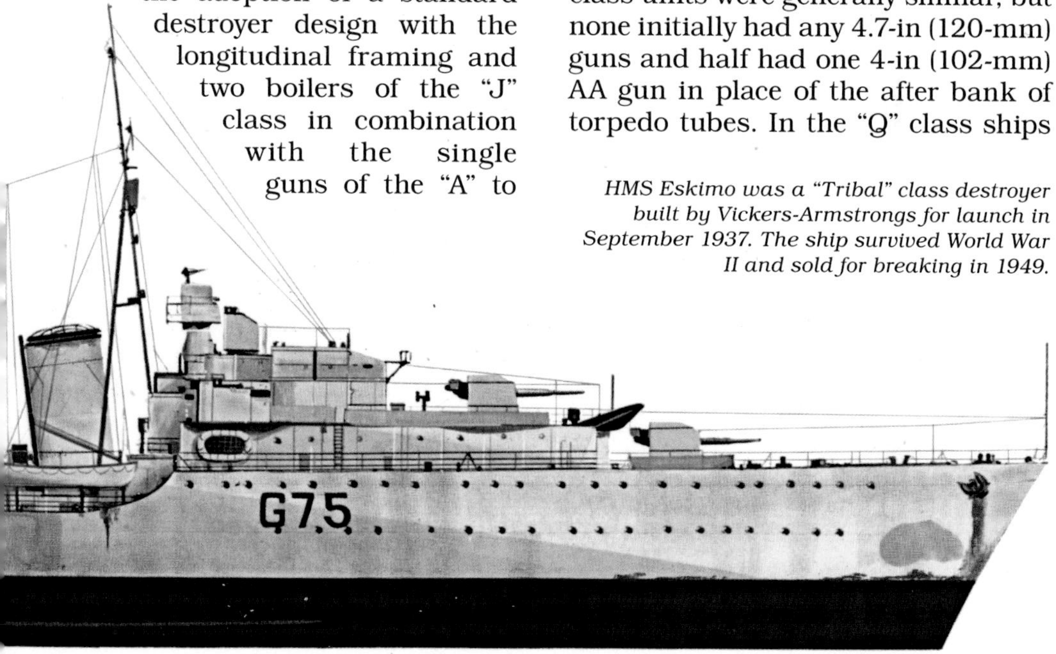

HMS Eskimo was a "Tribal" class destroyer built by Vickers-Armstrongs for launch in September 1937. The ship survived World War II and sold for breaking in 1949.

HMS Corunna was one of the eight units constituting the second group of "Battle" class fleet destroyers. The ships of the second group could be distinguished from the 16 ships of the first group by their slightly greater beam, 10 rather than eight 21-in (533-mm) torpedo tubes, and five rather than four 4.5-in (114-mm) guns.

had the quadruple 2-pdr mounting relocated to a position between the torpedo tubes and then replaced by one twin 40-mm or two twin 20-mm mountings, and all had eight 20-mm guns in addition by general adoption of twin mountings. The process was extended further in the "T" class ships, whose light AA armament comprised four twin and two single 20-mm guns later increased to 12 when the single mountings in the bridge wings were replaced by twin mountings, or one twin 40-mm and four twin 20-mm mountings. The ships of the "U" class saw the introduction of lattice masts, but their light AA armament was comparatively varied generally comprising one twin 40-mm or quadruple 2-pdr and four twin 20-mm mountings, or alternatively six twin 20-mm mountings. In the "V" class ships the light AA armament was based on one twin 40-mm or quadruple 2-pdr mounting and four twin 20-mm mountings. The "W" class ships were similar, but some had four or five single 40-mm guns

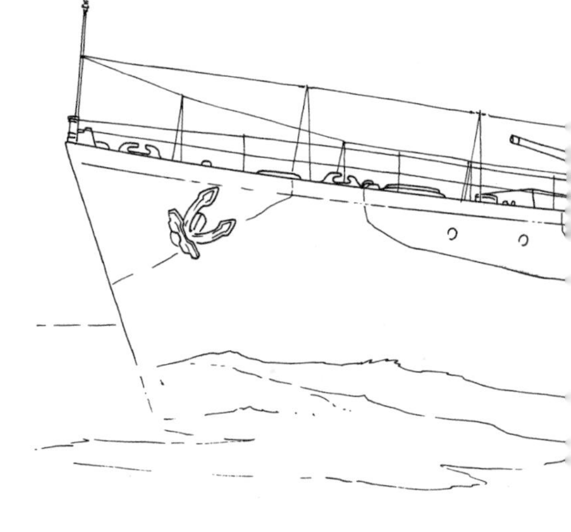

with the fifth gun in a superfiring position abaft the funnel. The "Z" class ships fully introduced the 4.5-in (114-mm) DP gun, and the light AA armament was generally one twin 40-mm and six 20-mm weapons, the latter in two twin and two single mountings. Finally the 32 ships of the four "C" class subgroups had a light AA armament of one twin 40-mm and six to eight 20-mm weapons, the latter comprising two twin and two single mountings or four twin mountings.

Wartime modifications were generally centered on the improvement of the ships' ability to cope with air attack, as reflected in their light AA armament, and with the delivery of anti-submarine attacks. The latter aspect was provided by an increase in depth charge stowage and the addition of a Hedgehog anti-submarine mortar. The number and capabilities of the radars was also increased considerably, and steadily more capable sonar was introduced.

With the end of the war with Germany in sight, the Admiralty switched its focus to the longer-range operations its ships would have to undertake against the Japanese in the Pacific. The standard destroyer was too small for effective service in such waters, and the "Battle" class destroyer (24 ships in two subgroups) was therefore created with a full-load displacement of 3,300-3,400 tons, length of 379 ft (115.5 m), 50,000 shp (37280 kW) delivered to two propellers for 35.75 kt, and a primary armament of four 4.5-in (114-mm) QF guns in two twin mountings as well as dedicated AA weapons, two quadruple or quintuple torpedo tube mountings, and depth charges. The "Battle" class destroyers provided much improved seaworthiness, longer range and greater capacity for self-support in extended operations away from a main base.

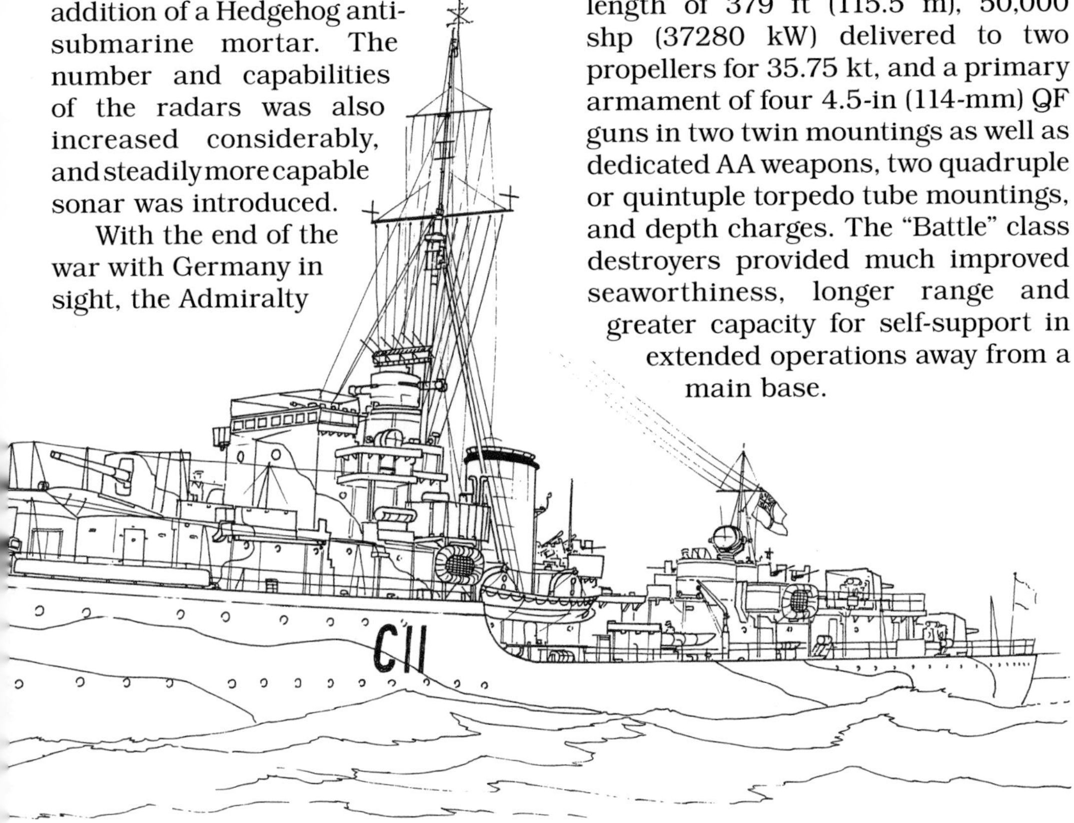

"Tribal" class (as completed)

Type:	fleet destroyer
Tonnage:	2,519 tons deep load
Dimensions:	length 377 ft (114.9 m); beam 36 ft 6 in (11.1 m); draft 13 ft 8 in (4.15 m)
Propulsion:	two geared steam turbines delivering 44,000 shp (32806 kW) to two propellers for 36.5 kt
Armour:	none
Armament:	eight 4.7-in (120-mm) QF guns, four 2-pdr pom-pom AA guns, eight 0.5-in (12.7-mm) AA guns, four 21-in (533-mm) torpedo tubes, and up to 30 depth charges
Complement:	190

KMS *Admiral Graf Spee* (1936)

The terms of the Treaty of Versailles, signed in 1919 and bringing to a conclusion Germany's involvement in World War I, allowed Germany to build warships with a maximum displacement of 10,000 tons and carryinggunsuptoamaximumcalibre of 11 in (280 mm). In determining these limits, the victorious Allies, and in particular the UK and probably with the new Swedish "Sverige" class ships in mind, estimated that these limits would make it possible for Germany to built only coast-defence battleships for operations in the Baltic Sea. During the periods immediate after the end of World War II, Germany's parlous political and economic situations combined to prevent the launch of any ambitious naval construction programs, and a the design of a small but capable new capital ship could only be taken in hand after the appearance in mature form of new technologies such as diesel propulsion and electric welding.

When this new capital ship did finally emerge, it was a genuinely remarkable if perhaps misconceived vessel of the type with the British nicknamed a "pocket battleship." This new "Deutschland" class design was in reality a commerce raider in which heavy armament, light protection and notably long range were combined. What the German design team achieved was a vessel which was more heavily armed than any British ship able to catch it, and faster than any British ship able to outgun it: the only exceptions to this rule were the battle-cruisers HMS *Hood*, HMS *Renown* and HMS *Repulse*. The "Deutschland" class ships posed a very real threat to the commercial traffic of any potential enemy, and if all the permitted eight units of the class had been built the three British battle-cruisers would not have been adequate to deal with them. The Washington Naval Treaty, signed in 1922 and limiting the naval strength of the five signatories, did not allow the UK to build more battle-cruisers, however, so France was persuaded to build two "Dunkerque" class fast battleships to complement the British battle-cruisers.

The key features of the design were a hull of welded light alloy, protection of only cruiser standard, propulsion by eight MAN double-acting nine-cylinder diesel engines which were lighter than any steam propulsion arrangement of comparable power and also offered significantly enhanced cruising range, and the main armament of six 11-in (280-mm) guns in two triple turrets fore and aft of the long but comparatively shallow superstructure.

To avoid claims that the Treaty of Versailles had been infringed, the "Deutschland" class vessels were officially designated as *Panzerschiffen* (armoured ships), but in 1940 they were reclassified as heavy cruisers. The initial three units were the KMS *Deutschland* built by Deutsche Werke and completed in April 1933, KMS *Admiral Scheer* built by Wilhelmshaven Naval Dockyard and completed in November 1934, and KMS *Admiral Graf Spee* also built by Wilhelmshaven and completed in January 1936. During the earlier stages of World War II all three units undertook successful cruises in the commerce-raiding role: the *Deutschland* sank 6,962 tons of shipping, the *Admiral Graf Spee* 50,089 tons, and the *Admiral Scheer* 137,223 tons. The *Admiral Graf Spee* put into Montevideo after the Battle of the River Plate in December 1939, and was then scuttled on December 17 of the same year in the Rio de la Plata estuary after a British intelligence operation had been instrumental in persuading her captain that a superior British force was awaiting his reappearance in international waters. After this, Adolf Hitler ordered the *Deutschland* to be renamed as KMS *Lützow* to avoid any possibility of a ship bearing the name "Germany" being sunk.

All three of the ships carried six 3.45-in (88-mm) AA guns in twin mountings from 1934 to 1939, and by 1945 the *Lützow's* AA armament had been boosted to 26 20-mm cannon in single and quadruple mountings. This ship received a new, curved bow in 1940, and a tall funnel cap in 1942. She was scuttled at Swinemünde on 4 May 1945 after suffering heavy damage from near-misses by "Tallboy" 12,000-lb (5443-kg) bombs. The *Admiral Scheer* was modified in appearance during the war with a curved bow, a funnel cap and a remodelled forward superstructure, and had her close-range armament increased to four 40-mm AA guns and 10 20-mm cannon in single and quadruple mountings. The ship was sunk on April 9, 1945 at Kiel by "Tallboy" bombs dropped by British bombers. The planned fourth and fifth units were redesigned to match the French *Dunkerque* and *Strasbourg*, and thus became the battle-cruisers KMS *Scharnhorst* and KMS *Gneisenau*.

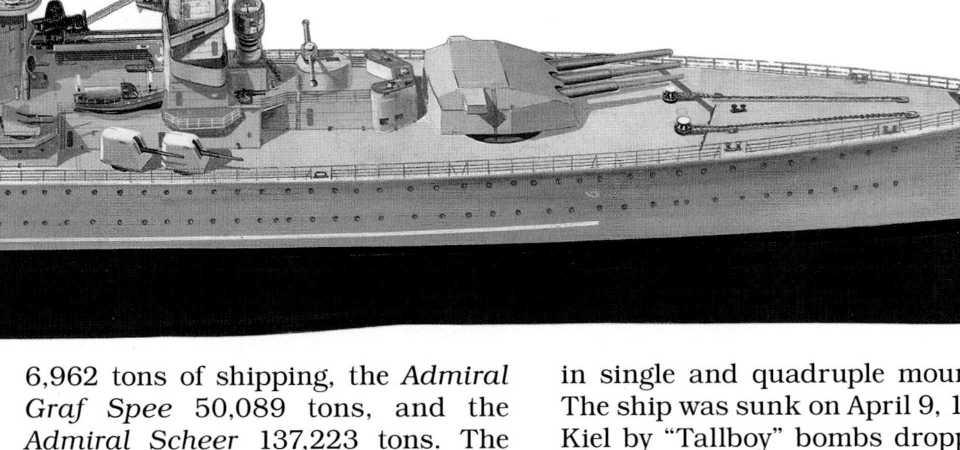

The pocket battleship KMS Admiral Graf Spee.

KMS *Admiral Graf Spee* (1936) *continued*

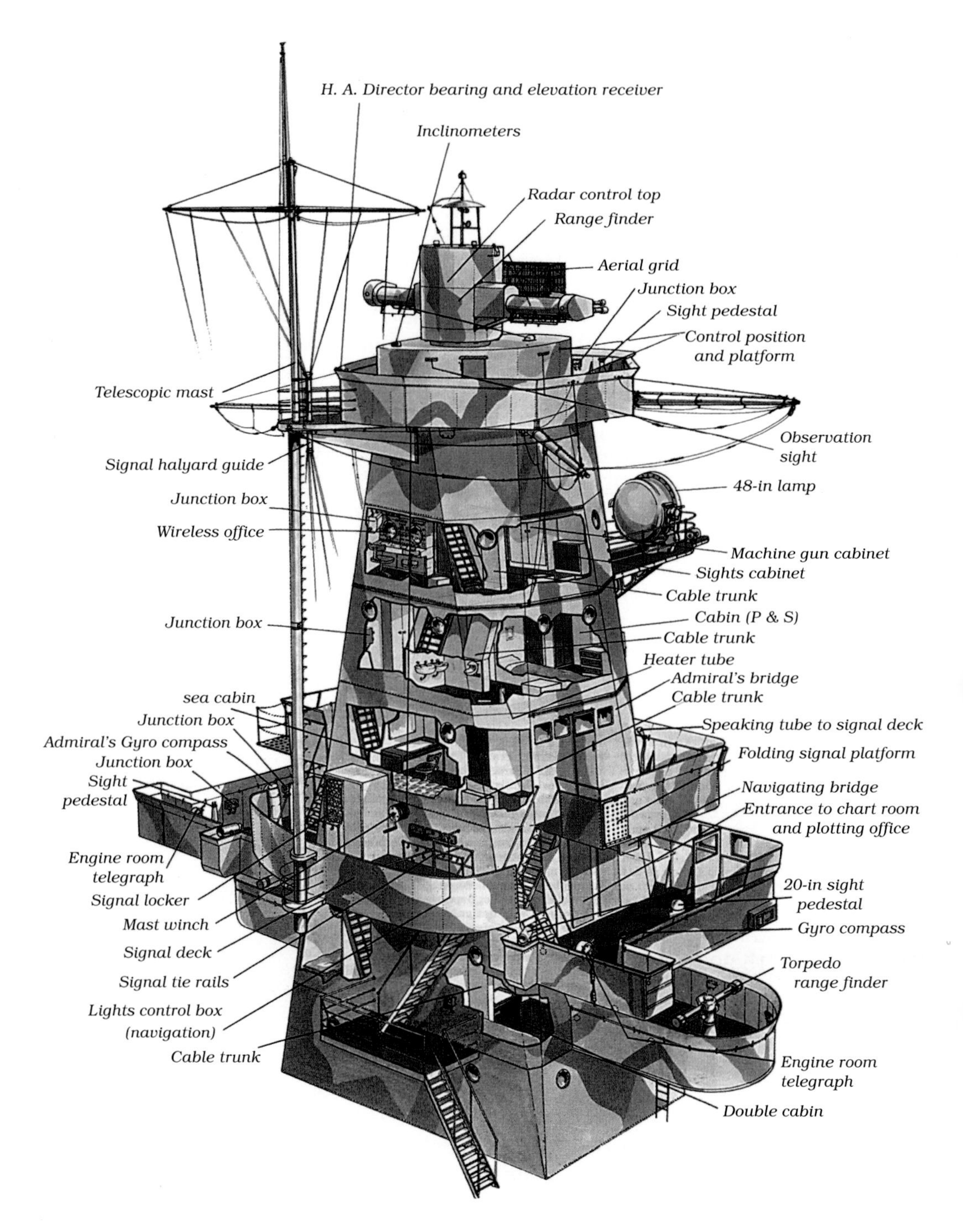

The armoured control tower of the Graf Spee surmounted by a range-finder and primitive radar aerial. The Germans were a long way behind in seaborne radar at the outbreak of war, but were the first to use gunnery radar in action.

The "Deutschland" class pocket battleships were attractive vessels, but of real utility only in the commerce-raiding role, for which their numbers were never adequate.

KMS Graf von Spee in action.

KMS *Admiral Graf Spee*

Type:	"pocket battleship"
Tonnage:	15,900 tons deep load
Dimensions:	length 610 ft 3 in (186 m); beam 70 ft 10 in (21.6 m); draft 24 ft 3 in (7.40 m)
Propulsion:	eight diesel engines delivering 54,000 bhp (40262 kW) to three propellers for 28 kt
Armour:	2.33/3-in (60/75-mm) belt, 1.5-in (40-mm) deck, 1.5/1.75-in (40/45-mm) torpedo bulkhead, 3.25/5.5-in (80/140-mm) main turrets, 0.5-in (13-mm) gun shields, and 5.9-in (150-mm) conning tower
Armament:	six 11-in (280-mm) guns, eight 5.9-in (150-mm) guns, six 4.2- in (105-mm) AA guns, eight 37-mm AA guns, six 20-mm AA cannon, eight 21-in (533-mm) torpedo tubes, and two aircraft
Complement:	1,150

"Nagato" class (1920)

The two "Nagato" class battleships introduced a new era as they were the world's first capital ships with 16-in (406-mm) guns. They were also well protected and notably fast for vessels of their protection and offensive punch. Though the hull was derived from that of the preceding "Hyuga" class, the use of 16-in (406-mm) rather than 14-in (356-mm) guns allowed a reduction in main armament twin turrets from six to four with only a marginal reduction in broadside weight, which was nonetheless fired to a greater range with enhanced hitting power. The secondary battery comprised 10 single 5.5-in (140-mm) casemated guns on each beam, seven on the upper deck and three one deck higher. The control top was located on the "pagoda" fore mast, which was the first of these wholly distinctive units. Another improvement was the protection, which was based on thicker and better armour. Possibly the only indifferent feature was the propulsion, which included 15 oil- and six oil/coal-fired boilers.

The *Nagato* was built by the Kure Navy Yard and completed in November 1920. The only other unit was the *Mutsu*, which was built by the Yokosuka Navy Yard and completed in November 1921. The most potent battleships of the early 1920s, the ships gave the Imperial Japanese navy an unrivalled combination of firepower, protection, speed and general seaworthiness. In the 1920s the fore funnel was swept aft at its top to keep smoke well clear of the fore mast, which evolved into a definitive "pagoda" type of structure from 1924 with the addition of more command and control positions.

In 1934/36 the ships were rebuilt with a longer stern increasing length to 738 ft (224.9 m), bulges increasing the beam to 113 ft 6 in (34.6 m), a triple bottom, and new machinery including 10 oil-fired boilers. The volume thus freed combined with the removal of the fore funnel to allow a significant enlargement of the "pagoda" mast. New main guns were installed with elevation increased from 30° to 43°, so raising the 16-in (406-mm) shell's range from 30,800 to 40,480 yards (28165 to 30015 m). Two of the 5,5-in (140-mm) guns were removed, the others had their elevation increased from 25° to 35°, the

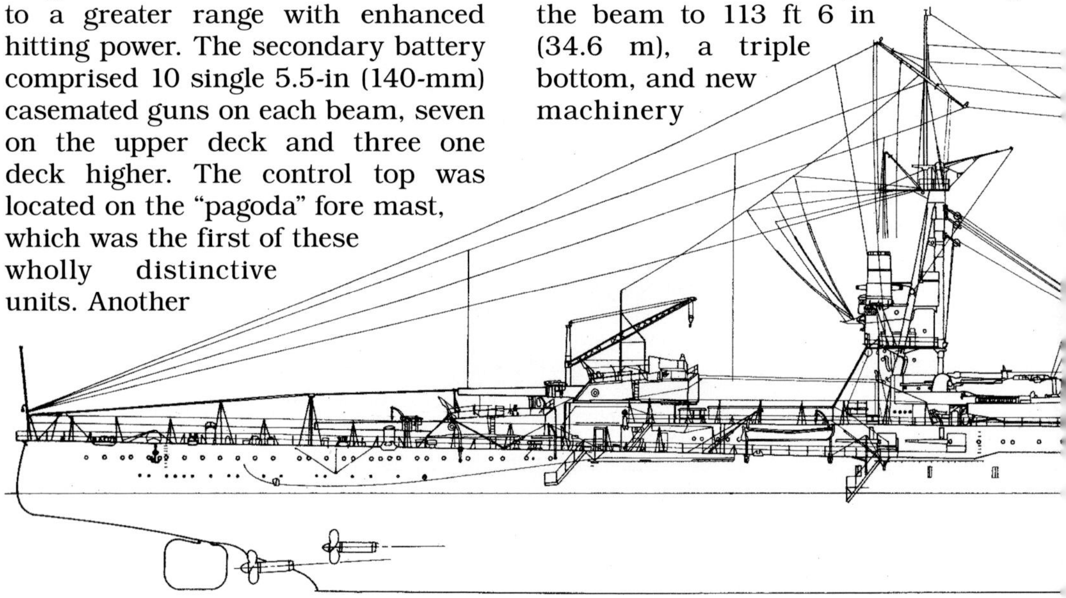

Rebuilt in the mid 1930s, Nagato emerged with a single funnel and a large pagoda foremast.

3-in (76-mm) AA guns were replaced by eight 5-in (127-mm) guns in four twin turrets, and 10 twin 25-mm AA cannon were added. A catapult was added for three floatplanes. The decks over the vital spaces were thickened to 7 in (178 mm) and the barbettes to 22 in (559 mm).

The displacement thus rose by 6,500 tons, but the speed dropped only slightly to 25 kt as the new machinery provided 82,300 shp (61363 kW).

The ships were much used in World War II. The *Mutsu* was lost to a magazine explosion in June 1943, but the *Nagato* survived the war after final service as a floating AA battery from January 1945 with a final radar-aided AA armament of her 5-in (127-mm) guns and 98 25-mm cannon. The ship was expended as a target in the Bikini atom bomb test of July 29, 1946.

A "Nagato" class battleship in its definitive form with only a single funnel.

Nagato (as completed)

Type:	battleship
Tonnage:	38,500 tons full load
Dimensions:	length 700 ft (213.4 m); beam 95 ft (29 m); draft 30 ft (9.1 m)
Propulsion:	four geared steam turbines delivering 80,000 shp (59648 kW) to four propellers for 26.5
Armour:	4/12-in belt, 1.5/3-in deck, 12-in turrets and barbettes, and 12-in conning tower
Armament:	eight 16-in (406-mm) guns, 20 5.5-in (140-mm) guns, four 3.1-in (79-mm) AA guns, and eight 21-in (533-mm) torpedo tubes
Complement:	1,333

HMS *Hood* (1920)

During November 1915 the Board of Admiralty suggested construction of an experimental battleship which would be characterised by the shallowest possible draft (allowing her to be used for operations against the North German coast in the Baltic Sea, for instance) and the incorporation of the very latest concepts about effective protection against underwater threats. The new battleship type was to be derived ultimately from the basic design of the "Queen Elizabeth" class fast battleships, but when it was submitted to him for criticism, the idea was wholly rejected by Admiral Sir John Jellicoe, the Grand Fleet's commander-in-chief. Jellicoe also indicated his strong preference for a 30-kt battle-cruiser to a battleship.

At this time the Admiralty was digesting reliable intelligence information suggesting that the Germans were preparing to build battle-cruisers with 15-in (380-mm) guns, so the initial shallow-draft battleship concept was revised by its designers, E. L. Attwood and Sir Stanley V. Goodall, as a 36,300-ton battle-cruiser with an 8-in (203-mm) belt and 32-kt speed. The Admiralty also agreed that any such ships would not have to fit into existing dry docks, a fact with gave the designers the opportunity to increase the length quite considerably. Somewhat more than the usual time was available for the design as no suitable building slips would be available until 1916.

The result was the "Hood" class battle-cruiser, of which four examples were projected. The design was designed to provide greater offensive

punch than that of the "Renown" class battle-cruisers in combination with better protection than that of the battle-cruiser HMS *Tiger*: in short the armament of a "Queen Elizabeth" class battleship combined with the much greater speed provided by a thinning of the armour and a doubling of the installed power in a much longer hull of finer length/beam ratio.

The first three ships were authorized in April 1916 as HMS *Hood*, HMS *Rodney* and HMS *Howe*, with HMS

Anson added in July. The Hood was laid down at John Brown's yard on May 31, 1916. During the Battle of Jutland, which started on the same day and ended in a tactical reverse but strategic victory for the Royal Navy, the loss of three British battle-cruisers persuaded the Admiralty to order an immediate cessation of work as the implications of these losses were considered. By August the basic design had been revised for the creation of a very fast 37,500-ton battleship differing from the initial battle-cruiser concept in its deepened belt and slightly decreased speed. Later in the same month the Director of Naval Construction offered his own suggestions for a modified design, which increased the displacement to 40,600 tons and increased the thickness of the belt to 12 in (305 mm). The opportunity was also taken to consider other options for what could now become decisive capital ships, these options including an armament still of 15-in (381-mm) guns but in a revised disposition of three triple or two triple and two twin turrets for a displacement of between 40,900 and 43,500 tons, and speed trimmed back to between 30.5 and 30.75 kt.

The original armament layout of four twin turrets in two superfiring pairs was finally retained in combination with many of the other changes, effectively turning the wheel full circle to the original notion of a faster "Queen Elizabeth" class battleship. As finally reauthorized for construction, with the keel relaid on September 1st, 1916, the *Hood* incorporated many of the lessons which had been learned up to this time in World War I. These lessons included the overriding importance of a secondary battery relocated one deck higher than had initially been standard (14 of the 16 5.5-in/140-mm guns at forecastle deck level and the other two as single port and starboard weapons abreast the fore funnel for improved capability in adverse conditions); and the significance of improved seakeeping through the incorporation in the hull of pronounced sheer and flare, the latter also being designed to prevent an incoming shell from striking the hull at 90°, thereby effectively increasing the thickness of the armour protection.

HMS Hood had a long and rangy appearance, and at speed her quarterdeck was virtually awash.

HMS *Hood* (1920) *continued*

Of the other three ships, the *Rodney*, *Howe* and *Anson* were laid down on October 9, October 16 and November 9, 1916 at the Fairfield, Cammell Laird and Armstrongs yards respectively. Then, during February 1917, the British government opted to continue with only the *Hood* as it had become clear from reliable intelligence sources that the Germans had stopped capital ship construction. Work on the *Rodney*, *Howe* and *Anson* was suspended in the following month, and in October 1918 the yards were authorized to clear the slips, with the last of the armour and machinery sold in August 1919.

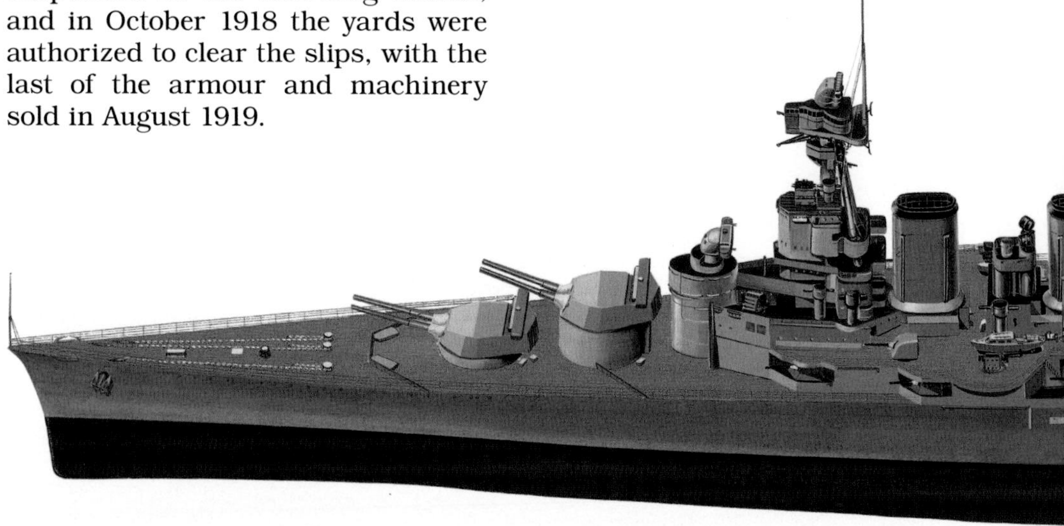

The *Hood* was launched on August 22, 1918 and completed in May 1920 with the Mk II mounting giving her 15-in (381-mm) guns elevation up to 30° rather than the 20° of the Mk I mounting. By this time the *Hood* had lost the aftermost four 5.5-in (140-mm) guns of her secondary battery and four of the eight 21-in (533-mm) torpedo tubes above the waterline. With regard to her protection, the *Hood* used the system typical of the time of her design, with the bulk of the armour disposed to provide protection against low-angle fire at shorter ranges rather than the plunging fire typical of longer-range engagements, but slightly adapted to provide additional horizontal protection against this type of high-angle fire and also against bombs. The belt was also angled outward to increase the impact angle of any incoming shell, thereby providing the effect of thicker armour. Anti-torpedo bulges were fitted, and the ship's bilges were filled with tubes to help absorb shock in the event of a torpedo strike.

Despite the weight-saving measures listed above, the new British capital ship was decidedly overweight as the result of additions made in 1918/19, which reduced freeboard and tended to submerge the belt. Even so, the ship was notably handsome and possessed a number of impressive aspects. But the reputation of the "Mighty" *Hood* resulted mostly from the press of the time, which assessed her fighting capability from her size rather than any objective criteria. In May 1920 the *Hood* was commissioned as flagship of the Battle-Cruiser Squadron and, as the Royal Navy's largest and most impressive warship, saw peacetime service in many parts of the world. This meant that the ship did not receive the major modernization she needed, however, and though a major refit and upgrade were finally scheduled for 1939, these were effectively prevented by World War II's start. All which could be achieved was a modest improvement of the AA armament to four twin 4-in (102-mm), three octuple 2-pdr and five quadruple 0.5-in (12.7-mm) guns.

The ship served with the Home Fleet and with Force H, and blew up in battle with KMS *Bismarck* and KMS *Prinz Eugen* on May 24,1941 after being hit by a salvo from the German battleship, all but three of her crew dying.

One of HMS Hood's main failings, and possibly the cause of her loss, was wholly inadequate armour protection against long-range fire with a steep final trajectory.

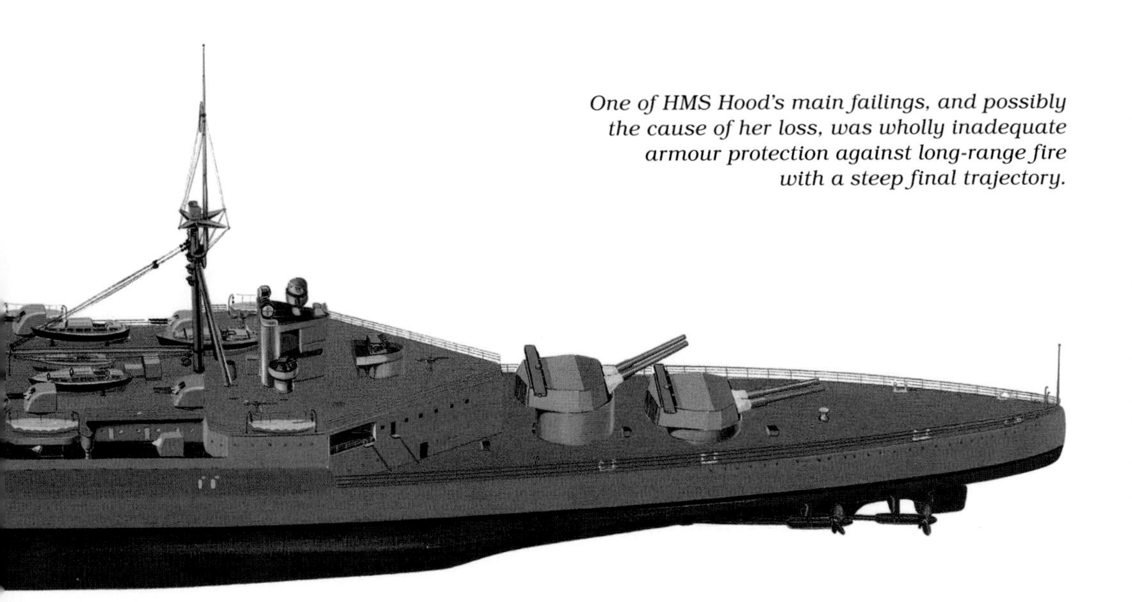

HMS *Hood* (as completed)

Type:	fast battleship
Tonnage:	45,200 tons deep load
Dimensions:	length 860 ft 7 in (262.3 m); beam 105 ft (32 m); draft 28 ft 6 in (8.7 m)
Propulsion:	four geared steam turbines delivering 144,000 shp (107366 kW) to four propellers for 31 kt
Armour:	5/12-in belt (127/305-mm), 4/5-in (102/127-mm) bulkheads, 1.5/3-in (38/76-mm) decks. 11/15-in (279/381-mm) turrets, 5/12-in (127/305-mm) barbettes, and 9/11-in (229/279-mm) conning tower
Armament:	eight 15-in (381-mm) guns, 12 5.5-in (140-mm) guns, four 4-in (102-mm) AA guns, four 3-pdr AA guns, and six 21-in (533-mm) torpedo tubes
Complement:	1,477

Motor Torpedo Boat (1939)

Despite the success of coastal motor boats and motor launches in World War I, the Royal Navy's interest in coastal forces declined rapidly from about 1920 to 1935. In the latter year, though, the threat of a revived German military machine persuaded the British and French that the time was ripe for the start of major rearmament programs. As part of this effort, the Royal Navy received considerably increased funding, and in 1935 placed the first orders signalling a revived British interest in coastal warfare. This order was placed with British Power Boat for torpedo boats with a wooden hull of the hard-chine type. Although this hull form offered greater resistance at cruising speeds (and therefore reduced range) and a slightly lowered maximum speed than the stepped hull of the CMB, it was better suited to the maintenance of speed in any type of sea.

The design which caught the Admiralty's attention was that of a 60-ft (18.3-m) developed by the company as a private venture. It was based on a hard-chine wooden hull with an aluminium deck. Two 18-in (457-mm) torpedoes were carried and, though launched over the stern as in earlier boats, the arrangement was different: the torpedoes protruded through ports in the transom and had their outboard halves supported on lattice outriggers that could be hinged back on deck when not required. The arrangement also meant that the engine room crew had to work with the torpedo warheads supported on overhead runways over the wing shafts. The launch of a torpedo meant that the weapons had to be run up, their restraints removed, and the boat swiftly accelerated to use inertia to drop the torpedoes. As the torpedoes had then to adjust their run in the disturbed water of the boat's wake, aiming was somewhat haphazard. The defensive armament fit seemed to be stronger than in fact it was: eight 0.303-in (7.7-mm) Lewis light machine guns in two quadruple mountings in pits at the extreme ends of the boat.

Though slower than that of the CMB, the hull design proved to be generally more sea-kindly but, like all of its kind, prone to pounding in a head sea. The BPB 60-ft boat was nonetheless

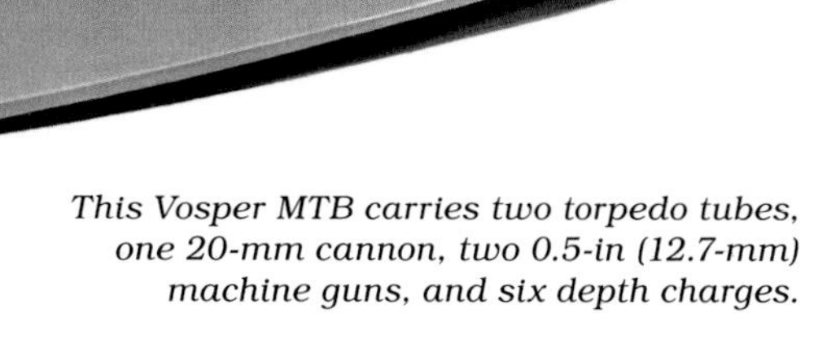

This Vosper MTB carries two torpedo tubes, one 20-mm cannon, two 0.5-in (12.7-mm) machine guns, and six depth charges.

Torpedo launch from an MTB at speed.

seaworthy and capable of staging as far as Malta. This was the first Royal Navy unit designated as a motor torpedo boat. Eighteen of the type were built in 1936/39 (*MTB 1* to *MTB 12* and *MTB 14* to *MTB 19*) with three petrol engines delivering 1,800 bhp (1342 kW) for 33 kt at a displacement of 22 tons. BPB then introduced a two-engined version in which the torpedoes were replaced by depth charges to create the MA/SB craft. These boats enjoyed only limited service in their initial anti-submarine form, and most were later refitted as early motor gun boat types to support MTBs in their operations. For this the boats were generally armed with one 2-pdr gun and four 0.5-in (12.7-mm) machine guns, but there were several other armament fits.

Considerably greater success attended the Vosper 70-ft (21.3-m) MTB, a type which had its origins in a single 68-ft (20.7-m) boat which Vosper built as a private venture in 1935/36 and was commissioned by the Royal Navy as *MTB 102.* Entirely wooden-built, the boat was powered by three Isotta-Fraschini gasoline engines delivering 3,450 bhp (2573 kW) for just less than 44 kt in calm water. An Italian powerplant was selected for lack of any British-made equivalent. Like all such high-powered engines, the Isotta-Fraschini units were very noisy, so a low-power Ford gasoline engine was also included: this could be clutched to the wing shafts for a slow but silent approach. The original armament fit included centerline torpedo tubes (one forward and one aft), but the Royal Navy disliked the arrangement and as a result there appeared what became the standard arrangement with two tubes mounted as one on each beam. It is also worth noting that *MTB 102* was the first Royal Navy vessel fitted with one 20-mm Oerlikon cannon in a mounting that became almost universal in British service.

Motor Torpedo Boat (1939) *continued*

BPB offered a rival 70-ft (21.3-m) MTB which it too had developed as a private venture, but the Admiralty opted for the Vosper design as being the stronger in heavy seas, though it should be added that the complete structural integrity of such wooden hulls in adverse conditions was a problem never adequately resolved. In 1938 the Admiralty ordered four Vosper and two essentially similar boats of Thornycroft design, and these were the real origins of the British MTB effort in World War II. The basic design remained unchanged except for a nominal increase in length to 72 ft 6 in (22.1 m) for enhanced sea-keeping capability and to offset the ever-growing weight of armament and other equipment. After Italy's entry into the war in June 1940 on the side of Germany, the powerplant became something of a problem. A few Rolls-Royce Merlin engines were extracted from the Air Ministry, but the Admiralty had to use the low-powered Hall-Scott engine until the powerful Packard unit became available from the USA. At first 20-mm Oerlikon cannon were in very short supply, so as an interim measure 0.303-in (7.7-mm) machine guns were used even though these were next to useless against targets such as the German S-boote. Eventually 6-pdr guns and 0.5-in (12.7-mm) machine guns were fitted and, after radar had also become available, this turned the MTB into an effective night-fighting type.

Sturdier but lighter hulls combined with more powerful engines meant that by 1944 the Vosper MTBs were able to carry 70 percent more weight of armament and equipment with virtually no significant decline in performance. The service contracted for 193 boats between 1939 and 1945, and most of these had been delivered before the end of World War II.

This late MTB carries a power operated 40-mm Bofors gun mounting aft.

MTB 376 was a Vosper MTB built in the USA by Annapolis Yacht Yard.

It should also be mentioned that one larger type of coastal warfare vessel could, but generally did not, carry torpedo armament. This was the Fairmile "D-type" design, which generally operated as a motor gun boat. With a displacement of 90 tons, a length of 110 ft (33.5 m) and a speed of 29 kt on the 5,000 bhp (3728 kW) delivered to four propellers by four gasoline engines, the "D-type" craft was generally operated in the escort and support roles with an armament of two 6-pdr guns, two 20-mm cannon on a single mounting and two twin 0.5-in (12.7-mm) machine guns, but could also be outfitted with the tubes for four 18-in (457-mm) torpedoes (two flanking the side-by-side pairs of machine guns forward of the bridge, and two flanking the 20mm cannon mounting on the deckhouse abaft the mast.

Vosper 72.5-ft motor torpedo boat

Type:	motor torpedo boat
Tonnage:	49 tons displacement
Dimensions:	length 72 ft 6 in (22.1 m); beam 19 ft 6 in (5.9 m); draft 5 ft 6 in (1.7 m)
Propulsion:	three Packard gasoline engines delivering 4,000 bhp (2983 kW) to three propellers for 40 kt
Armour:	none
Armament:	two 21-in (533-mm) torpedo tubes and a number of combinations of 6-pdr gun, 20-mm cannon, and 0.5- and 0.303-in (12.7- and 7.7-mm) machine guns
Complement:	13

USS *Texas* (1913)

The super-dreadnought battleship USS *Texas*, completed by Newport News in March 1914, was the sister ship of the USS *New York*, name ship of the class and completed by New York Navy Yard in April 1914. The design was similar to that of the preceding "Wyoming" class except for the replacement of the earlier two vessels' main armament of 12 12-in (305-mm) L/50 guns in six twin turrets by 10 14-in (356-mm) L/45 guns in five twin turrets, although the original plan was for 15 12-in (305-mm) guns in five triple turrets. Only with the advent of the new 14-in (356-mm) gun, initially proposed for the two battleships of the "Florida" class that immediately preceded the "Wyoming" class, did this super-dreadnought armament become possible: the turrets were disposed as superfiring pairs fore and aft, and a single unit amidships.

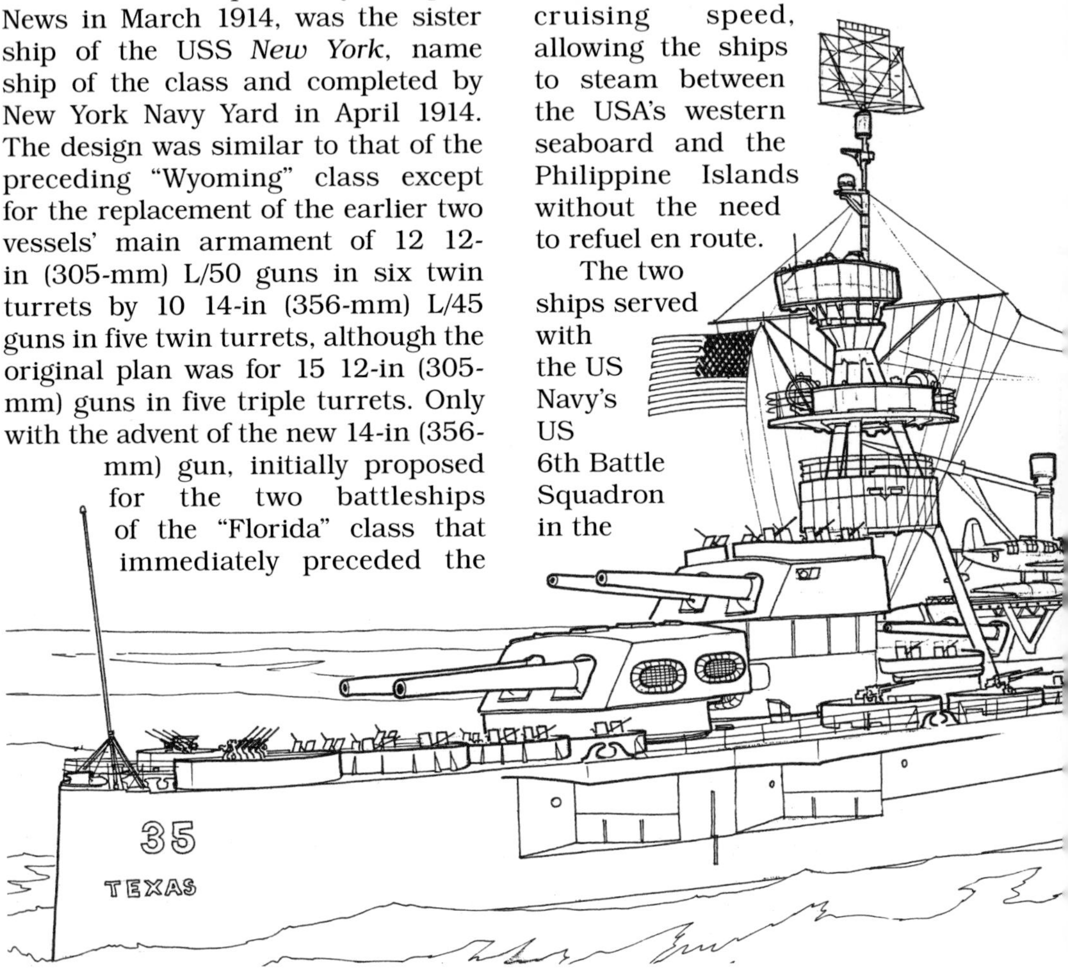

American manufacturers of steam turbines were unwilling to satisfy the US Navy's exacting requirements, even after long discussion of technical and price issues, so the Department of the Navy somewhat reluctantly reverted to reciprocating machinery for the two "New York" class ships. However, the use of such machinery did offer a 30 percent increase in range at typical cruising speed, allowing the ships to steam between the USA's western seaboard and the Philippine Islands without the need to refuel en route.

The two ships served with the US Navy's US 6th Battle Squadron in the British Grand Fleet during the later part of World War I, this revealing that the foremost and aftermost guns of the 5-in (127-mm) battery were effectively useless in all but the best of weather and sea conditions: therefore five of the guns were removed, and two 3-in (76-mm) guns were located at the tops the cranes" stump masts just forward of the after funnel.

The two ships underwent a major modernization in 1925/27, the torpedo tubes being removed, bulges added,

Though completed with the characteristic cage masts of US battleships up to the end of World War I, the USS Texas was later revised with tripod masts.

horizontal armour improved, more modern oil-fired boilers fitted, and cage masts replaced by tripod masts. The ships' poor sea-keeping characteristics were adversely affected by the increase of 10 ft 7 in (3.2 m) in beam and 4,224 tons in full-load displacement, and also reduced the speed to 19.5 kt. In 1940/41 the elevation of the main guns was doubled to 30° to give a maximum range of some 25,000 yards (22860 m). By the end of World War II the ships had steamed enormous distances in support of operations as far removed as the North African landings of November 1942 and Iwo Jima and Okinawa in spring 1945, and their secondary and AA armaments were six 5-in (127-mm), 10 3-in (76-mm) AA, 40 40-mm and 36 20-mm guns. The *New York* survived the atomic bomb tests at Bikini Atoll in July 1946 and was sunk as a target off Pearl Harbor in July 1948, while the *Texas* was taken over by her home state and is preserved as a memorial.

The USS Texas was used primarily as a shore bombardment weapon in World War II.

USS *Texas* (1945 standard)

Type:	super-dreadnought battleship
Tonnage:	34,000 tons full load
Dimensions:	length 572 ft 8 in ((174.6 m); beam 106 ft 1 in (32.3 m); draft 28 ft 6 in (8.7 m)
Propulsion:	two vertical triple expansion steam engines delivering 28,100 ihp (209512 kW) to two propellers for 21 kt
Armour:	6/12-in (152/305-mm) belt, 10-in (254-mm) bulkheads, 2-in (501-mm) decks, 8/14-in (203/356-mm) turrets, 12-in (305-mm) barbettes, 6-in (152-mm) battery, and 12-in (305-mm) conning tower
Armament:	10 14-in (356-mm) guns, five 5-in (127-mm) guns, 10 3-0in (76-mm) AA guns, 40 40-mm AA guns, and 36 20-mm AA cannon
Complement:	1,314

HMS *Abdiel* (1941)

The mine had played an important part in World War I, and great things were expected of it in the next war. An assessment of mine warfare in the immediate aftermath of World War I suggested to the Royal Navy that there was a distinct need for a dedicated warship with the size and speed to race into the area in which a minefield, or at least a large part of it, was to be laid in one fell swoop and then depart, all in the hours of darkness.

The first British warship to be built to the new cruiser minelayer concept was the 8,370-ton HMS *Adventure*, which was armed with four single 4.7-in (120-mm) QF guns, could carry up to 280 mines, and was completed by Devonport Dock Yard in 1927 as the first Royal Navy vessel with a transom stern. This last was found to be unsuitable for minelayers as a result of the fact that the mines, dropped into the dead water immediately abaft the stern, swung back and broke their horns on the transom. The *Adventure* was therefore rebuilt with a cruiser stern, increasing her length by 19 ft (5.8 m) to 539 ft (164.3 m). The *Adventure* could make only 28 kt and was only lightly protected, and in common with most other major warships of World War II was fitted with steadily more extensive light AA armament, and after twice being damaged by ground mines during World War II was relegated for conversion as a repair ship during 1944.

Much greater success attended the "Abdiel" class of six cruiser minelayers. Built by four yards in two batches as four original units completed between April and August 1941, and two later units completed in October 1943 and February 1944, the class comprised HMS *Abdiel*, HMS *Latona*, HMS *Manxman* and HMS *Welshman* in the first group, and HMS *Apollo* and HMS *Ariadne* in the second group. The *Apollo* and *Ariadne* differed from the other ships in having only four 4-in (102-mm) DP guns and two or, in the *Ariadne*, three twin 40-mm AA guns in place of the 2-pdr pom-pom guns. The Bofors twin guns were carried by tri-axial mountings for maximum stability, but in the *Ariadne* they were replaced

HMS Abdiel in camouflage. Note the minelaying hatches on each side of the stern.

by US bi-axial mountings in July 1945, the month in which five single Bofors guns also replaced 10 20-mm Oerlikon AA cannon. The *Apollo* retained the tri-axial mountings, and eventually had six single Bofors gun in place of 14 20-mm cannon. During their World War II careers, the other ships of the class received up to eight 20-mm cannon to beef up their short-range AA capabilities.

The "Abdiel" class cruiser minelayers were very successful, and their notably high speed proved invaluable for their primary role, and also for secondary tasks such as delivering special cargoes of ammunition to Malta. The *Abdiel* was sunk by a ground mine in September 1943, the *Latona* was scuttled in October 1941 after a 276-lb (125-kg) bomb in the engine room caused a serious fire and explosion among the munitions she was carrying, and the *Welshman* was torpedoed and sunk by the U-617 in February 1943. The *Manxman* survived a torpedo hit abreast the engine room, but was out of service for more than two years before returning to service and finally be sold for breaking in 1971.

HMS *Abdiel* (final form)

Type:	cruiser minelayer
Tonnage:	4,000 tons deep load
Dimensions:	length 418 ft (127.4 m); beam 40 ft (12.2 m); draft 14 ft 9 in (4.5 m)
Propulsion:	two geared steam turbines delivering 72,000 shp (53683 kW) to two propellers for 39.75 kt
Armour:	none
Armament:	six 4-in (102-mm) DP guns, four 2-pdr pom-pom guns, eight 0.5-in (12.7-mm) machine guns, and up to 156 mines
Complement:	246

USS *Baltimore* (1916)

The last class of heavy cruisers to be designed and, in some cases completed, during the course of World War II for the US Navy, the "Baltimore" class had basically the same ancestry as the preceding "Cleveland" class as an improved version of the USS *Wichita*, herself the heavy cruiser counterpart of the "Brooklyn" class large light cruisers. Despite the pressures mounting on the US Navy as the USA approached its involvement in World War II, the service's design department ensured that it had the time to consider carefully, and therefore produced a design based on a considerably lengthened but finer hull. This removed the threat of the topweight problems which beset the "Cleveland" class ships, and also allowed the incorporation of more potent propulsion machinery for a higher speed despite the greater displacement.

The armour was improved only slightly over the arrangement and thicknesses of the *Wichita*, which meant that most of the extra displacement was available for factors such as a stronger hull, better stability and, as proved desirable by the nature of the naval war in the Pacific, a larger and more effectively disposed combination of DP secondary and AA tertiary armaments. The main armament was disposed in three centerline triple turrets including a superfiring pair forward, the secondary armament in six twin turrets disposed in two centerline and four beam (groups of three round the forward and after parts of the superstructure), and the tertiary armament of 40-mm guns in 11 quadruple and two twin mountings clustered on and round the superstructure. The US Navy's standard 8-in (203-mm) shell weighed 260 lb (118 kg), but as the design of the "Baltimore" class was being completed the Bureau of Ordnance was introducing a new series of super-heavy shells including an 8-in (203-mm) projectile weighing 335 lb (152 kg) and offering significantly improved armour penetration. This suggested that the protection of the ships, should the Japanese proceed along the same course, might be inadequate, but operational demands necessitated construction rather than redesign. This limitation was addressed in the "Oregon City" subclass of the "Baltimore" class, whose first unit therefore appeared too late for service in World War II.

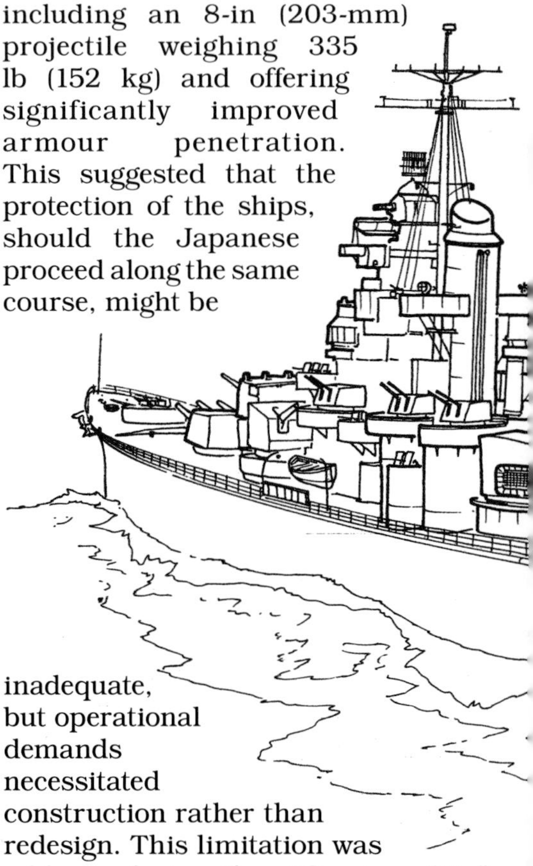

Orders were placed for 24 ships in all, only the first eight (USS *Baltimore, Boston, Canberra, Quincy, Pittsburgh, St Paul, Columbus* and *Helena*) and a later six to the baseline "Baltimore" class design. The first eight were built at Quincy by Bethlehem Steel, which laid down the ships in 1941/43 for completion between April 1943 and September 1945, and the later

The "Baltimore" class heavy cruisers were attractive and effective warships.

six (USS *Bremerton, Fall River, Macon, Toledo, Los Angeles* and *Chicago*) by New York Ship Building and Philadelphia Navy Yard for completion in 1945/46. Like another two "Baltimore" class ships, the last four of the eight "Oregon City" class ships were cancelled before being laid down.

The "Baltimore" class units remained in service after World War II, some serving as flagships and fire support ships in Vietnam, five being converted as missile cruisers, and all being stricken by 1980.

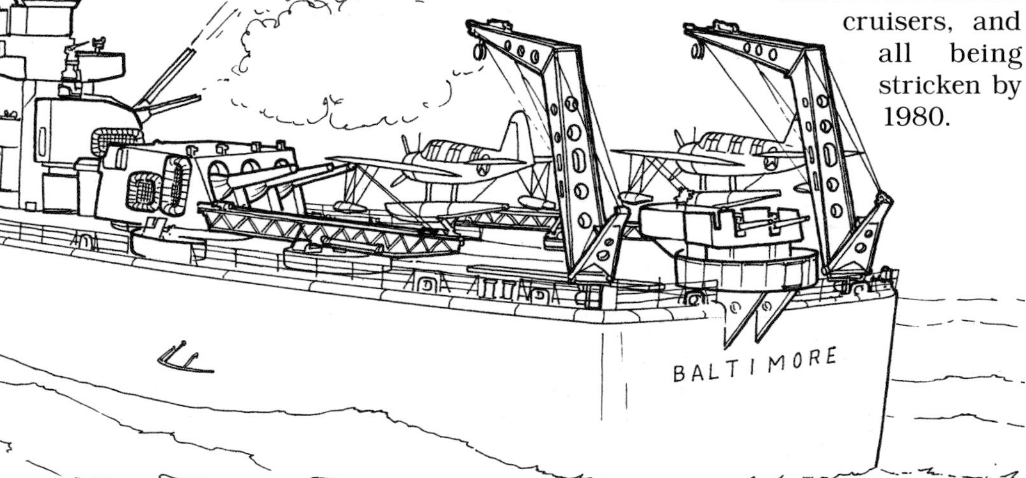

USS *Baltimore*

Type:	heavy cruiser
Tonnage:	17,031 tons full load
Dimensions:	length 673 ft 5 in (20.25 m); beam 70 ft 10 in (21.6 m); draft 24 ft (7.3 m)
Propulsion:	four geared steam turbines delivering 120,000 shp (89472 kW) to four propellers for 33 kt
Armour:	4/6-in (102/152-mm) belt, 2.5-in (64-mm) armoured deck, 1.5/8-in (38/203-mm) turrets, 6.3-in (160-mm) barbettes, 2.5/3-in (64/76-mm) magazine boxes, and 3/6-in (76/152-mm) conning tower
Armament:	nine 8-in (203-mm) guns, 12 5-in (127-mm) DP guns, 48 40-mm AA guns, 24 20-mm AA cannon, and two or four aircraft
Complement:	2,039

"V" & "W" class destroyers (1917)

In 1916 the Admiralty planned a new class of high-speed flotilla leaders. These were the five "V" class leaders capable of 34 kt on 27,000 shp (20131 kW), and having a 1,400-ton deep-load displacement and primary armament of four 4-in (102-mm) guns. Believing that the Germans were starting to build large and powerfully armed destroyers, the Admiralty then ordered 26 "V" class destroyers based on the hull, machinery and armament of the "V" class leaders but with a sturdier bridge and strengthening to allow the replacement of the standard twin mounting for 21-in (533-mm) torpedoes with a triple mounting. The ships were completed between August 1917 and June 1918, two of them as Thornycroft "specials" with their beam increased to 30 ft 8.5 in (9.4 m).

There followed 23 examples of the "W" class destroyer (including two Thornycroft "specials"), which were repeats of the "V" class ships with triple tube mountings and completed between November 1917 and October 1918, five of them as minelayers. Ordered to the extent of 16 units (including two Thornycroft "specials") in January 1918 and another 38 in March and April of the same year, the final development of this design concept was the "Modified W" class. A number of improvements was introduced, but in the event only 16 of the ships were completed, the others being cancelled at the end of World War I.

Three "V" class destroyers were lost in or immediately after World War I, and during the 1920s and 1930s the Royal Navy scrapped five "V" and one "W" class destroyers, and so approached World War II with 23 "V," 19 "W" and 14 "Modified W" class destroyers, these totals including the

A "W" class destroyer at sea.

HMS *Voyager* was a "V" class destroyer transferred to the Royal Australian Navy and sunk in September 1942.

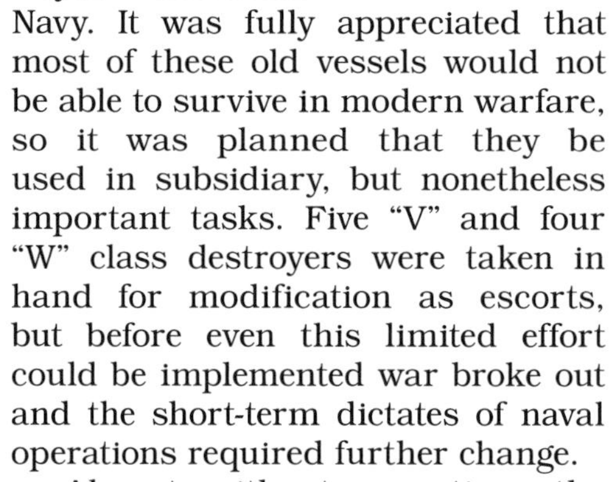

four Thornycroft "specials." Of these, three "V" and one "W" class ships had been passed to the Royal Australian Navy. It was fully appreciated that most of these old vessels would not be able to survive in modern warfare, so it was planned that they be used in subsidiary, but nonetheless important tasks. Five "V" and four "W" class destroyers were taken in hand for modification as escorts, but before even this limited effort could be implemented war broke out and the short-term dictates of naval operations required further change.

Almost without exception, the other destroyers were modified for escort work in three forms. Three "V" and one "W" class ships were adapted as escort destroyers along the lines established before the war and involving structural alteration and complete rearmament with AA and anti-submarine weapons. Some 11 ships were adapted as short-range escorts with enhanced AA and anti-submarine armament. The after torpedo tube mounting was replaced by a 3-in (76-mm) AA gun and the quarterdeck gun was removed to increase depth charge stowage. Four of the conversions were later further adapted to counter S-boote with a twin 6-pdr in place of the forecastle gun and a 2-pdr on the quarterdeck.

Finally, 22 ships were revised as long-range escorts with the forward boiler and its uptake replaced by additional bunkerage. The forecastle gun was replaced by an ahead-throwing Hedgehog anti-submarine weapon and the remaining torpedo tube mounting was generally removed, those which retained the mounting using it to fire heavy depth charges. Some 16 of the destroyers were lost in World War II.

HMS *Vanessa* (in World War II)

Type:	"V" class destroyer adapted as a long-range escort
Tonnage:	1,090 tons displacement
Dimensions:	length 312 ft (95.1 m); beam 29 ft 6 in (9 m); draft 9 ft 6 in (2.9 m)
Propulsion:	two geared steam turbines delivering 18,000 shp (13421 kW) to two propellers for 24.5 kt
Armour:	none
Armament:	two 4-in (102-mm) guns, one 3-in (76-mm) AA gun, two 2-pdr AA guns, two 20-mm AA cannon, three 21-in (533-mm) torpedo tubes, and one Hedgehog anti-submarine thrower
Complement:	125

De Ruyter (1936)

In 1915 the Royal Dutch navy ordered three "Sumatra" class cruisers designed with technical aid from Krupp of Germany, which also supplied some of the materials and skilled manpower. The design was far larger and better armed than the British and German cruisers of the period, and the *Java* and *Sumatra* were laid down in May and July 1916. It was planned that the vessels be completed in 1918, but the program was badly delayed and the ships were completed only in May 1926, by which time they were technically obsolete. A third unit was laid down as the slightly enlarged but lighter *Celebes* in 1917, but was cancelled in 1919.

The Netherlands considered that its East Indian empire required considerable military and naval forces, the latter including three cruisers. In 1930, therefore, the Dutch navy ordered the *De Ruyter* to replace the cancelled *Celebes* and operate with the *Java* and *Sumatra* in its East Indian navy. This was a period of great financial austerity, and the design was therefore fixed round a maximum displacement of 5,250

The De Ruyter had a massively capped funnel, and the single gun of her "B" turret was equipped to fire starshell.

tons, the primary armament of six 5.9-in (150-mm) guns in three twin turrets (one forward and two aft), protection generally similar to that of the "Sumatra" class, and a speed of 32 kt. The design was criticized for its inadequate size and limited armament at a time when most pundits wanted eight 5.9-in (150-mm) or six 8-in (203-mm) guns. The criticism was reflected in the modification of the design with a lengthened hull of improved lines and thus greater speed, and also able to carry one more 5.9-in (150-mm) gun forward in a superfiring turret, and a floatplane catapult abaft the single, massive funnel. At the same time careful consideration of the detail design, the introduction of aluminium wherever possible, and the use of welding rather than riveting in the construction yielded weight savings. The ship was ordered in August 1932 and laid down by Wilton-Fijenoord in September 1933 for completion in October 1936.

The protection was based on a waterline belt, 2 in (50 mm) thick in the center and tapering to 1.2 in (30 mm) at its ends, and this extended from the forward edge of "A" magazine to the after end of the steering compartment. The upper edges of the belt supported the outer sides of the 1.2-in (30-mm) thick protective deck, and was closed for and aft by 1.2-in (30-mm) bulkheads. The main conning tower (above a tower-like bridge structure), after control tower, turrets, barbettes and communication trunks were all protected by 1.2-in (30-mm) armour. The 5.9-in (150-mm) guns had a muzzle velocity of 2,953 ft (900 m) per second and fired a 101.5-lb (46-kg) projectile. There was no secondary anti-ship or medium-range anti-aircraft battery, while the short-range AA battery comprised five twin 40-mm gun mountings: these were stabilized and power-operated, and grouped on the after superstructure in an arrangement which limited the firing arcs and opened the possibility of a single hit destroying or disabling all five mountings. The advanced fire-control system included remote controls, stabilization and a significant element of automation.

The *De Ruyter* left the Netherlands for the East Indies in January 1937, and later became the Dutch flagship. It was in this ship that Rear Admiral Karel Doorman led the Allied force involved in the Battle of the Java Sea in February 1942. During the battle the ship was hit by gunfire and a "Long Lance" torpedo fired by the Japanese cruiser *Haguro*, and sank two hours later with some 345 of her crew including Doorman.

De Ruyter

Type:	light cruiser
Tonnage:	7,548 tons full load
Dimensions:	length 560 ft 4 in (170.8 m); beam 51 ft 6 in (15.7 m); draft 16 ft 9 in (5.1 m)
Propulsion:	two geared steam turbines delivering 66,000 shp (49210 kW) to two propellers for 32 kt
Armour:	1.2/2-in (30/50-mm) belt, and 1.2-in (30-mm) bulkheads, decks, turrets, barbettes and conning tower
Armament:	seven 5.9-in (150-mm) guns, 10 40-mm AA guns, eight 0.5-in (12.7-mm) AA machine guns, and two aircraft
Complement:	435

“South Dakota” class (1942)

The “South Dakota” class battleship had nine 16-in (306-mm) main guns in three triple turrets on the centreline forward and aft, and its secondary DP and tertiary AA armament clustered round

The four battleships of the US Navy’s “South Dakota” class were an interesting attempt to combine fully effective protection against 16-in (406-mm) projectiles and a standard displacement not exceeding the limit of 35,000 tons ordained by the 2nd London Naval Treaty of 1935. This combination was to be achieved without any reduction in speed from that of the preceding “North Carolina” class, with protection against the underwater hits which were likely to occur in long-range engagements, and with an immune zone against 16-in (406-mm) fire with a 2,250-lb (1021-kg) shell between 18,000 and 30,000 yards (16460 and 27430 m).

The designers therefore combined very acutely sloped internal side armour with a thick armoured deck, but this demanded considerable saving of weight elsewhere, and as a result the length of the protection was reduced by compressing the length of the ship containing the vital elements, and a higher-than-normal measure of blast interference was permitted round the superstructure, which was as cramped as the hull. In the latter the steeply angled belt, which not significantly thicker than that of the “North Carolina” class ships, was continued into the armoured bulkhead of the torpedo protection in an arrangement untested when the ships were laid down. Subsequent experiments suggested that the arrangement was not really adequate, but it was by

In retrospect, it is possible that the US Navy sought to pack too much offensive and defensive capability into a hull limited by treaty restrictions.

that time too late to alter both the "South Dakota" class and also the follow-on "Iowa" class battleships.

Another novel element of the design was the so-called "tunnel" stern, in which the two outboard propellers were carried by very large skegs, and the pair of inner propellers turned in the "tunnel" so created. The skegs thus provided a measure of torpedo protection for the inboard propellers, and the hydrodynamic refinements which allowed for sufficient hull volume to improve the torpedo protection for the after magazines.

The four ships were the USS *South Dakota*, USS *Indiana*, USS *Massachusetts* and USS *Alabama*. These were laid down between July 1939 and February 1940s by New York Ship Building, Newport News, Bethlehem and Norfolk Navy Yard respectively, and completed between March and August 1942. The *South Dakota* differed from her three sisters in being completed as a force flagship with an extra level in her conning tower, the additional topweight being offset by the omission of two 5-in (127-mm) DP guns mountings, with additional AA capability vested in two more quadruple 1,1-in mountings.

Originally only the *South Dakota* and the *Indiana* were authorised, but the *Massachusetts* and *Alabama* were then added despite the fact that work of the "Iowa" class ships was already well under way. In an effort to provide the 16-in (406-mm) guns of the US Navy's battleships with greater punch, in 1939 the Bureau of Ordnance developed a new 2.700-lb (1225-kg) shell which, it claimed, would provide the capability of an 18-in (457-mm) shell of the standard typified by the baseline 16-in (406-mm) shell. The other side of this coin, of course, was the fact that the development of a comparable shell by an enemy would effectively reduce the immune zone of the "South Dakota" class to between 20,500 to 26,400 yards (18745 and 24140 m). This factor was also relevant to the "Iowa" class ships, and was the single most compelling reason for the design of the considerably larger "Montana" class battleship, of which five were projected but not finally built.

"South Dakota" class (1942) *continued*

The "South Dakota" class battleships were used for the anti-ship and shore bombardment roles throughout World War II.

After they had been completely and had worked up to combat capability, the four ships had very active careers in the Pacific campaign of World War II. The *South Dakota*, for instance, fought in the battles of Santa Cruz, Guadalcanal, Gilbert Islands, Kwajalein, Truk and Palau raids, Hollandia, Saipan, Philippine Sea, Leyte, Luzon, China coast and Ryukyu raids, Iwo Jima, Okinawa, and Japanese home islands raids. She did not pass though the war without suffering damage and casualties, for as well as hitting an uncharted rock and colliding with an American destroyer, she suffered a bomb hit on "A" turret in the Santa Cruz battle, was damaged by shellfire and suffered 38 dead in the Guadalcanal battle, was hit by a bomb and suffered 27 dead off Saipan, and was damaged by a powder explosion one of her turrets. By August 1945 the *South Dakota's* light AA armament comprised 17 quadruple 40-mm and 72 single 20-mm mounts.

All the ships were withdrawn from service after World War II's end and decommissioned in 1947, although the *Massachusetts* was refitted for further service, this update reflecting the reduced threat of air attack and the need to economize on manpower in the considerable reduction in her light AA weapons. As none of the four was old or had been seriously damaged, right through the 1950s schemes were suggested for further use of the hulls, but none came to anything. The first two were sold for breaking in 1962/63, and the second two have been preserved as memorials.

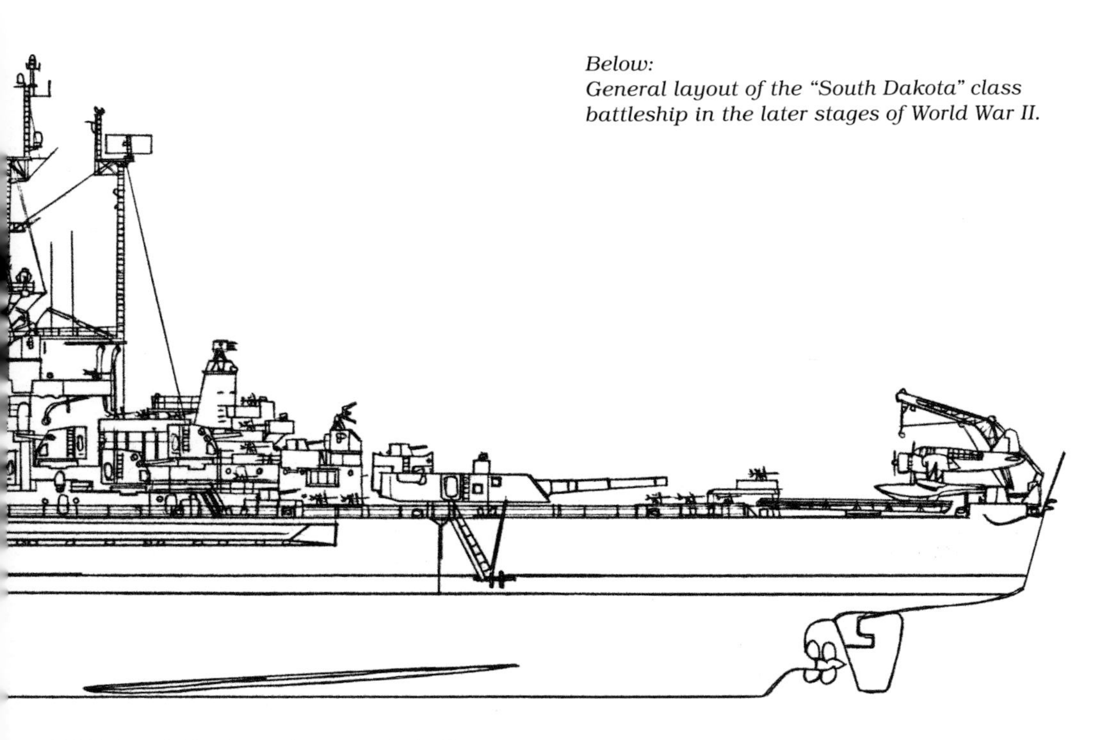

Below:
General layout of the "South Dakota" class battleship in the later stages of World War II.

USS *South Dakota* (as completed)

Type:	battleship
Tonnage:	44,519 tons full load
Dimensions:	length 680 ft (207.25 m); beam 108 ft 2 in (33 m); draft 35 ft 1 in (10.7 m)
Propulsion:	four geared steam turbines delivering 130,000 shp (97259 kW) to four propellers for 27.5 kt
Armour:	12.2-in (310-mm) belt, 1/12.2-in (25/310-mm) lower belt, 5.75/6-in (146/152-mm) armoured deck, 1.5-in (38-mm) weather deck, 11-in (279-mm) bulkheads, 7.25/18-in (184/457-mm) turrets, 11.3/17.3-in (287/439-mm) barbettes, and 7.25/16-in (184/406-mm) conning tower
Armament:	nine 16-in (406-mm) guns, 20 5-in (127-mm) DP guns, 12 1.1-in AA guns, 12 0.5-in (12.7-mm) AA guns, and three aircraft
Complement:	1,793

"Fletcher" class destroyer (1942)

On the same day in October 1939 the Boston Navy Yard launched the last two "Sims" class and the first two "Benson" class destroyers. Though both classes were based on the same hull and machinery, in the "Benson" class destroyers the boiler spaces were divided for improved damage control, even though his required reversion from one to two funnels. The armament was theoretically good, being based as it was one five 5-in (127-mm) DP guns and two quintuple launchers for 21-in

(533-mm) torpedoes, but wartime operational conditions revealed that this was too much, and as a result one gun and one set of torpedo launchers were removed from the first 24 units, which were the only ships completed with the full-specification armament. The basic design was nonetheless sound, and was retained for the first major destroyer class

Courtesy National Park Service, U.S. Department of the Interior, artist John Batchelor.

as the US Navy expanded rapidly in the face of war. Some 96 "Benson" class ships were built in 1939/43 and the last 64, though officially the separate "Livermore" class, differed only marginally as reflected a slightly greater displacement. These were the last American destroyers to have the European type of raised forecastle, which extended the maximum freeboard farther aft and produced a greater enclosed volume, but at the same time added greater structural stresses. Amidships the US Navy's destroyers had bulwarks to a point abaft the after funnel, which was a great aid to keeping the ship's waists dry, and was made possible by the fact that the continuous topside casing required the torpedo tubes to be located one deck higher than the upper deck, though this had adverse topweight implications.

Though the advent of the "Benson" and derived classes helped to put the US shipbuilding industry on a war footing it was apparent from an early stage that the basic design was too limited for effective use on the context of a Pacific campaign because of its limited endurance and cut-back armament fit. Even before the building had drawn to a close, therefore, the first units of the improved "Fletcher" class destroyers were being completed. The first two were launched in February 1942, and such was the intensity of the building effort during World War II that the last four of the 175 ships were launched on the same day in September 1944 at Puget Sound Navy Yard.

The hull of the "Fletcher" class destroyer was 28 ft (8.53 m) longer and 3 ft (0.91 m) beamier than that of the "Benson" class, and this allowed the retention of the full gun and torpedo armament at first specified for the "Benson" class, though a great improvement was the introduction of an AA battery initially comprising one quadruple 1.1-in gun and four single 20-mm cannon, the latter being licence-made European weapons. The nature of the war, especially in the Pacific, meant that the AA armament was steadily upgraded to a fit of licence-made weapons: these were initially three twin 40-mm weapons and 10 or 11 single 20-mm cannon, then five twin 40-mm weapons and seven single 20-mm weapons, and finally the latter fit supplemented by two more twin 40-mm guns. Some ships also had one bank of torpedo tubes removed to allow the replacement of two twin by two quadruple 40-mm mounts.

There was no main mast and the superstructure was both simplified and lightened, which helped the topweight problem, and the center of gravity was further lowered by reversion to a flushdecked hull, which was also stronger but more cramped. The funnels were shorter, and therefore completed with large caps.

Although the "Fletcher" class destroyers were generally deployed to the Pacific, where their endurance of 7,500 miles (12070 km) at 15 kt was a decided asset, but some of the ships built on the USA's East coast saw limited use in the Atlantic.

Later in the war the "Fletcher" class ships were complemented by

DD652 was the "Fletcher" class USS Ingersoll, built by Bath Iron Works and launched on 28 June 1943. The ship was stricken in January 1970 and broken up.

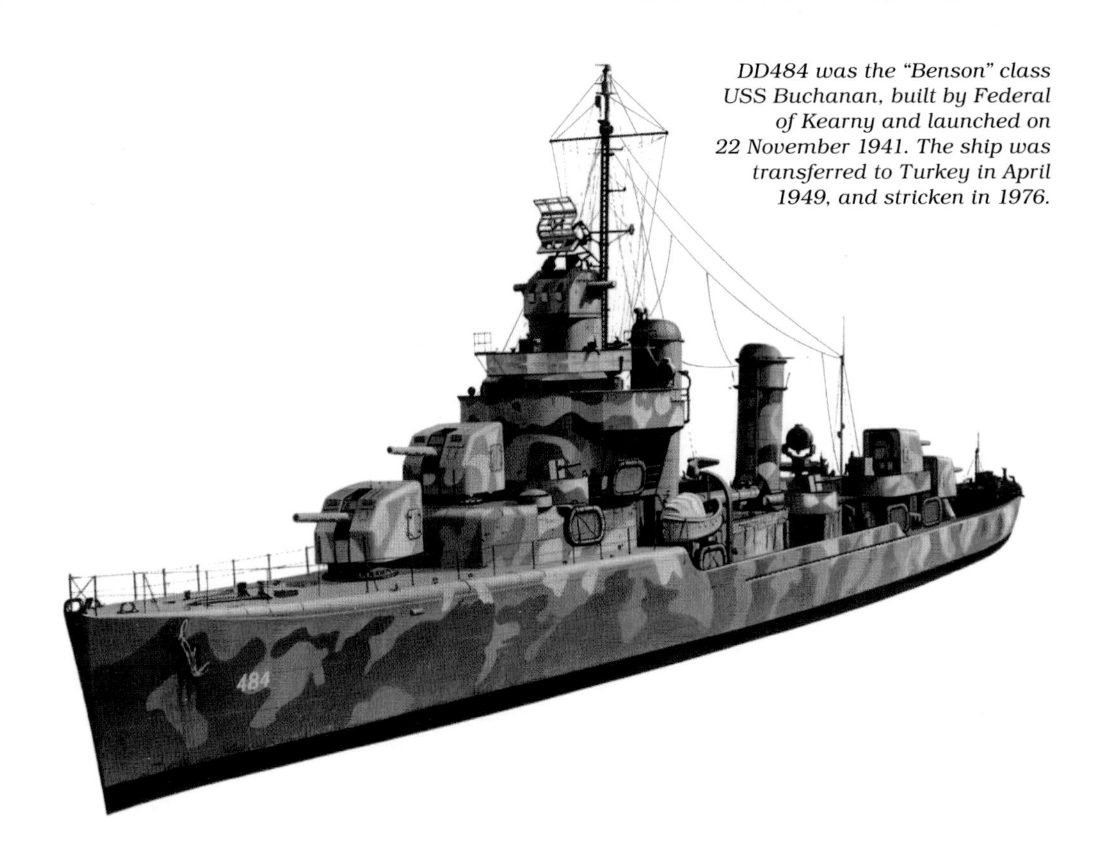

DD484 was the "Benson" class USS Buchanan, built by Federal of Kearny and launched on 22 November 1941. The ship was transferred to Turkey in April 1949, and stricken in 1976.

the first "Allen M. Sumner" class shorter-range destroyers with six 5-in (127-mm) guns in three twin mountings in place of the five 5-in (127-mm) guns in single mounts as carried by the "Fletcher" class destroyers, and then by the first "Gearing" class ships which were in effect lengthened "Allen M. Sumner" class units with greater fuel capacity. Most of the "Fletcher" class ships were reduced to reserve in the two years after World War II's end, but on the outbreak of the Korean War (1950/53), 39 were recommissioned in an upgraded form with four 5-in (127-mm) guns, 3-in (76-mm) AA guns and a quintuple torpedo

USS *Fletcher*

Type:	fleet destroyer
Tonnage:	2,924 tons full load
Dimensions:	length 376 ft 5 in (114.75 m); beam 39 ft 7 in (12.1 m); draft 13 ft 9 in (4.2 m)
Propulsion:	two double-reduction geared steam turbines delivering 60,000 shp (44736 kW) to two propellers for 38 kt
Armour:	0.75-in (20-mm) belt, and 0.5-in (13-mm) deck over machinery
Armament:	five 5-in (127-mm) DP guns, four 1.1-in AA guns, four 20-mm AA guns, 10 21-in (533-mm) torpedo tubes, six depth charge throwers, and two depth charge racks
Complement:	273

British armed trawler (World War II)

The Royal Navy made extensive use of trawlers, requisitioned and specially built, but turned most of these back to the fishing industry after 1918, so that by 1939 there survived in naval service just 14 "Mersey", three "Castle", one "Strath" and four "Axe" class vessels. The threat of war led to a hugely increased demand for these small but seaworthy vessels which could be used in a host of roles, and a first tranche of re-requisitioning saw naval ranks swelled by 30 "Mersey," 125 "Castle," 75 "Strath," two "Axe" and two "Military" class vessels.

During the mid-1930s the Admiralty had decided to test an improved trawler type, and HMS *Basset* was launched in 1935 with a large forecastle, the bridge more amidships, and slightly greater speed than mercantile trawlers. There followed, in the next 10 years, some 250 naval trawlers which differed but little from the *Basset's* basic design. Also in 1935, 20 modern trawlers were bought for anti-submarine and minesweeping work with "Gem" and "Tree" names respectively. Another 20 such vessels, together with six whalers, were acquired in 1936/39 for the anti-submarine, minesweeper, boom defence and depot ship roles. With 25 survivors from World War I and some six "Basset" class units, these were the trawlers available to the Royal Navy at the outbreak of World War II in 1939, another 40 "Bassets" ("Tree" and "Dance" classes) being under construction.

With the start of the war, some hundreds of trawlers and drifters were mobilized for Royal Navy service, which initially involved the coastal anti-submarine and minesweeping roles but came to include oceanic anti-submarine work in the escort task. Their weatherliness meant that trawlers were often the only escorts operative in heavy weather.

The trawlers used by the British and some of their allies were very weatherly, and could remain at sea in conditions that defeated destroyers.

War construction was limited mainly to the "Basset" type ("Shakespearian" and "Isles" classes). A small number of mercantile-type trawlers was also built on the basis of designs by Hall Russell, Cochrane and Cook, and Welton & Gemmell.

The trawlers were usually armed with one 4-in (102-mm) or 12-pdr gun when outfitted for the anti-submarine or minesweeping roles respectively, though old 6- and 3-pdr weapons were used at first. Similarly, the anti-aircraft machine guns were later replaced by 20-mm cannon. In the naval trawlers the mast stepped before the bridge was always re-stepped abaft it, warning radar was fitted as it became available, and an all-steel bridge replaced the former mattress- protected wooden units. Reciprocating machinery, in which engine room reservists were experienced, was standard, as were coal-fired boilers.

"Isles" class trawler

Type:	naval trawler
Tonnage:	545 tons displacement
Dimensions:	length 164 ft (50 m); beam 27 ft 6 in (8.4 m); draft 10 ft 6 in (3.2 m)
Propulsion:	one vertical triple expansion steam engine delivering 850 ihp (634 kW) to one propeller for 12 kt
Armour:	none
Armament:	one 12-pdr AA gun, and three 20-mm AA cannon
Complement:	40

Akitsuki (1941)

During the later 1930s the increasingly capable threat of air attack persuaded the world's more advanced navies to plan enhanced protection for their major warships, most especially their primary assets such as capital ships, aircraft carriers and cruisers, against the increasing threat of air attack. Thus the Imperial Japanese navy designed its new "Type B" destroyer with two pairs of superfiring turrets each mounting two 3.9-in (100-mm) L/65 high-velocity AA guns. The resulting escort design was the heaviest yet produced for a destroyer. The new gun was very capable, with a high rate of fire and a surface range of 20,000 yards (18290 m) and thus offer capabilities somewhat better than the US Navy's 5-in (127-mm) L/38 DP gun. The guns were mounted in large power-operated and fully protected turrets, and to increase the efficiency with which the pairs of turret could operate, separate fire-control positions were fitted fore and aft. It was then decided to change the requirement so that the destroyers could operate in an offensive as well a defensive role through the addition of a quadruple mount amidships for the truly formidable 24-in (610-mm) Type 93 or "Long Lance" torpedo. Fuelled with liquid oxygen and carrying a large warhead able to penetrate thick armour, the Type 93 could be set to run a long distance at moderately high speed, or a shorter distance at considerable higher speed. The Japanese rightly believed that salvoes of such torpedoes could be genuinely decisive in shorter-range engagements, especially in the type of night operations for which the Japanese had specially trained.

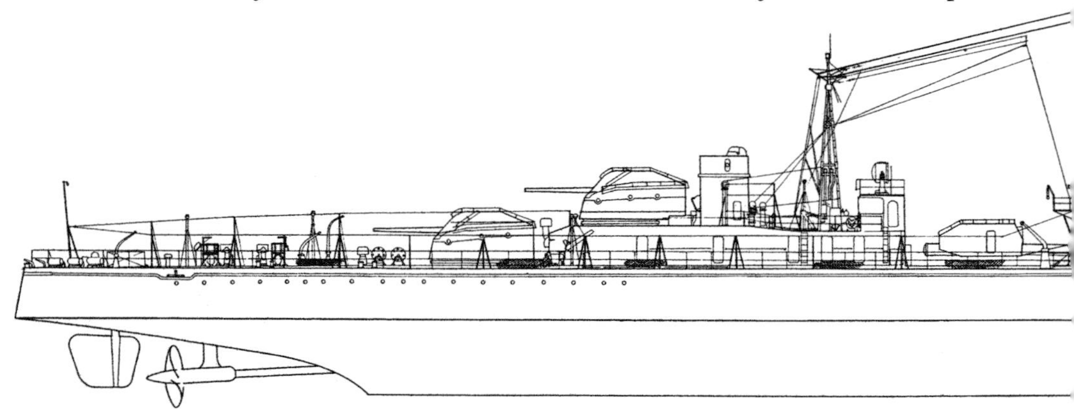

This change created the "Akitsuki" class design, of which the first six units were ordered under the 1939 program and another 10 added under the 1941 program. In the event only 12 of the destroyers were completed, between June 1942 and April 1945, as vessels whose distinctive silhouette included one large funnel containing all three boiler uptakes and turrets that were in fact larger than the 5-in (127-mm) turrets of the "Kagero" and "Yugumo" class destroyers. Soon after the first ships had been completed, their minesweeping gear was removed and the vessels were given an anti-submarine capability through the provision of four throwers for 54 depth charges or, in the case of the ships completed in 1944/45, 72 depth charges. During 1943 the light AA weapons complement was upgraded to 15 25-mm guns, and the ships received air and surface search radars with their antennae on the fore mast. After June 1944 the *Akitsuki*, the *Hatsutsuki*, the *Shimotsuki*, the *Suzutsuki* and the *Wataksuki* had their light AA capability further strengthened to 29 25-mm and four 13-mm guns. The *Fuyutsuki, Hanutsuki, Harutsuki, Natsutsuki* and *Yoitsuki* were completed with some 40 to 51 25-mm guns (five to seven triple and 25 to 30 single mounts).

Four of the first 16 ships were cancelled (one of them after being laid down), and a further 39 (16 to the current standard and 23 to an enlarged standard with a standard displacement of 2,933 rather than 2,701 tons) were ordered but then cancelled. Six of the 12 completed ships were lost in World War II (one, two and three to US submarine, carrierborne air and surface ship attack), and of the other six two were too badly damaged to be worth repairing, and the other four were transferred to China, the USSR, the USA and the UK, the latter two scrapping their single vessels.

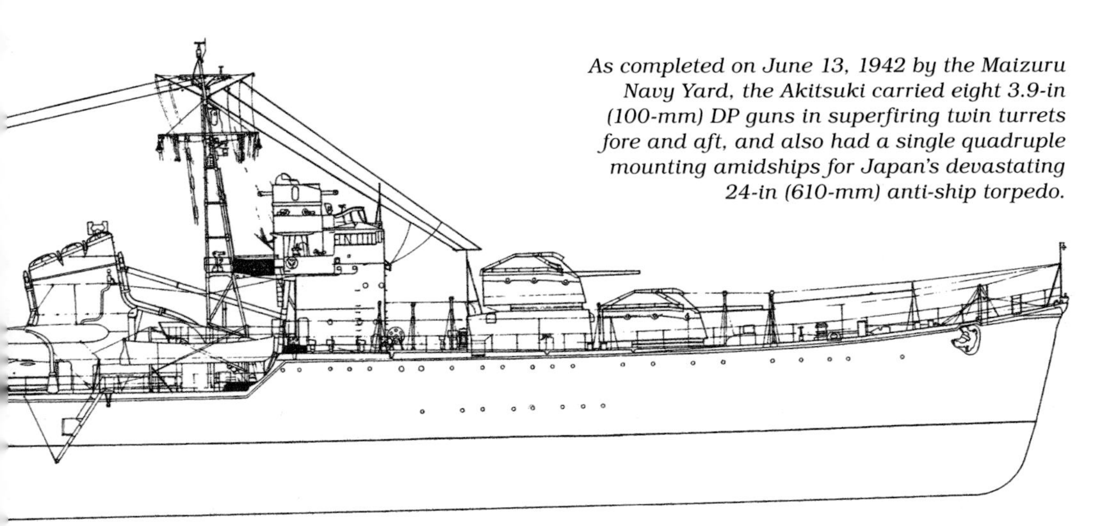

As completed on June 13, 1942 by the Maizuru Navy Yard, the Akitsuki carried eight 3.9-in (100-mm) DP guns in superfiring twin turrets fore and aft, and also had a single quadruple mounting amidships for Japan's devastating 24-in (610-mm) anti-ship torpedo.

Akitsuki (as completed)

Type:	fleet destroyer
Tonnage:	3,700 tons full load
Dimensions:	length 440 ft 3 in (134.2 m); beam 38 ft 1 in (11.6 m); draft 13 ft 7 in (4.15 m)
Propulsion:	two geared steam turbines delivering 52,000 shp (38771 kW) to two propellers for 33 kt
Armour:	none
Armament:	eight 3.9-in (100-mm) DP guns, four 25-mm AA guns, four 24-in (610-mm) torpedo tubes, and 72 depth charges
Complement:	290

USS *Massachusetts* (1942)

The four vessels of the "South Dakota" class, the penultimate US battleship class, were an effort to achieve good protection against 16-in (406-mm) shell fire and torpedo hits on a displacement limited by the London Treaty to 35,000 tons, but without any sacrifice of the speed achieved in the "North Carolina" design. The was achieved by reducing habitability, allowing great blast interference between the secondary armament turrets, and reducing hull length by some 50 ft (15.2 m) to permit the introduction of greater horizontal and underwater protection through the combination of steeply sloped internal side armour and a heavy armoured deck.

The four ships were the USS *South Dakota*, USS *Indiana*, USS *Massachusetts* and USS *Alabama*, which were laid down in 1939/40 in four yards and completed between March and August 1942. The *South Dakota* differed from her sisters in being completed as a force flagship with an additional conning tower level and, to offset this extra topweight, eight rather than 10 5-in (127-mm) twin DP gun turrets with improved AA defence provided by 20 1.1-in guns in five quadruple mounts. With much sacrificed for superior protection, greater offensive capability was provided by a new 2,700-lb (1225-kg) projectile for the 16-in (406-mm) L/45 main guns.

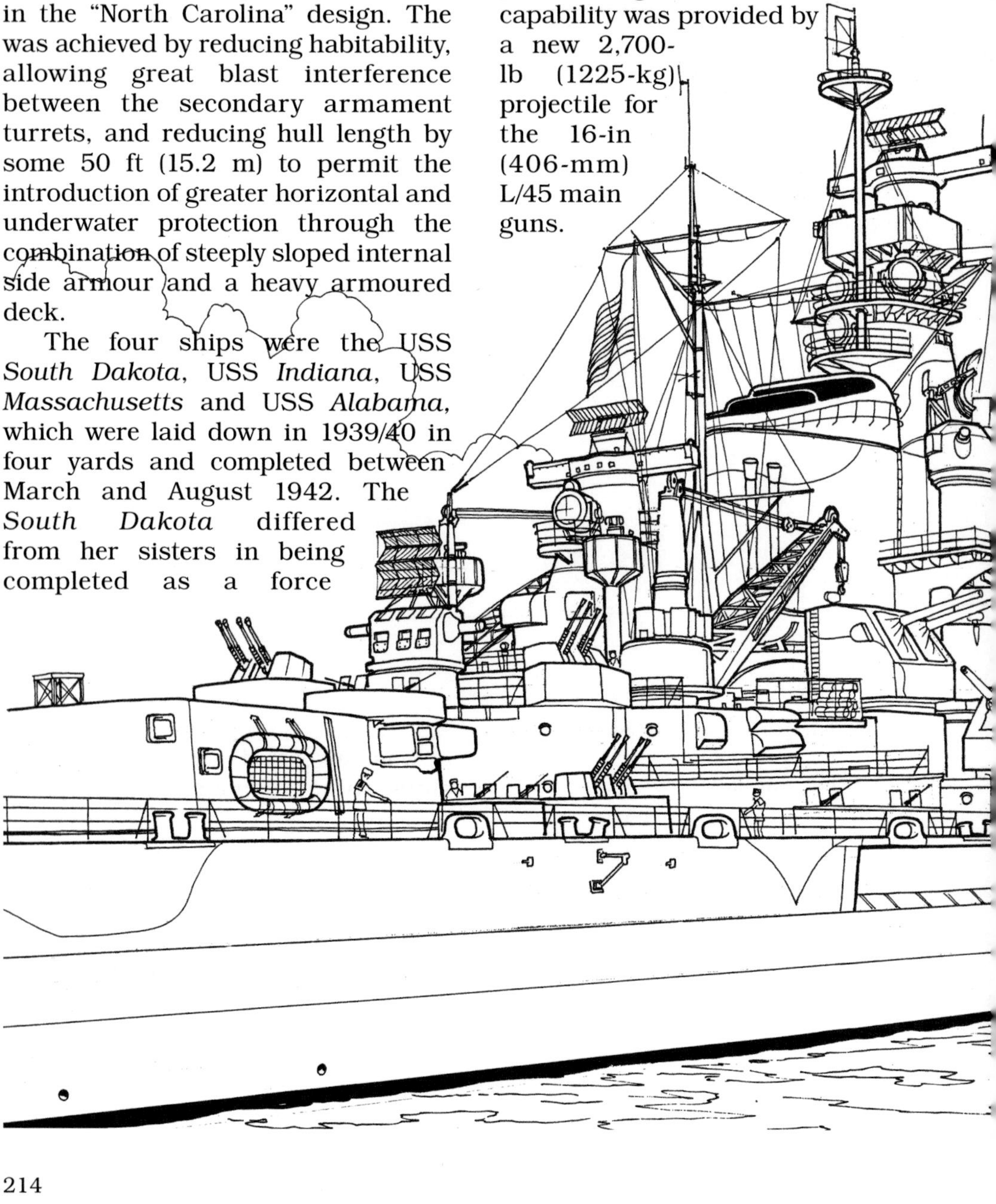

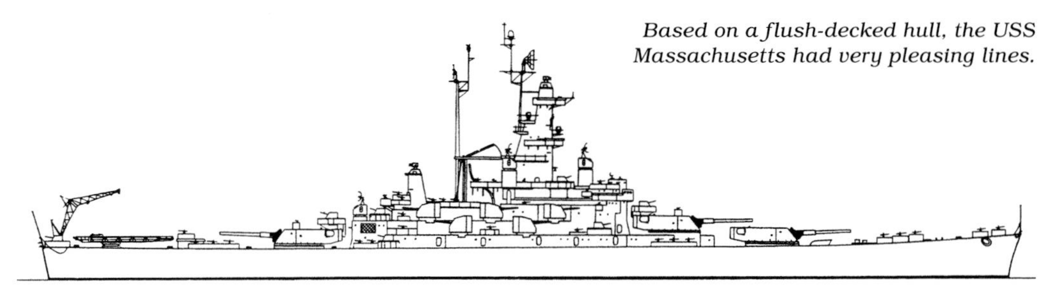

Based on a flush-decked hull, the USS Massachusetts had very pleasing lines.

USS *Massachusetts* (1945 standard)

Type:	battleship
Tonnage:	44,216 tons full load
Dimensions:	length 680 ft 9 in (207.5 m); beam 108 ft 2 in (33 m); draft 35 ft 1 in (10.7 m)
Propulsion:	four geared steam turbines delivering 130,000 shp (96928 kW) to four propellers for 27.5 kt
Armour:	12.25-in (311-mm) belt, 11-in (279-mm) bulkheads, 5.75/6-in (146-152-mm) decks, 11.3/17.3-in (287/439-mm) barbettes, 7.25/18-in (287/457-mm) main turrets, 0.75/1-in (19/25-mm) secondary turrets, and 7.25/16-in (184/406-mm) conning tower
Armament:	nine 16-in (406-mm) guns, 20 5-in (127-mm) DP guns, 56 40-mm AA guns, 40 20-mm AA cannon, and three aircraft
Complement:	2,232

The ships saw very extensive service in World War II, in which their AA defences were much enlarged, principally by the addition of an eventual 14 power-operated 40-mm quadruple mounts (with radar as well as optical directors) and 40 20-mm cannon. All the ships were withdrawn from service in 1946/47, soon after the end of World War II. The *Massachusetts* was taken in hand for the improvement designed to provide her with a capability for further service. Though the ships had seen extensive service, none had suffered major damage, and right through the 1950s there appeared a variety of schemes to make further use of the ships. For a short time, for instance, it was suggested that one of these ships, rather than a cruiser, might be adapted as the first US fleet missile ship. It was even mooted for a short time that the ships' power be raised to allow them to operate at the new fleet speed of 33 kt, but that would have been extraordinarily costly. The *South Dakota* and *Indiana* were sold for breaking in 1962/63, while the *Massachusetts* and *Alabama* were handed over to their name states in 1964/65 for preservation.

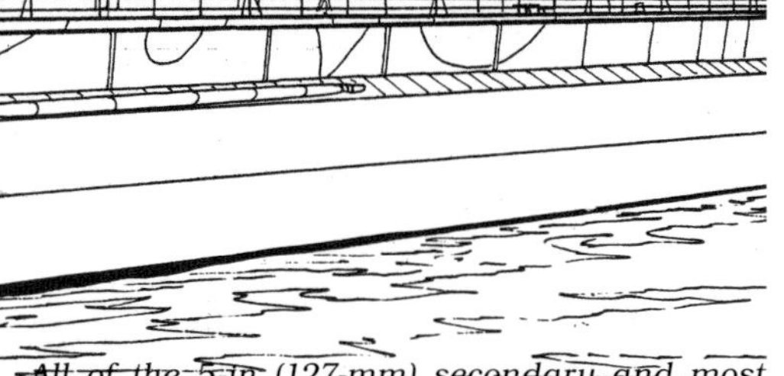

All of the 5-in (127-mm) secondary and most of the 40-mm quadruple gun mountings were clustered on and round the USS Massachusetts' superstructure and main armament turrets.

HMS *Repulse* (1916)

It had been intended that the Royal Navy's "Revenge" class super-dreadnought battleships should comprise eight ships, but in August 1914, shortly after the outbreak of World War I, the Admiralty suspended initial work on the sixth and seventh units and cancelled the eighth, all in the belief that the war would be over before the ships could be completed. Only four months later, two battle-cruisers' success in the Battle of the Falklands, when they sank two German armoured cruisers and a number of smaller ships, persuaded Admiral Sir "Jackie" Fisher that his original battle-cruiser concept was sound, and he therefore ordered the sixth and seventh "Revenge" class battleships to be redesigned and built in just 15 months as the two "Renown" class battle-cruisers.

HMS Repulse as revised in 1934/36 with additional armour and AA armament as well as a hangar, spotter floatplane and catapult.

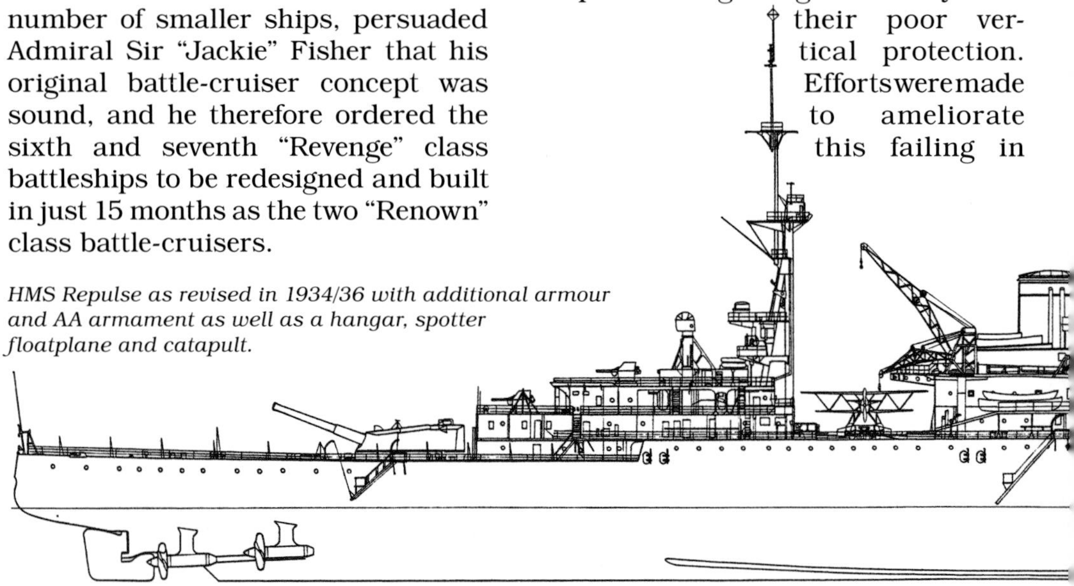

The ships were HMS *Renown* and HMS *Repulse*, which were laid down by Fairfield and John Brown and completed in September and August 1916 respectively. This was a considerable feat, especially as more horizontal armour was worked into the structure at the last stage as a result of the hammering which the British battle-cruisers received in the Battle of Jutland.

The two "Renown" class ships were the first British battle-cruisers with two funnels and also the first with 15-in (381-mm) guns. However, each ship carried only six of these weapons because of manufacturing limitations during the very short time of the ships' construction. However, an inescapable fact is that, despite a speed of 30 kt, the "Renown" class ships were a tactically and technically regressive step at a time when the UK was building the fast and well-protected "Queen Elizabeth" class super-dreadnought battleships. The ships' most glaring deficiency was their poor vertical protection. Efforts were made to ameliorate this failing in successive modernizations, but this was a very difficult task as the lower edge of the shallow main belt was carried, just beneath the waterline, on the upper slope of the large anti-torpedo bulges which, for the first time, had been made an integral part of the hull structure. Another poor feature, directly attributable to Fisher's desire for massed small-calibre fire to defeat torpedo boats, was a secondary battery of 4-in (102-mm) rather than 6-in (152-mm) guns, most of them in five triple mountings that proved very indifferent.

Only the *Repulse* saw any real action during World War I, being involved in the indecisive affair of November 1917 in the German Bight. Great efforts were made between the wars to rectify the ships' shortcomings, the *Renown* being extensively modernized: with her protection improved, secondary armament revised to 20 4.5-in (114-mm) DP guns, main guns revised for greater elevation, and a tower superstructure, she proved effective both offensively and defensively, especially in the Gibraltar-based Force H. The *Renown* was sold for breaking in 1948. The *Repulse* was less extensively upgraded, and as a result succumbed on December 10, 1941, with the comparatively new battleship HMS *Prince of Wales*, to a carefully planned and executed Japanese air assault which hit her with five torpedoes.

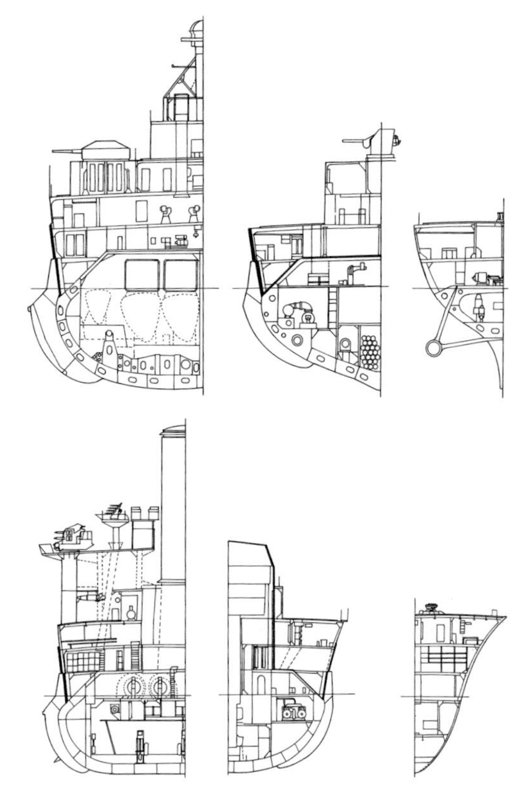

Half-sections of the Repulse's hull showing the compartmentalization and (thicker lines) armour.

HMS *Repulse* (as completed)

Type:	battle-cruiser
Tonnage:	30,835 tons full load
Dimensions:	length 794 ft (242 m); beam 90 ft (27.4 m); draft 25 ft 6 in (7.8 m)
Propulsion:	four steam turbines delivering 112,000 shp (83507 kW) to four propellers for 30 kt
Armour:	1.5/6-in (38/152-mm) belt, 3/4-in (76/102-mm) bulkheads, 0.5/3-in (13/76-mm) decks, 7/11-in (178/279-mm) turrets, 4/7-in (102/178-mm) barbettes, and 10-in (254-mm) conning tower
Armament:	six 15-in (381-mm) guns, 17 4-in (102-mm) guns, two 3-in (76-mm) AA guns, and two 21-in (533-mm) torpedo tubes
Complement:	967

La Lorraine (1915)

France produced only one class of dreadnought battleships, (the four units of the "Courbet" class laid down in 1910/11) before moving one rung up the calibre ladder to produce its first super-dreadnought battleships in the form of the three "Bretagne" class ships *La Bretagne*, *La Lorraine* and *La Provence*. The ships were completed between June and September 1915.

The ships had what were in essence the hull and dimensions of the "Courbet" class in combination with a larger-calibre main armament in centreline twin turrets including superfiring units fore and aft and one turret amidships which replaced the earlier class's two wing turrets.

The ships were notably wet forward as a result of their short bows, and were the only French ships fitted from the start with net defences against torpedoes, though these were removed in 1917. Another limitation was their main armament, which had a shorter range than most other guns of this period with a similar calibre: the maximum range was a mere 15,855 yards (14500 m), but in 1917 the range of La Lorraine's main armament was boosted to 19,685 yards (18000 m) by increasing the elevation of the aftermost turret's guns from 12° to 18°. A comparable enhancement of *La Bretagne* and *La Provence*, as well as to *La Lorraine's* other turrets, was not made before November 1918.

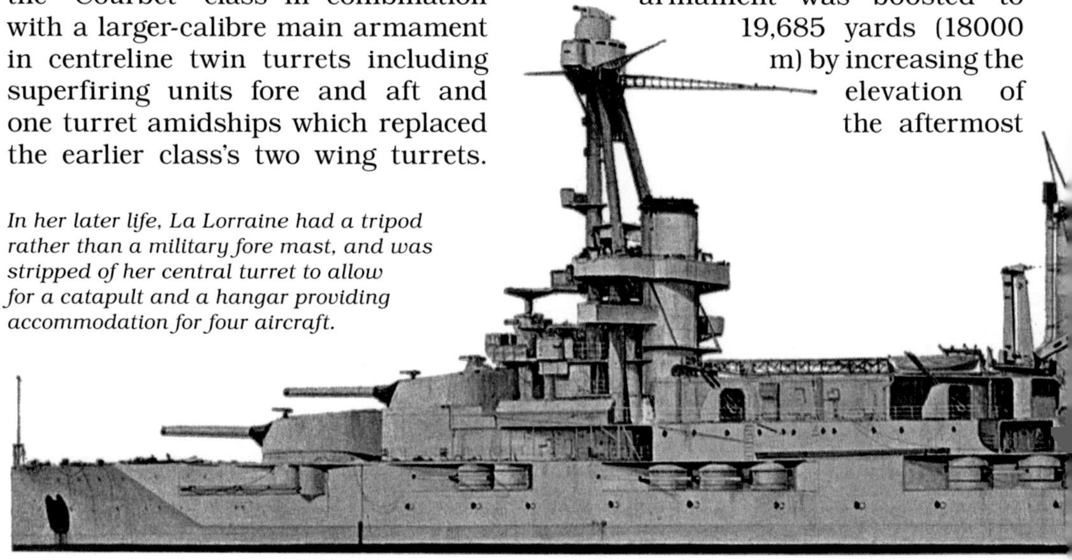

In her later life, La Lorraine had a tripod rather than a military fore mast, and was stripped of her central turret to allow for a catapult and a hangar providing accommodation for four aircraft.

The main armament was based on the 13.4-in (340-mm) L/45 gun, and the secondary armament remained unaltered as 22 5.5-in (139-mm) L/55 guns in casemated mountings.

The "Bretagne" class ships were comparatively well designed in overall terms, the main exception being their underwater protection, which was decidedly insufficient. Features which received special attention by the standards of the time were fire direction, weapon control, and command and control, all of which were advanced.

The battleships entered full service with the French navy during 1916, *La Provence* being the service's flagship until 1919 and beginning her service with operations in Greek waters to ensure the survival of a pro-Allied government. *La Lorraine* was detached to Cattaro in the Adriatic Sea between January and March 1919. *La Bretagne* sank on July 3, 1940 at

Mers-el-Kébir in North Africa, with the loss of 977 members of her crew, as a result of British action designed to prevent any possibility of French ships falling into German hands: the wreck was salvaged and sold for breaking in 1952. *La Lorraine* was disarmed under French control at Alexandria in July 1940, but was back in service by June 1943 as a Free French vessel in the Mediterranean. Between 1945 and 1953 the vessel was a training ship before being hulked and stricken in February 1953, and broken up from January 1954. *La Provence* was damaged in the Mers-el-Kébir operation and in November of the same year was brought to Toulon for repair before being scuttled on November 27, 1942 as the Germans seized Vichy France.

In her later life, La Lorraine had a tripod rather than a military fore mast, and was stripped of her central turret to allow for a catapult and a hangar providing accommodation for four aircraft.

La Lorraine

Type:	super-dreadnought battleship
Tonnage:	28,500 tons full load
Dimensions:	length 544 ft 8 in (166 m); beam 88 ft 3 in (26.9 m); draft 32 ft 2 in (9.8 m)
Propulsion:	two steam turbines delivering 29,000 shp (21622 kW) to two propellers for 20 kt
Armour:	6.3/10.6-in (160/27-mm) belt, 1.2/1.6-in (30/40-mm) decks, 13.4-in (340-mm) end turrets and barbettes, 15.7-in (400-mm) center turret, 9.8-in (250-mm superfiring turrets and barbettes, 7-in (180-mm) battery, and 12.4-in (314-mm) conning tower
Armament:	10 13.4-in (340-mm) guns, 22 5.5-in (139-mm) QF guns, four 2.95-in (75-mm) QF guns, and four 17.7-in (450-mm torpedo tubes
Complement:	1,124

"Flower" class corvette (1940)

The anti-submarine escorts of the "Flower" and "Modified Flower" classes (145 and 113 built in the UK and Canada respectively for launch in 1940/42) came to be regarded by the British as the archetypical oceanic escort ship. Though they made their reputation in the early days of the Battle of the Atlantic, the ships were in fact not ideally suited to the deep-ocean, long-endurance task as the type had initially been developed for the coastal escort role with minesweeping capability. This seemed to be somewhat anomalous, however, as the hull of the "Flower" class corvette was based on that of a commercial whale catcher, a hull designed to survive and work in the worst of weather and sea conditions.

The rapid development of the North Atlantic convoy war combined with the general shortage of escorts to compel the Admiralty to consider these small ships for the ocean role. Given their design origins, the "Flower" class corvettes were excellent seaboats, but their short length made them very uncomfortable and wet in oceanic conditions. As a result even the best crews were exhausted within days in a period when a capability for refuelling at sea often kept them out for very much longer. It was the limitations thus revealed which persuaded the Admiralty to switch its thinking to larger vessels such as the frigate.

The "Flower" class corvettes were workmanlike vessels whose design origins were evident in a hull characterised by a pronounced sheer, strong flare and cutaway forefoot Early examples had a short forecastle with the single mast stepped forward of what was still essentially a mercantile

K180 was the second "Flower" class ship named HMS Lotus (ex-Phlox), and was built by Robb in 13 months and 13 days for completion in May 1942.

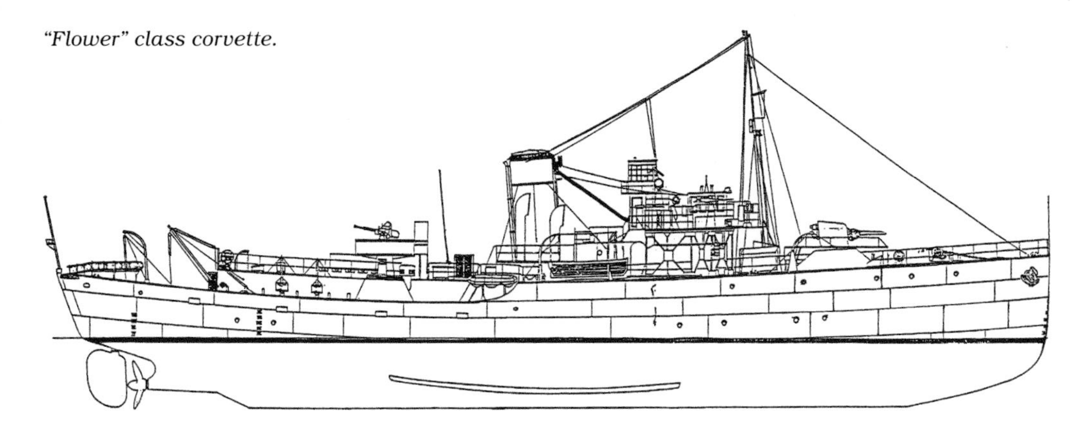
"Flower" class corvette.

bridge structure, but most were later modified to the layout of the later "Modified Flower" class ships, 208 ft 4 in (63.5 m) long, which had their forecastles extended aft to the funnel, thereby providing an increase in accommodation and offering an improvement in overall seaworthiness and reduced wetness.

For speed of construction, lowering of cost, maximization of reliability, ease of maintenance, and simplicity of operation by hastily trained personnel, the machinery was kept as simple as possible. The propulsion arrangement was therefore based on a four-cylinder triple expansion engine taking its steam from two Admiralty single-engined cylindrical boilers which occupied much of the hull's depth amidships and had their uptakes trunked into a single funnel. The "Flower" class corvettes were also somewhat different from most Royal Navy warships of the period in having only one propeller.

All of the ships were armed with an obsolete 4-in (102-mm) gun on a bandstand forward, but the original AA outfit of machine guns was clearly inadequate and was soon replaced by a 2-pdr pompom weapon and as many 20-mm Oerlikon cannon as could be found. Later ships incorporating all modifications certainly possessed a more workmanlike appearance and, somewhat surprisingly, many went on to serve m a mercantile role after the war. The corvettes served under a variety of Allied flags, including that of the USA in 1942. Wartime losses were 31, and the ships sank more than 50 U-boats.

"Flower" class corvette (original type)

Type:	anti-submarine escort
Tonnage:	1,245 tons deep load
Dimensions:	length 205 ft (62.5 m); beam 33 ft 2 in (10.1 m); draft 13 ft 7 in (4.15 m)
Propulsion:	one vertical triple expansion steam engine delivering 2,750 ihp (2050 kW) to one propeller for 16.5 kt
Armour:	none
Armament:	one 4-in (102-mm) gun, one 2-pdr or four 0.5-in (12.7-mm) AA guns, and 40 depth charges or, in later vessels one Hedgehog projector and 72 depth charges
Complement:	85-109

HMS *Victorious* (1941)

Following a small number of aircraft carriers completed or converted from other types of ship, the Royal Navy's first purpose-built fleet carrier was HMS *Ark Royal*, built by Cammell Laird and completed in 1938. The Ark Royal was a one-off type, but there then followed the three fleet carriers of the "Illustrious" class, which were the first aircraft carriers to be built anywhere in the world with fully armoured hangars whose roof was provided by the armoured flight deck. The protection scheme was based on the ability to withstand air-dropped bombs as well as the projectiles of 6-in (152-mm) guns at longer range and the smaller-calibre guns of destroyers as short range.

The weight of so much armour high above the waterline, with the flight deck 38 ft (11.6 m) above the deep-load waterline, meant that the design could incorporate only one hangar, which had an adverse effect on the number of aircraft which could be embarked.

The three ships were HMS *Illustrious*, HMS *Victorious* and HMS

Formidable, of which the first pair was built by Vickers-Armstrongs (the first at Barrow and the second on the Tyne) and the last ship by Harland & Wolff in Belfast. The ships were laid down between April and June 1937, and completed in May 1940, May 1941 and November 1940 respectively. The design had the now standard starboard-side island incorporating the funnel, and the flight deck had an effective length of 620 ft (189 m) in the *Illustrious* and 670 ft (204.2 m) in the other two ships, later increased to 740 ft (225.6 m) in all of the ships by reducing the long round-down sections at the front and rear of the flight decks. The flight deck's width remained at 95 ft (29 m), and a single catapult was provided, this being able to launch an airplane weighing between 11,000 and 14,000 lb 4990 and 6350 kg) at 76 mph; 122 km/h). The hangar below the flight deck was 458 ft (139.6 m) long, 62 ft (18.9 m) wide and 16 ft (4.9 m) high, and the flight and hangar decks were connected by two unarmoured lifts each measuring 45 ft (13.7 m) by 22 ft (6.7 m) and able to carry a 14,000-lb (6350-kg) load. At 50,540 Imp gal (191315 litres), the aviation fuel capacity was sized to the original aircraft complement, and proved a tactical limitation in the last

A biplane torpedo bomber rises from the flight deck of HMS Victorious, which fought with great success if many theatres during World War II. Note the flight deck's long round-down over the bows, later largely flattened out with that over the stern to lengthen the usable length of the flight deck.

HMS *Victorious* (1941) *continued*

part of World War II after it had been found possible to increase the aircraft complement to 52 or 54 aircraft by means of permanent deck parking with outrigger stowage.

The protective belt amidships was taken as far up only as the hangar deck, to the flight deck only on the starboard side abreast the island, and to the upper deck for the last 30 ft (9.15 m) forward and aft. Most notably for the aircraft carriers of the periods, the side armour of the hangar was complete, and in fact extended well beyond the ends of the belt, which it joined only by the island. The thickness of the armoured flight deck was 3 in (76 mm) over the hangar armour and 1.5 in (38 mm) at both ends and in the section beneath the island The hangar deck was 1 in (25 mm) thick outside the central citadel where it formed the hangar floor and 2.5/3 in (64/76 mm) thick between the hangar walls and the belt. The lower deck was 3 in (76 mm) thick aft, and the underwater protection scheme was an improved version of that developed for the *Ark Royal*, and therefore of the sandwich type with longitudinal bulkheads well inboard of the compartmented sides.

The propulsion arrangement was based on three sets of Parsons geared turbines in three engines rooms using steam generated by six Admiralty three-drum boilers in three boiler rooms. The defensive armament was based on 16 4.5-in (114-mm) high-angle guns paired in shallow mountings on the beams between the decks, and this primary defence against air attack at medium altitude and range was complemented by a light AA armament which was considerably altered and augmented during World War II. Thus the six octuple 2-pdr pom-pom weapons with which each ship was completed gradually gave way to the war in the *Illustrious* to five octuple 2-pdr mountings, three single 40-mm mountings and 52 single 20-mm mountings, in the *Formidable* to six octuple 2-pdr mountings, 12 single 40-mm mountings, 34 single 20-mm mountings, and in the *Victorious* to five octuple 2-pdr mountings, 21 40-

The island of the aircraft carrier HMS Victorious with the boiler uptake and funnel rising through it.

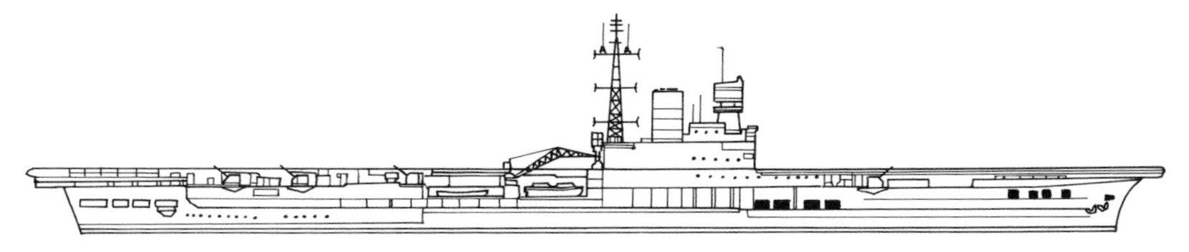

Above and below: HMS Victorious, one of the Royal Navy's mainstays in World War II.

mm guns (two quadruple, two twin and single mountings), and 45 single 20-mm mountings.

The protective capability of the ships' vertical armour remained untested by gunfire during the war, but the horizontal protection was tested to the full. In the Mediterranean on January 10, 1941, for example, the *Illustrious* survived seven bomb hits and one near miss, mostly by 1,102-lb (500-kg) weapons with delay-action fuses, although one 2,205-lb (500-kg) bomb penetrated the armoured flight deck and burst about 10 ft (3,05 m) above the hangar deck. While at Malta the ship received another bomb hit as well as several near misses, the shock disabling the port element of the propulsion machinery. The *Illustrious* was inoperative for almost 11 months. The *Formidable* was also out of action for 6 months after being hit by two 2,205-lb (1000-kg) bombs, neither of them on the flight deck, during May 25, 1941. On August 12, of the following year the *Victorious* took a single bomb which bounced off her armour, but also several which damaged the unarmoured parts of the flight deck and the lifts.

Both the *Formidable* and the *Victorious* served with the British Pacific Fleet in 1945, and here their armoured flight decks proved their worth: both ships were twice struck by *kamikaze* aircraft but survived relatively unscathed; the worst damage was caused to the *Formidable*, where the flight deck had been holed by a bomb released shortly before the crash of a *kamikaze* airplane. The ships were sold for breaking in 1956, 1969 and 1953 respectively.

HMS *Victorious* (as completed)

Type:	fleet aircraft carrier
Tonnage:	29,240 tons deep load
Dimensions:	length 753 ft 3 in (229.6 m); beam 95 ft 9 in (29.2 m); draft 28 ft 6 in (8.7 m)
Propulsion:	three geared steam turbines delivering 111,000 shp (82762 kW) to three propellers for 30.5 kt
Armour:	4.5-in (114-mm) belt, 4.5-in (114-mm) hangar side, 3-in (76-mm) flight deck, and 2.5/4.5-in (64/114-mm) bulkheads
Armament:	16 4.5-in (114-mm) DP guns, 48 2-pdr pom-pom AA guns, and 33 aircraft
Complement:	1,229

Allied landing craft (World War II)

Amphibious operations started to mature only when the right dedicated craft became available. It was the Japanese who first made use of a purpose-designed landing craft with a hinged bow ramp in 1938, in landings along the Yangtse river, and the success of this type soon caught the attentions of the world's most ambitious military powers. The British designed two similar craft, and 10 plywood-built LCAs (Landing Craft, Assault) for infantry and LCMs (Landing Craft, Motor) for vehicles and matériel, were first used in April 1940 during the Norwegian campaign. This was the first use of landing craft in European war. The UK's lack of landing craft was underlined at Dunkirk, where for lack of any way of swiftly re-embarking them, the British army had to abandon most of the 63,400 vehicles, 20,500 motorcycles, and 2,500 heavy guns it had taken to France. The German forces belatedly started to convert Rhine river barges for the invasion of England planned in July 1940 but never undertaken.

Modern landing craft were developed most realistically in the USA, where the US Marine Corps experimented with the several types of assault craft in the 1930s.

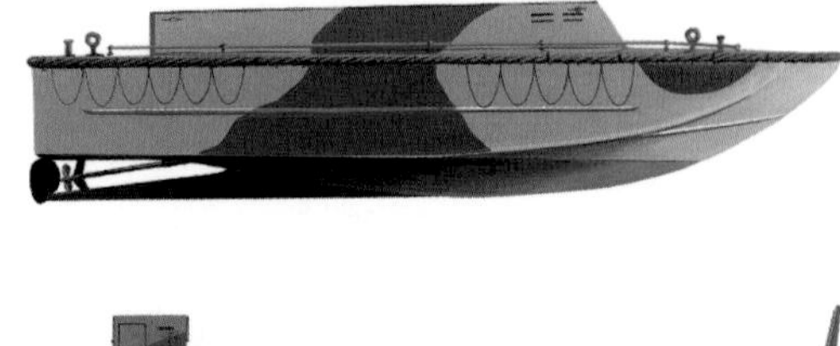

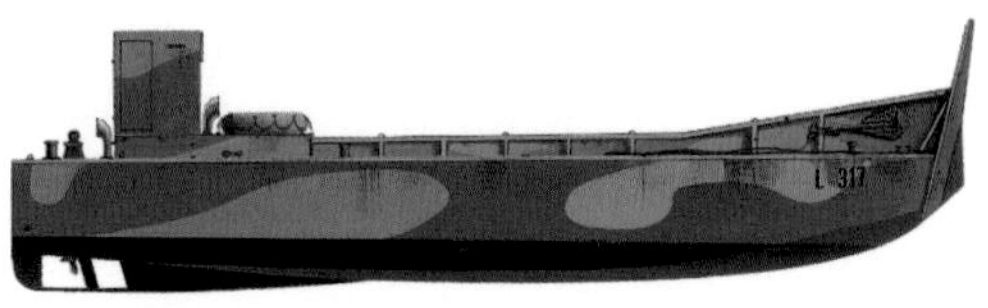

The British LCPL (Landing Craft, Personnel, Large) carrying 25 men and (lower) the US LCM Mk 3 (Landing Craft, Mechanised Mk 3) able to carry troops or a 30-ton tank.

A private marine engineer, Andrew Higgins, produced the best of these by combining his 36-ft (11-m) Eureka boat with the Japanese type of hinged bow-ramp, the basic landing craft of today was born. Able to carry an infantry platoon of 36 men, or 8,000 lb (3630 kg) of freight, or a 3-ton truck, his plywood design was known as the LCVP (Landing Craft Vehicle, Personnel) and had armour on the ramp and sometimes the sides. The British used many of the type, which was better than their own LCA (Landing Craft, Assault), and from 1941 some 23,400 LCVPs were manufactured in the USA. There was also a less satisfactory wooden LCPL (Landing Craft Personnel, Large) which could carry a platoon but lacked a

The LCIL (Landing Craft, Infantry, Large) could carry up to 210 troops as well as its crew of 29.

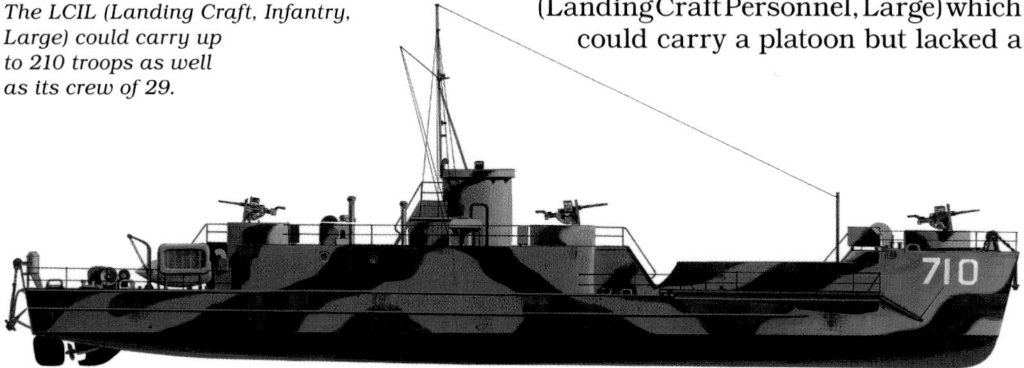

The "amtrack" (amphibious tractor) was the workhorse of the Pacific and Southwest Asia campaigns. This is an LVT Mk 2 without a ramp but able to carry 24 men or 6,500 lb (2950 kg) of freight.

ramp, the assault force jumping from the bow. In 1942 Higgins also designed a larger craft capable of carrying a single 30-ton tank. This was the 50-ft (15.2-m) LCM (Landing Craft, Mechanized), of which 11,400 were produced, replacing the earlier British LCM. A larger tank landing craft was designed separately in the UK during 1940. This LCT (Landing Craft, Tank) could carry six tanks or 13 trucks, and nearly 1,500 were mass-produced in the USA for the UK as flat-bottomed, shallow-draft craft, and were lowered from the davits of larger troop-carrying merchantmen. The LCT was also developed in more specialized form for assault purpose as the LC, Gun (with two 4.7-in/120-mm guns, 25-pdr field guns or 17-pdr anti-tank guns) and LCT, Rocket) with no fewer than 792 or 1,064 surface-to-surface rockets for the saturation of target areas.

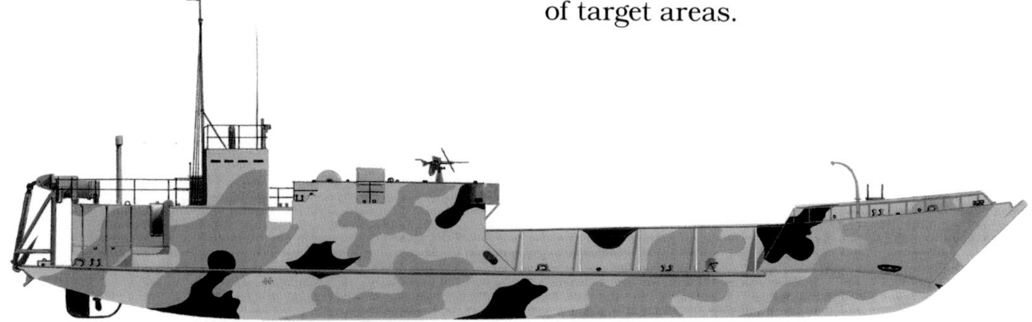

The LCT (Landing Craft, Tank) could typically carry five medium or three heavy tanks, as well as 54 troops. A kedging anchor was fitted over the stern to allow the vessel to haul itself off the beach.

Landing Ship, Tank Mk 2

Type:	tank landing ship
Tonnage:	2,160 tons full load
Dimensions:	length 328 ft (100 m); beam 50 ft (15.2 m); draft 9 ft 6 in (2.9 m) full load
Propulsion:	two diesel engines delivering 1,800 shp (1341 kW) to two propellers for 10.5 kt
Armour:	none
Armament:	one 5-in (127-mm) gun and/or eight 40-mm AA guns, and six to 12 20-mm AA cannon
Complement:	211, plus two LCVPs, or 18 heavy tanks, or 27 trucks or one LCT Mk 5, and up to 163 troops

Allied landing craft (World War II) *continued*

Early LSTs (Landing Ships, Tank) such as the British Bachaquero (able to carry between 22 and 33 tanks depending on size) were converted shallow-draft tankers with an extending bow ramp.

With an invasion across the English Channel always in mind, the British also needed larger assault vessels that could travel from port direct to the invasion beach. As a result, the seagoing 158-ft (48.2-m) LCIL (Landing Craft Infantry, Large), able to carry up to 200 troops, was designed. Slightly more than 1,000 of these were constructed, primarily for British and Canadian use. Instead of a forward ramp, the LCIL had a lowering gangway on each side of the bow.

The LCIL was complemented by the LST (Landing Ship, Tank) designed by the British and Americans to carry 20 tanks on a lower deck and lighter vehicles on an upper deck, with an elevator connecting the two. The LST was built to the extent of 1,050 units. As a seagoing vessel, it had a ballast system that enabled it to take on sea water and sail with a deep draft for stability, but when approaching land it pumped out the water, becoming a shallow-draft vessel, which could be beached to disgorge its load. Several cross-Channel ferries had earlier been converted to a similar design, by way of experiment, and there were several hospital, anti-aircraft and HQ variants. This range of craft was first employed in the November 1942 landing in French North Africa, and then saw large-scale use in the

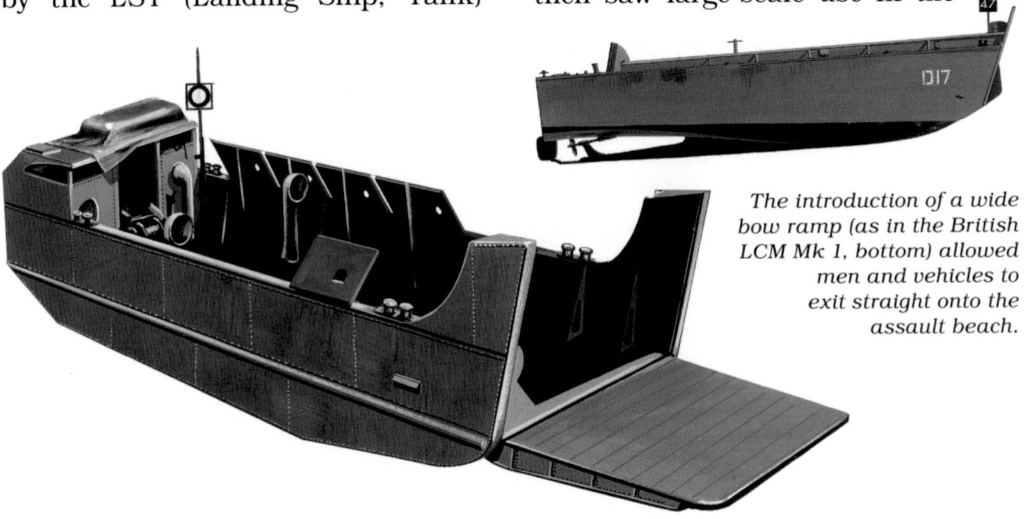

The introduction of a wide bow ramp (as in the British LCM Mk 1, bottom) allowed men and vehicles to exit straight onto the assault beach.

A tank leaves an LCT (Landing Craft. Tank) by means of the powered bow ramp.

The payload area of most small landing craft could carry light vehicles, such as a jeep, as an alternative to men.

The LVT(A) Mk 4 (Landing Vehicle, Tracked, Armoured Mk 4) was the LVT Mk 4 adapted with the turret of the M8 Howitzer Motor Carriage complete with its 75-mm (2.95-in) short-barrel howitzer.

Salerno, Anzio, southern French and Normandy invasions, where 4,126 of all types were used. The demand for landing craft of all types, but especially LSTs, always exceeded availability, particularly with the various Pacific theatres vying for the same vessels.

Just as important were amphibious craft, capable of driving ashore with troops or supplies, as typified by the LVT (Landing Vehicle, Tracked). This was 8 ft (2.4 m) tall, weighed 12 tons unladen, and had land and water speeds of 20 and 7 mph (32 and 11.2 km/h) respectively. First used in 1942 at Guadalcanal as an armoured ship-shore ferry, it was subsequently used in a direct assault role. Some of the 18,620 variants produced carried a turret that converted it into an amphibious tank. It was known to the British as Buffalo, which was used to clear the Scheldt and to cross into the Rhineland. Also relevant was the DUKW six-wheeled amphibious truck, which was developed in 1942. Some 21,000 DUKWs were built, and the type could carry 25 troops or 5,000 lb (2270 kg) of freight. It is worth noting that there was also an amphibious jeep.

Landing Craft. Assault

Type:	assault landing craft
Tonnage:	13 tons full load
Dimensions:	length 41 ft 6 in (12.6 m); beam 10 ft (3.05 m); draft 2 ft 3 in (0.7 m)
Propulsion:	two petrol engines delivering 130 bhp (97 kW) to two propellers for 7 kt
Armour:	none
Armament:	two of three 0.5- or 0.3-in (12.7- or 7.62-mm) machine guns
Complement:	4, plus 35 troops and 800 lb (363 kg) of equipment

HMS *Cavalier* (1944)

The "C" class comprised a total of 32 fleet destroyers built for the Royal Navy and launched between 1943 ands 1945. As was standard with British destroyers of the period, the class was built in four flotillas, each of eight vessels. The destroyers on these flotillas were known as the "Ca," "Ch," "Co" and "Cr" subclasses as they each had names starting with the relevant pairs of letters. The ships were ordered as part of the War Emergency Programme, which was based on the hull and machinery of the earlier "J" class but incorporated whatever armament was available as well as any and all developments in naval radar and electronics. Only a proportion of the ships were completed in time for service in World War II, and the subclasses were ordered as the 11th, 12th, 13th and 14th Emergency Flotillas.

The "Ca" subclass, whose eight units were built as pairs by John Brown, Scotts, White and Yarrow, was in essence a repeat of the preceding "Z" class, itself a descendant of the "S" class via the "T," "U," "V" and "W" classes. The "Ca" subclass was basically the "W" class with improved fire control and four single 4,5-in (114-mm) rather than 4.7-in (120-mm) guns. The smaller-calibre gun had a lower muzzle velocity but fired a heavier and less "draggy" projectile, which translated as greater destructive effect at longer range. The AA armament was based on two 40-mm Bofors guns on a tri-axial mounting, and four single 2-pdr pom-pom guns.

The other three subclasses of the "C" class had only one rather than two quadruple mountings for 21-in (533-mm) torpedoes to offset the additional weight of remote power control gunlaying equipment for the 4.5-in (114-mm) guns. With HMS *Contest* they also introduced the all-welded hull into Royal Navy destroyer construction. A fifth flotilla, the "Ce" subclass, was planned but terminated in favor of the "Weapon" class.

The "Ca" class destroyers were upgraded in the 1960s to serve as fast fleet escorts. Notable ships were HMS *Caprice*, the last destroyer built for the Royal Navy with the quadruple 2-pdr "pom-pom" AA gun, and HMS *Cavalier* which is now preserved as the sole British example of a World

Above:
HMS Cavalier, last survivor of the British destroyer in World War II.

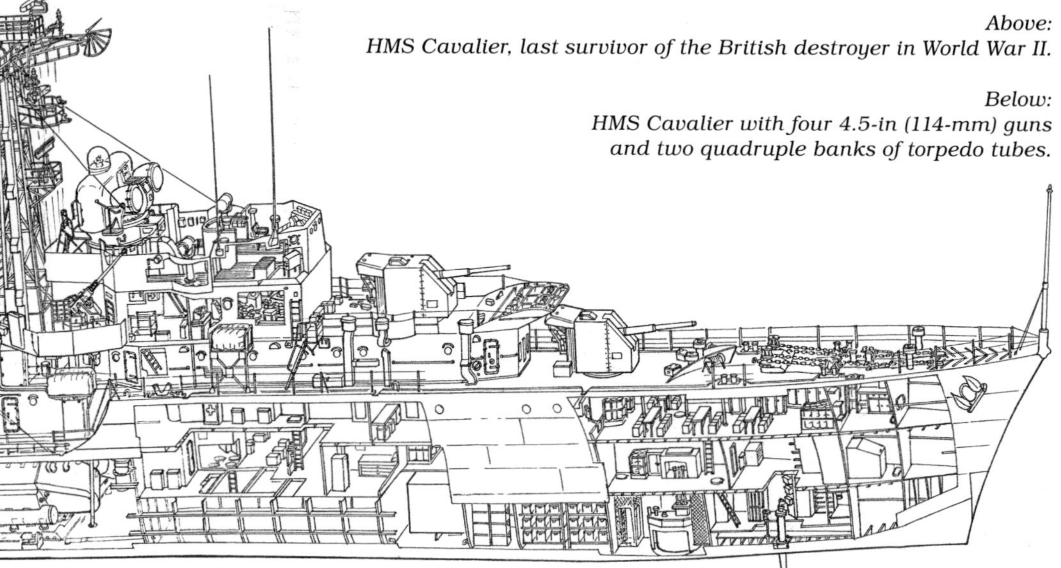

Below:
HMS Cavalier with four 4.5-in (114-mm) guns and two quadruple banks of torpedo tubes.

HMS *Cavalier*

Type:	fleet destroyer
Tonnage:	2,575 tons deep load
Dimensions:	362 ft 9 in (110.6 m); beam 35 ft 8 in (10.9 m); draft 14 ft 6 in (4.4 m) m)
Propulsion:	two geared steam turbines delivering 40,000 shp (29824 kW) to two propellers for 37 kt
Armour:	none
Armament:	four 4.5-in (114-mm) DP guns, two 40-mm AA guns, four 2-pdr pom-pom AA guns, eight 21-in (533-mm) torpedo tubes, and up to 130 depth charges
Complement:	222

Guided Explosive Boats (World War II)

As the tide of World War II turned against them, the three leading nations of the Axis or Tripartite Pact had recourse to a number of increasingly desperate expedients in an effort to regain the initiative, at last at the tactical level.

The best known of the these expedients were the *kamikaze* suicide aircraft attacks by pilots of the Imperial Japanese armed forces, who reckoned that the loss of one life and one airplane was a small price to pay for the destruction or crippling of an Allied warship. The equation was by means so simple, however, and the combination of good tactics and potent defences, by defensive fighters and shipboard AA guns, cost the Japanese very heavy losses for limited results. The Imperial Japanese navy added a suicide boats to its aircraft for an enhanced attack capability. Some 6,000 of the "Shinyo" type explosive-filled motor boats had been built before Japan's surrender in 1945, most of them with an explosive charge or two depth charges in their bows, However, it was only in the Okinawa campaign of April 1945 that they saw real service, when some 200 to 300 of 700 suicide boats were used, sinking one landing craft and damaging five other vessels including one destroyer and one landing craft which had to be scrapped, and another destroyer and a cargo ship whose repairs were completed only after the war's end.

A German equivalent of the "Shinyo," developed in 1944/45 and intended for mass production in the many boatyards along Germany's northern coast, was the so-called Sprengboot (explosive boat). This was small and of wooden construction with power provide by one or two car engines, and was fitted with an ejection seat powered by compressed

"Shinyo" type

Type:	suicide attack motor boat
Tonnage:	1.35 to 2.15 tons displacement
Dimensions:	length 16 ft 9 in (5.1 m) to 21 ft 4 in (6.5 m); beam 5 ft 6 in (1.67 m) to 6 ft 1 in (1.86 m); draft 1 ft 1 in (0.33 m)
Propulsion:	one or two gasoline engines delivering between 62 and 134 bhp (46 and 92.5 kW) to one or two propellers for 20 to 28 kt
Armament:	one 4,409-lb (2000-kg) TNT charge or two 264-lb (120-kg) Type 98 depth charges, and two 4.7-in (120mm) rockets
Complement:	1

Sprengboot

Type:	attack motor boat
Tonnage:	not available
Dimensions:	length 14 ft 3 in (4.35 m); beam 4 ft 1 in (1.25 m); draft not available
Propulsion:	one or two car engines delivering power to one or two propellers for 35 to 40 kt
Armament:	661-lb (300-kg) explosive charge
Complement:	1

air: after setting his boat on collision course with the target vessel and activating the impact fuse, the driver departed at a distance of about 110 yards (100 m) from the target. It is hard to see what worthwhile targets Germany saw for this weapon as by this time the country was on the verge of defeat through land advances from east and west. It is also believed that another type of Sprengboot was designed with a pulse-jet engine and an enclosed cabin mounted above the struts connecting two aircraft floats.

The Italian MTM (Motoscafo di Turismo Modificato, or modified tourist motor boat) was developed from 1938 on the basis of the MAT two prototypes of 1936. The canvas-decked but otherwise wooden boat was small and light enough to be carried by a Savoia-Marchetti S.55 flying boat. The driver departed over the stern once he had set the boat on a collision course with the target, and on this the boat broke apart, releasing a charge to sink and explode at a set depth or on reaching the seabed. Some 28 were built in 1938/39, and two sank the cruiser HMS York in March 1941. The MTR was a narrower-beam version for submarine delivery, the MTS was a miniature torpedo boat, the MTSM was an improved MTS and one sank the British escort destroyer HMS Eridge in August 1942, and the MTSMA was the MTSM modified with a larger hull for greater warload (154- rather than 110-lb/70- rather than 50-kg depth charges) and more fuel for a range of 290 miles (465 km).

MTM

Type:	attack motor boat
Tonnage:	1 ton displacement
Dimensions:	length 20 ft (6.1 m); beam 5 ft 3 in (1.6 m); draft not available
Propulsion:	one petrol engine delivering 95 hp (71 kW) to one propeller for 29 kt
Armament:	661-lb (300-kg) explosive charge
Complement:	1 or 2

HMS *Belfast* (1939)

The 10 cruisers of the "Town" class marked the final stages of the British adherence to the limitations imposed by naval armament treaties of the 1920s and early 1930s. The immediate spur for the class was the US Navy's "Brooklyn" class created to match the Japanese "Mogami" class. The Admiralty decided that it too must move to the creation of a more modern cruiser capability optimized for the fleet role rather than commerce protection task. The resulting "Town" class was based on a lighter displacement and smaller hull than its Japanese and US counterparts, but nonetheless carried a primary armament of 12 very reliable 6-in (152-mm) guns in a new design of triple turret, and also offered good seakeeping qualities.

With its greater size, more purposeful appearance, two raked funnels, and 12 rather than eight main guns in superfiring triple rather than twin turrets, the "Town" class vessel was essentially a "super" light cruiser intermediate in capability between

the light and heavy cruiser. The first five ships, were the "Town Type I" HMS *Birmingham*, HMS *Glasgow*, HMS *Newcastle*, HMS *Sheffield* and HMS *Southampton*, and these were built by four yards for completion between March and November 1937. They had a deep-load displacement of 11,350 tons rising later to 12,190 tons, and an overall length of 591 ft 6 in (180.3 m) with a beam of 61 ft 8 in (18.8 m). The *Southampton* was bombed in January 1941 and so severely damaged that she had to be sunk, but the other four, though badly damaged at various times, survived extensive service in World War II.

HMS Belfast's lightweight lattice mast provided a stable and rigid mounting for a growing number of antennae.

Between August 1938 and January 1939 there followed the "Town Type II" class HMS *Gloucester*, HMS *Liverpool* and HMS *Manchester*, which were again built by three different yards. They had a deep-load displacement of 11,650 tons rising later to 12,330 tons, the same length, the beam increased to 62 ft 4 in (19 m), and the machinery increased from 75,000 shp (55920 kW) for 32 kt in the first subclass to 82,500 shp (61512 kW) for 32.3 kt. The most important improvement was the enhanced protection of the turrets with armour increased from 1 in (25 mm) to 2/4 in (51/102 mm), and the deck over the machinery spaces was also increased slightly.

HMS Belfast wearing the Type 25 camouflage in which she fought in the Battle of the North Cape in December 1943.

HMS *Belfast* (1939) continued

The crane was needed to hoist heavy items, such as HMS Belfast's reconnaissance and spotter floatplanes, onto and off the water.

The AA defences of the *Manchester* had been boosted by the addition of three single 40-mm guns and five single 20-mm cannon by the time of her loss in August 1942, when she had to be scuttled after taking a surface-launched torpedo hit.

The *Liverpool* was severely damaged in October 1940 by an air-launched torpedo, and eventually lost her bow after leaking aviation fuel caused an explosion. The repair lasted one year, and then in June 1942 another air-launched torpedo hit an engine room and disabled three of the ship's four shafts. The repair and a refit lasted to July 1945, and in this the ship had her catapult and "X" turret removed to allow for the addition of six quadruple and four single 2-pdr pom-pom guns, seven single 40-mm guns, and five single 20-mm cannon. The *Gloucester* was sunk by at least four heavy bombs and three near misses during May 1941.

Originally to have had a standard displacement of 10,000 tons but emerging from the yards of Harland & Wolff and Swan Hunter in August and July 1939 at a displacement of 10,550 tons, HMS *Belfast* and HMS *Edinburgh* were the two units of the "Town Type III" subclass. They differed significantly from the ships of the "Town Type I" subclass. Their

HMS Belfast's "A" and "B" turrets, forward of the bridge, each carrying three 6-in (152-mm) guns.

The "Town" class ships were intermediate cruisers with a larger number of the types of weapon normally carried by light cruisers.

guns still elevated to 45° and were rammed but hand, but now had shell and cordite lifts right into the gun houses without any manual lifting. The after pair of superfiring turrets was raised by one deck level. The 4-in (102-mm) AA guns were increased from eight to 12 in six rather than four twin mountings, and the 2-pdr pom-pom guns were doubled in number from eight to 16, but the ammunition arrangements were poor, with the 4-in (102-mm) magazines well forward of the guns. The magazines' previous box protection was replaced by a lengthening of the belt, and the horizontal protection was also much thickened.

The *Belfast* was severely damaged by the detonation of a magnetic mine in November 1939, when her back was broken, and returned to service only in October 1942, her repairs having included the addition of bulges which increased her beam by 3 ft (0.9 m). The ship was refitted between August 1944 and April 1945, the catapult and four 4-in (102-mm) guns being removed and four quadruple and four single 2-pdr pom-poms, as well as 14 single 20-mm cannon, being added. The *Belfast* had a very active life when she was in service, and is now preserved in London.

In April 1942 the *Edinburgh* was hit by two torpedoes from the *U-456*. The damage was very serious, and her stern later broke away, but two days later she sank one of three destroyers which made a further attack on her, but was hit by another torpedo. The ship was abandoned and sunk by a torpedo from a British destroyer.

HMS *Belfast* (final form)

Type:	cruiser
Tonnage:	14,900 tons deep load
Dimensions:	length 613 ft 6 in (187 m); beam 66 ft 4 in (20.2 m); draft 23 ft 2 in (7.1 m)
Propulsion:	four geared steam turbines delivering 80,000 shp (59648 kW) to four propellers for 32.5 kt
Armour:	4.5-in (114-mm) belt, 2.5-in (64-mm) bulkheads, 2/4-in (51/102-mm) turrets, and 1/2-in (25/51-mm) ring bulkheads
Armament:	12 6-in (152-mm) guns, 12 4-in (102-mm) AA guns, 16 2-pdr pom-pom AA guns, six 21-in (533-mm) torpedo tubes, and three aircraft
Complement:	850

USS *Bogue* (1942)

One of the early lessons of World War II's maritime war was that the German U-boat arm was going to be a threat at least as formidable as it had been in World War I. The British responded to the threat with a convoy system in which merchant vessels were protected by potent escorts. Larger escorts were useful against commerce raiders but of no use against U-boats, while the smaller escorts offering greater capability against U-boats were lacking in numbers and limited and valuable for use in the convoy escort role, but a solution was found in a small aircraft carrier, which was pioneered by the British and became known as the escort carrier. Such vessels were simple and therefore cheap to build and, while at first based on incomplete mercantile hulls, were quickly produced as purpose-built vessels.

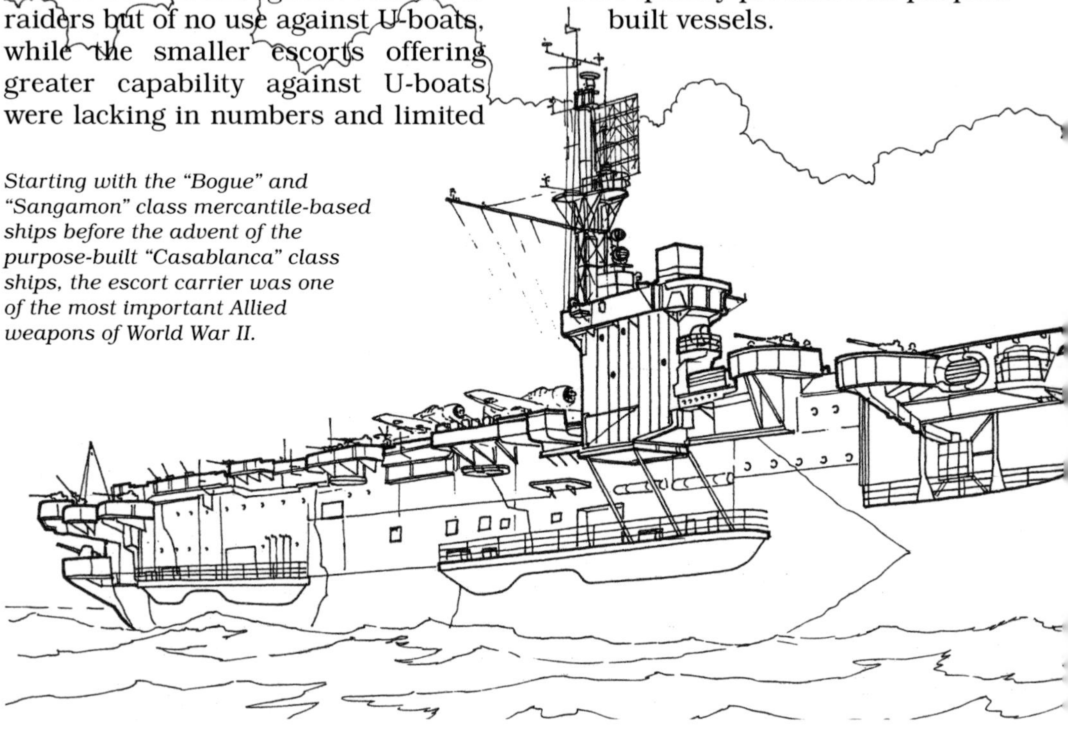

Starting with the "Bogue" and "Sangamon" class mercantile-based ships before the advent of the purpose-built "Casablanca" class ships, the escort carrier was one of the most important Allied weapons of World War II.

to purely defensive operations. It soon became clear that aircraft were the answer, for when available these could take the war to U-boats, respond quickly to perceived threats, and force the U-boats to spend more time below the surface, where their speed and endurance were lower.

However, even large land-based aircraft lacked the range to operate deep into the Atlantic and, like their flying boat brethren were also unavailable in adequate numbers. Fleet aircraft carriers were too large

The US Navy here followed the Royal Navy's lead, and the service's first escort carrier, the USS *Long Island*, was converted from the cargo ship *Mormacmail* for completion in June 1941: at first her role was that of an aircraft transport, but she was soon reclassified as a combatant. The conversion benefited somewhat from British experience with the *Empire Audacity*, converted at about the same time, and many later US conversions were allocated to the Royal Navy. With a full-load displacement

USS *Bogue* (as completed)

Type:	escort carrier
Tonnage:	15,400 tons full load
Dimensions:	length 495 ft 8 in (151.1 m); beam 69 ft 6 in (21.2 m); draft 23 ft 3 in (7.1 m)
Propulsion:	one geared steam turbine delivering 8,500 shp (6338 kW) to one propeller for 18 kt
Armour:	none
Armament:	two 5-in (127-mm) guns, four 40-mm AA guns, 10 20-mm AA guns, and 28 aircraft
Complement:	890

of 15,126 tons, speed of 16,5 kt and complement of 16 aircraft (10 observation and six attack), the *Long Island* was originally a diesel-powered cargo ship and considered too slow, so future US conversions were of steam-powered ships. The ship had a catapult-equipped flight deck 102 ft (31.1 m) wide. In 1944 the *Long Island* was modified as an aircraft transport with a lightened flight deck as it no longer had to absorb landing loads, and her catapult replaced by a more powerful type.

The *Long Island's* steam-powered successors, the 21 units of the "Bogue" class completed in 1942 and including 11 for transfer to the Royal Navy, had a longer flight deck with a width of 111 ft 6 in (34 m) and two rather than one lift. There was one or sometimes two catapults, and in 1942 the air group comprised 16 fighters and 12 torpedo-bombers.

In February 1942 it was decided to add an island, as in the first British diesel-powered ships. By comparison with the first purpose-built escort carrier type, the "Casablanca" class, the "Bogue" class was slower but had a longer operational radius as well as greater cargo and fuel capacities. The ships" habitability was good, and despite the use of only a single propeller they were manoeuvrable. But they also had cambered flight decks, which could make aircraft handling difficult in rough weather, and the British thought they lacked adequate survivability and therefore rebuilt their ships. The utility of the "Bogue" class, of which nine out of 10 US units survived, was proved by the ships" retention as aircraft transports. In 1945 the ships were armed with two 5-in (127-mm) DP, 10 twin 40-mm AA, and 27 (25 in the USS *Card*) single 20-mm guns.

USS *Hornet* (1941)

By the mid-1930s the US Navy had experience with the operation of two sizes of aircraft carrier, namely the pioneering but small USS Langley converted from a collier, and the altogether larger USS *Lexington* and USS *Saratoga* converted from incomplete battle-cruisers. These paved the way for the service's first purpose-built carrier, the 17,580-ton USS *Ranger*, and with the treaty tonnage allocation left to it the US Navy decided to order two 20,000-ton carriers and the smaller USS *Wasp*. The former were the initial pair of "Yorktown" class ships, the USS *Yorktown* and USS *Enterprise* for completion in September 1937 and May 1938 respectively. These can be regarded as the US Navy's first truly modern aircraft carriers, and thus in essence the immediate precursors of the classic "Essex" class of fleet carriers instrumental in the USA's maritime victory over Japan in World War II.

The "Yorktown" class was created on the basis of experience with the carriers mentioned above, and the availability of two sister ships fitted nicely into the US Navy's thinking that a two-ship group offered tactical advantages. Naval aviators wanted flush-decked ships, as they had with the Ranger, but it was decided that high speed (requiring the disposal of much smoke) and a hinged funnel arrangement were incompatible. With the need for a large funnel appreciated, it became logical to make this the core of an "island" superstructure also including the bridge and the flight operations control position such as was already proving its worth on the Lexington and Saratoga, and would soon be added to the *Ranger* while building.

Armoured flight and hangar decks were planned for a time, but there was insufficient armour for the task and protection was therefore limited to the belt and the deck covering its two halves: this was designed to protect against 6-in (152-mm) gun fire between 10,000 and 20,000 yards (9145 and 18290 m). Torpedo protection was also included, but this was reckoned to possess only four sevenths of the capability of that included in later battleships. The flight deck was slightly longer than the hull, and had a maximum width of 109 ft 6 in (33.4 m). The flight deck carried two catapults, and was connected to the open hangar deck by three lifts. The air group in the late 1930s comprised

The USS Hornet was last of a three-ship class that paved the way for the larger and more capable "Essex" class.

Right and below: A B-25 Mitchell bomber lumbers into the air on the "Doolittle raid."

18 fighters, 36 torpedo-bombers, 37 dive-bombers and five general-purpose aircraft.

The USS *Hornet* was built as a repeat *Yorktown* since the creation of a new design would have entailed a unacceptable delay. The ship was again built by Newport News, and was completed in October 1941. She differed from her near-sisters in being slightly larger, having a flight deck width of 114 ft (34.75 m) as a feature later added to the *Enterprise*, and having a pair of athwartships catapults on the hangar deck. The *Hornet* was lost within a year of her completion, being so badly damaged by air-launched torpedoes and bombs in the Battle of Santa Cruz on 26 October 1942 that she was abandoned and later sunk by Japanese destroyers. Before this, on April 18, the ship had secured a place in history by launching the "Doolittle raid" by North American B-25 Mitchell twin-engined bombers of the US Army Air Forces against the Japanese home islands. The *Yorktown* was sunk in June 1942, and though often damaged the *Enterprise* survived, in better protected and armed form, to be sold for breaking in 1958.

USS *Hornet* (as completed)

Type:	fleet aircraft carrier
Tonnage:	29,100 tons full load
Dimensions:	827 ft (252.1 m); beam 83 ft 3 in (25.35 m); draft 28 ft (8.5 m)
Propulsion:	four geared steam turbines delivering 120,000 shp (89472 kW) to four propellers for 32.5 kt
Armour:	2.5/4-in (64/102-mm) belt, 4-in (102-mm) bulkheads, 1.5-in (38-mm) armoured deck, and 2/4-in (51/102-mm) conning tower
Armament:	eight 5-in (127-mm) DP guns, 16 1,1-in AA guns, 24 0.5-in (12.7-mm) AA guns, and up to 85 aircraft
Complement:	2,175

"Nelson" class (1927)

Completed in August and November 1927 after construction by Armstrongs and Cammell Laid respectively, HMS *Nelson* and HMS *Rodney* were designed and built to satisfy maxima ordained in the 1922 Washington Naval Treaty. These included a displacement of 35,000 tons and main armament calibre of 16 in (406 mm). displacement at a maximum of 35,000 tons (35,560 tonnes) and gun calibre at a maximum of 16m (406mm). The design task faced by E. L. Attwood and S. V. Goodall was very demanding, for they had to create the two ships allowed to the UK to balance the Japanese "Nagato" and US "Maryland" classes, both with 16-in (406-mm) guns. Their solution was a curtailed version of the 1921 "G3" battle-cruiser design with the same main armament and protection level but, to meet the treaty displacement limit, a low-power propulsion arrangement and a trimming of the volume covered by the armour. The need to economize on armour also led to the location of the three main turrets forward of the bridge. Other novelties, in British capital ship practice, were 16-in (406-mm) guns, triple turrets, all-turreted secondary armament, a tower bridge, engine rooms forward of the boiler rooms, and separate conning towers surmounted by armoured and revolving director control positions. The main turret arrangement was successful in reducing the weight of armour needed, but it also made it impossible to fire abaft the beam.

Each 16-in (406-mm) guns turned the scales at 103.5 tons and fired and fired a 2,461-lb (1116-kg) shell with a muzzle velocity of 2,953 ft (900 m) per second to a range of 35,000 yards (32005 m). The 6-in (152-mm) secondary armament was grouped in six twin turrets (power-operated for the first time in a Royal Navy ship), and was located toward the truncated stern. The AA armament was located abreast of and abaft the bridge, and was considerably boosted by the end of World War II to six 4.7-in (120-mm), 48 2-pdr, 16 40-mm and 61 20-mm weapons in the *Nelson*.

The protection was schemed on the "all or nothing" basis with protection afforded only to vital areas such as the waterline, turrets, magazines, barbettes, machinery spaces and conning tower. Forming part of the basic structure, the armour provided very good protection in both the vertical and horizontal planes, but by the start of World War II it had become evident that the horizontal armour was vulnerable to the penetration by amour-piercing bombs.

As noted above, one of the elements which had to be sacrificed to keep the ships' displacement within treaty limits was propulsive machinery, and as a result the ships were undoubtedly slow. Both ships were also inadequate seaboats, possessing poor rolling qualities and being slow in their response to the helm. Even so, both of the ships completed very satisfactory service in home waters, the Arctic, the Mediterranean and, in the case of the *Nelson*, the Far East. Both were damaged (the *Nelson* once by a mine and twice by torpedoes, and the *Rodney* once by a bomb) but survived to be sold for breaking in February 1948.

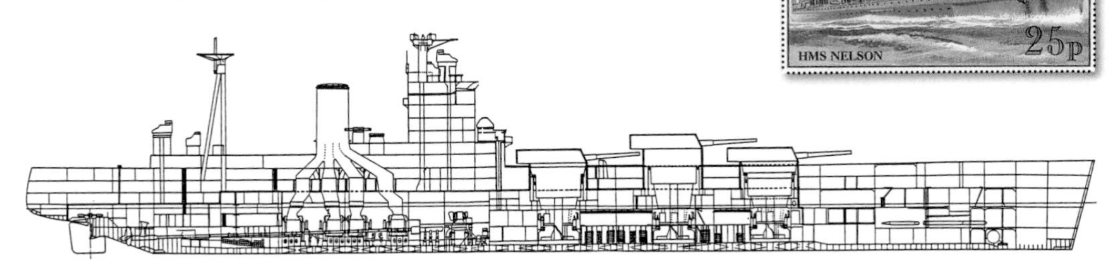

The "Nelson" class battleships had their main armament grouped forward, and their secondary armament massed on the after section.

"Nelson" class

Type:	battleship
Tonnage:	41,250 tons deep load
Dimensions:	length 710 ft (216.4 m); beam 106 ft (32.3 m); draft 33 ft 6 in (10.2 m)
Propulsion:	two geared steam turbines delivering 45,000 shp (33552 kW) to two propellers for 23 kt
Armour:	13/14-in (330/356-mm) belt, 4/12-in (102/305-mm) bulkheads, 7/9-in (178/229-mm) funnel uptakes, 7.25/16-in (184/406-mm) turrets, 12/15-in (305/381-mm) barbettes, and 6.5/14-in (165/356-mm) conning tower
Armament:	nine 16-in (406-mm) guns, 12 6-in (152-mm) guns, six 4.7-in (120-mm) AA guns, eight 2-pdr pom-pom AA guns, and two 24.5-in (622-mm) torpedo tubes
Complement:	1,314

"Four-Stack" Destroyers (World War II)

These "four piper" or "flush-deck" survivors of a very large group of American destroyers were nearly as important to naval operations in World War II as they had been in World War I. However, whereas in the earlier war they had epitomised something of the "state of the art," in the later war they were technically obsolete.

Designed to provide the US Navy with the modern destroyer force it so desperately needed as the USA edged toward involvement in World War I (the USA declared war on Germany in April 1917), the first of the new classes was the "Caldwell" class, of which six were built to a design developed from that of the "Tucker" class of "thousand tonners." The new class had the same major dimensions and displacement, but did away with the European type of raised forecastle. Thus the "Caldwell" prototype ships had a hull with a long, easy sheerline, and the two amidships 4-in (102-mm) guns resited from the break of the forecastle to a house between the second and third funnels. The additional topweight had an adverse effect on a hull which was already tender. The 21-in (533-mm) torpedo armament was based on two triple launchers on each beam.

The "Caldwell" class three-stackers paved the way for the first true "four-stackers," namely the 111 units of the "Wickes" class, which was a 35-kt development of the 30-kt "Caldwell" class to operate with the US Navy's new battle-cruisers and scout cruisers. The greater speed was provided by modification of the hull shape and incorporation of steam turbines delivering some 33 percent more power. The ships were built by eight yards for launch between August 1916 and July 1919, and completion with basically the same armament (four 4-in/102-mm guns, two 1-pdr or one 3-in/76-mm AA guns, and four triple torpedo launchers) as the "Caldwell" class.

There followed 156 "Clemson" class destroyers, with greater fuel capacity. The last of these "Clemson" class ships were launched in 1921, and the "Wickes" and "Clemson" classes provided he bulk of the US destroyer force into the late 1930s. Some 93 were scrapped under the terms of the London Naval Treaty of 1930, and most of the others were laid up.

Immediately after the retreat of the British Expeditionary Force from France in June 1940, carried out in the Dunkirk and other evacuations, the UK faced

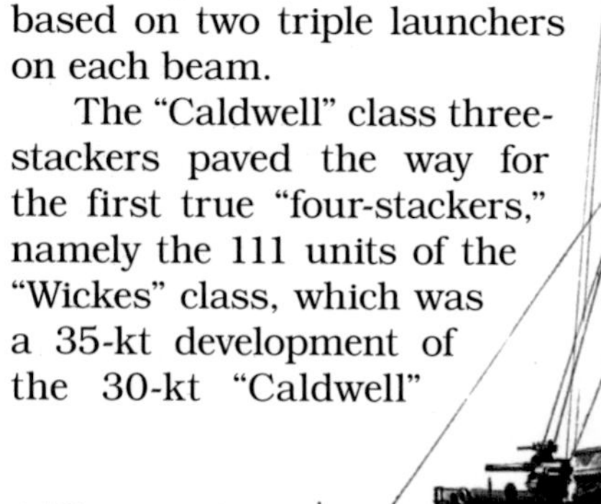

A "Clemson" class destroyer of the "four-stacker" series in her original form.

"Clemson" class (as built)

Type:	destroyer
Tonnage:	1,308 tons full load
Dimensions:	length 314 ft 4 in (95.8 m); beam 30 ft 10 in (9.4 m); draft 9 ft 10 in (3 m)
Propulsion:	two geared steam turbines delivering 27,000 shp (20134 kW) to two propellers for 35 kt
Armour:	none
Armament:	four 4-in (102-mm) guns, one 3-in (76-mm) AA gun, and four triple launchers for 21-in (533-mm) torpedoes
Complement:	114

the prospect of a German seaborne invasion at a time when she had other vital commitments all over the world. In July 1940 the Royal Navy was so short of escorts that the British government negotiated a deal for 50 obsolescent "four-stackers" in exchange for 99-year US leases on British bases between the Caribbean and Newfoundland.

This was not the deal which provided the Royal Navy with the "50 Ships that Saved the World", as the fellow journalists of the time liked to describe them, but the ships-for-bases deal did signal the increasing willingness of President Franklin D. Roosevelt's administration to support the UK, and also provided the Royal Navy with a useful number of additional ships at a time when it was sorely overextended. There was never any intention that these obsolescent vessels be used for any type of fleet purpose, but they more than proved their worth as escorts, and by 1945 the surviving ships were generally armed with one 4-in (102-mm) QF gun, one 12-pdr AA gun, three or four 20-mm AA cannon, one triple 21-in (533-mm) torpedo launcher, and between 60 and 80 depth charges. The ships were delivered from September 1940, and some were revised with their funnels removed or trunked, or converted to escorts, minelayers, minesweepers or small auxiliaries. The most famous of these ships was HMS *Campbeltown*, the ex-USS *Buchanan* of the "Wickes" class, which had her bows filled with explosives to ram and destroy the lock gates at St Nazaire on March 28, 1942.

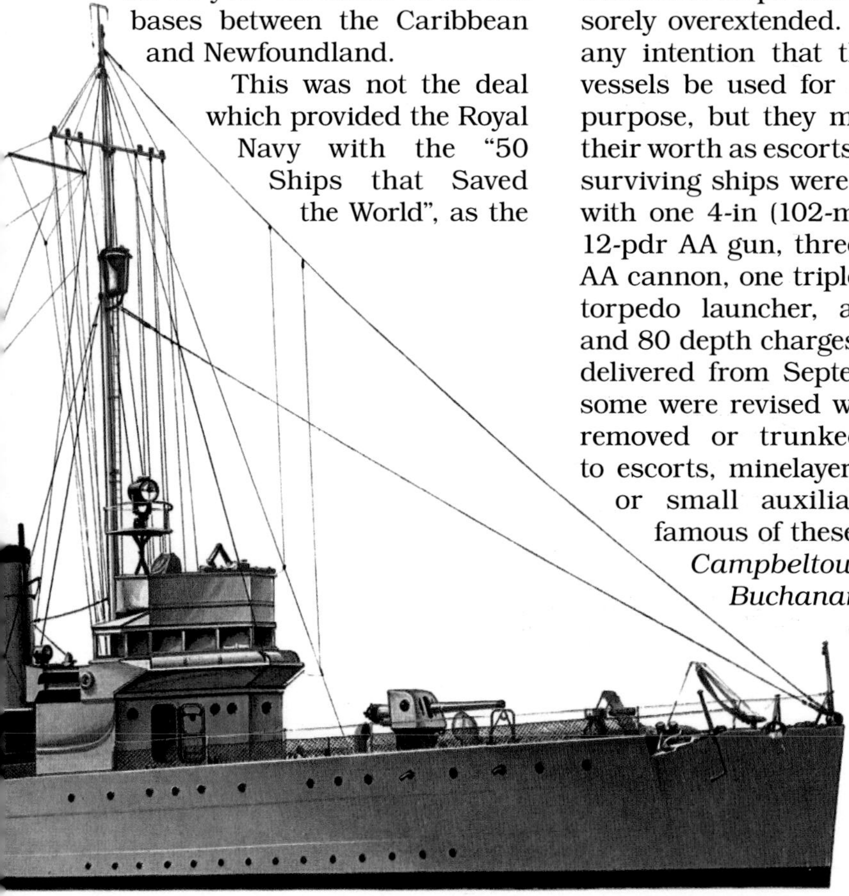

USS *North Carolina* (1941)

The two capital ships of the "North Carolina" class were the first battleships designed and built for the US Navy after the expiry of the 1922 Washington Naval Treaty's "building holiday," although as conceived the two ships adhered to the 1930 London Naval Treaty's limit on main-armament calibre to 14 in (356 mm). The ships were thus initially conceived within the context of the final stages of the US Navy's preference not for outright speed but rather for heavy firepower and excellent protection even if this meant reduced speed. By 1935, though, the US Navy felt that the time was ripe for evaluation of the somewhat different battleship type being created in other countries with speed as important as firepower and protection, The US Navy therefore ordered that its next battleship design should provide high speed in combination with good armament and good protection. The decision was taken not just to create a battleship class comparable with those being created by other nations,

The USS North Carolina in action.

such as the Imperial Japanese navy's "Kongo" class battle-cruisers in their rebuilt 26-kt battleship forms, but also with the performance to work with fast task forces based on the latest generation of high-speed fleet aircraft carriers. At this stage the service's two ablest carriers were the USS *Saratoga* and USS *Lexington*, which had been laid down as battle-cruisers, and it was recommended that each of these carriers should operate with two fast battleships as the core of any long-range task group.

On this basis, therefore, the US Navy ordered the design of a new 30-kt battleship armed with nine 14-in (356-mm) guns in three triple turrets and protected against plunging fire from the same calibre of weapon. The reasoning was basically similar to that which was later adopted for the "Iowa" class battleships, but at a late stage in the process the chief of naval operations intervened, rejecting the design in favor of a more

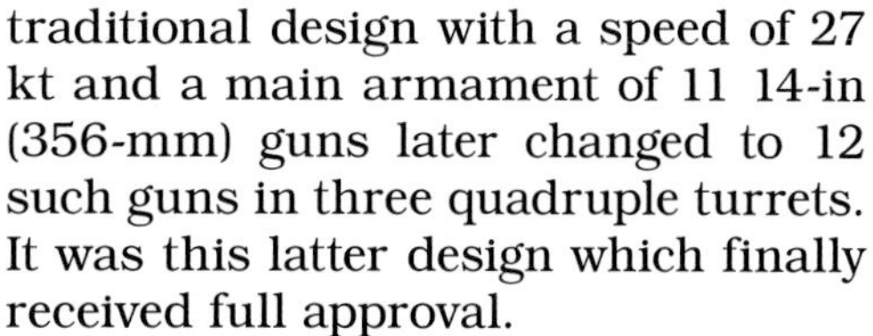

traditional design with a speed of 27 kt and a main armament of 11 14-in (356-mm) guns later changed to 12 such guns in three quadruple turrets. It was this latter design which finally received full approval.

Though the possibility of using 16-in (406-mm) guns had been considered at the draft design stage, the 2nd London Naval Treaty of 1936 preserved the main armament calibre limitation of 14 in (356 mm) for new battleship construction, and it was this which formed the basis of both the main armament and the protection levels designed into the "North Carolina" class. The ships were to be generally proof against 14-in (356-mm) fire at ranges between 20,000 and 30,800 yards (18290 and 28165 m), though lower limits of 19,000 yards (17375 m) for the battery and 33,000 yards (10060 m) for the magazines were fixed. The realities of the current world situation and the steady improvement of technology were also reflected in the provision in the design for the new 14-in (356-mm) quadruple turret to be replaced by a 16-in (406-mm) triple turret, as would be permitted if an escalator clause in the 2nd London Naval Treaty was invoked. This clause was based on whether or not the Japanese accepted the 14-in (356-mm) limit, and when Japan withdrew from the treaty negotiations the US government invoked the escalator clause. Thus all the new US battleships were armed with 16-in (406-mm) guns.

However, what this clause could not manage was a change in armour thicknesses, which were already embedded in the basic design. Thus, in the face of the standard 16-in (406-mm) shell, which weighed only 2,250 lb (1021 kg) and was less capable than the later 2,700-lb (1225-kg) shell which was adopted, the

USS *North Carolina* (1941) *continued*

protection of the "North Carolina" class battleship provided an immunity zone only between 21,000 and 27,000 yards (19200 and 24690 m) for the magazines, and between 23,200 and 26,000 yards (21215 and 23775 m) for the machinery spaces.

The two ships were the USS *North Carolina* and USS *Washington*. The former was built by the New York Navy Yard between October 1937 and June 1940 for completion in April 1941, while the latter was built by the Philadelphia Navy Yard between June 1938 and June 1940 for completion in May 1941. When the USA was drawn into World War II by the Japanese attack on Pearl Harbor in December 1941, both ships were very new in service but not fully operational until a time early in 1942 as a result, at least in part, of propeller vibration.

Both ships enjoyed intensive operational careers in World War II, the *Washington* gaining the distinction of being the only modern US battleship to engage another capital ship, in this case the Japanese battle-cruiser *Kirishima*, which with the USS *South Dakota* she sank during the night of 13/14 November 1942 off Savo Island in the Solomons group.

The *South Carolina* was involved in the Guadalcanal, Eastern Solomons, Gilbert Islands, Kwajalein, 1944 Truk and Palau Islands raids, Hollandia, Saipan, Philippine Sea, 1944 Philippines, Taiwan and China coast raids, 1945 Kyushu and Ryukyu Islands raids, Iwo Jima, Okinawa, and 1945 Japanese home islands campaigns and battles. On 15 September 1942 the ship was hit by a torpedo fired by the Japanese submarine *I-19* off Espiritu Santo Island, and on April 6, 1945 she was hit by "friendly" fire off Okinawa. As assessment of the two ships' overall capabilities later suggested that the "North Carolina" class battleships were generally superior to the four units of the succeeding "South Dakota" class, largely as a result of the latters' shorter, more cramped hulls.

The "North Carolina" class ships had their light AA armament greatly enhanced during the war. The 16 1.1-in guns and 12 0.5-in (12.7-mm) machine guns were replaced by 60 40-mm guns (15 quadruple mounts) and 56 single 20-mm cannon, although

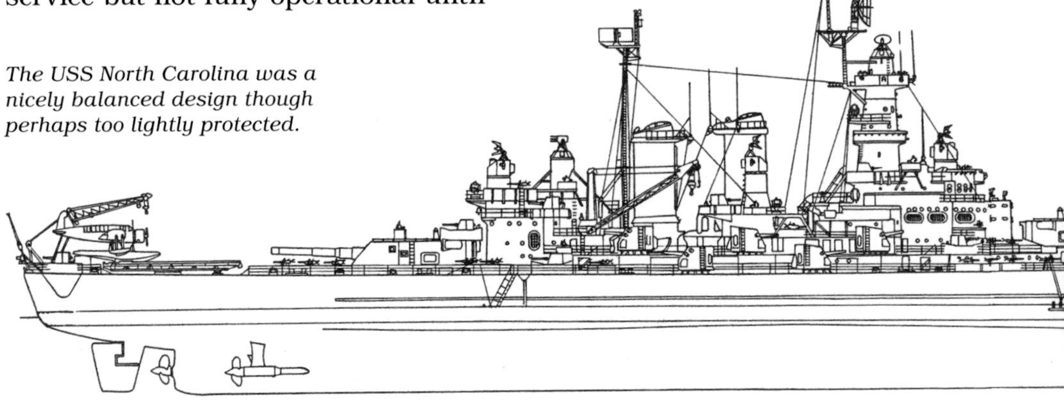

The USS North Carolina was a nicely balanced design though perhaps too lightly protected.

The USS North Carolina had only a short operational career.

the North Carolina ended the war with 96 40-mm guns (24 quadruple mounts) and 36 20-mm cannon (eight twin and 20 single mounts), and the Washington with 15 40-mm quadruple mounts and 83 20-mm cannon in one quadruple, eight twin and 63 single mounts. The capabilities of this tertiary AA armament were enhanced by the provision of many optical directors and, later, radar.

The *North Carolina* was used for a short time after World War II as a training ship before being decommissioned in June 1947 and stricken in June 1960. In September of the following year the ship was transferred to her name state, where she is preserved as a memorial at Wilmington. The *Washington* was decommissioned in June 1947, stricken in June 1960, and sold for breaking in May 1961.

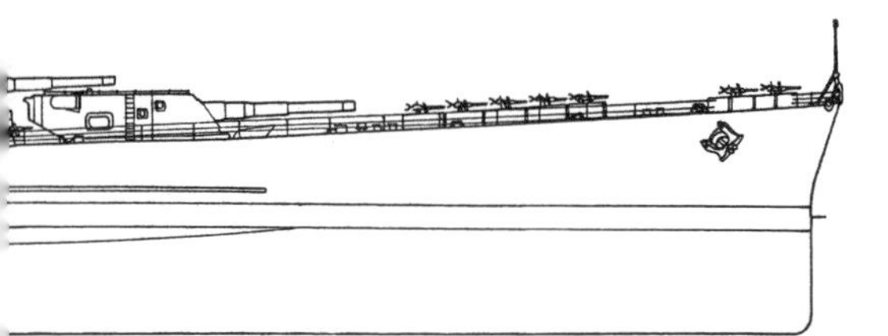

USS *North Carolina* (as completed)

Type:	battleship
Tonnage:	46,770 tons full load
Dimensions:	length 728 ft 9 in (222.1 m); beam 108 ft 4 in (33 m); draft 33 ft (10 m)
Propulsion:	four geared steam turbines delivering 121,000 shp (90218 kW) to four propellers for 28 kt
Armour:	6.6/12-in (168/305-mm) belt, 5/5.5-in (127/140-mm) armoured deck, 11-in (279-mm) bulkheads, 7/16-in (178/406-mm) turrets, 14.7/16-in (373/406-mm) barbettes, and 7/16-in (178/406-mm) conning tower
Armament:	nine 16-in (406-mm) guns, 20 5-in (127-mm) DP guns, 16 1.1-in AA guns, 12 0.5-in (12.7-mm) AA guns, and three aircraft
Complement:	1,880

KMS *Gneisenau* (1938)

KMS *Scharnhorst* and KMS *Gneisenau*, completed January and May 1938 respectively, were of a compromise design. Adolf Hitler originally wanted ships possessing the same armament and speed as the "Deutschland" class "pocket battleships" but with a 19,000-ton displacement to allow better protection, but the German navy felt that such a vessel, carrying only six 11-in (280-mm) main guns, would be poorly balanced, and therefore wanted at least a third triple turret, increasing the displacement to 26,000 tons. Hitler reluctantly agreed, and the German navy saw in the ships its answer to France's two "Dunkerque" class fast battleships.

The Anglo-German Naval Agreement of 1935 permitted gun calibres up to 16 in (406 mm), and Hitler soon revised his thinking to demand that the ships be completed with 15-in (380-mm) guns. The 11-in (280-mm) triple turret was readily available and a new 15-in (380-mm) twin turret would take some years to develop, so Hitler agreed that the new ships should be completed with the smaller weapons but be retrofitted with the larger guns as soon as these were ready.

In the winter of 1938/39 the ships had their original straight stems replaced by clipper bows, increasing overall length by 16 ft 9 in (5.1 m) and reducing wetness forward. In 1938/39 the *Scharnhorst* received a new tripod main mast, and the vessels' short-range AA fit was boosted in World War II, the Scharnhorst gaining an extra 24 and the *Gneisenau* 12 more 20-mm cannon. The *Scharnhorst* was also revised, late in her career, with the two triple launchers for 21-in torpedoes removed from the light cruiser KMS *Nürnberg*.

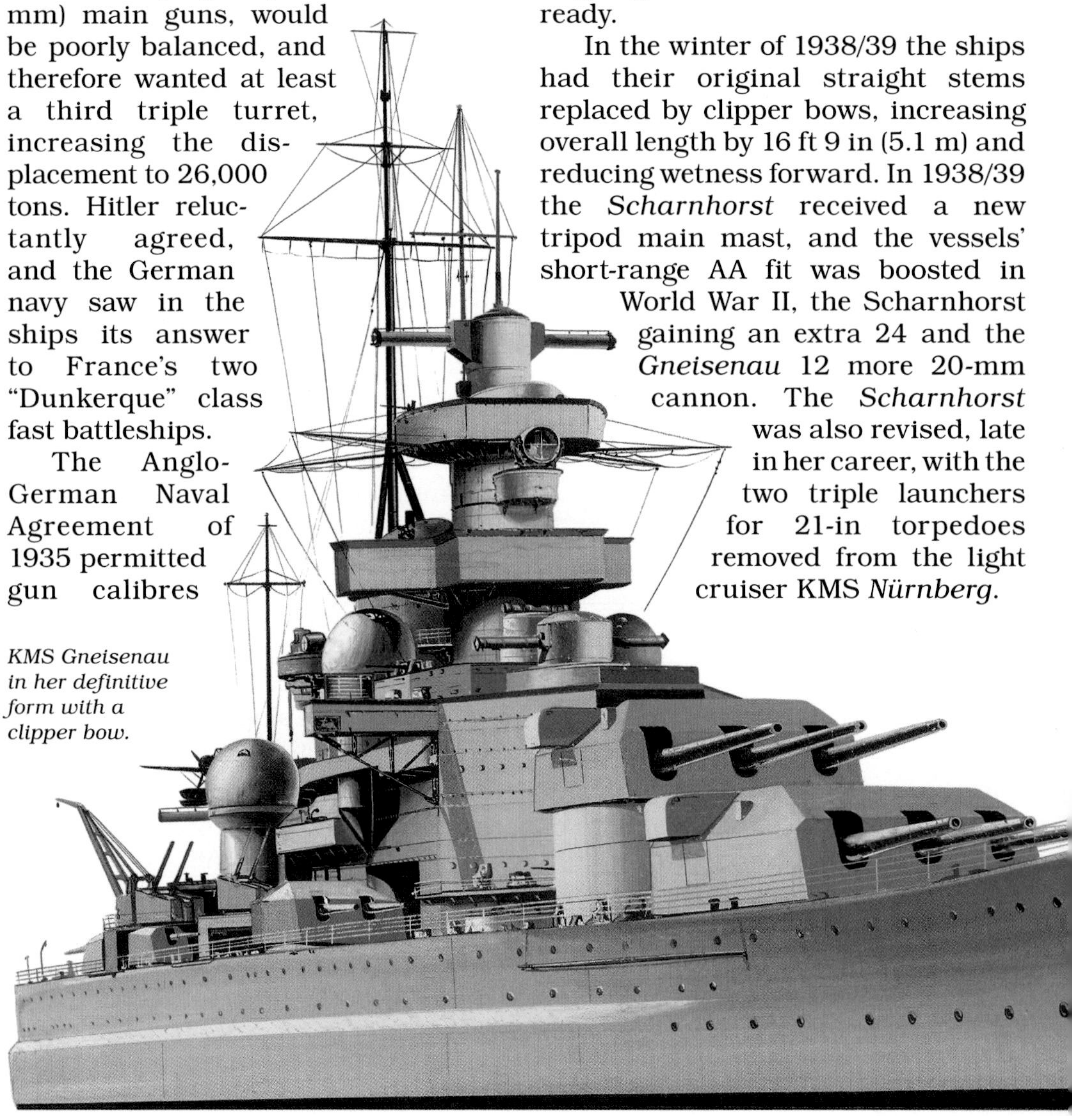

KMS Gneisenau in her definitive form with a clipper bow.

KMS Gneisenau under way in the North Sea.

KMS *Gneisenau* (as completed)

Type: battle-cruiser

Tonnage: 38,900 tons deep load

Dimensions: length 753 ft 11 in (229.8 m); beam 98 ft 5 in (30 m); draft 32 ft 6 in (9.9 m)

Propulsion: three geared steam turbines delivering 165,000 shp (123024 kW) to three propellers for 32 kt

Armour: 6.75/13.75-in (170/350-mm) belt, 1.75-in (45-mm) torpedo bulkhead, 2-in (50-mm) deck, 3-in (75-mm) armoured deck, 3.9-in (100-mm) slopes, 5.9/14-in (150/355-mm) main turrets, 2/5,5-in (50/140mm) secondary turrets, 2-in (50-mm) gun shields, and 3.9/13,75-in (100/350-mm) conning tower

Armament: none 11-in (280-mm) guns, 12 5.9-in (150-mm) guns, 14 4.1-in (105-mm) DP guns, 16 37-mm AA guns, eight 20-mm AA cannon, and three or four aircraft

Complement: 1,840

After the ship had been damaged in a British air raid on Kiel during 26/27 November 1942, it was decided that the *Gneisenau* should be reconstructed with 15-in (380-mm) guns. The concept was dropped in 1943, and the ship was left without her bow section forward of "A" turret, the guns of her main battery being used for coastal defence, and those of the secondary battery for other land service. Late in the war the vessel was towed to Götenhafen (Gdynia) and scuttled as a block ship. The *Scharnhorst* was sunk on December 26, 1943 in the Battle of the North Cape by the battleship HMS *Duke of York* and the cruisers HMS *Belfast*, HMS *Jamaica* and HMS *Norfolk*.

KMS *Bismark* (1940)

The only two battleships of the German navy in World War II, KMS *Bismarck* and KMS *Tirpitz* exercised a very considerable effect on British naval operations through World War II, for as long as either of the ships survived the Royal Navy felt itself compelled to retain in home waters major and modern parts of its surface fleet, which could otherwise have been deployed usefully in other theatres.

Though visually impressive and possessing good firepower, the two ships of the "Bismarck" class did not in fact reflect the latest in naval thinking. This resulted from the fact that there was a significant gap in the design and construction of major warships, beginning with the Treaty of Versailles in 1919. This meant that while major naval powers such as the UK, USA and Japan could experiment with older or redundant ships in assessing the capability of shells and armour, Germany could not and, at the same time, lost ground in the process of uninterrupted battleship evolution. The best that the German navy could manage was secret theoretical work, but this meant that after the 1935 signature of the Anglo-German Naval Treaty, the German navy was nicely positioned for the speedy completion of the design of two of the three 35,000-ton battleships the treaty permitted it.

The design of the hull was based on that of the "Baden" class, the last super dreadnought class completed in Germany during World War I. However, to provide for a 6-kt kt increase in speed, much enhanced underwater protection and very considerably heavier AA armament, the design was revised for greater length and a finer length/beam ratio. The recycling of a World War I design saved time, but it also preserved several flawed features: the rudders and steering gear were poorly protected, and the location of the main armoured deck toward the lower edge of the belt (other major powers had shifted its position toward the belt's upper edge) meant that most of the data-transmission and communications systems effectively unprotected, and both of these were key elements in the loss of the *Bismarck*. Another aspect of the design which reflected the interval in Germany's capital ship experience was the lack of a dual-purpose secondary armament: this meant an increase in size and displacement to provide for separate anti-ship and anti-aircraft batteries. Mention should also be made of the poor quality of the armour protection scheme by comparison with that of

The sole operational cruise of KMS Bismarck.

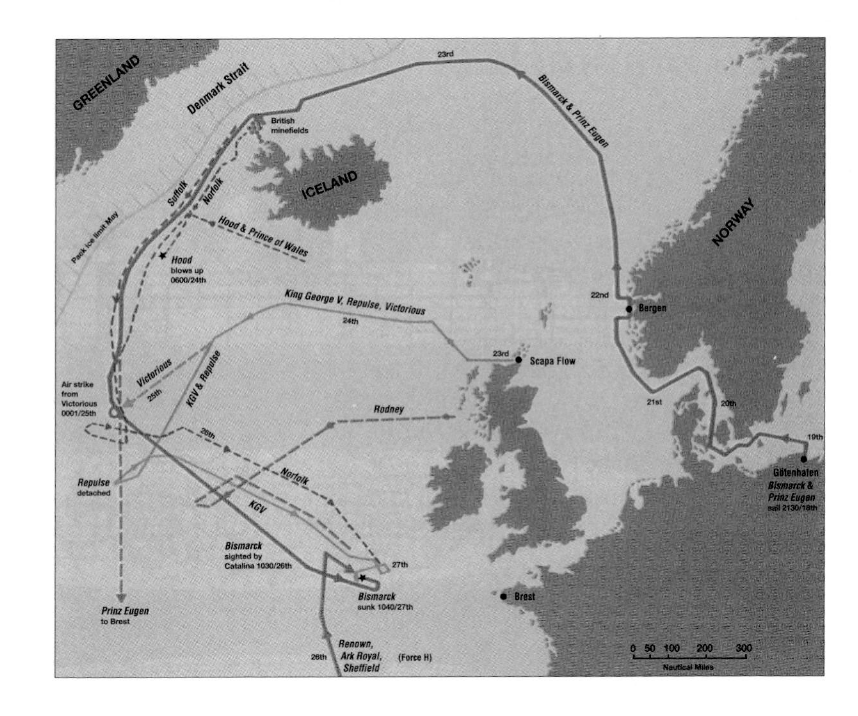

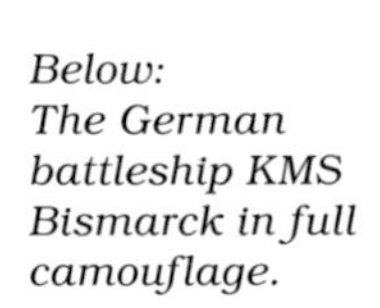

Below: The German battleship KMS Bismarck in full camouflage.

countries which had been able to test World War I ships to destruction: thus the *Bismarck's* conning tower, which was theoretically proof against 15-in (381-mm) projectiles, was in fact penetrated by British 8-in (203-mm) projectiles.

As noted above, the two ships of the class were the *Bismarck* and the *Tirpitz*, the former laid down by Blohm und Voss of Hamburg in July 1946 for completion in August 1940, and the latter laid down by Wilhelmshaven Navy Yard in October 1936 for completion in February 1941. For all their subsequently perceived faults, though, the two ships were of very impressive appearance and were generally perceived as extremely formidable. Their construction was very good, which made them very difficult to sink, their fire-control systems (especially that for the AA battery) were excellent, they carried gunnery radar, and they were well planned for their primary task of attacking the UK's maritime lines of communications, especially those plied by mercantile traffic across and along the Atlantic.

The armament layout was based on eight 15-in (380-mm) main guns in superfiring pairs of twin turrets on the centreline forward and aft, 12 5.9-

KMS *Bismark* (1940) *continued*

in (150-mm) anti-ship guns in six twin turrets abreast the superstructure, and 16 4/1-in (105-mm) AA guns in eight twin mountings also abreast the superstructure. The main and anti-ship secondary batteries there were three separate directors each in the forward and after command positions, while the foretop command post had four directors to control both batteries at the same time.

After working up in the Baltic, the *Bismarck* was dispatched from Götenhafen (Gdynia) on May 18, 1941 for a commerce raiding foray into the Atlantic in company with the heavy cruiser KMS *Prinz Eugen*. However, the ship was reported as she passed through the Kattegat and sighted by air reconnaissance while in harbour near Bergen taking on additional fuel. Attempting to break out into the Atlantic through the Denmark Strait between Iceland and Greenland, she was again sighted and reported by two patrolling British cruisers, which then shadowed her, reporting her movements and course changes. Meanwhile the Royal Navy's Home Fleet had sailed from Scapa Flow. A northern squadron, consisting of the old battle-cruiser HMS *Hood* and the newly commissioned but as yet unready battleship HMS *Prince of Wales*, was south of Iceland; the commander-in-chief in the battleship HMS *King George V*, with the battle-cruiser HMS *Repulse*, the aircraft carrier HMS *Victorious*, three cruisers and seven destroyers sailed on a more southerly course to cover outward and homeward bound convoys.

The *Hood* and the *Prince of Wales* sighted the *Bismarck* and *Prinz Eugen* as they emerged from the Denmark Strait early on May 24, and in the short action with followed the *Hood* was hit and blew up, and the *Prince of Wales* was damaged. However, the *Bismarck* was also hit three times, the detonation of one of these shells isolating 1,000 tons of oil fuel in forward tanks. After the loss of the *Hood*, the *Prince of Wales* joined the cruisers HMS *Suffolk* and HMS *Norfolk* as they continued to shadow the German squadron.

Cutaway of KMS Bismarck.

Later that day the British commander-in-chief detached the carrier *Victorious* for an air attack, one torpedo hitting but not damaging the *Bismarck*. The British Admiralty had meanwhile ordered the Gibraltar-based Force H (the battle-cruiser HMS *Renown*, aircraft carrier HMS *Ark Royal* and cruiser HMS *Sheffield*) to steam north, and the battleship HMS

Rodney, then well to the north-east, to close the German ships. Early in the morning of May 25, the *Bismarck*, now becoming short of fuel, and the *Prinz Eugen* separated, the former steering south-east toward France, and the latter south into the mid-Atlantic.

It was not until 10:30 on May 26, that a British flying boat relocated the *Bismarck*, and then aircraft from the *Ark Royal* shadowed her throughout the day. The *Ark Royal's* aircraft attacked during the evening, scoring three hits, one of them on the rudders making the battleship all but unsteerable and reducing her speed to some 6 kt. A destroyer flotilla detached from a convoy attacked during the night and scored another five hits. Throughout the night the *King George V* and *Rodney* closed in, sighting the *Bismarck* soon after 08:00 on May 27. The British battleships opened fire and soon reduced the German ship to a shambles which was either scuttled or finished off by torpedoes from the cruiser HMS *Dorsetshire*. There were only 110 survivors.

From January 1942 to November 1944 the *Tirpitz* was based in Norwegian waters as a permanent threat to the British convoys to northern Russia. The ship fired her main armament in anger for the only time on September 9, 1943 during a bombardment of Barentsburg on Spitsbergen. She survived many air, midget submarine and human torpedo attacks, though she often sustained damage and casualties, before finally being sunk by air attack on November 12, 1944.

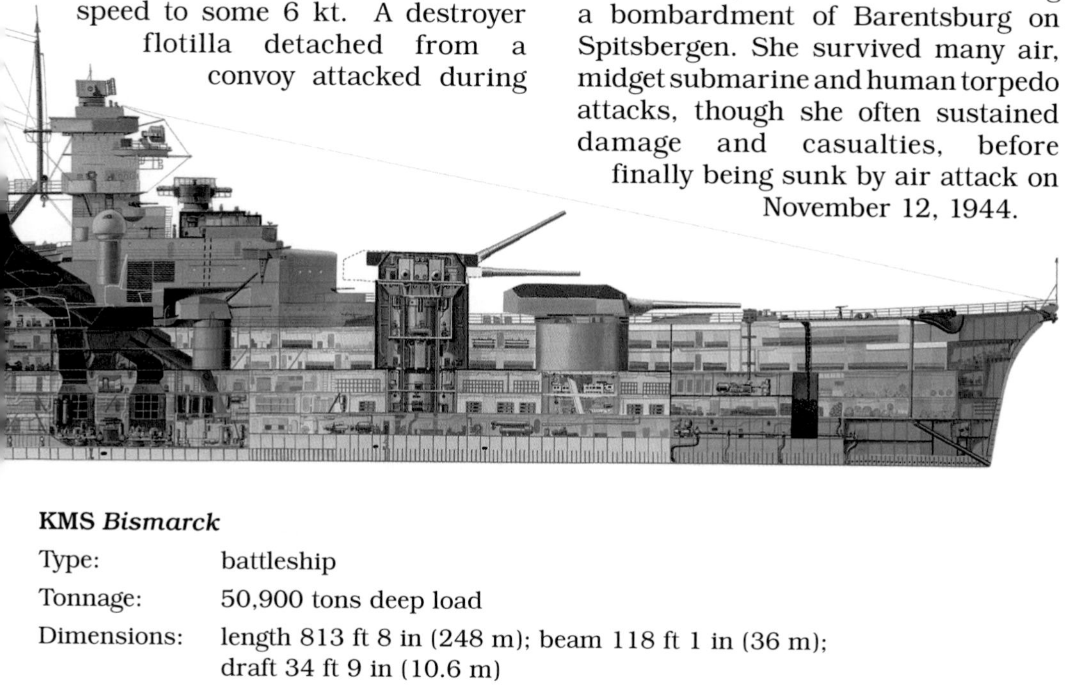

KMS *Bismarck*

Type:	battleship
Tonnage:	50,900 tons deep load
Dimensions:	length 813 ft 8 in (248 m); beam 118 ft 1 in (36 m); draft 34 ft 9 in (10.6 m)
Propulsion:	three geared steam turbines delivering 138,000 shp (102893 kW) to three propellers for 29 kt
Armour:	10.5/12.5-in (265/320-mm) belt, 3.25/4.75-in (80/120-mm) armoured deck, 2-in (50-mm) deck, 1.75-in (45-mm) torpedo bulkhead, 7/14.25-in (180/360-mm) main turrets, 1.5/3.9-in (40/100-mm) secondary turrets, and 2/13.75-in (50/350-mm) conning tower
Armament:	eight 15-in (3880-mm) guns, 12 5.9-in (150-mm) guns, 16 4.1-in (105-mm) AA guns, 16 37-mm AA guns, 12 20-mm AA cannon, and up to six aircraft
Complement:	2,092

"Liberty" ship (1941)

Though intended primarily for mercantile use, replacing Allied tonnage sunk by the Germans, Italians and Japanese, the "Liberty" ship was so important to the eventual Allied victory in World War II that it can be regarded in many respects as a weapon. The type was created for mass production in US yards on the basis of a standardised design using an all-welded steel hull. The ships were produced in 18 shipyards located along the Atlantic, Pacific and Gulf coasts of the USA between 1941 and 1945, and totalled 2,770 vessels (by far the largest number ever completed to a single design) amounting to some 29.292 million deadweight tons. This total included 24 equipped as colliers, eight as tank carrier ships, 36 as aircraft transports, and 62 as tankers.

The original design was produced by J. L. Thompson and Sons of Sunderland in the north-east of England as early as 1879, and this design was adopted by the Americans because it emphasized simple design and operation, rapid construction, maximum freight-carrying capability and, as it emerged, an excellent capacity to withstand damage. With the whole of US turbine and diesel engine building capacity already allocated to combatant vessels, it was decided that the "Liberty" ships would be powered by triple-expansion steam engines, and also use steam for all their auxiliary machinery.

The manufacture of the "Liberty" ship was organized and controlled, on the basis of a major industrial undertaking, by the construction magnate Henry Kaiser, most of whose previous experience had been in road and dam building. It was Kaiser to whom the definitive "Liberty" ship concept should also be attributed.

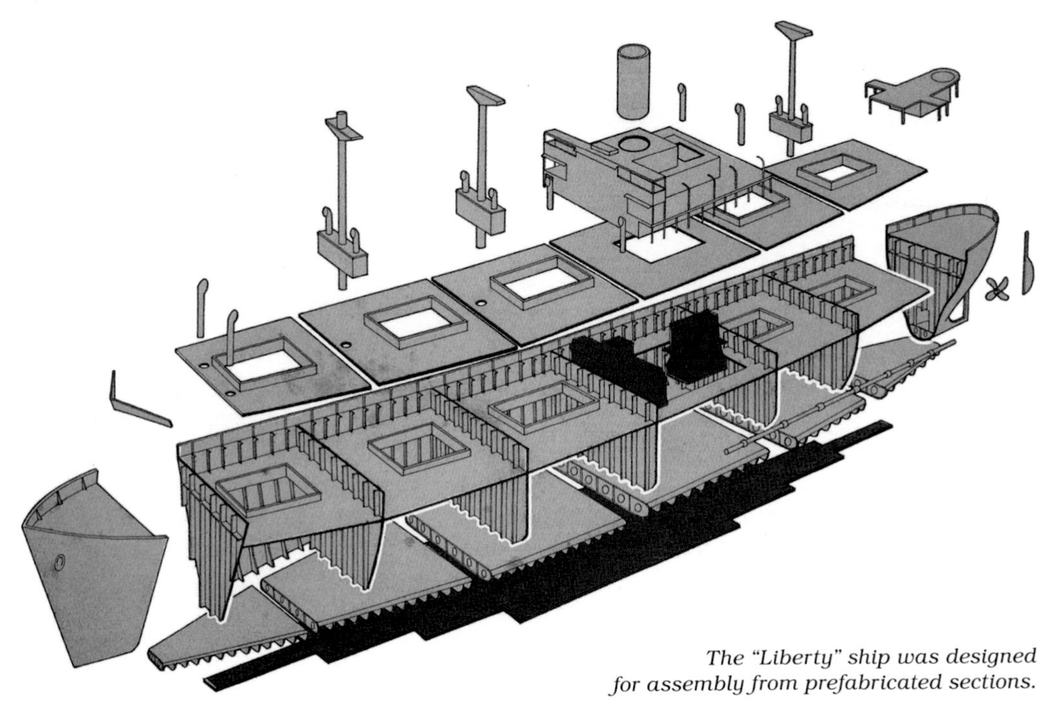

The "Liberty" ship was designed for assembly from prefabricated sections.

It is arguable that without the "Liberty" ship the Allies would have found it very considerably harder to prevail over the Axis nations.

Kaiser established the procedures to be used to maximize and streamline the production effort on a truly huge scale, and also performed the task of overseeing the entire process.

The "Liberty" ship was optimised for the carriage of cargo, and was both cheap and simple to build. The concept was based directly on ships ordered by the UK from US yards to replace tonnage lost principally to German aircraft, surface raiders and, most significantly of all, submarines. The ships were then bought for the US merchant marine and also for delivery to US allies under the terms of the Lend-Lease Act.

The production of the "Liberty" ships echoed, on a very much larger scale, the building of the "Hog Island" and other standardised ship types in World War I, and also paved the way for the post-World War II "Victory" ship. This latter was completed to a standard less austere than that of the "Liberty" ship, and was based on a lengthened and strengthened hull with a forecastle and seam turbine machinery. The standard "Victory" ship had a gross tonnage of 7,607 and speed of 16 kt.

It was in 1940 that the British government ordered 60 tramp steamships from US yards to replace war losses and boost the merchant fleet. The units of this "Ocean" class were simple but fairly large with a single propeller driven by a single 2,500-ihp (1864-kW) reciprocating engine working on the steam generated by coal-fired boilers, this fuel being specified as the UK had an abundance of coal but no indigenous oil. The order specified an 18-in (0.45-m) increase in draft to increase the displacement by 800 tons to 10,100 tons, the accommodation, bridge and main engine located amidships, and a long tunnel to connect the main engine shaft with its aft extension to the propeller. The first "Ocean" ship was the *Ocean Vanguard*, launched on August 16, 1941.

This design was then further developed by the US Maritime Commission to accord with US

Stamp featuring the "Liberty" ship.

construction practices and also to simplify them still further for ease and speed of construction. The American version was the EC2-S-C1, in which most of the riveting (one-third of the labor cost) was replaced by welding. The order was given to Kaiser's "Six Companies" engineering and construction conglomerate.

The number of Lend-Lease ships was increased to 200 in March 1941, and then in April of the same year to 306, of which 117 would be "Liberty" ships. The ships had a poor public image at the time, and in an effort to swing the public behind the program September 27, 1941 was became "Liberty Fleet Day," and the first 14 EC-2 units were launched on this day. The first to enter the water was the *Patrick Henry,* which was launched by President Franklin D. Roosevelt. The president said that the new class of ships would bring liberty to Europe, and this led to the appellation "Liberty" ship.

At first it took about 230 days to build each ship Early on, each ship took about 230 days (the *Patrick Henry* took 244 days), but as the process bedded down and the work force became more skilled the average dropped finally to a mere 42 days. As a publicity stunt, the *Robert E. Peary* was launched only 4 days

The "Liberty" ship was optimized for ease and speed of construction on the basis of the extensive use of non-strategic materials and simple processes.

Though not without their structural problems, the "Liberty" ships often survived major attacks to reach port with precious cargoes.

and 15.5 hours after the laying of her keel. The ships were made from prefabricated sections joined on an assembly-line basis, and in 1943 three new "Liberty" ships were completed every day. The ships were named mainly for famous Americans, starting with those who had signed the Declaration of Independence in 1775,

A particularly notable "Liberty" ship was the *Stephen Hopkins*, which sank a German commerce raider during 1942, and in the process became the first US ship to sink a German surface combatant.

The "Liberty" ships were often far from perfect. Many suffered hull and deck cracks, and some were lost to such structural problems. During World War II almost 1,500 serious fracture were reported, and 19 ships broke in half without warning, the latter including the *John P. Gaines*, which sank on November 24, 1943 with the loss of 10 lives. The reasons for this problem were the fact that the ships were built in great haste, often by inexperienced people, in the era before the embrittlement problems of steel were fully comprehended, and the ships were often very considerably overloaded. The losses generally occurred after storms, when the hulls were very severely stressed, but they were among the factors that led to the follow-on "victory" ship being designed with greater strength and less stiffness.

The last "Liberty" ship to be completed was the *Albert M. Boe* delivered on October 30, 1945. Most of the "Liberty" ships survived to become a major element in the post-war cargo fleet.

"Liberty" ship (typical)

Type:	general-purpose freighter
Tonnage:	7,000 tons deadweight
Dimensions:	length 441 ft 6 in (134.6 m); beam 56 ft 11 in (17.35 m); draft 27 ft 9 in (8.45 m)
Propulsion:	two triple expansion steam engines delivering 2,500 ihp (1864 kW) to two propellers for 11.5 kt
Capacity:	9,140 tons of cargo
Armament:	one 4-in (102-mm) gun, and an assortment of light anti-aircraft gun
Complement:	41

"Buckley" class (1943)

Despite the fact that both their nations made extensive use of the sea for mercantile as well as naval purposes, in the period before World War II the Americans and Japanese both saw little need for escort vessels to convoy their merchant fleets and also protect the slow-moving transports on which their far-flung naval and military operations would be dependent. Thus American and Japanese destroyer design and building efforts were concentrated during the 1930s on fleet destroyers optimised for support of major surface forces and therefore capable of high speeds, possessing only modest range, and armed primarily for the anti-ship role with 5-in (127-mm) guns and banks of torpedo launchers. However, once the fallacy of this thinking had been made apparent, initially by the British experience in the Atlantic Ocean and Mediterranean Sea, the Americans reacted with great speed in the creation of destroyer escorts smaller than their fleet destroyer counterparts, characterized by lower speed but considerably greater range, armed with smaller numbers of lighter dual-purpose guns and also light AA weapons, and possessing a much enhanced anti-submarine capability.

The requirement which led to this type was created in 1941 by the Royal Navy, which contracted with the USA, in the period between November 1941 and January 1942, for the construction of 300 such escorts. In the middle of this period the Japanese attack on Pearl Harbor catapulted the USA into World War II, and the Americans immediately set in motion plans for the rapid construction of more than 1,000 examples of what the US Navy designated the DE (Destroyer Escort) type.

There was a clear conceptual link between the DD (fleet destroyer) and DE in the use of a flush-decked hull, with a prominent sheer line, in both types, but the weapons layout was different, with space available forward for a Hedgehog anti-submarine weapon and the after portion reserved for depth charges (200 or more in the 78 "Captain" class units completed for the British) and their throwers and racks. The machinery was also considerably lower-powered than that of the DEs as the ships needed to be somewhat faster than convoys rather than fleet forces. The ships fell into several classes depending on a number of factors including their use

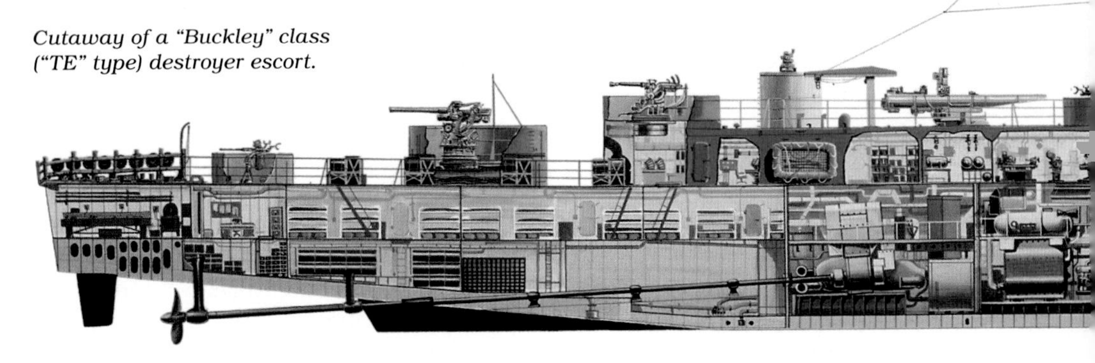
Cutaway of a "Buckley" class ("TE" type) destroyer escort.

of diesel propulsion (85 "Edsall" or "FMR" class ships), or diesel-electric propulsion (97 "Evarts" or "GMT" and 76 "Bostwick" or "DET" class ships) or turbo-electric propulsion (152 "Buckley" or "TE," 74 "John C. Butler" or "WGT" and 81 "Rudderow" or "TEV" class ships).

The US Navy would have preferred the ships to be powered by geared steam turbines for a speed of 24 kt, but gear-cutting was a production bottleneck so diesel engines of the type used in submarines were selected as the alternative despite the fact that their use had to be omitted, resulting in a 4.5-kt reduction in speed. The vessels of this type were the "GMT" (General Motors Tandem diesel drive) type. Next came a turbo-electric propulsion arrangement with the same power output but demanding a lengthened hull, the latter balancing out the greater displacement and giving these "TE" type vessels a speed of some 24 kt. The longer hull was then standardized. Other arrangements were a Westinghouse geared turbine, using relatively small gears, in the "WGT" type, the original diesel-electric system in a long hull as the "DET" type, and a geared diesel drive in the "FMR" (Fairbanks Morse Reduction geared) type.

The ship numbers for which contracts were issued inevitably rose swiftly past the original 50 units and, at its apogee, the DE building effort called for the construction of 1,005 ships: 105 "GMT," 154 "TE," 252

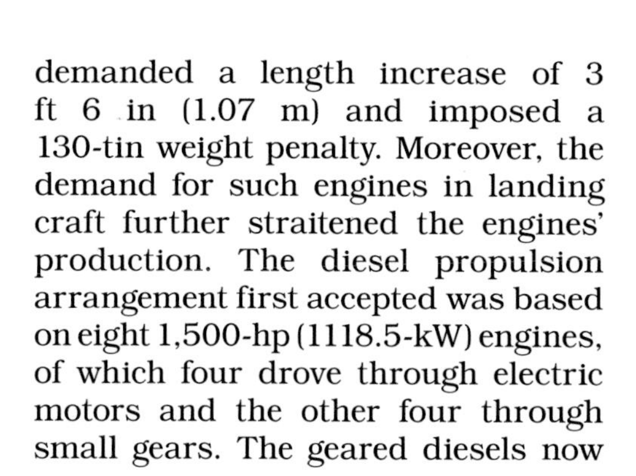

demanded a length increase of 3 ft 6 in (1.07 m) and imposed a 130-tin weight penalty. Moreover, the demand for such engines in landing craft further straitened the engines' production. The diesel propulsion arrangement first accepted was based on eight 1,500-hp (1118.5-kW) engines, of which four drove through electric motors and the other four through small gears. The geared diesels now

"TEV" ("TE" with 5-in/127-mm guns), 293 "WGT," 116 "DET" and 85 "FMR" units. Many of these were ordered to ensure that 260 ships were completed in 1943, and in fact more than 300 were completed in this period. This magnificent industrial effort in fact saw the completion of 425 ships in the year between April 1943 and Aril 1944. The ship completed most rapidly, by the Bethlehem Iron Works,

The USS Osberg was a "John C. Butler" class ("WGT" type) DE built by Boston Navy Yard and launched on December 7, 1943 with a main armament of two 5-in (127-mm) enclosed guns.

was the "Buckley" class USS *Underhill*, which was completed in less than two months. Mass cancellations began in the autumn of 1943, and totalled 305 in September and October of that year. Another 135 were axed in 1944, and two in 1946. Many of the DEs were converted to APD (fast light transports) standard; the program called for 50 each of the "TE" and "TEV" types to be modified, but the totals were 44 and 51 respectively. Another program was launched for 20 to be converted as radar pickets, but only seven were completed at the end of the war, although many others were converted in the 1950s as part of the North American Air Defense System.

The armament varied greatly. The original design included provision for two enclosed 5-in (127-mm) guns in place of the standard 3-in (76-mm) weapons, and the "TEV" and "WGT" types were built to this standard. The "GMT" type were the only DEs which never mounted torpedo tubes, and the Royal Navy, which had originally specified tubes, asked that they be deleted from all the DEs slated for delivery to the UK and Canada. The Royal Navy was the service which first specified the installation of the Hedgehog anti-submarine weapon, and this was in fact fitted in all DEs. All but the "TEV" and "WGT" type ships had the originally specified original British-style tall bridge, and ships completed with, but not

The USS Maloy was a "Buckley" class ("TE" type) DE built by Consolidated and launched on August 18, 1943 with a main armament of three 3-in (76-mm) open guns.

those converted to, 5-in (127-mm) guns had a lower bridge similar to that of the "Allen M. Sumner" class DDs and ultimately based on British experience. The "TE" type ships converted as radar pickets in 1945 had two 5-in (127-mm) guns, a heavier mast to carry the antenna of the search radar, and a new combat information center. In many of the ships the torpedo launchers were removed during refits and replaced by four 40-mm single AA guns. Several late vessels were completed without torpedo launchers, and this allowed the incorporation on six "WGT" type ships of one quadruple 40-mm gun aft, three twin 40-mm guns and 10 single 20-mm cannon.

Total DE construction was 565 ships.

USS *Joseph C. Hubbard* ("TE" type)

Type:	destroyer escort
Tonnage:	1,823 tons full load
Dimensions:	length 306 ft (93.3 m); beam 37 ft (11.3 m); draft 11 ft 3 in (3.4 m)
Propulsion:	two steam turbo-electric engines delivering 12,000 shp (8947 kW) to two propellers for 23 kt
Armour:	none
Armament:	three 3-in (76-mm) DP guns, four 1,1-in AA guns, eight 20-mm AA cannon, one triple launchers for 21-in (533-mm) torpedoes, one Hedgehog anti-submarine weapon, eight depth charge throwers, and two depth charge racks
Complement:	186

HMS *Vanguard* (1946)

Built by John Brown and completed in August 1946 as what was by then a completely outmoded concept, HMS Vanguard was the last British battleship. The ship's origins can be traced back to a time early in 1939, when Sir Stanley Goodall, the Director of Naval Construction, suggested that the four existing 15-in (381-mm) twin turrets removed from the battle-cruisers HMS *Courageous* and HMS *Glorious*, when they were turned into aircraft carriers in 1924/25, to create a 30-kt battleship. It was recognized that these turrets were no longer in the flush of their youth, and in some respects were obsolescent, but they were also reliable, could be modernised and provided with thicker face and roof armour, and carried guns whose elevation angle to be increased to 30°. Moreover, the guns were only marginally less potent than the latest 15-in (381-mm) weapons, and this was deemed acceptable for Far Eastern service. The one main problem was that the turrets had been designed for use in ships with their shell rooms below their magazines, and for what had by this time became standard, the magazine handing rooms had to be on the lower deck above the shell rooms with fixed hoists from the magazines below.

The *Vanguard* was basically an improved "King George V" class ship lengthened to accommodate four rather than three centerline turrets (superfiring pairs forward and aft), the main belt extended but thinned by 1 in (25 mm) to save weight, bows characterized by pronounced sheer and, again to save weight, a transom stern. The result was a ship of impressive appearance with seakeeping to match and no tendency to take water over the bows.

The secondary armament was based on 16 5.25-in (133-mm) DP guns in eight twin gun houses abreast the two funnels, but no provision was made for aircraft operations. The belt was reduced in thickness to 14 in (356 mm) abreast the magazines and 13 in (330 mm) elsewhere with a uniform thickness of 4.5 in (114 mm) on its lower edges, and the lower strake was continued for some distance as it tapered from 13 to 11 in (330 to 281 mm) with a lower edge again 4.5 in (114 mm) thick. The main deck armour was 6 in (152 mm) thick over the magazines and 5 in (127 mm) thick over the machinery spaces. The secondary armament gun houses had 1.5/2.5-in (38/64-mm) protection, and there was

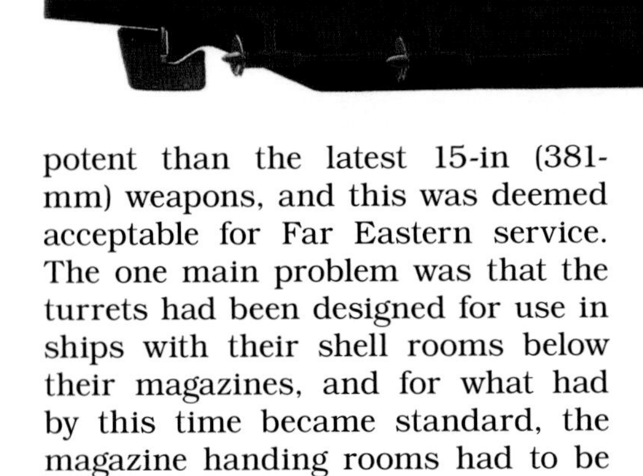

HMS Vanguard was obsolete when completed, but was a fine seaboat.

more splinter protection than in the "King George V" class. The torpedo protection was similar to that of the "King George V" class.

The main machinery was also disposed as in the "King George V" class, with the boiler and engine rooms constituting four separate units which could operate independently of each other. Habitability was notably good, and the ship included both central heating and air conditioning to allow her deployment anywhere in the world.

The contract was issued in March 1941, and it was expected that the ship would be completed in 1943. Weights increased as the ship was built, and another 770 tons had therefore to be added to the upper deck to cope with the higher stresses which resulted. The ship was completed only after World War II, and was used mainly for training and as an HQ vessel before being sold for breaking in 1960.

With HMS Vanguard, the Royal Navy's involvement with the battleship came to an end with an obsolete but nonetheless stately vessel.

HMS *Vanguard*

Type:	battleship
Tonnage:	51,420 tons full load
Dimensions:	length 814 ft 4 in (248.2 m); beam 108 ft (32.9 m); draft 36 ft (11 m)
Propulsion:	four geared steam turbines delivering 130,000 shp (96928 kW) to four propellers for 30 kt
Armour:	4.5/14-in (114/356-mm) belt, 4/12-in (102/305-mm) bulkheads, 5/6-in (127/152-mm) main deck, 6/13-in (152/330-mm) turrets, 11/13-in (279/330-mm) barbettes, and1/3-in (25/76-mm) conning tower
Armament:	eight 15-in (381-mm) guns, 16 5.25-in (133-mm) DP guns, and 73 40-mm AA guns
Complement:	1,893

Fast Attack Craft (1945/55)

After World War II's end in 1945, development of fast combat craft such as motor torpedo boats, PT-boats came to a virtual end in the navies of the victorious western Allies. The UK and USA decided that their fast combat craft had achieved only a comparatively indifferent success in their naval efforts of World War II, and that they should therefore return to the type of pre-war navies whose large surface combatants and submarines had dominated operations in the Atlantic and Pacific Oceans in the war. Substantial numbers of fast combat craft were therefore deleted or transferred to smaller navies. These latter used the craft mainly for the patrol role, but the navies of some middle-rank nations used them as technical and tactical stones toward the re-creation of conventional navies out of the maritime ashes left to them after World War II.

Many of the world's navies, including a large number without any claim to a long-standing naval or even maritime tradition, now operate forces of small but comparatively heavily armed fast combat craft. These can be defined as vessels possessing a displacement of up to 600 tons and a top speed of 25 kt or more, and fall into two basic categories. These are the fast patrol boat (FPB) and fast attack craft (FAC). The FPB is generally fitted with only light armament (generally machine guns and cannon of up to 40-mm calibre) together with minimal sensor and fire-control suites. The FAC is a considerably more formidable type usually capable of higher speeds and carrying a heavier, longer-ranged armament that can include anti-ship guided missiles, guns of up to 3-in (76-mm) calibre, heavyweight anti-ship torpedoes of up to 21-in (533-mm) calibre, and anti-submarine weapons such as lightweight homing torpedoes, rocket-propelled grenades and depth charges, all controlled with the aid of a considerably more sophisticated sensor and fire-control suites. The nature of the primary armament is generally indicated by a suffixed letter: thus the FAC(G) carries a medium-calibre gun, the FAC(M) carries anti-ship missiles, the FAC(T) carries anti-ship torpedoes etc.

The FPB is significantly inferior to the FAC in combat capability, but is still worthy of examination. Many countries use such FPBs for patrol and protection of their territorial waters

An Israeli reworking of the late-standard 73-ft British MTB of Vosper design and construction with a 40-mm Bofors gun over the stern.

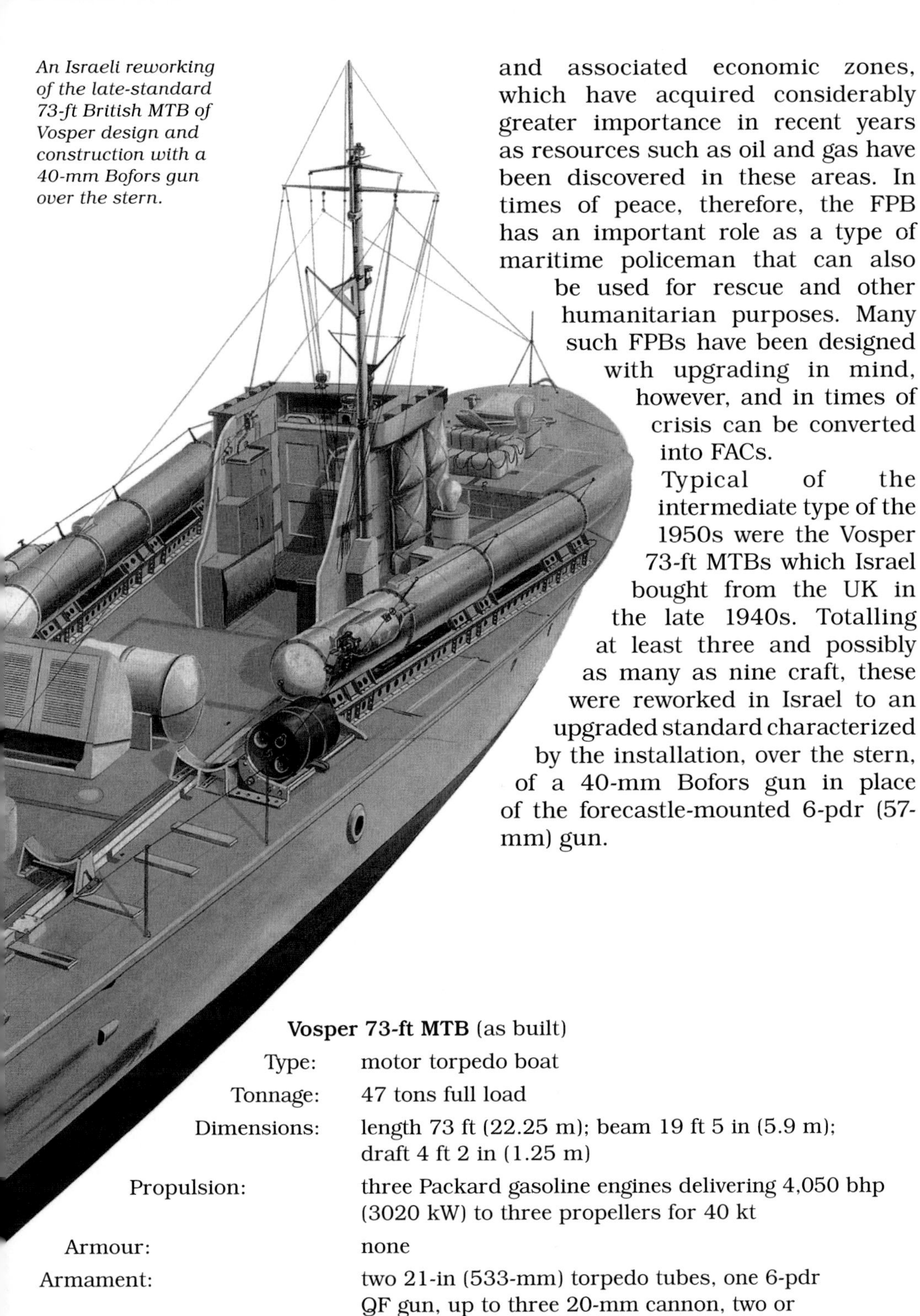

and associated economic zones, which have acquired considerably greater importance in recent years as resources such as oil and gas have been discovered in these areas. In times of peace, therefore, the FPB has an important role as a type of maritime policeman that can also be used for rescue and other humanitarian purposes. Many such FPBs have been designed with upgrading in mind, however, and in times of crisis can be converted into FACs.

Typical of the intermediate type of the 1950s were the Vosper 73-ft MTBs which Israel bought from the UK in the late 1940s. Totalling at least three and possibly as many as nine craft, these were reworked in Israel to an upgraded standard characterized by the installation, over the stern, of a 40-mm Bofors gun in place of the forecastle-mounted 6-pdr (57-mm) gun.

Vosper 73-ft MTB (as built)

Type:	motor torpedo boat
Tonnage:	47 tons full load
Dimensions:	length 73 ft (22.25 m); beam 19 ft 5 in (5.9 m); draft 4 ft 2 in (1.25 m)
Propulsion:	three Packard gasoline engines delivering 4,050 bhp (3020 kW) to three propellers for 40 kt
Armour:	none
Armament:	two 21-in (533-mm) torpedo tubes, one 6-pdr QF gun, up to three 20-mm cannon, two or four 0.5- or 0.303-in (12.7- or 7.7-mm) machine guns, and two depth charges
Complement:	12/13

USS *Mitscher* (1953)

The USS *Mitscher*, *John S*, *McCain*, *Willis A. Lee* and *Wilkinson* of the "Mitscher" class, built in pairs by the Bath Iron works and Bethlehem Steel for completion between May 1953 and September 1954, were at first designated as destroyers and then as frigates in a US Navy category that lasted to 1975. Designed for high speed in a seaway while deeply loaded, these were large vessels designed in 1944/46 as substantial but orthodox destroyers whose main innovation was a semi-automatic twin mounting for 5-in (127-mm) L/54 guns. As it became more evident that aircraft carrier escorts would need a more fully optimized AA capability, in terms of armament and fighter-direction facilities, a new battery was planned on the basis of the new 3-in (76-mm) L/70 gun in fully automatic twin mountings. However, some 5-in (127-mm) guns were eventually retained to deal with light ships and surfaced submarines. However, the most important "weapon" was the combat information centre and its associated radars, allowing fully optimized control of a fast carrier task force's fighters. Anti-submarine capability was now secondary as the task force's high sustained speed would offer virtually complete immunity. The most important anti-submarine weapon was the guided torpedo, fired from a fixed tube, backed by two trainable and elevating Weapon Alfa rocket launchers.

A very compact machinery arrangement was required to pack maximum power into a fairly small hull, and reliability was therefore a constant problem and largely responsible for the ships' decommissioning in 1969/78.

The ships were all extensively modified in service. They were completed with 3-in (76-mm) L/50 guns in open mountings, the L/70 enclosed mountings being retrofitted only in 1957 and demanding the removal, for weight reasons, of the depth charges and after Weapon Alfa installation. In 1960 the ships were adapted to carry the DASH remotely controlled anti-submarine helicopter on a platform replacing the after twin 3-in (76-mm) mounting. The first pair of ships had the SQS-23 sonar, while the latter pair had prototypes SQS-26.

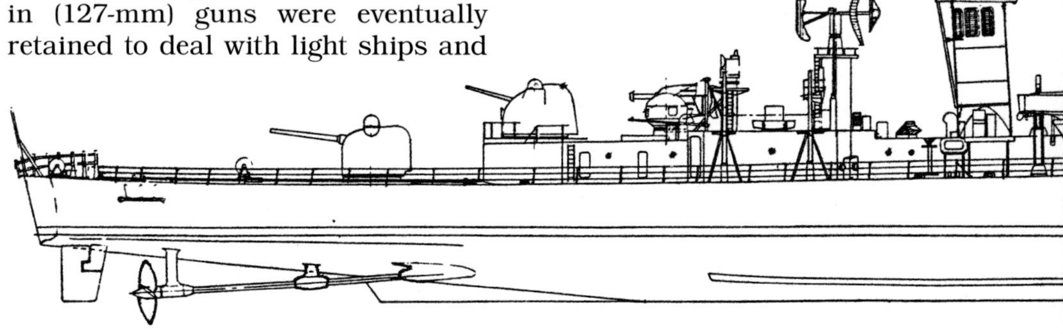

Right:
"Mitscher" class fleet escort.

Below:
The USS Mitscher in early definitive form with two 5-in (1127-mm) and four 3-in (76-mm) guns, the latter in two twin mountings, as well as two Weapon Alfa launchers.

Missile conversions were suggested as early as 1959, the Tartar and Terrier surface-to-air weapons appearing feasible. The first two units were converted as Tartar guided missile destroyers in the later 1960s, but the two other ships were not similarly adapted. The conversion was based on replacing the surviving superfiring weapons forward by an octuple launcher for 16 ASROC anti-submarine rockets, and aft by two triple launchers for 12.75-in (324-mm) lightweight anti-submarine torpedoes and one single-arm launcher for 40 Tartar SAMs. The conversion made the ships top heavy, and they were stricken after little more than 10 years of service.

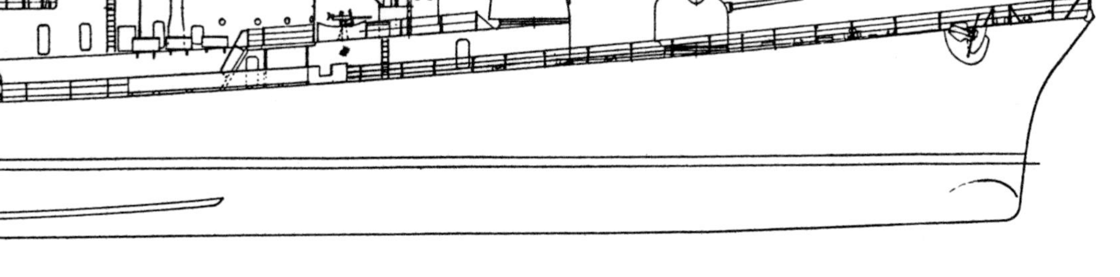

USS *Mitscher*

Type:	fleet escort
Tonnage:	4,855 tons full load
Dimensions:	490 ft (149.4 m); beam 47 ft 6 in (14.5 m); draft 14 ft 8 in (4.5 m)
Propulsion:	two geared steam turbines delivering 80,000 shp (59648 kW) to two propellers for 36.5 kt
Armour:	none
Armament:	two 5-in (127-mm) guns, four 3-in (76-mm) DP guns, eight 20-mm AA guns, four 21-in (533-mm) torpedo tubes, two Weapon Alfa anti-submarine mortars, and one depth charge rack
Complement:	378

Centauro (1957)

Financially and morally exhausted by World War II, Italy was at first content to enter the post-war world with the surviving units of its World War II navy supplemented by a number of ex-US Navy vessels. So far as frigates were concerned, the only units in service during the first part of the 1950s were three "Cannon" class ships supplied by the USA. By the beginning of the 1950s, however, plans were being made for a larger and more modern navy based on ships designed and built in Italy even if there still included US sensors and other equipment.

The first post-war frigates of Italian construction were the four units of the "Canopo" class, namely the *Canopo, Castore, Centauro* and *Cigno.* The *Centauro* was built by Ansaldo, and the other three by the Cantieri Navali Triestini, the ships being laid down in 1952/55 and completed between March 1957 and April 1959. The first and third ships were built with Italian funding, while second and fourth were based on US offshore procurement aid.

There was little remarkable about the design of what were, for their time, wholly orthodox vessels optimized for the anti-submarine role with the Italian Menon mortar as their primary weapon. This was mounted in the "B" position above and behind the forward mountings for two of the design's four 3-in (76-mm) main guns. When completed, the ships had Italian search radar, in the form of the MLA-1 equipment, but by 1960 this had been replaced by the US SPS-6 equipment. The guns and the most of the fire-control systems remained Italian, but most of the other sensors were of American origin even if, like the MLT-4 main armament fire-control radar, it was an Italian version of an American system, in this instance the Mk 39. The two 21-in (533-mm) torpedo tubes were mounted between the funnels, and were angled to fire obliquely forward in the manner of fast attack craft. During 1964 two of the four depth charge throwers were removed, and more modern sonar was fitted.

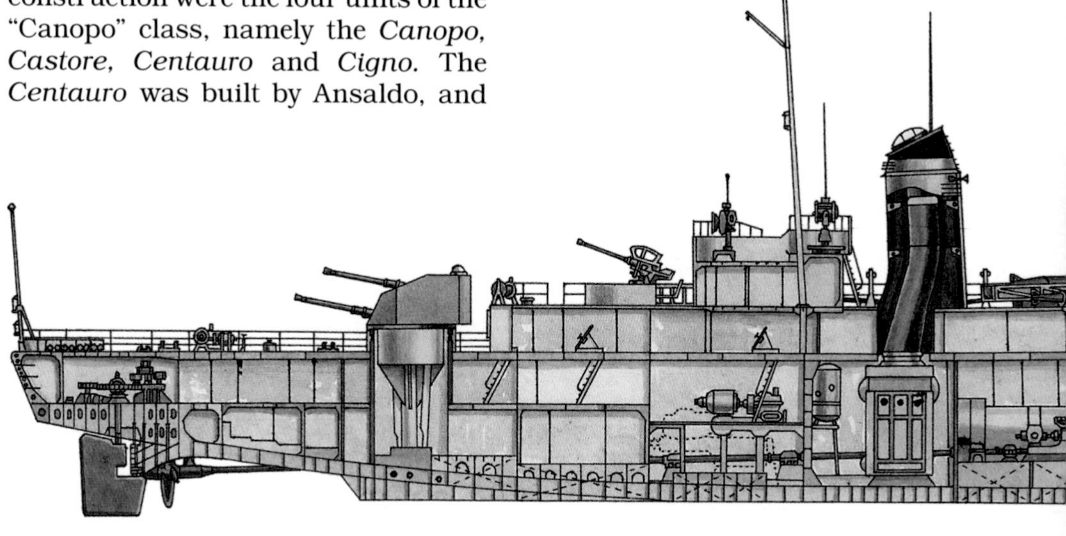

The ships' four 3-in (76-mm) guns were installed in vertically staggered pairs with the elevating gear between the barrels. These mountings did not prove successful, however, and were superseded by single rapid-fire mountings. This new type was very successful, and was the direct ancestor of the ubiquitous OTO Melara (now Otobreda) 76/62 Compact and Super Rapido mountings.

The *Castore* was rebuilt in 1966/67 with three single 3-in (76-mm) mountings, one of them replacing a pair of 40-mm AA guns, and two triple launchers for 12.75-in (324-mm) lightweight anti-submarine torpedoes. The sensor and fire-control suites were also upgraded, principally with new radar and sonar equipment, and at a later stage the ships were fitted with an electronic warfare suite. The other ships were also rebuilt, the last in the early 1970s. All four ships were stricken in the first half of the 1980s.

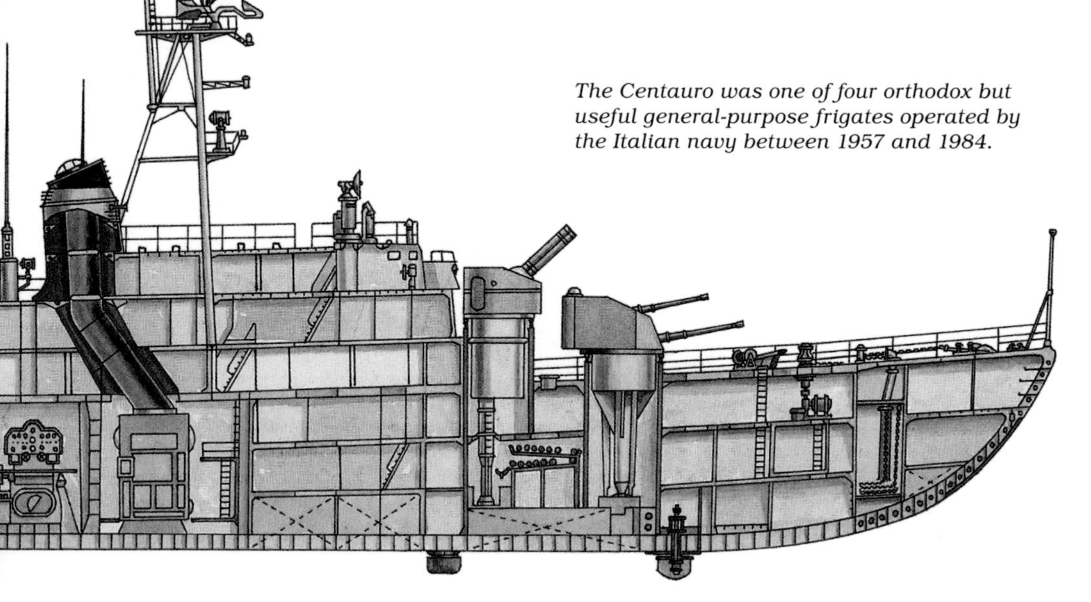

The Centauro was one of four orthodox but useful general-purpose frigates operated by the Italian navy between 1957 and 1984.

Centauro (as completed)

Type:	general-purpose frigate
Tonnage:	2,250 tons full load
Dimensions:	length 338 ft 4 in (103.1 m); beam 39 ft 4 in (12 m); draft 12 ft 6 in (3.8 m)
Propulsion:	two geared steam turbines delivering 22,000 shp (16403 kW) to two propellers for 26 kt
Armour:	none
Armament:	four 3-in (76-mm) DP guns, four 40-mm AA guns, one Menon anti-submarine mortar, and two 21-in (533-mm) torpedo tubes
Complement:	207

Alpino (1968)

Originally planned at four units, of which only the *Alpino* (ex-*Circe*) and *Carabiniere* (ex-*Climene*) were built by CNR at Riva Trigosa for completion in January and April 1968 respectively, this class was schemed as an improved version of the "Canopo" class anti-submarine frigate. In the event a major revision of the design created ships more akin to the "Bergamini" class frigates with CODAG (Combined Diesel and Gas turbine) rather than diesel propulsion. Each of the two shafts was powered by a pair of Tosi diesels and a Tosi-Metrovick G6 gas turbine, the cruising speed on diesels alone being 24 kt.

The hull was clearly derived from that of the "Canopo" class but with a superstructure characterized by one large uptake rather than two smaller and taller funnels. The armament had originally been specified as two 3-in (76-mm) guns, 40-mm AA guns in two beam mountings, one Menon anti-submarine mortar in the "B" position, and one Agusta-Bell AB.204 helicopter. What finally emerged, however, was six 3-in (76-mm) guns as a superfiring pair forward (with the Menon mortar abaft the gun in the "B" position) and two on each beam abreast the funnel and the hangar, which was enlarged to accommodate two helicopters. The rotary-wing aircraft operated from a platform above the quarterdeck, so leaving the extreme stern free for the first variable-depth sonar introduced in an Italian ship. Such a sonar system, with a fixed hull as well as towed elements, was a major enhancement in anti-submarine capability for the type of waters in which the Italian navy generally operated.

The ships were completed with adequate electronic systems, with area made available for the addition of other systems at a later date, Both of the ships were taken in hand for large-scale refits during the 1980s, the *Alpino* being completed in the course of July 1985. The upgrade involved the installation of new sonar with separate hull and variable-depth systems, a more capable combat information system derived from that used in the later "Lupo" and "Maestrale" class guided-missile frigates, and a modem electronic warfare system with large spherical radomes in place of the earlier arrangement's cylindrical radomes.

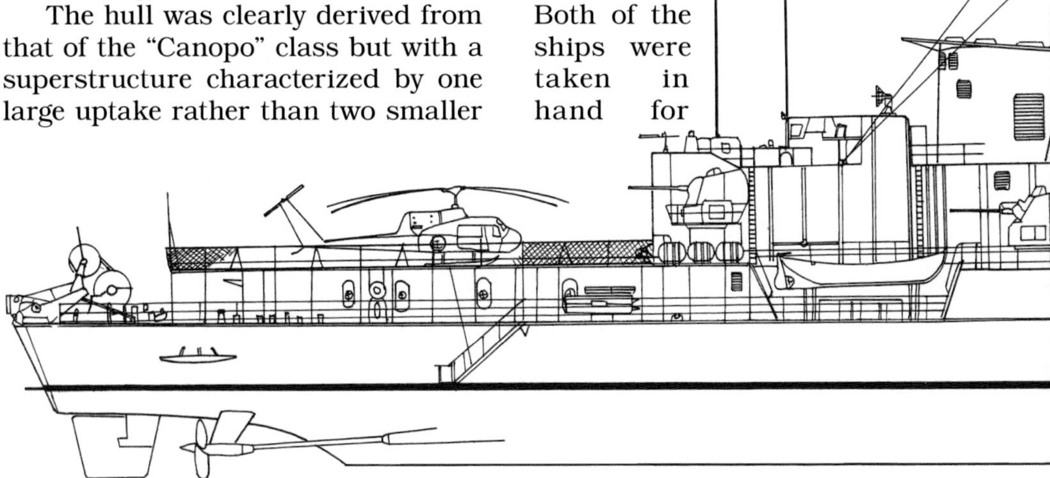

Right:
The Alpino was the end of the Italian navy's commitment to anti-submarine frigates without missile armament.

Below:
Side view of the Alpino, with the Menon mortar abaft "B" gun mounting.

its pair of spherical jammer radomes (for directional jammers) replacing the earlier cylinders alongside the big uptakes

The place of the unbuilt second pair of "Alpino" class frigates was taken by the first two of the succeeding "Lupo" class. The *Carabiniere* became an auxiliary in January 1993. Her new task was that of a weapon trials ship: in this capacity her Menon mortar was replaced by a single Milas anti-submarine missile box launcher. The ship also undertook the trials of a new radar system. Both ships were retired in the late 1990s.

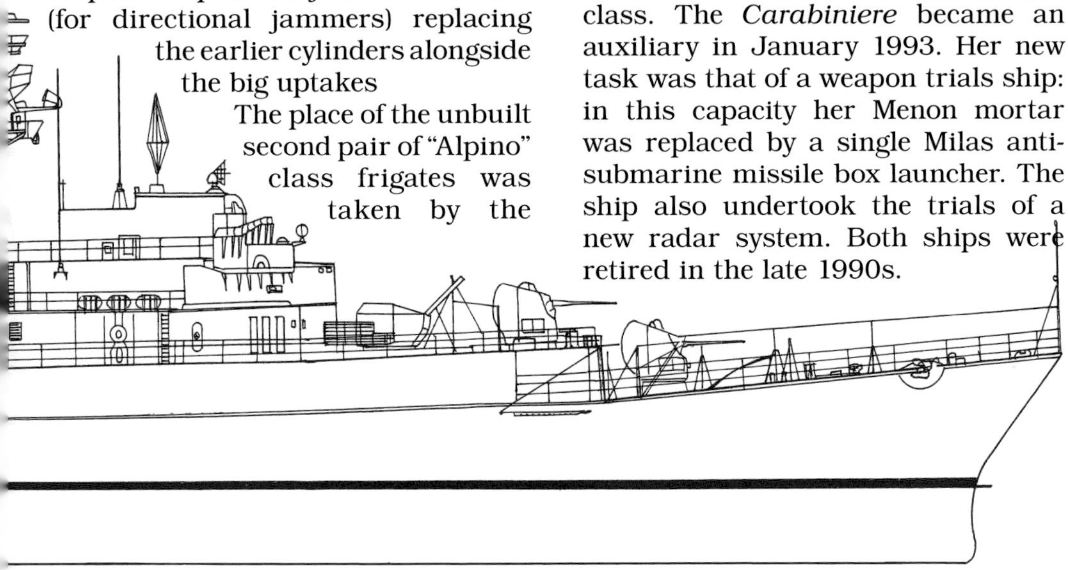

Alpino

Type:	frigate
Tonnage:	2,700 tons full load
Dimensions:	length 371 ft 10 in (113.3 m); beam 43 ft (13.1 m); draft 12 ft 4 in (3.8 m)
Propulsion:	CODAG arrangement with two gas turbines delivering 15,000 shp (11184 kW) and four diesel engines delivering 16,800 bhp (12526 kW) to two propellers for 29 kt
Armour:	none
Armament:	six 3-in (76-mm) DP guns, one Menon anti-submarine mortar, two triple launchers for 12.75-in (324-mm) lightweight anti-submarine torpedoes, and two helicopters
Complement:	263

"La Combattante" class (1972)

In purely commercial terms, the most successful FAC (Fast Attack Craft) developed and built in France has been a series which, perhaps somewhat surprisingly, the French navy did not adopt in either its basic "La Combattante II" or improved and enlarged "La Combattante III" class forms. The "La Combattante II" type uses a common hull created by Lürssen of Vegesack in Germany on the basis of its "Type 141" FAC for the West German navy and, together with its larger version, has proved very popular with a number of navies. The hull is fabricated of steel and carries a light alloy superstructure, and the overall flexibility of the design made it possible for purchasers to choose their own electronics and weapon fits, although the French preferred the section of French equipment and weapons such as Thomson-CSF radars and fire-control systems in association with Aerospatiale MM.38 or MM.40 Exocet anti-ship missiles.

Characterized by a full-load displacement of 275 tons and a length of 154 ft 2 in (47 m), and a propulsion arrangement of four diesel engines driving four propellers for 36 kt, export customers for the "La Combattante II" class included Greece (four with MM.38s), Iran (12 with Harpoon SSMs), Libya (10 with Otomat SSMs), Malaysia (four with MM.38s) and West Germany (20 "Type 148" class units with MM.38s). The Iranian "Kaman" class craft saw extensive service in the Iranian-Iraqi Gulf War of the 1980s, losing two of their number but also scoring a number of successes.

Both "La Combattante" variants have a high degree of habitability, which is obviously an asset for operators in the hotter parts of the world, and the larger "La Combattante III" class craft were designed for longer endurance and the capability for use as command vessels for smaller craft "La Combattante III" class craft were adopted by Greece (four with MM.38s plus six locally built with cheaper machinery, electronics and Penguin Mk II anti-ship missiles), Nigeria (three with MM.38s), Qatar (three with MM.40s) and Tunisia (three with MM.40s).

The builder of both "La Combattante" versions was the Constructions Mécaniques de Normande at Cherbourg. It is also worth noting that the Greek "La

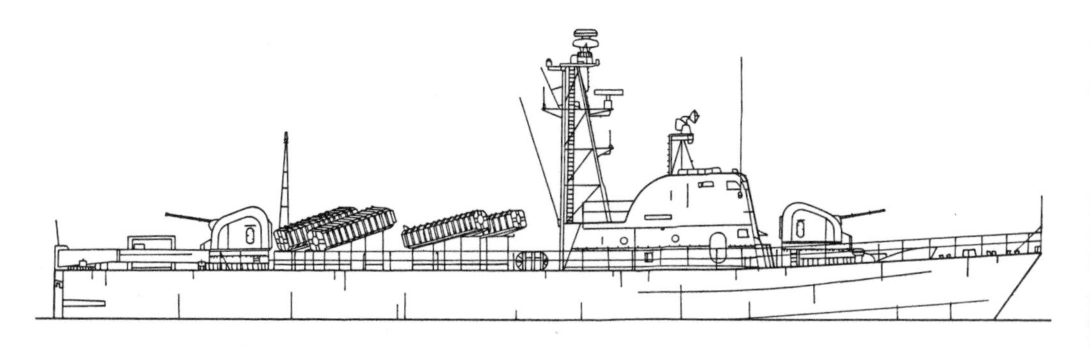

The French-built "La Combattante II" class FAC was very versatile, and was completed in a number of forms with different electronic and armament fits.

The Iranian fast attack craft Kaman, a Combattante II Class vessel built by Construction Mécanique de Normandie. The egg-like fairing on her mast protects a Hollandse Signaalapparaten WM 28 tactical fire and control radar. She is armed with two Harpoon missile launchers and has one 3-in (76-mm) OTO-Melara and one 1.57-in (40-mm) Bofors gun. Iran ordered 12 boats which were due to be delivered by April 1979. The Kaman Class boats differ considerably from the original Combattante I, and like the Greek Calypso Class are Combattante IIs with Thomson CSF Triton radar and Plessey IFF Mk 10. The complement of the original French boat was 25, the Iranian is 30, while the Greek boats have a crew of 40 - though the French boat was slightly smaller and did not have the full armanent of missiles and guns deployed on later versions of the class.

Combattante IIIG" craft of the French-built first type differ from the rest in having a higher-rated propulsion arrangement and four MM.38 rather than six Penguin missiles, this allowing each of the craft to ship two rearward-firing 21-in (533-mm) torpedo tubes. These latter carry the German SST4 wire-guided anti-ship torpedoes with active/passive acoustic homing, a 573-lb (260-kg) warhead and a maximum range of about 12.5 miles (20 km).

"La Combattante IIIG Type I" class

Type:	fast attack craft (missile and torpedo)
Tonnage:	425 tons full load
Dimensions:	length 184 ft 3 in (56.15 m); beam 26 ft 3 in (8 m); draft 8 ft 2 in (2.5 m)
Propulsion:	four diesel engines delivering 18,000 shp (13420 kW) to four propellers for 36.5 kt
Armour:	none
Armament:	two 3-in (76-mm) DP guns, two twin 30-mm AA guns, four MM.39 Exocet anti-ship missiles, and two 21-in (533-mm) torpedo tubes
Complement:	42

HMS *Kent* (1966)

The eight "County" class area defence ships were built for the Royal Navy by six yards in two batches. The first four (HMS *Devonshire*, *Hampshire*, *London* and *Kent*) were the "County Batch 1" class vessels completed in 1962/63 with the Seaslug Mk 1 system, and the second four (HMS *Fife*, *Glamorgan*, *Antrim* and *Norfolk*) were the "County Batch 2" class vessels completed in 1966/70 with the Seaslug Mk 2 system and updated electronics requiring revised mast heads. The major identifying feature was the prominent AKE-2 "double bedstead" antenna of the Type 965 air-search radar, and a taller fore mast carrying the Type 992Q low-angle search radar.

The whole of the Seaslug beam-riding missile system was on a large scale (the missile, handling arrangements and electronics), and shoe-horning a single system into a ship of the size even of the "County" class was a major challenge. The missile itself was enormous and was stowed vertically in a large magazine that took up much volume. The missile was then moved horizontally along

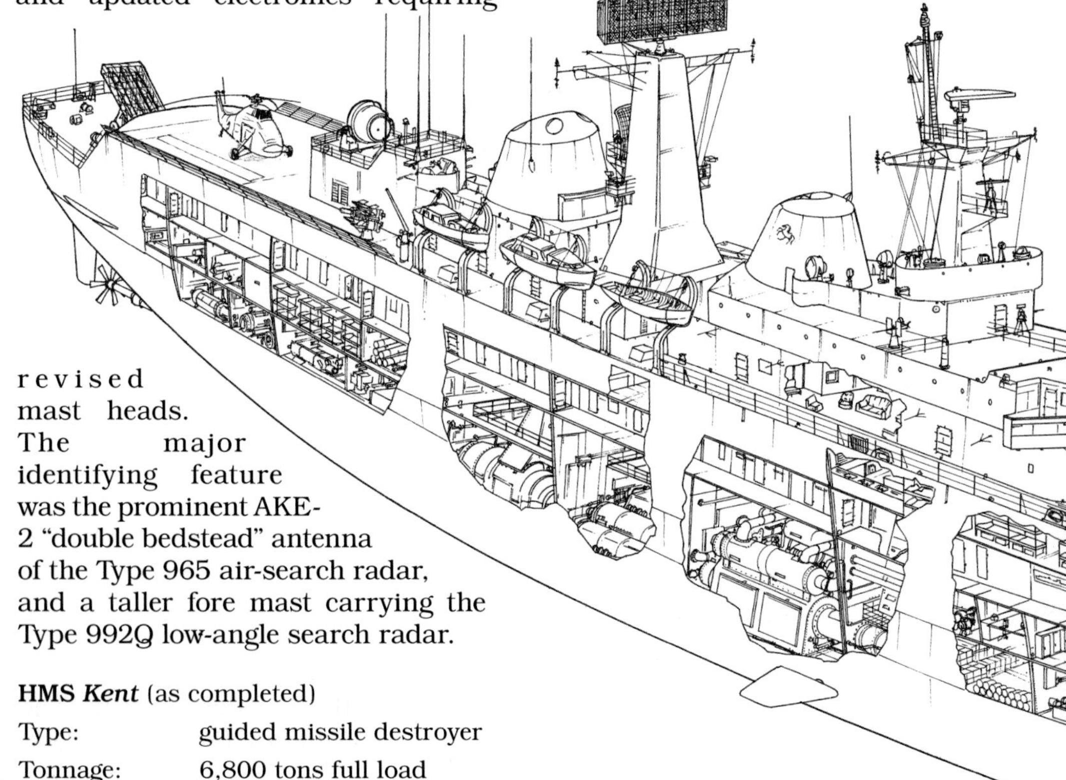

HMS *Kent* (as completed)

Type:	guided missile destroyer
Tonnage:	6,800 tons full load
Dimensions:	521 ft 6 in (158.9 m); beam 54 ft (16.4 m); draft 20 ft 6 in (6.2 m)
Propulsion:	COSAG arrangement with two geared steam turbines delivering 30,000 shp (22368 kW) and four gas turbines delivering 30,000 shp (22368 kW) to two propellers for 32.5 kt
Armour:	none
Armament:	four 4.5-in (114-mm) DP guns, one twin launcher for Seaslug long-range SAMs, two quadruple launchers for Seacat short-range SAMs, two 20-mm AA cannon, and one helicopter
Complement:	471

In 1966 the technical artist John Batchelor spent five days as a guest on HMS Kent, gaining an intimate knowledge of the ship's arrangements.

a large tunnel to a handling room in which the wings and solid-fuel wraparound launch boosters were attached before the weapon passed out of an airlock onto the large twin launcher. The electronics required were the large Type 901 fire-control and Type 965 air-search radars, whose large antennae required a great deal of weight carried high on the ship.

In the 1970s the second batch's four ships had their after superfiring 4.5-in (114-mm) twin turret replaced by four canister launchers for the MM.38 Exocet anti-ship missile. The armament was completed by a hangar and flight deck for one Westland Wessex (later Westland Lynx) anti-submarine helicopter.

This cutaway illustration of HMS Kent reveals the very large volume devoted to the early-generation Seaslug missile, its handling arrangements and all the associated systems.

The *Antrim* and *Glamorgan* saw service in the 1982 Falklands war, the latter suffering serious damage as a result of an Exocet hit. The ships were replaced from the mid-1970s by the "Type 42" class destroyers with the more modern Sea Dart SAM system, and the last "County" to be decommissioned from British service, in 1987 after service as a training ship, was the Fife.

In 1982 the *London* was sold to Pakistan as the *Babur*, which was decommissioned in 1993. The four "County Batch 2" ships were sold to Chile, the *Blanco Encalada* (ex-*Fife*) and *Almirante Cochrane* (ex-*Antrim*) being updated with a enlarged flight deck and hangar (for two helicopters) in place of the Seaslug system. The *Capitán Prat* (ex-*Norfolk*) was refitted in 2001 for the carriage of one large helicopter, and in 1996 all four had been fitted with the Israeli Barak SAM system in place of the Seacat. The *Almirante Latorre* and *Blanco Encalada* were decommissioned in 1998 and 2003, and the other two are being phased out as ex-Dutch frigates reach Chile.

HMS *Fearless* (1966)

The two British assault ships, or more formally LPDs (Landing Platforms, Dock) HMS *Fearless* and HMS *Intrepid,* were designed and constructed as the Royal Navy's first modern purpose-built amphibious warfare vessels, and were created specifically to provide the capability

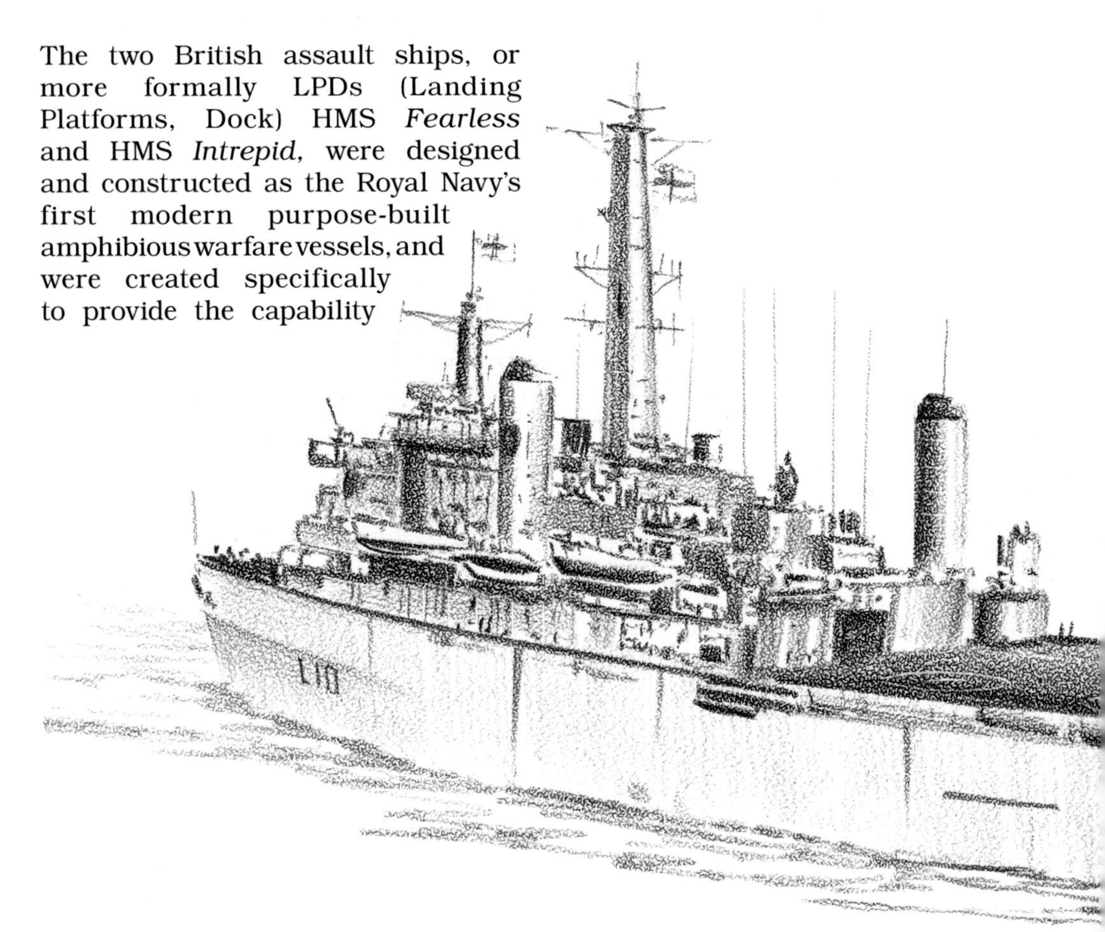

for transporting and landing troops from the sea be means of helicopters and/or LCUs (Landing Craft, Utility). The ships were built by Harland & Wolff and John Brown for completion in November 1965 and March 1967 respectively, and their continued existence was threatened in 1981 by a misconceived defense review which ordained their disposals in 1984 and 1982 respectively. In February 1982 the Ministry of Defence sensibly decided that both ships would continue in service, their value soon being proved during the Falkland Islands war, since without them there could not have been a British assault landing to recapture the islands.

The role allocated to the two "Fearless" class ships was amphibious assault lift for between 400 and 700 troops supported by an onboard naval assault group/brigade headquarters using the facilities of a fully equipped assault operations room to allow the force commanders to plan, launch and control every aspect of the air, sea and land forces involved in the relevant operation.

The ships each carried an amphibious detachment comprising an assault squadron subdivided into a landing craft squadron with four LCUs (ex-LCM9s) and four LCVPs, an amphibious beach unit (ABU) with its own Land Rover and a Centurion

BARV (Beach Armoured Recovery Vehicle) to aid stranded vehicles and landing craft, and a vehicle deck party (VDP) to control vehicles during their embarkation on the landing craft Each LCU could carry as its payload one Chieftain or two Centurion tanks, or four 4-ton trucks, or eight Land Rovers and their trailers, or 100 tons of cargo, or 250 troops. Each LCVP could carry either 35 troops or two Land Rovers.

Over the well deck in each ship's after section, opened to the sea by the lowering of a ramp after the ship's after end had been flooded down, was a flight deck 165 ft (50.3 m) long by 75 ft (22.85 m) wide, and capable of allowing operations by most NATO helicopter types and also, when opportune, BAe Sea Harrier VTOL multi-role fighters aircraft Three vehicle decks were built into each ship, in the form of one for tracked vehicles (tanks, self-propelled guns and other AFVs), one for wheeled trucks, and one half-deck for Land Rover vehicles and trailers.

The overload troop capacity of 700 men was sufficient for a light infantry battalion or Royal Marine Commando with an attached artillery battery. Additional area for the parking of light vehicles could be provided by use of the flight deck.

The *Intrepid* was put into reserve in 1991 and then used as a source of spares for the *Fearless* before being finally withdrawn from service in August 1999. The *Fearless* was kept in service to the end of 2002.

HMS Fearless with her docking well open and a helicopter above the flight deck.

HMS *Fearless*

Type:	assault ship
Tonnage:	12,120 tons deep load
Dimensions:	length 520 ft (158.5 m); beam 80 ft (24.4 m); draft 20 ft 6 in (6.3 m)
Propulsion:	two geared steam turbines delivering 22,000 shp (16403 kW) to two propellers for 21 kt
Armour:	none
Armament:	two 40-mm AA guns, four quadruple launchers for Seacat short-range surface-to-air missiles, and up to five medium and three light helicopters
Complement:	580

"Brown Water Navy" (1965/72)

The US naval aspect of the Vietnam War started in August 1964, but it was another year before riverine operations by the "brown water navy" began in any significant way with the object of halting the delivery of food, ammunition, other supplies and reinforcements to the Viet Cong. In much of Vietnam the rivers and their estuaries were the only highways. In August 1965 Operation "Market Time" for coastal surveillance was entrusted to Task Force 115, but is soon became clear that the operation would have to be expanded to include the country's rivers, for the Viet Cong were operating there with impunity. In December 1965 a new River Patrol Force, codenamed "Game Warden" was set up as Task Force 116. In October 1967 the "Game Warden" patrols were reinforced by the "Seawolves" of Helicopter Support Squadron One flying Bell UH-1 "Huey" ground-support helicopters They made a deadly combination with the 40 river patrol craft in the Rung Sat and 80 operating in the Mekong delta. In February 1969 virtually the entire riverine force (242 "Game Warden" and "Market Time" craft) was handed over to the South Vietnamese navy as a start in the over-ambitious and hasty attempt to "Vietnamize" the war effort. The Mobile Riverine Force was formally disbanded in August 1969, and in its place was left SEALORDS, the South East Asian Lake/Ocean River Delta Strategy, which was an impressive name for a steadily diminishing capability. This was not the end of riverine warfare, however, for in April 1970 the South Vietnamese military command started an attack on the Viet Cong sanctuaries in Cambodia. As part of this offensive it

Riverine craft such as this monitor were often protected by rodded screens to provide protection against the hollow-charge warheads of rocket-propelled grenades.

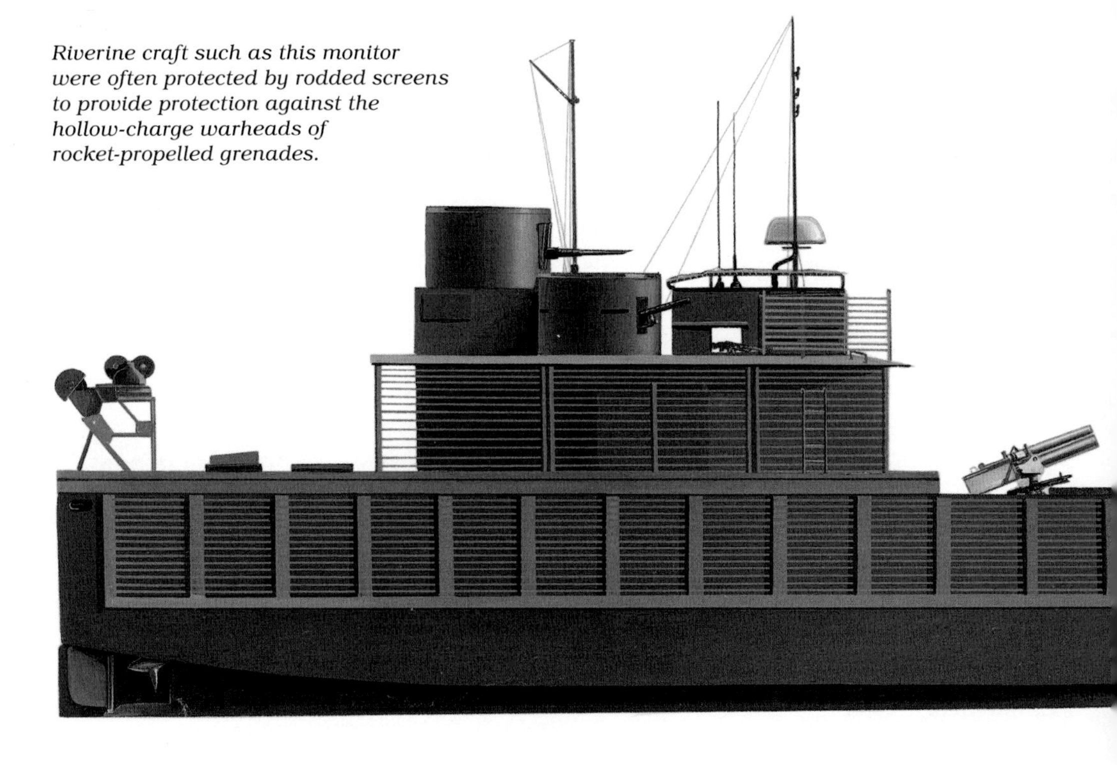

A 0.5-in (12.7-mm) machine gun and mortar combination mount on a "Swift" type patrol boat used mainly for coastal interdiction.

was essential to keep open the Mekong river, which flows from Phnom Penh in Cambodia down into Vietnam. In May Cambodian forces failed in their attempt to open the Mekong, but a flotilla of South Vietnamese vessels fought its way through. When the ground offensive ended, retention of the river route became even more crucial as a means of evacuating large numbers of people.

The "Game Warden" craft patrolled the Rung Sat, a swamp lying between Saigon and the sea, as well as the Mekong delta. Special river patrol boats of fiberglass construction were built, and a number of elderly ex-French landing craft were also pressed into service. Modern craft were adapted as riverine monitors, and work began on steel-hulled assault boats carrying an impressive armament, including 81-mm mortars, 20-mm cannon and flamethrowers.

Typically, a riverine operation involved floating barracks and supply barges known as the Mobile Afloat Force (MAF) and protected, at anchor, by assault support patrol boats (ASPBs) and monitors to become the Mobile Riverine Base (MRB). The MAF generally operated up to 30 miles (48 km) from a main base The task of the ASPBs was to interdict attempts by the Viet Cong to withdraw by water, and covering fire could be called down from the Fire Support Base, and from fixed- and rotary-wing aircraft. Armoured troop carriers (ATCs) were used to land assault troops, in conjunction with US Army troops on the landward side to prevent the communists from withdrawing successfully.

The joint task forces created by the US Navy and US Army to fight the riverine war were based on river assault squadrons with purpose-designed assault craft based mainly on "LCM6" landing craft. The squadrons comprised 52 ATCs, five Command and Control Boats (CCBs), 10 fire-support Monitors (MONs) and two

"Brown Water Navy" (1965/72) *continued*

Riverine patrol craft were optimized for speed and agility, and had a shallow draft.

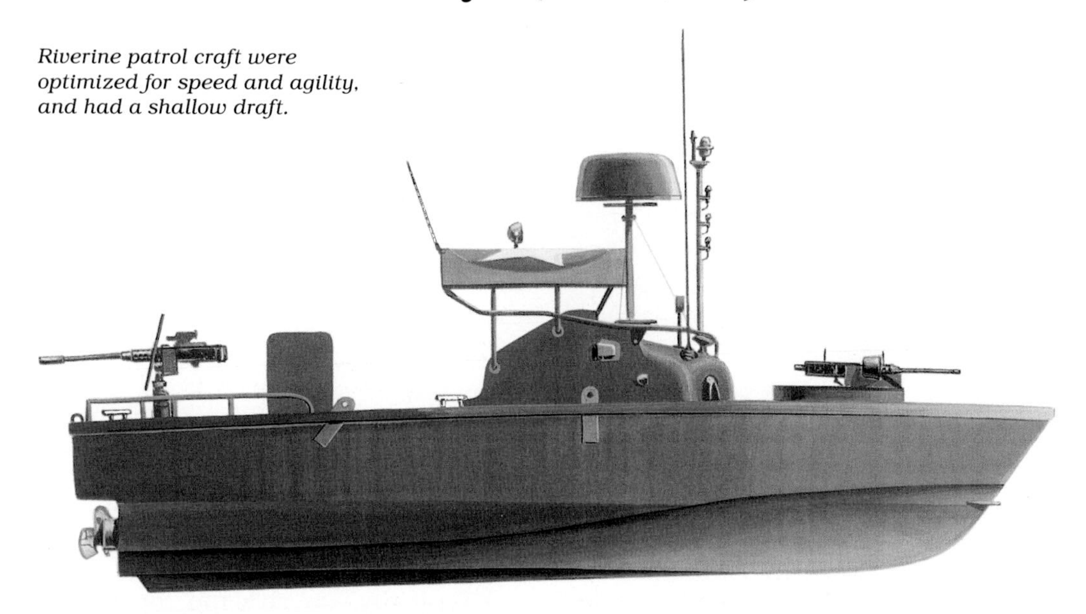

ATC refuelling craft They also had 32 ASPBs, which were of the only craft created specifically for riverine war. The ASPB was built in two versions during in 1967/68 with a welded steel hull, aluminium alloy superstructure and engine silencing system fitted with underwater exhaust outlets. The craft were normally used to lead assault forces, sweeping ahead with a chain drag to counter command-detonated river mines, were also operated as escort, patrol and counter-ambush vessels, and were also used in riverine minesweeper and command craft. The standard armament was one 20-mm gun in a forward turret, a 0.5-in (12.7-mm) twin machine gun in an aft turret above the conning position, two 0.3-in (7.62-mm) machine guns in two turrets just forward of the 0.5-in (12.7-mm) turret, and two 40-mm grenade-launchers; some craft also had an 81-mm (3.2-in) mortar and 0.5-in (12.7-mm) machine gun in an open well aft.

The monitors were either adapted "LCM6s" or specially constructed MON Mk V craft that differed primarily in having rounded bows instead of the landing craft's bow door arrangement. The armament varied widely, but a typical fit comprised one 40-mm gun in an armoured turret forward, one 20-mm gun in a small turret aft above the conning position, two 0.5-in (12.7-mm) machine guns in similar port and starboard turrets just forward of this, an 81-mm (3.2-in) mortar or two flamethrowers in a well located between the control position and the forward turret, and provision for small arms fire on each beam. The MON had screen and bar protection against hollow-charge rocket projectile and recoilless rifle fire.

The CCB was an adaptation of the MON with the mortar well replaced by a modular command and communications facility. The armament was the bow turret with either one 20-mm or 40-mm gun, the aft turret with one 0.5-in (12.7-mm) and the two other turrets each armed with one 0.3-in (7.6-2mm) machine gun; one 60-mm (2.36-in) mortar was

A type used by the South Vietnamese navy was the landing support ship, of which seven ex-French but US built examples were operated. The type had a high bridge which was vulnerable but also offered a good vantage point.

carried by some craft.Analternative armament fit was three 20-mm guns in single turrets, two 0.3-in (7.62mm) machine guns and two 40-mm grenade-launchers. And like the MON, the CCB had the ability to tow disabled craft by means of towing rig on its stern.

Able to carry a platoon of 40 fully equipped infantrymen, the ATC was a converted "LCM6" with bar armour on the hull and superstructure and bullet-proof awnings over the troop and cargo deck. A few of the craft were also fitted with a helicopter pad in place of the awnings to act as battalion medical aid stations for casualty evacuation, and some of the craft had a 1,200-US gal (4540-litre) tank on the cargo deck for transfer of diesel fuel to other craft. Another important type produced in limited numbers as an "LCM6" conversion was the Combat Salvage Boat (CSB).

The numbers of the types built or converted for the riverine warfare role are not known in details, but it is known that at least nine CCBs, 84 ASPBs, 42 MON Mk Vs, 22 MON conversions, 100 ATCs and four CSBs were transferred to South Vietnam in the 1960s and early 1970s Numbers were also lost in combat, and the

MON Mk V

Type:	riverine monitor
Tonnage:	75.5 tons full load
Dimensions:	length 60 ft (18.3 m); beam 17 ft 5 in (5.3 m); draft 3 ft 3 in (1 m)
Propulsion:	two diesel engines delivering 330 hp (246 kW) to two propellers for 8.5 kt
Armour:	screen and bar armour
Armament:	either one 40-mm gun, one 20-mm gun, two 0.5-in (12.7-mm) machine guns, one 81-mm (3.2-in) mortar and two flamethrowers, or alternatively two 20-mm guns, one 81-mm (3.2-in) mortar, two 0.5-in (12.7-mm) machine guns and four 0.3-in (7.62-mm) machine guns; in some craft the 20-mm guns and 81-mm (3.2-in) mortar were replaced by a 105-mm (4.1-in) howitzer
Complement:	11

Obraztsovy (1965)

The world's first class of major warships with all-gas turbine propulsion, in the form of a COGOG (Combined Gas turbine Or Gas turbine) arrangement based on four gas turbines, the 20-strong "Project 61" class (known to NATO as the "Kashin" class) was constructed from 1963 onward at the Zhdanov Shipyard in Leningrad (five units completed in 1964/66), and at the 61 Kommuna (North) Shipyard at Nikolayev near the Black Sea (16 units completed in 1963/72). The ships were designed and built for the area-defence role with an armament optimised for the anti-aircraft role with only secondary anti-ship and anti-submarine roles, the former with four 3-in (76-mm) DP guns in two twin mountings and the latter with two RBU-6000 and two RBU-1000 rocket launchers.

The last unit to be completed was the *Sderzhanny*, and this introduced the revised "Project 61M" (NATO "Kashin (Mod)") class standard with a slightly increased full-load displacement, the hull lengthened by 9 ft 10 in ((3 m), modernized electronics including a variable-depth sonar, the replacement of the 3-in (76-mm) guns by container-launchers for four SS-N-2C "Styx" anti-ship missiles, and the addition of four 30-mm ADG-630 close-in weapon system mountings for improved self-defence against air attack. The five Zhdanov-built ships (*Ognevoy, Obraztsovy, Odarenny, Slavny* and *Steregushchiy*) were then converted to the revised standard in the period 1973/80.

In 1974 the *Otvazhny* of the standard type foundered in the Black Sea following a catastrophic explosion and fire that lasted for five hours, more than 200 of her crew being killed. In 1981 the *Provorny* re-entered service with the Black Sea Fleet after being converted as the trials ship for the SA-N-7 SAM system. The other units of the "Project 61" class, which was termed a *"bolshoy protivolodochny korabl"* (large ASW ship) by the Soviets, were the *Komsomolets Ukrainy, Soobrazitelny, Otvazhny, Stroyny, Krasny Kavkaz, Reshitelny, Smyshlenny, Stroigiy, Smetlivy, Smely, Krasny Krim, Sposobny* and *Skory*.

The powerplant was so light, by comparison with the steam plant typical of the era, that there were concerns that the ships would be made top heavy by their mass of

The stern of the "Kashin" class guided-missile destroyer Obraztsovy of the Soviet navy.

The "Kashin" class destroyers were fine seagoing destroyers optimized for the anti-aircraft and anti-submarine escort roles.

Above: Lattice masts were located forward and aft of the two outward-canted forward funnels.

Below: A pair of twin-arm launchers for SA-N-1 surface-to-air missiles was fitted, seen here being the after unit.

Above and right:
A multitude of electronic antennae characterized the upper works and masts of the "Kashin" class destroyer.

antennae at the heads of the two lattice masts. As a result a new hull design was adopted, this having a knuckle from amidships to the transom stern and with a very sharp bow line. These were also the first Soviets ships specifically designed to withstand the effects of a nuclear explosion, with a primary ship control station located far from the bridge in the bowels of the hull, and with fore-and-aft access by means of an enclosed passageway. The ships were decommissioned and scrapped from the late 1980s.

One "Project 61M" class ship, the *Smely*, was transferred to the Polish navy in 1987 as the *Warszawa*, and decommissioned in 2003. Five other ships, called "Kashin II" class by NATO, were also built for India, whose

The Obraztsovy was the second of the five "Kashin" class destroyers built at the Zhdanov yard.

navy placed these units in service from the late 1970s as the *Rajput, Rana, Ranjit, Ranvir* and *Rangivay.* These are considerably modified in comparison with the Soviet ships, having only one 3-in (76-mm) gun mounting, four SS-N-2B "Styx" SSM launchers in pairs on each side of the bridge, and a platform and hangar aft for one ASW helicopter m place of the after 3-in (76-mm) gun mounting.

The "Kashin" class destroyer had a notably impressive external appearance.

All photographs taken by John Batchelor during a visit to Portsmouth.

Obraztsovy

Type:	guided missile area-defence destroyer
Tonnage:	4,650 tons full load
Dimensions:	length 482 ft 3 in (147 m); beam 51 ft 10 in (15.8 m); draft 15 ft 9 in (4.8 m)
Propulsion:	COGAG arrangement with four gas turbines delivering 96,000 shp (71578 kW) to two propellers for 35 kt
Armour:	none
Armament:	four launchers for SS-N-2C "Styx" anti-ship missiles, two twin launchers for 32 SA-N-1 "Goa" surface-to-air missiles, four 30-mm ADG-630 close-in weapon system mountings, five 21-in (533-mm) torpedo tubes, and two RBU-6000 anti-submarine rocket launchers
Complement:	300

"Sparviero" class (1974)

Together with the US Navy, Italy was unique among NATO navies in having FAHs (missile-armed hydrofoils) as part of its operational surface fleet. In the early 1960s, both the USA and Italy became interested in the possibilities of the hydrofoil for high-speed combat craft, and in 1964 the Italian government, in the form of its IRI research and development organization, joined an Italian builder of commercial hydrofoils (the Carlo Rodriguez company of Messina in Sicily) and the American company Boeing to establish Alinavi. Through the rest of the 1960s, this organization examined the potential of the Boeing-designed "Tucumcari" design and finalized the detailed plans for the all-aluminium Sparviero as a prototype which was built between 1971 and 1974. This was based on the Boeing jetfoil system with three retractable foils in the form of one unit forward and two aft.

The potential of the *Sparviero* was fully confirmed by the craft's successful trials, and the Italian navy therefore ordered anther six production-standard craft as the *Nibbio, Falcone, Astore, Grifone, Gheppio* and *Condore.* which were launched between February 29, 1980 and January 25, 1983.

The craft were powered in the foilborne mode by a waterjet driven by a single Rolls-Royce Proteus gas turbine delivering 4,500 shp (3357 kW), and in hullborne mode by a single propeller driven by one General Motors diesel engine delivering 180 shp (134 kW). The hull was fabricated entirely of aluminium alloy, and revealed adequate durability as well as the light weight that was also important in providing the craft with a high level of agility. The two most adverse factors discovered during early evaluation of the craft were their short range and limited armament, but these were deemed acceptable by the Italian navy as they craft were intended, and were indeed ideal, for use only in Italy's extensive coastal

The "Sparviero" class FAH packed a considerable punch into a single small, agile and speedy package.

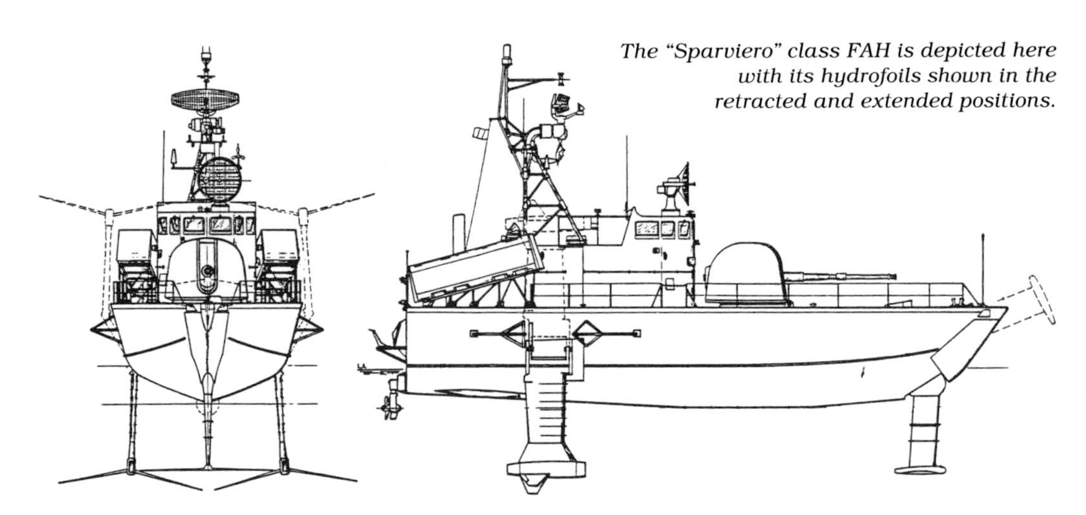

The "Sparviero" class FAH is depicted here with its hydrofoils shown in the retracted and extended positions.

waters with ready access to refuelling and rearming facilities.

All seven of the craft carried a 3-in (76-mm) Otobreda (originally OTO Melara) Compact dual-purpose gun in a fully automated mounting on the foredeck ahead of the bridge, providing a high rate of fire and considerable accuracy in short-range surface-to-air and surface-to-surface engagements, but while the *Sparviero* had a single-cell launcher for one Otomat Mk 1 anti-ship missile, the later units had the more capable Teseo system with two launchers (angled out from the centerline over the stern) for improved and longer-ranged Otomat Mk 2 missiles, whose maximum range capability was best exploited by the availability of a helicopter for mid-course guidance update.

The six later craft also had a more modern surface search radar than the *Sparviero*, and this radar was fitted with an IFF interrogator unit. The design of the "Sparviero" class paved the way for the US Navy's "Pegasus" class hydrofoil, but interest in the concept then waned and only modest number of FAHs were actually built and placed in service. The *Sparviero* was stricken in September 1991, and the other six craft followed by the early part of the 21st century.

"Sparviero" class

Type:	fast attack hydrofoil (missile and gun)
Tonnage:	62.5 tons full load
Dimensions:	length 80 ft 89 in (24.6 m) with the foils retracted and 75 ft 6 in (23 m) with the foils extended; beam 39 ft 4 in (12 m) with the foils retracted and 35 ft 5 in (10.8 m) with the foils extended; draft 14 ft 1 in (4.3 m) hullborne with the foils extended and 5 ft 11 in (1.8 m) foilborne
Propulsion:	one diesel engine delivering 161 shp (120 kW) to one retractable propeller for hullborne operation at 8 kt and one gas turbine delivering 5,000 shp (3728 kW) to one waterjet for foilborne operation at 50 kt
Armour:	none
Armament:	one 3-in (76-mm) DP gun and two launchers for Otomat Mk 2 anti-ship missiles
Complement:	10

“Osa” class (1961)

Even as the first “Komar” class craft were entering service, the Soviets were creating a successor as the “Osa” class, designed for excellent seakeeping qualities and full capability in coastal operations. Based on a larger displacement-type hull, the type was built of steel with a steel/aluminium superstructure. The gun armament was comprises four 30-mm cannon in two remotely controlled mountings, and while intended primarily for AA use also possess a capability against light surface vessels. The sensors include surface-search and fire-control radars, other mast-mounted antennae are associated with the IFF (identification friend or foe) system. The design was fully optimized for the carriage and launch of the SS-N-2 “Styx” anti-ship missile, of which two are carried in launchers on each side of the deck abaft the bridge. The launchers provide the missiles with full protection against atmospheric and water conditions.

The first “Osa” class craft were laid down in 1959/60, and the type entered service in 1961. Production continued up to 1966, and amounted to some 175 craft excluding more than 100 built in China as the “Huangfeng” class. The Soviet craft served with all four of the Soviet navy's main surface forces, but many of them were later transferred to the navies of satellite, allied and client states as more modern craft entered Soviet service.

The first of these more modern types was the “Osa II” class, which entered service in 1966 and resulted in the NATO redesignation of the initial type as the “Osa I” class. The “Osa II” class is notably different from the “Osa I” class in its revised missile arrangement. This comprises four cylindrical rather than box-like launchers. The arrangement is much lighter than that it replaces, and is associated with an improved variant of the “Styx” missile. Succeeding what

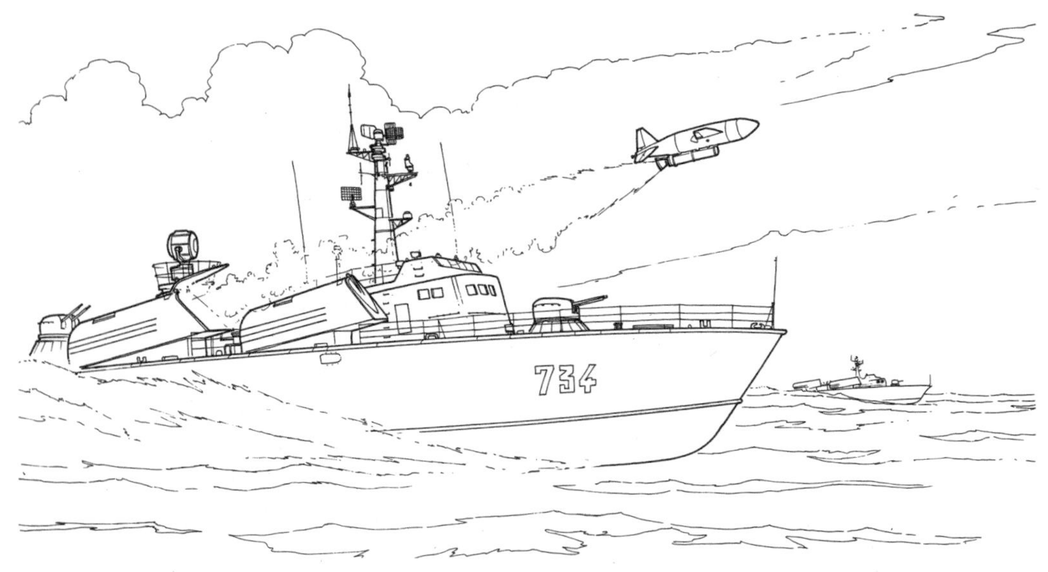

Both types of “Osa” class FAC offered seakeeping characteristics superior to those of the preceding “Komar” class.

The two types of "Osa" class FAC can be differentiated by their missile containers, the "Osa I" having box-like containers and the "Osa II" cylindrical containers.

now became the SS-N-2A, this was dubbed SS-N-2B by the Americans and was a more compact weapon with folding wings and probably infra-red terminal homing as an alternative to the original active radar homing.

"Osa II" production continued up to 1970 and amounted to perhaps 115 craft. Both "Osa" classes have a three-shaft propulsion arrangement, but whereas the "Osa I" class has three 4,025-shp (3000-kW) M503A diesels for a speed of 38 kt at a full-load displacement of 210 tons, the "Osa II" class has a considerably more potent arrangement for higher performance at a greater displacement. In service, many of the "Osa II" class craft have been upgraded with superior weapons, most notably the SS-N-2C version of the "Styx" and the SA-N-5 naval version of the SA-7 "Grail" man-portable surface-to-air missile. Introduced in the early 1970s and sometimes known as the SS-N-2 (Mod), the SS-N-2C is a longer-range derivative of the SS-N-2B with the choice of active radar or IR terminal guidance and updated electronics, the latter permitting a sea-skimming approach to the target.

"Osa I" class craft were used in combat by the navies of several countries including India in 1971 when the Pakistani destroyer *Khaibar* was sunk, Egypt in 1973 against Israel, Syria in 1973 against Israel, and Iraq between 1980 and 1990 against Iran. The only navy which has used craft of the "Osa II" class in combat is that of Iraq in the same 10-year Persian Gulf war with Iran. Most of the craft have now been retired.

"Osa II" class

Type:	fast attack craft (missile)
Tonnage:	245 tons full load
Dimensions:	length 128 ft (39 m); beam 25 ft 3 in (7.7 m); draft 6 ft 3 in (1.9 m)
Propulsion:	three diesel engines delivering 15,090 shp (11250 kW) to three propellers for 40 kt
Armour:	none
Armament:	four SS-N-2B "Styx" anti-ship missiles, one quadruple launcher for SA-N-5 short-range surface-to-air missiles, and two twin 30-mm cannon
Complement:	30

USS *Buchanan* (1962)

The "Charles F. Adams" class destroyer, carrying the Tartar medium-range SAM as its primary weapon system, was initially schemed as a modified "Forrest Sherman" class gun-armed destroyer with the twin 3-in (76-mm) gun mounting nearer the missile launcher replaced by an area for underway replenishment of missiles and the other by a twin anti-submarine weapon launcher, and there was to have been a quintuple torpedo tube mounting between the funnels. The proposed RAT anti-submarine system was then terminated for ASROC, whose octuple launcher replaced the torpedo tubes. The design also received the standard triple launchers for lightweight anti-submarine torpedoes. It soon became clear that the hull would have to be lengthened for the new ASROC-associated sonar and an enlarged combat information center.

Several modifications were incorporated during the construction of the 23 ships, which were completed between September 1960 and September 1964 by several yards in a program which was terminated at an earlier stage than had been anticipated as a result of the reliance placed on the advanced Typhon missile whose further development was then cancelled. The first 13 ships, ending with the USS Buchanan, were completed to the initial standard described below, while the last 10 were had single- rather than twin-arm Tartar launchers (with 40 missiles) for greater reliability, and the last five also had bow-mounted sonar. Australia and West Germany both purchased very similar vessels: the former's three "Perth" class units had a single Ikara launcher in place of the ASROC launcher, while the latter's three "Lütjens" class units had a "mack" (combined mast/stack) arrangement.

The ships were completed without computer-based combat direction systems, but by 1971 the availability of a new and more compact central computer made feasible a low-volume NTDS (Naval Tactical Data System), which was to have been retrofitted to all the ships but was, for financial reasons, installed in only four units as the JPTDS (Junior Participating Tactical Data System). Attempts for other modernizations of the ships were complicated by the shortage of spare volume and thus the complexity (and therefore the cost) of trying to shoe-horn

more equipment into the hulls. Modernization therefore proceeded on a somewhat piecemeal basis and seldom extended right through the class. Major upgrade elements included the Mk 86 gun and missile fire-control system adding a third missile-control channel forward, the SLQ-32 and SLQ-20 countermeasures system in place of the earlier ULQ-6B, new radars (SPS-40C/D air search unit in place of the less reliable SPS-40B, SPS-52C 3D unit in place of SPS-39, and LN-66 navigation unit) and, most importantly, a three-computer NTDS and with the SYS-1 integrated combat system; countermeasures capability was also enhanced by the installation of launchers for SRBOC (Super-Rapid Blooming Offboard Chaff). These electronic systems demanded greater generating and air-conditioning capabilities. Other changes included upgrade of the AQS-23 sonar to SQQ-23 two-dome standard, and the Tartar missile launchers modified to fire the Harpoon anti-ship missile, of which four or six were normally carried.

The US Navy took its last "Adams" class destroyer, the USS *Goldsborough*, on April 29, 1993. Four of the class were transferred to the Greek navy, which retired the vessels in the first part of the 21st century. Australia and Germany decommissioned their last ships in 2003.

The USS Buchanan was completed as the last of the first standard to which the "Charles F. Adams" class destroyers were completed, with a twin-arm SAM launcher.

USS *Buchanan*

Type:	guided-missile fleet escort destroyer
Tonnage:	4,526 tons full load
Dimensions:	length 437 ft (133.2 m); beam 47 ft (14.3 m); draft 15 ft (4.6 m)
Propulsion:	two geared steam turbines delivering 70,000 shp (52192 kW) to two propellers for 33 kt
Armour:	none
Armament:	two 5-in (127-mm) guns, one twin-arm launcher for 42 Tartar medium range surface-to-air missiles, one octuple ASROC launcher for eight anti-submarine torpedoes, and two triple launchers for 12.75-in (324-mm) lightweight anti-submarine torpedoes
Complement:	333/350

SR.N6 "Winchester" class (1966)

The hovercraft or air cushion vehicle was created in the UK during the 1950s. Essentially a flat platform carrying the crew, payload, power unit and propulsion system on top, the hovercraft is supported just above the surface being crossed by a cushion of air directed downward by a lift fan and trapped under the vehicle by semi-flexible surrounding "curtains". Able to operate over land, water and virtually all combinations of these two such as swamp, the hovercraft is an extremely versatile transport, but limited by its inability to undertake quick maneuvers and its restriction to operations over essentially flat surfaces. Military fields in which the hovercraft has excelled are therefore those such as amphibious assault from the sea onto a flat shore, and patrol of riverine and swamp areas such as the marshes of southern Iraq and the delta of the Mekong and other rivers in South-East Asia.

One of the most successful hovercraft in military and para-military service has been the SR.N6 or "Winchester" class air-cushion vehicle, which was created by the British Hovercraft Corporation as a fast car ferry for sheltered waters. The type then evolved into a number of variants. Though evaluated by the Royal Navy and the British army in many parts of the world (including the Falkland Islands) for an assessment of its capabilities under any and all operating conditions, all the SR.N6 craft were sold during 1982 after the disbandment of the Hovercraft Trials Unit.

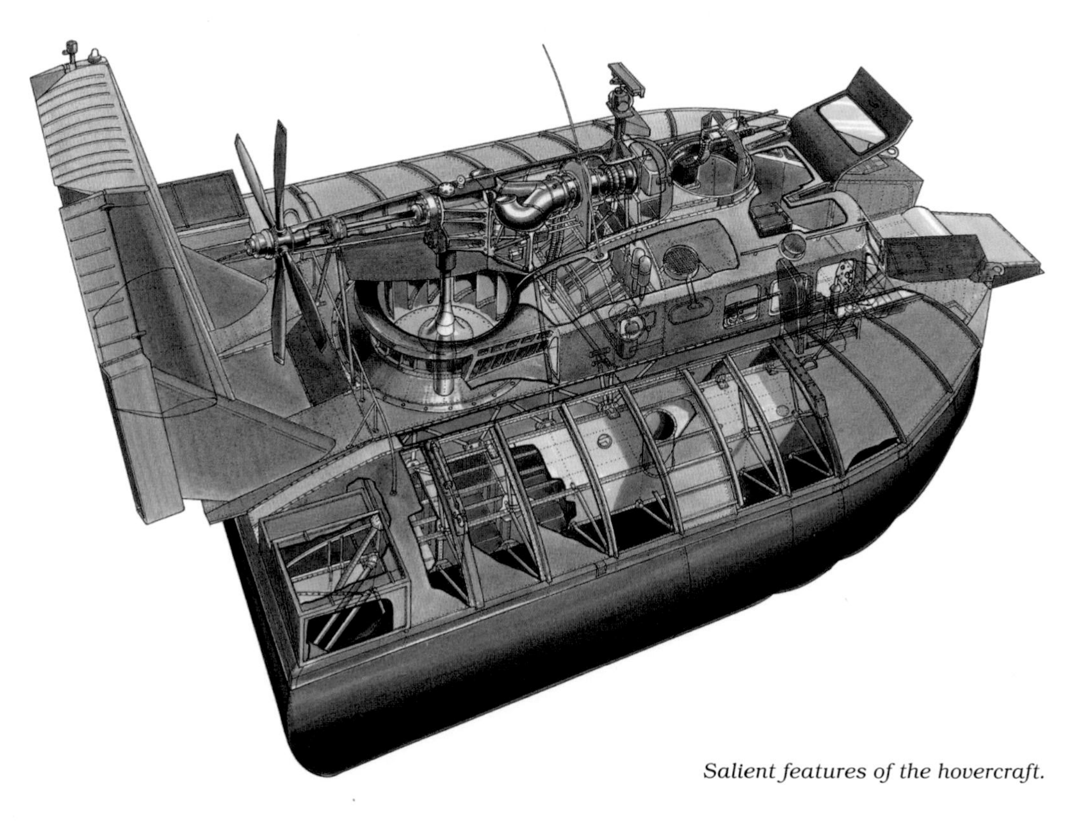

Salient features of the hovercraft.

The hovercraft rides on a cushion of air trapped under the vehicle, and is driven by one or more propellers. Photo: US Navy.

Characterized by a long cabin ending at its rear in the powerplant compartment, the SR.N6 is driven by one or two pusher propellers and controlled by means of a pair of fin-and-rudder units behind the propeller(s). The baseline two-propeller SR.N6 Mk 1 can carry 38 passengers or 3 tons of supplies, and was sold to the Egyptian navy and the Royal Saudi Arabian Frontier Force and Coast Guard, which received one and eight craft respectively. There followed the wholly military SR.N6 Mks 2 and 3 for the logistic support role: these feature a roof loading hatch and specially strengthened side decks for long 0.5-ton loads, and one machine gun. The maximum payload is 5 tons of cargo or up to 30 fully armed troops. The operators, which each received two Mk 2 craft, were the Egyptian and Iranian navies, the former also having its earlier craft brought up to a similar standard, including the ability to carry six 1,102-lb (500-kg) mines. The Iranian navy also bought six SR.N6 Mk 4 craft for coast defence purposes with armament capability including a 20-mm cannon or short-range SS.12 wire-guided tactical missiles as alternatives to the more usual machine gun armament. The Iraqi customs service purchased six basically similar craft but in the SR.N6 Mk 6C general-purpose form with a larger cabin to accommodate up to 55 passengers or 6 tons of freight. Saudi Arabia bought eight SR.N6 Mk 8 craft each able to carry 55 troops in the assault role. This variant had a single propeller.

SR.N6 Mk 8

Type:	general-purpose military hovercraft
Weight:	37,400 lb (16965 kg)
Dimensions:	length 60 ft (18.3 m); beam 28 ft (8.5 m)
Propulsion:	one gas turbine delivering 1,050 shp (785 kW) to one lift fan and one propeller for 50 kt
Armour:	none
Armament:	one machine gun or cannon, or light missiles
Complement:	crew of two and 55 troops

USS *Albany* (1962)

The USS *Albany*, USS *Chicago* and USS *Columbus* were the most fully optimized conversions (of three "Baltimore" class heavy cruisers) undertaken after World War II to provide the US Navy with fleet defence based on surface-to-air missiles. Among the 11 conversions, these were the only units to receive the Talos long-range system as initially envisaged with magazines extended deep into the hull fore and aft. The conversions were planned without gun armament, and had a secondary shorter-range battery of one Tartar launcher on each beam, as well as a single launcher for eight ASROC anti-submarine rockets. The shaping of the bridge was dictated by the need to provide clearance for the paired missile-control radars forward of it, and the unusual "mack" (mast/stack) arrangement was adopted to reduce radar interference from the funnels. The initial plans also featured the Regulus II surface-to-surface missile system, but this was soon deleted. Three later conversions, not effected, were planned with eight Polaris nuclear-armed surface-to-surface missiles amidships.

After conversion, the ships were recommissioned in November 1962, May 1964 and December 1962 and, at presidential insistence, also had limited gun armament in the form of two 5-in (127-mm) weapons amidships.

The three additional ships were to have had improved missile-control radar, but their conversions were cancelled in favour of the greater capabilities apparently offered by the in-development Typhon missile system, which was itself abandoned a few years later. The last conversion, the *Chicago*, was completed with an interim Naval Tactical Data System, and the *Albany* received a full NTDS system as part of an anti-air warfare modernization completed between February 1967 and June 1969, in which the Talos system was revised with a digital fire-control system. The same ship was refitted in 1974/75 with a satellite

In her late form, the USS Albany was a missile conversion of a gun-armed heavy cruiser dating from the end of World War II.

A "double-ended" missile ship, the USS Albany was able to undertake the simultaneous engagement of four aerial targets at long range.

communications capability as the flagship of the 2nd Fleet. The *Chicago* received a more limited modernization between August 1972 and August 1973 with an improved NTDS and upgraded defensive electronics. The *Albany* had already had the latter fitted in 1970 after her modernization. The *Columbus* was not modernized, and was therefore the first of the ships to be laid up, in May 1975, before being stricken in 1976. The *Albany* and *Chicago* were decommissioned in 1980, their Talos missile system having been withdrawn for financial reasons, even though they were to have been retained until 1985. Even so, the ships were not stricken as a result of the precarious nature of the "Cold War" at this time.

The *Chicago* served as the key air protection ship during the US mining of Haiphong harbour in North Vietnam during 1972, she and other air-defence warships being deemed more capable and less vulnerable than carrierborne fighters. When radar detected interceptors nearing the aircraft carrying out the mining, the *Chicago* shot one down with a Talos missile at a range of 55 miles (88.5 km), the other fighters then withdrawing.

USS *Albany*

Type:	anti-aircraft and anti-submarine fleet escort
Tonnage:	18,777 tons full load
Dimensions:	length 674 ft 11 in (205.8 m); beam 69 ft 9 in (21.3 m); draft 25 ft 9 in (7.9 m)
Propulsion:	four geared steam turbines delivering 120,000 shp (89472 kW) to four propellers for 32 kt
Armour:	(as built) 4/6-in (102/152-mm) belt, 2.5-in (64-mm) deck, 1.5/8-in (38/203-mm) turrets, 2.5/3-in (64/76-mm) magazines, 6.3-in (160-mm) barbettes, and 3/6-in (66/152-mm) conning tower
Armament:	two Talos twin-arm long-range SAM systems with 52 missiles each, two Tartar twin-arm short-range SAM systems with 42 missiles each, two 5-in (127-mm) DP guns, one ASROC anti-submarine system with eight rockets, and two triple launchers for 12,75-in (324-mm) lightweight anti-submarine torpedoes
Complement:	1,266

USS *Pegasus* (1977)

In the late 1950s the US Navy became interested in hydrofoil craft for very high speeds. The first concrete expression of this interest was the USS *High Point*, a three-foil unit commissioned in 1963 as a test bed for the possible anti-submarine application of hydrofoil concepts. Two more experimental platforms, the USS *Flagstaff* and USS *Tucumcari*, were commissioned in 1968 as prototypes for the US Navy's PHM (missile-armed patrol hydrofoil) requirement. This had been schemed for green water coastal operations, was also to involve the navies of Canada, Germany, Italy and the UK, and possibly comprise 100 craft. But as costs started to rise the other four nations dropped out. The US Navy at first remained true to the initial concept, and planned a class of 30 units with a CODOG (Combined Diesel or Gas turbine) propulsion arrangement with waterjets for both hullborne and foilborne operation. The US Navy then started to revise its thinking and diverted most of the funding. This delayed Boeing's completion of the USS *Pegasus*, and the other vessels had not been started before the service terminated the program in 1977. Just one month later the US Congress ordered the US Navy to complete the six craft which had originally been specified, and the Pegasus was commissioned three months later. The other five units were the USS *Hercules*, *Taurus*, *Aquila*, *Aries* **and** *Gemini*, commissioned in 1981/82.

The units were each armed with a single 3-in (76-mm) Mk 75 gun forward and two quadruple launchers for

The "Pegasus" class hydrofoil offered speed and agility, but was severely limited by anything but good sea conditions.

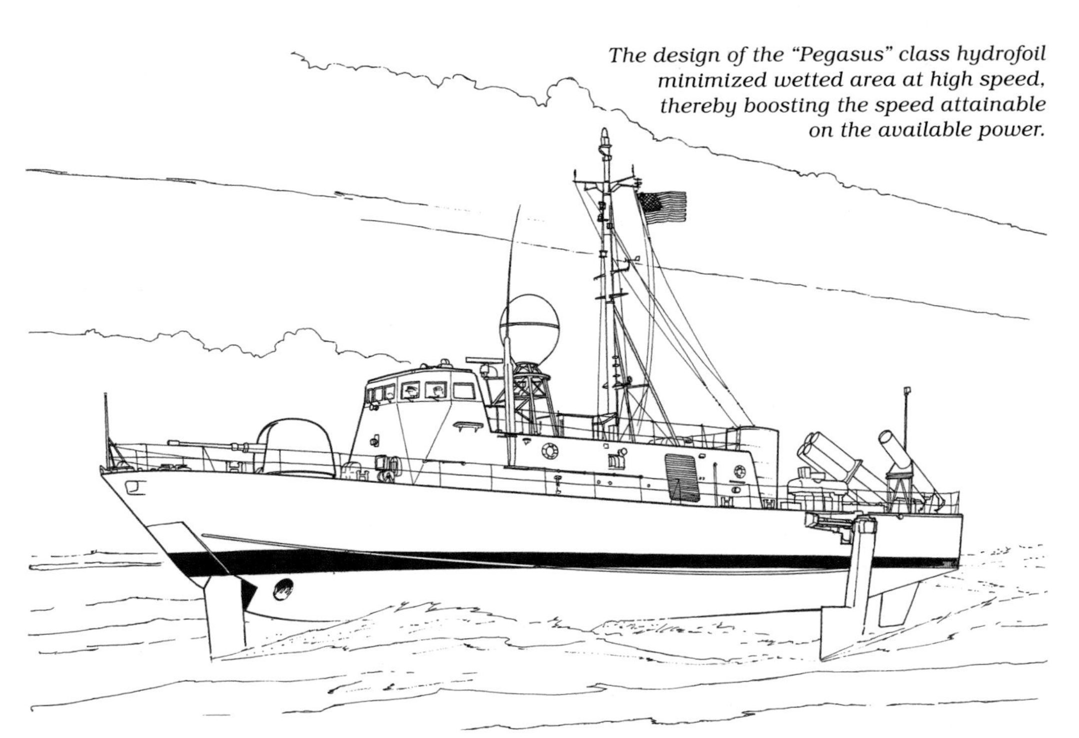
The design of the "Pegasus" class hydrofoil minimized wetted area at high speed, thereby boosting the speed attainable on the available power.

RGM-84 Harpoon anti-ship missiles above the stern. Trials revealed that the craft could be highly effective in the right conditions, but that they lacked the range, endurance and versatility of larger warships. The "Pegasus" class thus fell outside the main tactical precepts of its operating service. Until their retirement in 1993, the "Pegasus" class craft constituted a special squadron based at Key West, off the coast of Florida, and undertook surveillance missions in the Caribbean Sea and Gulf of Mexico when not continuing work on the development of fast combat craft tactics and how such tactics can be countered.

USS *Pegasus*

Type:	fast attack hydrofoil (missile/gun)
Tonnage:	240 tons full load
Dimensions:	length 132 ft 11 in (40.5 m) with the foils extended and 145 ft 4 in (44.3 m) with the foil retracted; beam 47 ft 6 in (14.5 m) with the foils extended and 28 ft 2 in (8.6 m) with the foils retracted; draft 23 ft 2 in (7.1 m) with the foils extended and 6 ft 2 in (1.9 m) with the foils retracted
Propulsion:	two diesel engines delivering 1,635 shp (1220 kW) to two waterjets for hullborne operation for a speed of 12 kt, and one gas turbine delivering 18,000 shp (13420 kW) to two waterjets for foilborne operation for a speed of 48 kt
Armour:	none
Armament:	one 3-in (76-mm) gun and two quadruple launchers for anti-ship missiles
Complement:	24

"Oliver Hazard Perry" class (1979)

The "Oliver Hazard Perry" class of frigates was procured by the US Navy during the 1970s and 1980s, and the frigate was created as a general-purpose escort able to do most tasks adequately, yet cheap enough to be bought in large quantities to replace ageing World War II destroyers. The frigates were built in 445-ft (135.7-m) short-hull (Flight I) and 455-ft (138.7-m) long-hull (Flight III) variants. The 30 long-hull ships, including four converted from short-hull standard, carry the Sikorsky SH-60 Seahawk helicopter, while the 21 short-hull ships have the less capable Kaman SH-2 Seasprite helicopter. The long-hull ships also have the RAST (Recovery Assist Securing and Traversing) system attached to the Seahawk in flight and allowing the helicopter to be winched down onto the deck in adverse conditions.

Two American yards built the US Navy's ships as well as four of Australia's six "Adelaide" class vessels: of the latter, the US-built units were of the short-hull type later revised to the long-hull standard to which the Australian-built ships were completed. Spanish and Taiwanese yards built the six "Santa Maria" and eight "Cheng Kung" class long-hull ships: the former have greater beam than the US Navy's vessels, and the latter have different armament and electronic fits.

Though the cost of the "Oliver Hazard Perry" class increased very considerably during the production run, all 50 ships planned for the US Navy were eventually built for completion in 1979/87, with a 51st unit added in 1989. Some of the long-hull ships are scheduled to remain in American service for some years to come, but others have already been decommissioned. A proportion of the latter have been transferred to the navies of allied nations, including Bahrain, Egypt, Poland and Turkey. In the US Navy, the in-service ships are being adapted to reduce operating costs and the missile launcher is being removed as the Standard SM-1MR missile is obsolescent. This leaves the embarked helicopter as the only means of engaging a target (ship or submarine) at longer range, and even the shorter-range offensive capability may disappear if the 3-in (76-mm) gun is removed, as rumored, for financial reasons. The weapons left would then allow only for short-range defence against submarines, missiles and aircraft.

"Oliver Hazard Perry" class frigates twice reached the headlines during the 1980s. In the Persian Gulf, on May 17, 1986, the USS *Stark* was attacked, apparently in error, by an Iraqi warplane: some 37 US American sailors died in this episode, which took place just before the launch of Operation "Earnest

Will," in which Kuwaiti oil tankers were reflagged as US vessels for safer passage through the gulf during the Iraqi-Iranian Gulf War of the 1980s. On April 14, 1988 the USS *Samuel B. Roberts* hit an Iranian mine in the same region and nearly sank: the ship suffered no dead, but 10 of its wounded sailors had to be airlifted from the ship for treatment. Days later the USA responded with a one-day offensive against Iranian oil platforms used as bases for raids on shipping.

The "Oliver Hazard Perry" class was intended to provide adequate capability in combination with great affordability. The 3-in (76-mm) automatic gun was mounted above the superstructure block abaft the lattice main mast.

"Oliver Hazard Perry Flight III" class long-hull frigate with a Seahawk helicopter.

"Oliver Hazard Perry Flight I" class

Type:	guided missile oceanic escort frigate
Tonnage:	3,486 tons full load
Dimensions:	445 ft (135.7 m); beam 47 ft 5 in (14.5 m); draft 14 ft 5 in (4.4 m)
Propulsion:	two gas turbines delivering 40,000 shp (29824 kW) to one propeller for 28.5 kt
Armour:	none
Armament:	one 3-in (76-mm) DP gun, one single-arm launcher for 40 Standard SAM and Harpoon anti-ship missiles, one 20-mm close-in weapon system mounting, two triple launchers for 12.75-in (324-mm) lightweight anti-submarine torpedoes, and one or two helicopters
Complement:	176

HMS *Amazon* (1974)

The origins of the "Amazon" class frigate can be found in two places, namely the Royal Navy's need to replace older diesel-engined frigates, and the pressure exerted by private yards for the opportunity to build a frigate without what they claimed were the overly high standards imposed by the Ministry of Defence's Ship Department.

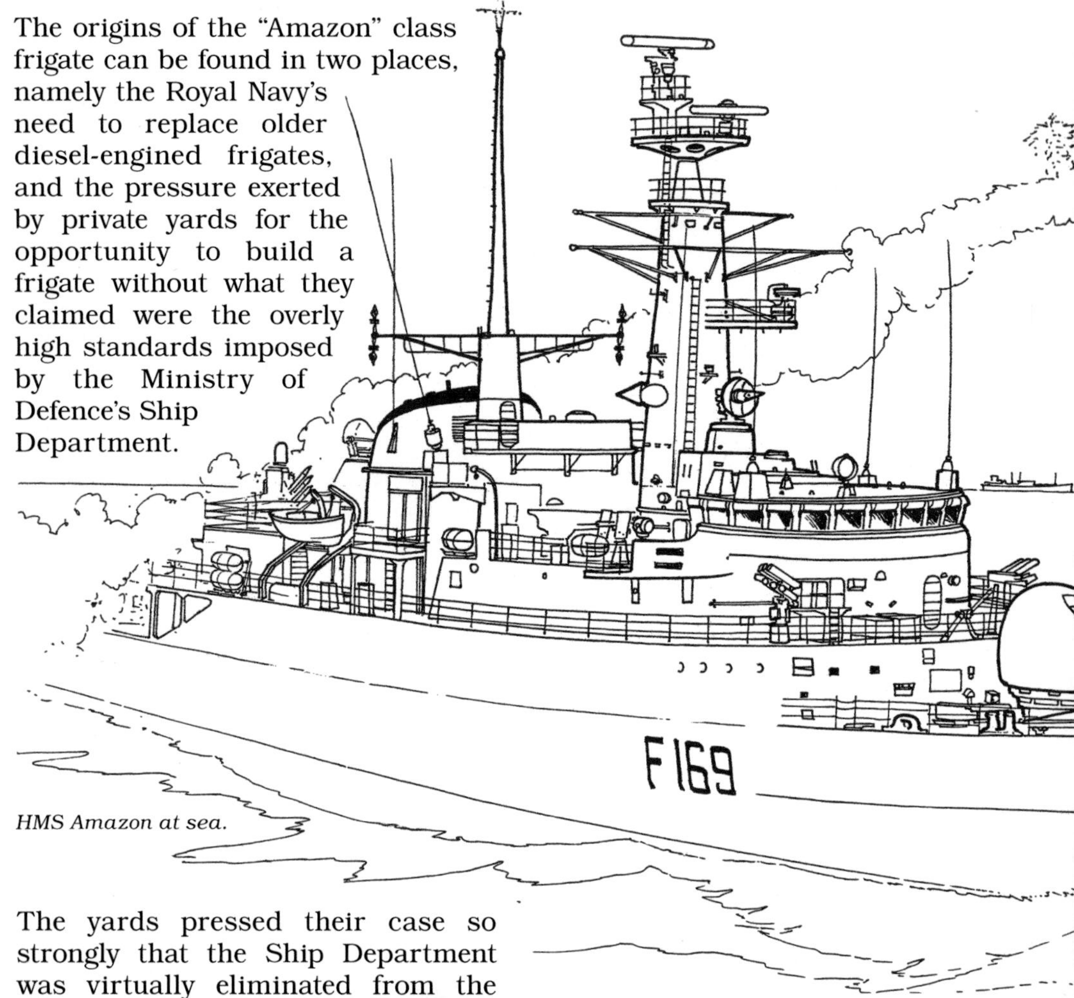

HMS Amazon at sea.

The yards pressed their case so strongly that the Ship Department was virtually eliminated from the design process, and thus was lost a chance to combine official and private talents. Some design details did not meet naval requirements, the cost was high, and the design lacked the "stretchability" needed to introduce later weapon and electronic systems.

Eight ships were ordered (three from Vosper Thornycroft and five from Yarrow), and these were completed between May 1974 and April 1978 as HMS *Amazon, Antelope, Active, Ambuscade, Arrow, Alacrity, Ardent* and *Avenger*. From the third unit the ships were completed with two twin launchers for Exocet long-range heavyweight anti-ship missiles, and triple launchers for anti-submarine torpedoes were retrofitted. The anti-aircraft capability was vested mainly in one quadruple launcher for obsolescent Seacat short-range SAMs, but there was never sufficient topweight allowance for the retrofit of the more modern Seawolf system. A Westland Lynx helicopter was also carried. Australia contributed to the design process but ordered no ships, and the only other interested party

Attractive and popular with their crews, HMS Amazon and her sisters were slightly too small to fulfil the roles demanded of them by the Royal Navy.

was Argentina, which also failed to order the type.

During a Far East deployment in 1977, the *Amazon* suffered a severe fire, persuading designers of the dangers inherent in the use of an all-aluminium superstructure, and this fact was confirmed by operations in the Falklands war of 1982. After this the Admiralty demanded steel superstructures. During the 1982 Falklands war with Argentina, the *Ardent* was badly damaged by air-launched rockets on May 21, and sank, while the *Antelope* was hit by bombs on May 23, and blew up on the following day while an explosives expert was trying to defuse an unexploded weapon. The six remaining vessels, which had their hulls stiffened after the war, were sold to Pakistan in 1993/94. The ships have been stripped of the Seacat and Exocet systems, the latter being replaced by US-supplied Harpoon missiles, and in 2005 it was reported that a Chinese LY-60N SAM system was being installed on the frigates by the Pakistani navy.

HMS *Amazon*

Type:	general-purpose frigate
Tonnage:	3,600 tons deep load
Dimensions:	length 384 ft (117m); beam 41 ft 9 in (12.7 m); draft 19 ft (5.8 m)
Propulsion:	COGOG arrangement of two Rolls-Royce Olympus TM3B gas turbines delivering 56,000 shp (41754 kW) and two Rolls-Royce Tyne RM1A gas turbines delivering 8,500 shp (6338 kW) to two propellers for 30 kt
Armour:	none
Armament:	one 4.5-in (114-mm) gun, two 20-mm AA cannon, one quadruple launcher for Seacat SAMs, two triple launcher for 12.75-in (324-mm) anti-submarine torpedoes, and one helicopter
Complement:	175/192

HMS *Invincible* (1980)

The Royal Navy's "Invincible" class light aircraft carriers were initially conceived as 12,500-ton anti-submarine escort carriers for the proposed "CVA-01" class of fleet carrier. The latter was cancelled in 1966 and the former was reworked into anti-submarine cruiser with six helicopters, later increased to nine before the vessel was redesigned into a 19,500-ton carrier, known at the time, for political reasons, as a "through-deck cruiser." The BAe Harrier's emergence paved the way for a further design to carry the half-sister Sea Harrier multi-role STOVL warplane, and the design ended with a flight deck 557 ft 9 in (170 m) long and 115 ft (35 m) wide, two aircraft lifts and, to boost the Sea Harrier's ability to take-off after a short run with maximum weapons load, a "ski jump" forward edge to the flight deck, its slope initially set at 7° for HMS *Invincible* and HMS *Illustrious* and 12° for HMS *Ark Royal*. The ships were built by Vickers-Armstrongs (first) and Swan Hunter (second pair), and were commissioned in 1980/85.

Up to 1982, the *Invincible's* air group typically comprised nine Westland Sea King anti-submarine helicopters and five Sea Harrier. The Falklands war, in which the *Invincible* was a vital British asset, changed this balance, and the later complement became 12 Sea Kings (including three conversions for the airborne early warning role) and up to nine improved Sea Harriers. Other changes were effected during the 1980s and early 1990s, probably the most important being the increase of the "ski jump" angle on the *Invincible* and *Illustrious* to match the 12° slope of the Ark Royal. In the period after this another three major changes were effected. One was the removal of the Sea Dart SAM system, the elimination of the twin-arm launcher ahead of the flight deck's starboard forward end opening the way to increased deck parking for aircraft and giving the ships an appearance considerably more akin to that of pure aircraft carriers than that of the hybrid cruiser/aircraft carrier form in which they were built. The Sea Dart magazines were converted to increase the stowage volume available for air-to-surface weapons, and new aircrew briefing facilities were also established below the extended flight deck for both the standard Sea Harrier force and also the Harriers of the Royal Air Force which were increasingly tasked with operations from the "Invincible" class ships.

The short-range AA defense was also considerably strengthened, and the ships were also revised to operate the more modern EHI Merlin helicopter which has succeeded the Sea King in the anti-submarine role.

Right:
Showing HMS Ark Royal with a Sea Harrier taking off.

Below:
HMS Ark Royal in her initial form with a Sea Dart SAM launcher near the forward edge of the flight deck.

However, with the increasing integration of Fleet Air Arm and RAF STOVL warplane capability, the Merlin helicopter has increasingly operated from the carrier's escorting "Fort" class replenishment ship.

In their most recent operational deployments, the ships have operation mainly in the helicopter cruiser role as there was little scope for the use of STOVL warplanes, and among their aircraft in this deployments have been Boeing Chinook heavy helicopters of the RAF. The Sea Harrier was retired from service in 2006, and after that time ships' most important air asset will be the Harrier GR.Mk 9 operated by two FAA and two RAF squadrons. The *Invincible* was decommissioned in July 2005 and mothballed but with an 18-month facility for reactivation up to 2010. The *Illustrious* has taken her place as the fleet flagship, and is scheduled for decommissioning in 2012, with the *Ark Royal* following in 2015, as two much larger carriers enter service.

HMS *Invincible* (as completed)

Type:	light aircraft carrier
Tonnage:	20,400 tons full load
Dimensions:	677 ft (206.3 m); beam 90 ft (27.5 m); draft 24 ft (7.3 m)
Propulsion:	COGOG arrangement with four gas turbines delivering 112,000 shp (83507 kW) to two propellers for 28 kt
Armour:	none
Armament:	one twin launcher for Sea Dart medium-range SAMs, and up to 14 aircraft
Complement:	875

USS *Nimitz* (1975)

The super-carriers of the US Navy's "Nimitz" class are currently the world's largest capital ships, and constitute the most powerful single element in the USA's ability to project vast military power to most parts of the world. Named for Fleet Admiral Chester W. Nimitz, who had commanded the US Navy's forces in the Pacific through most of World War II with superb skill, and built by Newport News Shipbuilding (now Northrop Grumman Newport News), the USS *Nimitz* was laid down on June 22, 1968, launched on May 13, 1972 and commissioned on May 3, 1975. The ship's operational career since that time is in many ways a mirror of the US Navy's history in the last days of the "Cold War" with the USSR and the USA's emergence as the "world's policeman" since the collapse and dissolution of the USSR during the early 1990s.

The *Nimitz's* first deployment began on July 7, 1976 when the ship departed Norfolk, Virginia, for the Mediterranean. Included in the task force were the nuclear-powered cruisers USS *South Carolina* and USS *California*, and this deployment marked the first time in 10 years that nuclear-powered ships had deployed to the Mediterranean. The ship returned to Norfolk after a seven-month deployment. The *Nimitz* sailed toward the Mediterranean once more on December 1st, 1977, returning once more to Norfolk on July 20, 1978. During her third cruise to the Mediterranean, from September 10, 1979, the *Nimitz* was dispatched to strengthen the US naval presence in the Indian Ocean area as tensions heightened over Iran's seizure of 52 US citizens and hostages. Four months later, the "Evening Light" operation was launched from the *Nimitz* in an attempt to rescue the hostages, but the effort was aborted in the Iranian desert after the number of helicopters fell below the minimum

The USS Nimitz was one of the 11 capital ships available to the US Navy in the middle of the 21st century's first decade.

needed to transport the attack force and hostages out of Iran. During this deployment, the ship was continuously at sea for 144 days, and she returned to Norfolk on May 26, 1980.

On May 15, of the following year, the *Nimitz* departed Norfolk for the final phases of the work-up for her forthcoming Mediterranean cruise, but on the night of May 25 a Grumman EA-6B Prowler electronic warfare airplane crash-landed on the flight deck, killing 14 crewmen and injuring 45 others. The carrier returned to Norfolk for repair of her damaged catapults, but returned to sea less than two days later to complete her work-up. During her fourth deployment to the Mediterranean, on August 18/19, 1981 the *Nimitz* and the USS *Forrestal* conducted an open ocean missile exercise in the Gulf of Sidra near the so-called "Line of Death" proclaimed by the Libyan leader, Colonel Ghadafi. On the morning of August 19, Libyan aircraft fired on two of the *Nimitz's* aircraft, which returned the fire and destroyed both of the Libyan aircraft. On June 14, 1985, two Lebanese Shiite Muslim gunmen hijacked TWA Flight 847, carrying 153 passengers and crew, including many Americans. In response, the *Nimitz* was instructed to reach the eastern Mediterranean, off the coast of Lebanon, as swiftly as possible. Here she remained until August. After another extended deployment, the *Nimitz* left the Mediterranean on May 21, 1987, crossed the Atlantic Ocean, rounded the rough waters off Cape Horn, and entered the Pacific Ocean en route to her new home port, Bremerton in Washington state, where she arrived on July 2, 1987. In September 1988 the *Nimitz* operated off the coast of South Korea providing additional security for the Olympic games in Seoul. On October 29 of the same year the carrier took up station in the North Arabian Sea, where she was involved in the program to protect shipping lanes and escort Kuwaiti tankers re-registered in the USA. On February 25, 1991 the *Nimitz* departed Bremerton for the western Pacific and the Arabian Gulf, where she took over from the USS *Ranger* during "Desert Storm" before returning to the USA on August 24, 1991. The *Nimitz* was again deployed to the Arabian Gulf on February 1st, 1993, relieving the USS *Kitty Hawk* and taking part in "Southern Watch," returning to the USA in August 1993.

In November 1995 the *Nimitz* embarked on a deployment which took her successively to the western

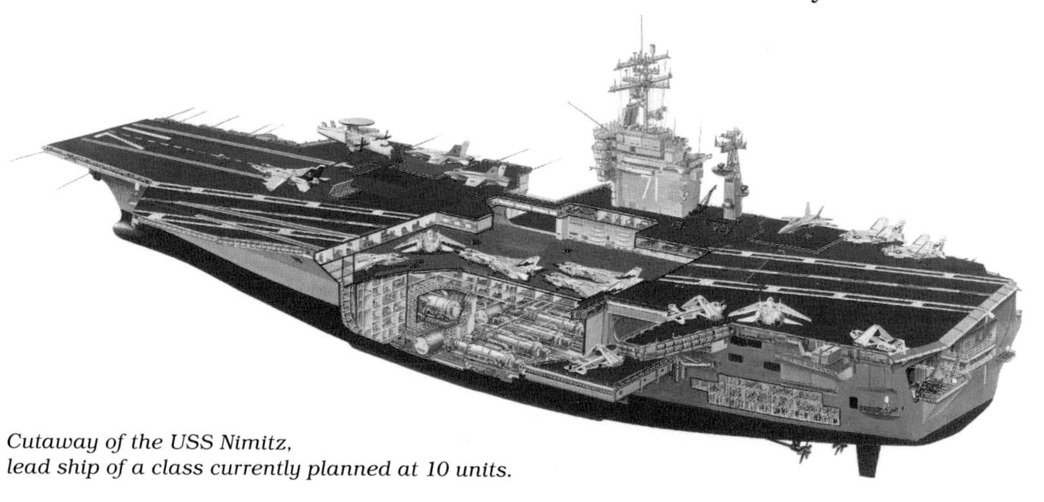

Cutaway of the USS Nimitz, lead ship of a class currently planned at 10 units.

USS *Nimitz* (1975) *continued*

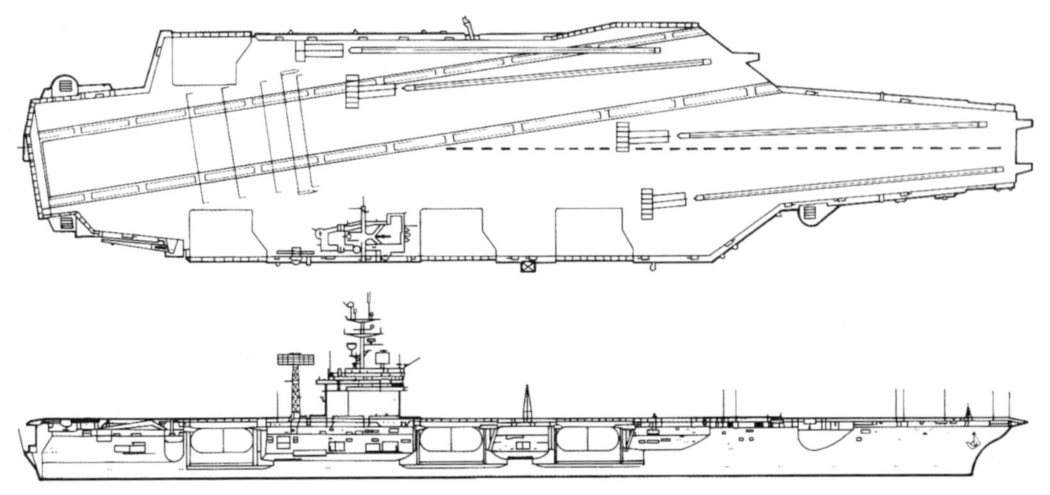

The nuclear-powered aircraft carrier USS Nimitz.

Pacific, Indian Ocean, Arabian Gulf, and the waters off Taiwan, where once again the presence of carrier forces at sea helped to defuse the tensions attendant on the dispute between Taiwan and China. On September 1st, 1997 the carrier started on what was scheduled as virtually a circumnavigation of the world ending at Norfolk, where she was to be cycled through a long overhaul. However, the *Nimitz* was diverted to the Arabian Gulf in support of "Southern Watch" and various United Nation initiatives, finally reaching the USA on March 1st, 1998. Eight weeks later the *Nimitz* began a SLEP (Service Life Extension Program) mid-life major overhaul and reactor refuelling to provide the capability for another quarter-century of unrefuelled operations. The ship was scheduled to re-enter service in mid-2001 before departing to her new home port of San Diego in southern California in preparation for her tenth deployment, in this instance to the western Pacific. The *Nimitz's* refuelling was completed in June 2001 and she left Norfolk on September 21, 2001, rounding Cape Horn to reach her new home port on November 8. The ship began a four-month shakedown in January 2002 and then undertook sea trials and damage control exercises and training before returning to San Diego in mid-September.

The *Nimitz* relieved a sister ship, the USS *Abraham Lincoln*, in the Persian Gulf during the middle of April 2003, and her aircraft flew large numbers of missions over Iraq in support of the allied ground forces committed during the "Iraqi Freedom" operation. The aircraft carrier returned to San Diego on November 2nd, 2003, and here she was taken in hand for a scheduled period of maintenance and repair as required after any deployment. The *Nimitz* departed on yet another deployment to the Persian Gulf in May 2005, returning from an uneventful deployment on November 8 of the same year.

The last ship of the class, the USS *George H. W. Bush*, will be the transition ship to the new "CVN-21" class of carriers whose

Despite its great size, the hangar deck of the USS Nimitz can accommodate only about half of the aircraft carrier's aircraft complement.

construction is due to start in 2007, and will incorporate advanced-technology features such as a new multi-function radar system, volume search radar and open-architecture information network, and will also have significantly reduced crew requirements. To lower costs, some new technologies were also incorporated into the ninth unit, the USS *Ronald Reagan*, though not nearly as many as will be involved with the *Bush*.

USS *Nimitz*

Type:	multi-role aircraft carrier
Tonnage:	about 97,000 tons full load
Dimensions:	length 1,092 ft (332.8 m); beam 134 ft (40.8 m); draft 36 ft 8 in (11.2 m)
Propulsion:	four geared turbines powered by two nuclear reactors and delivering 280,000 shp (208768 kW) to four propellers for 35 kt
Armour:	not revealed
Armament:	two octuple launchers for RIM-7 Sea Sparrow SAMs, three Phalanx 20-mm close-in-weapons system mountings, two 21-cell launchers for RIM-116 Rolling Airframe Missile SAMs, and up to 90 fixed- and rotary-wing aircraft
Complement:	5,621

USS *Abraham Lincoln* (1989)

With its combination of nuclear propulsion, a large flight deck and sizeable hangar volume able to handle large numbers of aircraft, advanced command, control and communications electronics, and provision for under-way replenishment of all essential and many non-essential consumables, the aircraft carriers of the US Navy's "Nimitz" class represent the ultimate in modern power projection by sea. All built by Newport News Shipbuilding and powered by two nuclear reactors, the ships of the class were completed from May 1975 and in 2006 comprised nine units with a tenth building for completion in 2009. In order of completion, the ships are the USS *Nimitz*, USS *Dwight D. Eisenhower*, USS *Carl Vinson*, USS *Theodore Roosevelt*, USS *Abraham Lincoln*, USS *George Washington*, USS *John C. Stennis*, USS *Harry S Truman*, USS *Ronald Reagan* and USS *George H. W. Bush*.

Following the three conventionally powered "Kitty Hawk," the single nuclear-powered "Enterprise" class and single conventionally powered "John F. Kennedy" class carriers, the "Nimitz" class carriers represented the US Navy's whole-hearted return to the concept of very large aircraft carriers with a nuclear powerplant. The "Nimitz" class ships are based on a new type of twin-reactor powerplant, developed from a project for a single reactor destroyer/frigate plant, and so have even more internal space than the huge USS *Enterprise* with her complement of eight reactors. The pressurized water-cooled reactors deliver steam to four sets of geared turbines which drive the four propellers. In addition, the "Nimitz" class ships incorporate the more volume-economical torpedo defence system of the USS *John F. Kennedy*. In their general arrangement and their electronics suite the "Nimitz" class carriers are essentially identical to the *John F. Kennedy*, and were defensively armed on completion with two or three octuple launchers for the RIM-7 Sea Sparrow medium-range surface-to-air missiles, of which no reloads are carried.

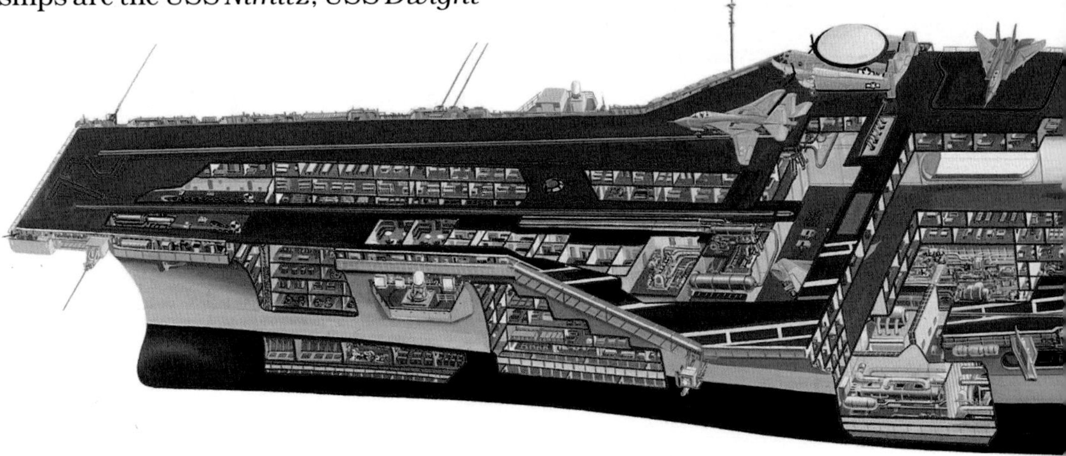

The flight deck extends the full length of the ship and is 257 ft 6 in (78.5 m) wide. The flight deck is of the angled type, with aircraft coming

Right:
A Grumman F-14 Tomcat two-seat fleet defence fighter lands on the angled part of the USS Abraham Lincoln's flight deck.

Below:
A cutaway illustration highlights the huge volume and complexity of the USS Abraham Lincoln's interior arrangements.

in over the stern at a port angle to the ship's centerline to engage any of three arrester wire or, as a last resort, a single arrester net, and has four steam catapults (two at the forward end of the flight deck and two at the forward end of the angled section where it overhangs the port side of the ship: the angled flight deck section is 780 ft (237.7 m) long. Access between the flight deck and the hangar deck is provided by four deck-edge elevators, three on the starboard side (two forward of and one abaft the island) and one on the port side roughly in line with the aftermost starboard-side elevator. The hangar deck is 25 ft 7 in (7.8 m) high, and is large enough to accommodate about half of the ship's aircraft complement as any one time. The ship's capacities in terms of aircraft consumables include 2,570 tons of ordnance and 2.8 million US gal (10.6 million litres) of fuel, each of

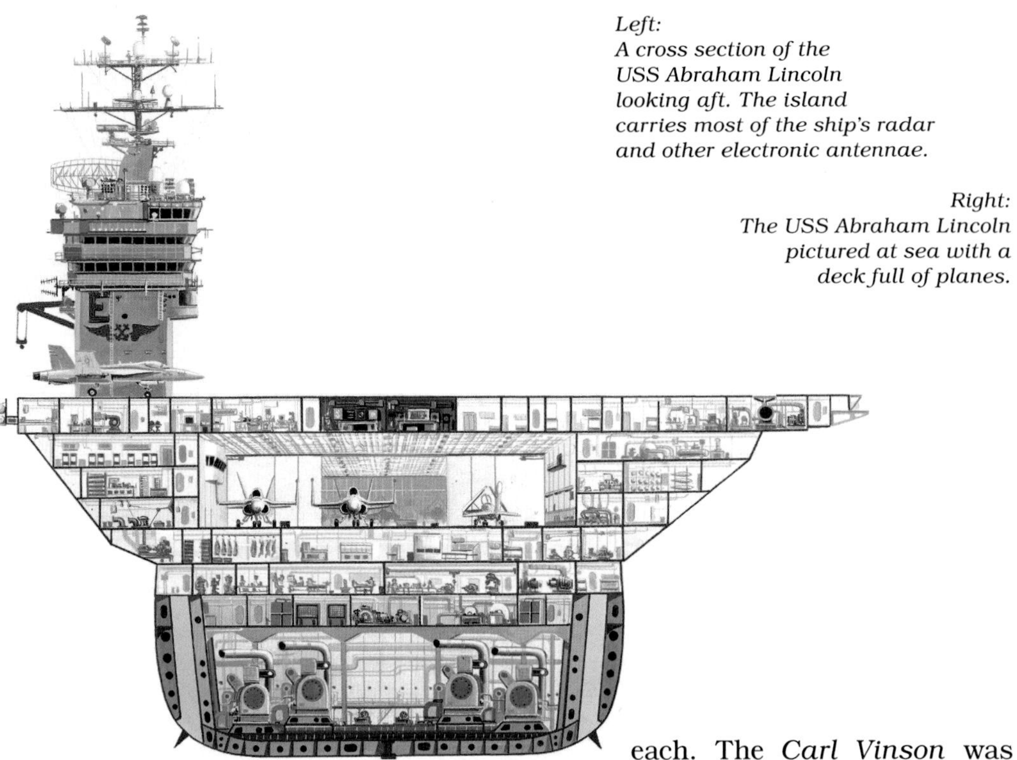

Left:
A cross section of the USS Abraham Lincoln looking aft. The island carries most of the ship's radar and other electronic antennae.

Right:
The USS Abraham Lincoln pictured at sea with a deck full of planes.

these figures being greater than the equivalent figure for the *Enterprise*, and provide the ship with the ability to complete 16 days of sustained air operations before resupply becomes necessary.

The first three ships constitute a separate sub-class, the *Dwight D. Eisenhower* and *Carl Vinson* being further distinguishable by their single rather than twin bridge-catching booms. From the *Theodore Roosevelt* onward, the ships have no such boom, current carrierborne aircraft incorporating a catapult attachment in their landing gear and therefore not needing the wire bridles of the past. The *Carl Vinson* was completed with four 20-mm Phalanx CIWS mountings for last-ditch defence, mainly against missiles, and the others had three each. The *Carl Vinson* was also completed with three Sea Sparrow launchers, while her two sister ships received their third launchers during refits.

The US Navy claims that these ships can absorb three times the damage which the "Essex" class fleet carriers survived in 1944/45. The first three units were later fitted with Kevlar splinter armour of the type installed in the later ships that were built. The ships have been steadily upgraded in electronic capability for both offensive and defensive purposes. As well as radars and defensive electronics, the ships have the ASCAC (Anti-Submarine warfare Classification and Analysis Center) for data sharing with aircraft and surface escorts in the anti-submarine role, and the NTDS (Naval Tactical Distribution System) whose data links provide a secure means

(Kevlar over vitals, and better hull protection), the reduction in their aviation ordnance to 1,954 tons presumably reflecting the greater volume allocated to their protection. Otherwise these ships are similar to the first three units, but the *Abraham Lincoln* and *George Washington* were completed with a new type of lower-pressure catapult and enhanced aircraft landing aids. The air group originally embarked comprised two Grumman F-14 fleet defence fighter, one Grumman A-6 medium attack, and two Vought A-7 light attack squadrons as well as detachments of electronic warfare, airborne early warning and anti-submarine aircraft, but is now more streamlined through the greater use of Boeing F/A-18 multi-role aircraft and the declining submarine threat.

of sharing tactical information with aircraft and other ships. A satellite communications system is standard, and each ship has facilities allowing it to be used as a fleet flagship.

The seven later ships are considerably improved in many aspects, particularly in self-defence

USS *Abraham Lincoln*

Type:	multi-role aircraft carrier
Tonnage:	about 97,000 tons full load
Dimensions:	length 1,092 ft (332.8 m); beam 134 ft (40.8 m); draft 36 ft 8 in (11.2 m)
Propulsion:	four geared turbines powered by two nuclear reactors and delivering 280,000 shp (208768 kW) to four propellers for 35 kt
Armour:	not revealed
Armament:	two octuple launchers for RIM-7 Sea Sparrow SAMs, three Phalanx 20-mm close-in-weapons systems mountings, two 21-cell launchers for RIM-116 Rolling Airframe Missile SAMs, and up to 90 fixed- and rotary-wing aircraft
Complement:	5,621

Future Surface Combatant

Since the 1990s several nations have undertaken much work on the evaluation of future warships offering good combat capability, low manning levels, and modest cost of building, running and maintenance. The Royal Navy's effort was centered on examination of the so-called Future Surface Combatant, which was projected for a service entyry in 2013 as successor to the "Type 22" and "Type 23" class frigates but was effectively cancelled in 2004/05. At first planned as a type optimized for the anti-submarine role, from 2001 the FCS was increasingly schemed as a general-purpose type reflecting the more diverse nature of modern naval operations. The design of the ship had not been fixed, but possibilities included a hull based on that of the "Type 45" class destroyer or on a more radical trimaran form of hull. For evaluation of the latter, the RV *Triton* was built as a technology demonstrator.

The *Triton* is the world's largest motor-propelled vessel of the trimaran (triple-hull) configuration. The design and construction of the vessel was funded by QinetiQ, the semi-privatized defence research organization which was formerly the government's DERA (Defence Evaluation and Research Agency), and its brief was to quantify the structural and seakeeping performance of the trimaran hull, and to test whether or not the trimaran configuration was fully suitable for a vessel as large and as complex as the planned FCS. This would have included advanced weapons including a fully automatic gun and vertical-launch missile units forward of the bridge, provision for a rotary-wing aircraft as large as the Bell/Boeing V-22 Osprey tilt-proprotor machine on a wide platform extending out from the central hull over the after parts of the outer hulls, a number of close-in weapon systems mountings over the after part of the ship, advanced propulsion arrangements, and antennae for advanced sensor and other electronic systems on the

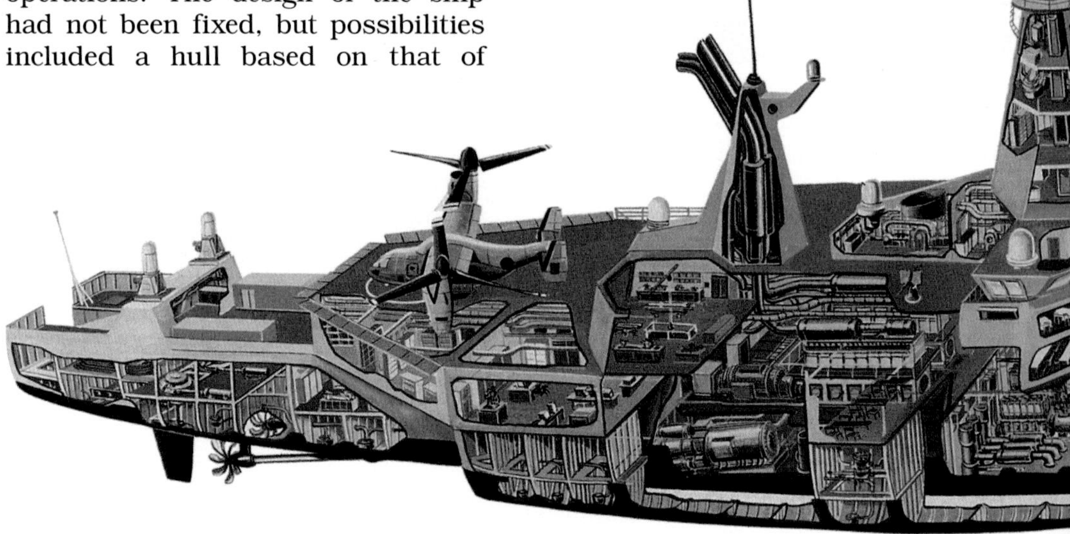

pyramidal "mast" above the low superstructure, as revealed in the accompanying cutaway illustration. The ship was also to have been characterized by low radar, thermal and other signatures to make it as difficult as possible for any opponent to detect.

In August 1998, the UK Ministry of Defense awarded a contract to Vosper Thornycroft to construct the *Triton*, which was launched in May 2000 and delivered in August of the same year. The *Triton* then undertook a two-year risk-reduction trials program for the ministry of Defense and its US counterpart, the Department of Defense. After the end of the trials program, the *Triton* has been used in the trials of other QinetiQ technologies, including a propeller of composite construction. In January 2005 the *Triton* was bought by Gardline Marine Sciences, a British company based in East Anglia, for use in the hydrographic survey role under contract to the Maritime and Coastguard Agency. For this the vessel is being outfitted with a special sensor and processing suite.

The US Department of Defense is now considering its options, and among these are the Medium-Size Vessel Derivative, the Versatile Surface Combatant and the Global Corvette. The first is based on the need for a type to replace at least the four "Type 22 Batch 3" frigates. Here the options are an "off the shelf" procurement of the Franco-Italian FREMM multi-role frigate, a variant of the "Type 45" class destroyer optimized for the anti-submarine and surface warfare roles, or a private enterprise design such as the DML Group's Frigate Concept 65. This last would be a surface combatant offering high speed and long endurance on the basis of a hull some 492 ft (150 m) long with a 6,600-ton displacement. Two gas turbines would power four waterjets for a speed in the order of 35 kt.

RV *Triton*

Type:	trimaran research vessel
Tonnage:	1,100 tons displacement
Dimensions:	length 321 ft 6 in (98 m); beam 65 ft 7 in (20 m); draft not available
Propulsion:	two diesel generators delivering 5365 hp (4000 kW) to two propellers for 20 kt
Armour:	none
Armament:	none
Complement:	12 plus up to 28 civil and naval trials personnel

Index

T

W